# BOLD DRAGOON

Also available from the
**VINTAGE CIVIL WAR LIBRARY**

*Sherman's March* by Burke Davis

# BOLD DRAGOON

## The Life of J.E.B. Stuart

## Emory M. Thomas

**Vintage Books**
A Division of Random House
New York

First Vintage Books Edition, May 1988

Copyright © 1986 by Emory M. Thomas

Maps by Jean Paul Tremblay

Library of Congress Cataloging-in-Publication Data
Thomas, Emory M., 1939–
Bold dragoon.
Reprint. Originally published: New York: Harper &
Row, c1986.
Bibliography: p.
Includes index.
1. Stuart, Jeb, 1833–1864.    2. Generals—United
States—Bibliography.    3. United States. Army—Biography.
4. Confederate States of America. Army—Biography.
5. United States—History—Civil War, 1861–1865—
Campaigns.    I. Title.
[E467.1.S9T45    1988]       973.7'3'0924       87-45928
ISBN 0-394-75775-0 (pbk.)

Grateful acknowledgment is made for permission to reprint from the following works:
John Esten Cooke, *Wearing of the Gray*, edited by Philip Van Doren Stern (Indiana
University Press: 1959). Reprinted by permission of Indiana University Press. Heros
Von Borcke, *Memoirs of the Confederate War for Independence*, 2 volumes (Peter
Smith Publisher: 1938). Reprinted by permission of Peter Smith Publisher, Inc.,
Gloucester, MA. W. W. Blackford, *War Years with Jeb Stuart* (Charles Scribner's Sons:
1945). George Cary Eggleston, *A Rebel's Recollections* (Indiana University Press: 1959).
Reprinted by permission of Indiana University Press. Peter W. Hairston, editor,
"J. E. B. Stuart's Letters to His Hairston Kin, 1850–1855" from the July 1974 issue of
the *North Carolina Historical Review*. Passage from a poem by John Thompson from
*Poems of John R. Thompson*, edited by John S. Patton (New York: 1920). Poem from
*Singing Soldiers*, edited by Paul Glass (New York: 1964). Passage from "Childe Harold's
Pilgrimage" from *Byron: Poetical Works*, New Edition, edited by
Frederick Page (London: 1970).

*For my first wife*

# Contents

# MAPS

*A section of photographs follows page 210*

# *Preface*

Wittingly and otherwise, many people have contributed to this book. I wish I could name them all.

Virginia Davis, who is J. E. B. Stuart's granddaughter (her mother was Virginia Pelham Stuart Waller), rummaged through her belongings until she found a box of papers in the back of her blanket closet. She allowed me to see this material; she answered questions about her grandparents; and she told me some of the stories her grandmother (Flora Stuart) told by the family fireside. Stuart B. Campbell, Jr., who descends from William Alexander Stuart, allowed me to see a collection of letters which no scholar, as far as I know, has ever before used. He also offered insight and encouragement which I much appreciate.

At manuscript repositories and libraries, directors and staff members were often more than kind. Howson Cole of the Virginia Historical Society and I became good friends during the course of my research visits, and Howson's help has been vital. Robert L. Krick of the Fredericksburg and Spotsylvania National Military Park heard I was doing this book and called to offer his help. Several times during the last year he sent me copies of material relating to Stuart which I would never have known existed otherwise. Edward D. C. Campbell, Jr. (Kip), offered me assistance from three locations: the Museum of the Confederacy, Virginia Historical Society, and Virginia State Library. And he and Patty Campbell also offered the only occasion I can recall in which I ate as many broiled scallops as I wanted.

At the Virginia Historical Society Paul Nagel continued to be the good friend he had been as a colleague at the University of Georgia, and Virginius Hall, Waverly Winfree, Rebecca Perrine, and Nelson Lankford all went out of their way to be helpful. Betsy McKemie, who directs the Museum of the Confederacy and Charlene Alling, Curator of Manuscripts and Archives at the Museum, offered their knowledge and interest in the tradition of Eleanor Brokenbrough whose kindness to itinerant scholars is indeed legendary. Dick Sommers of the U.S. Army Military History Institute, Carlisle Barracks, Pennsylvania, shared his encyclopedic mind as well as materials about Stuart in the collection he has built.

Staff members in libraries at the University of Virginia, University of North Carolina at Chapel Hill, Duke University, U.S. Military Academy at West Point, University of South Carolina, Virginia State Library, the Huntington Library, San Marino, California and the University of Georgia have my thanks for their assistance. At the Huntington, for example, Harriet McLoone not only helped me use the collection of Stuart papers, she also found and furnished Stuart items scattered in other manuscript collections at the library.

Graduate students at the University of Georgia who served as research assistants at various stages of this project have my great appreciation for their efforts. Bill Stevens became a Stuart bibliophile and shared his copious notes on the novels of John Esten Cooke. Terri Blair read countless unit histories and embarked cheerfully (!) upon "fishing expeditions" in Confederate newspapers and magazines. Brian Wills tracked down Stuart material in the *Confederate Veteran* and in the *Southern Historical Society Papers*. And Jim Jones found the published version of Tom Price's diary, having begun his hunt with the single clue that the diary was in "some Northern newspaper after May 3, 1863."

Friends and colleagues at the University of Georgia have added substantive meaning to the phrase "community of scholars." Bud Bartley listened to some of my early ideas and responded with characteristic enthusiasm. Lester Stephens not only provided me with time and some travel funds in his capacity as department head, he also read a portion of the manuscript and offered his encouragement. Jean Friedman lent her sensitive insight to my efforts to understand the relationship between Stuart and Flora. And Ben Wall enlivened many long Saturday and Sunday afternoons in LeConte Hall with his stories and homespun sagacity.

Within that larger community of scholars beyond Clarke County, Georgia, I have had the benefit of conversations and correspondence about Stuart with Tom Connelly, Jim McDonough, Jack Davis, and Tom Watson Brown. And at a critical juncture in my writing Bill McFeely agreed to give a "quick read" to nine draft chapters. Bill did read the material; he read it two times and then offered ideas and insight which were truly brilliant. This was a supreme act of friendship, and I am ever grateful.

My praise goes to Nancy Heaton, Kathy Coley, and Donna Marshall, who transformed my barely legible legal pad pages into clear typescript. I thank them for their skills and good humor throughout this process.

Fran, Em, and John (aka J.T.) have read and listened and provided comic relief. I thank them, too.

*Athens, Georgia*
*1985*

# BOLD DRAGOON

# Man As Metaphor:
## An Epilogue by Way of Introduction

HE FASHIONED HEROISM from the human condition and crammed an incredible lot of life into the thirty-one years that he lived. But James Ewell Brown Stuart lives in the American memory more as antique metaphor than as man—as figure of speech rather than flesh and blood.

Near the beginning of William Faulkner's novel *Sartoris,* there is a wonderful vignette about Bayard Sartoris and J. E. B. Stuart. For the sake of coffee, "or the lack of it rather," Stuart's "military family" sweeps down upon an outdoor breakfast in the camp of a Yankee general. While the general and his staff scatter in confusion, Rebel horsemen quaff coffee directly from a steaming pot "as with a loving-cup" and then spur away. During the dash back to Southern lines, a captured Yankee expresses his relief that the raiders had not discovered the general's anchovies. Anchovies! Immediately Sartoris turns his horse and gallops again for the enemy headquarters. Stuart, too, wheels about, intending to compound his derring-do only to be restrained by his staff. Thus Sartoris rides alone into the already ravaged mess tent to search for the anchovies. Then a Yankee cook who lay hidden amid the rubble thrusts a hand and a derringer pistol from concealment and shoots Sartoris in the back.

Faulkner uses this story, among other purposes, to illumine the character of Bayard Sartoris, and by extension the Sartoris family. The vignette is about a "hare-brained prank of two heedless and reckless boys wild with their own youth." On the other hand, it is also about "a gallant and finely tragical focal point to which the history of the race had been raised from out of the old miasmic swamps of spiritual sloth by two angels valiantly fallen and strayed, altering the course of human events and purging the souls of men."[1]

Bayard Sartoris is a figment of Faulkner's fiction created to introduce the main character of the novel. And in his novel Faulkner wrote, not only about "the goddamnedest army the world ever saw," or about Mississippi or the southern United States. He used his local characters and regional settings to write about universals —to reveal the world as he knew it.

What about J. E. B. Stuart? He was real—not fiction, but fact. If an imagined Bayard Sartoris can speak to the truths of the human condition, what has the real J. E. B. Stuart to say? Is there universality, transcendence from his time to this time, in the experience of J. E. B. Stuart?

William Faulkner never spoke to these questions; that was not his purpose. Yet in *Sartoris* he uses history, and he uses Stuart. He makes Stuart the soul mate of Bayard Sartoris and thus reinforces the image of Sartoris as "heedless and reckless" at the same time he is "valiantly fallen and strayed," capable of "altering the course of human events and purging the souls of men." Faulkner's Bayard Sartoris does not ride with just any cavalry; he is a member of Stuart's "military family" and because he is, he is an authentically gallant, dashing, romantic fellow. For Faulkner, and presumably for his readers, Stuart stands for gallantry, dash, and romance. He is a symbol—a metaphor instead of a man.

Nor is Stuart's cameo appearance in *Sartoris* an isolated literary occurrence. In generations of American poetry and prose, he is a "gay knight-errant of the elder time," "flower of cavaliers," "genius of cavalry," "a fool at running around his enemy," "the singing, rollicking, daring young Cavalier," and more.[2]

One very good reason for the simple, one-dimensional image of Stuart in American fiction is the work of friends, relatives, historians, and buffs who have offered nonfiction about him. Here again Stuart is consistently *beau sabreur*, "the very image of a cavalier," "the gayest of the gay," "the last cavalier."[3]

Some have questioned Stuart's military merit; but they have done so on the grounds that he was an anachronism in the blood and mud of "modern war." This is the only variation in the Stuart image, and it is really no variation at all. Stuart is still the Cavalier. At issue is only whether any Cavalier could long succeed in a war with Roundheads.

Stuart deserves better than to be a lifeless symbol, however heroic, standing in fiction and fact for antique, and thus irrelevant, values and virtues. Stuart was once a man instead of a metaphor. His humanity deserves a hearing—in order to know him alive and whole.

To discover Stuart, I have consulted many sources. Most revealing have been the letters and documents of Stuart himself, and in my research I have used Stuart materials that no one else has. Testimony about Stuart by his friends, enemies, and comrades, in print and otherwise, has also been quite helpful. In a number of instances, however, I have interpreted stories and observations about Stuart in ways other than those who told or made them. For example, H. B. McClellan, who was Stuart's adjutant and first biographer, recalled Stuart's deathbed instructions as evidence of his composure and thoughtfulness. I have offered a significantly deeper meaning for this incident. In order to discern the life within the Stuart legend, I have had to examine that legend, which developed and grew even while Stuart lived. Accordingly I have incorporated newspaper and magazine articles, songs, and even rumors and gossip into my research and then into the narrative. Because Stuart was a professional soldier, I have dealt extensively with his military record. However, those who seek here a comprehensive chronicle of cavalry operations in the Army of Northern Virginia will, I fear, be disappointed.

I have attempted to keep my focus clearly upon Stuart and to emphasize Stuart the human being. Indeed, I have found him to be a fascinating human being. Stuart's life is more intriguing, and in some ways more heroic, than his legend.

# I

## *Young James*

JAMES EWELL BROWN STUART was born a Virginian into an established and prominent Virginia family. True—but that statement requires some explaining and considerable qualification.

Stuart's mother was Elizabeth Letcher Pannill Stuart. One of her grandfathers was something of a local hero in Patrick County, southwest Virginia. William Letcher had been active in the patriot cause during the American Revolution, so active that a notorious Tory had come to his home and shot him dead. Members of Elizabeth Stuart's family owned large tracts of land and numerous slaves in southwest Virginia and northwest North Carolina, and two of her cousins became state governors. In June of 1817, while still in her mid-teens, she had married Archibald Stuart.[1]

Archibald Stuart, too, could claim a grandfather who had served the American Revolution; Major Alexander Stuart had commanded a regiment at the Battle of Guilford Court House. Archibald Stuart's father was a lawyer, judge, and politician who maintained Virginia roots and property even while he was United States judge in Illinois and Missouri and Speaker of the Missouri legislature. Archibald Stuart himself had been an officer in the United States Army during the War of 1812. At the time of his marriage he was embarking upon a career in law and politics.[2]

At this career Archibald Stuart was visibly a success. He achieved local fame as a lawyer renowned for his speeches to juries and judges. He represented Patrick County in the Virginia Constitutional Convention of 1829–30, and there displayed no lit-

[ 5 ]

tle courage in voting for reform—a "white basis" of representation, excluding the slave population in determining the number of representatives from the state's legislative districts. Such a stand was calculated to win Stuart no friends among Virginia's conservative slaveholders. Maybe this was the reason Stuart was unseated in a contested election when he ran for the General Assembly in 1830. He rebounded, however, and won a seat in the United States House of Representatives during the fall of 1836; Stuart was a Whig member of Congress for one term, 1837–39. He was also a delegate to the Virginia Constitutional Convention of 1850–51, and he served in the Virginia Senate from 1852 to 1854. Stuart's record of public service, though not spectacular, was surely solid. Indeed, before 1860 Abraham Lincoln's political credentials were no better than Archibald Stuart's.[3]

However prominent he was, Archibald Stuart was never prosperous. Perhaps he lacked talent or discipline in the mundane affairs of business; maybe his clients were simply slow to pay his fees. Or maybe Archibald Stuart was to some degree a dissolute person. A description of his portrait notes "a certain weakness about the mouth." Certainly he was a bon vivant. Descriptions of him include such phrases as "no gathering of gentle folk . . . was complete without Arch Stuart"; "wonderful wit and humor"; "trill songs in his golden voice"; "center of attraction at every social gathering"; "when the cloth was drawn and the bottle passed." Family tradition among the Stuarts also links Archibald with games of chance.

Whatever the cause, Archibald Stuart "lost the farm," his inheritance, quite literally. James Ewell Brown Stuart was born at Laurel Hill, the place his mother had inherited from her martyred grandfather, William Letcher. And when young James was twelve years old, Elizabeth Stuart required him, as she had required all her sons, to take a solemn oath never to touch a drop of liquor. Indeed, if a small sample of her letters be any indication, Elizabeth Stuart responded to her husband's conviviality by becoming something of a shrew. She was full of negative opinions of people and supported her judgments with biblical quotations. It appears that Archibald's conduct first inspired and fueled Elizabeth's tirades, and perhaps because of them, Archibald spent a lot of time away from home.

Good lawyer that he was, Archibald Stuart might attack this interpretation of the character and conduct of himself and his wife as based upon hearsay and circumstantial evidence. If so, he would have a point. Yet the evidence is quite strong, if not overwhelming. Whatever the details, it is incontrovertibly true that Archibald Stuart was a "hell-of-a-fellow," that Elizabeth Stuart had "no special patience with nonsense," and that young James was not born into affluence. And all these circumstances had an impact upon the boy who grew up among them.[4]

James, or Jim, or Jimmy, as he was variously known then, was born at eleven thirty on the morning of February 6, 1833. He was the seventh child and youngest son in a brood that eventually included ten children, four boys and six girls. His Christian name honored an uncle, Judge James Ewell Brown, second husband of Archibald Stuart's sister.[5]

He spent his boyhood at Laurel Hill in southwestern Patrick County. Patrick County is technically in the Virginia Piedmont; yet it lies at the western border of the Piedmont on the eastern fringe of the Blue Ridge Mountains. The Patrick County portion of the Virginia Piedmont was far away from the Piedmont of Thomas Jefferson's Albemarle County or James Madison's Orange County. Patrick County was simply far away, remote from traditional centers of Virginia society and culture, nearer to the mountains and to North Carolina than to established circles of power and influence.

When Virginian jurist and Southern ideologue Nathaniel Beverly Tucker wrote his political novel *The Partisan Leader* in 1836, he set his partisans in Patrick County, where they might find safety in the rugged terrain of this wild, backwater region. James Stuart spent his boyhood in rough country marked by place-names such as Troublesome, Turkey Cock Mountain, Goblin Town Creek, No Business Mountain, Roaring Fork, and Buffalo Knob.

Patrick County was overwhelmingly rural; in contrast to the South of large plantations and numerous slaves, most landholdings in the county were farms and in 1840 slaves constituted only 24 percent of the total population (8,032). Patrick County farmers raised tobacco, corn, and livestock for market; but much of the local agriculture during James's youth was subsistence farming. The county seat was Taylorsville (now Stuart), which in 1849 contained only fifty houses. The nearest city worthy of the name (incorporated 1852) was Lynchburg, more than fifty miles away.[6]

Laurel Hill was in Virginia, but just barely; the Stuarts' post office was Mt. Airy, North Carolina. A grove of oak trees surrounded the spacious house, and the land around was rolling hills. It was essentially a farm, as opposed to a plantation, although by 1850 Archibald Stuart owned real estate valued at $10,000. James's father was more lawyer/politician than he was farmer, and his profession kept him away from Laurel Hill for extended periods, riding the legal circuit in southwestern Virginia or fulfilling his political obligations in Washington or Richmond. In his absence Elizabeth Stuart assumed responsibility for managing the place. And a significant responsibility this was. In 1830, for example, the Stuart extended household included twelve whites and nineteen blacks. In 1840 there were forty-one people living at Laurel Hill —thirteen whites and twenty-eight blacks. Among Laurel Hill slaves in 1840, eleven of twenty-eight were less than ten years old and thus less than productive laborers. Paradoxically James Stuart grew up in rural isolation within an active community.[7]

Young James spent his early youth at home; he played with his brothers and sisters, performed a share of farm chores, and roamed the hills of Laurel Hill. He developed an appreciation of nature, in grand vistas and single leaves, that he never lost. Later he would write a poem "Lines Addressed to a Pressed Geranium Leaf," and still later would begin letters describing his life at West Point with remarks on the "natural beauty" of the site, "the picturesque mountain scenery, the magnificent view of the Hudson, the delightful river breezes . . ." During his young years on the farm, James also absorbed a feeling for animals. At age thirteen he closed a letter to his mother with a request she kiss his sister and brother for him; then he added, "I would tell you to kiss Black and Dallas [horses? dogs?], but I know you wouldn't do that." Throughout his life Stuart referred to his horses with much the same feeling and familiarity as he devoted to family and friends. He even wrote a poem which honored "Maryland," one of his war horses.[8]

During his youth, James developed a sensitive side. He displayed it in his concern for the feelings of others and in an aesthetic bent that inspired him to write bad poetry and appreciate beauty in people as well as nature. There was a tenderness about young Stuart. Sometimes he concealed it beneath the hearty facade with which he imitated his father. Sometimes he hid it behind a rigid zeal for principles reminiscent of his mother. Often he affected something like tenderness, put it on like a mask, to make himself appear properly genteel. But underneath all this was the genuine article, the soul of a sensitive human being.

Of course it was dangerous for boys and young men to be tender, and especially in James Stuart's circumstance. He lived within a large family in which he was the youngest male, among a larger extended family in a region where cousins kept closely in touch and made long visits. He came of age in a patriarchal setting in which boys were supposed to act like men, in a rural, mountain environment where refinement was rare. In such a situation, to be tender was to be vulnerable; the setting seemed to demand toughness and reward manifestations of strength. James placed great stock in physical courage and sought opportunities to assert his manhood even while a boy.

There is a story in Stuart family tradition, told by James's brother William Alexander, concerning young James and a hornets' nest. The nest was among the branches of a large tree, and the boys, William Alexander about fifteen and James around nine, wanted it as a trophy. First they stalked the nest; then they tried without success to bring it down by throwing short sticks at it. Finally they climbed into the tree with long sticks for an assault at closer range. As they neared the nest, the hornets emerged and began to sting their assailants. William Alexander did the logical thing: he tumbled out of the tree and ran out of range. James took a deep breath, squinted his eyes, and pressed the attack. He suffered the stings and secured the prize. The story may be apocryphal, but it is much in character. Young James seemed to feel the need to prove himself, to himself and to others, and in the course of doing so, he took lots of dares and considerable punishment.[9]

Elizabeth Stuart took charge of James's early education, but beyond basic skills the boy needed more formal schooling. And to pursue his education he had to leave Laurel Hill. To all intents and purposes, James left home to make his way in the world at age twelve. He returned from a succession of schools only for visits. He left Laurel Hill, in many ways, a "normal" boy; his experiences, upbringing, and interests were typical of his time and place. But, like all people, James was unique. He had inherited both his "Pa's" zest for good times and his "Mama's" demanding standards. Though possessed of tender feelings and an aesthetic consciousness, at the same time he acted out a puerile sort of machismo. He took care of himself and took pride in his independence. James was aware that members of his family had made their mark in the world, and this record of accomplishment challenged him to make something of himself. He had lofty expectations for himself, and he knew that his family and friends shared and supported his ambitions. He also knew that whatever success he achieved would have to be largely his own doing. He was not an "advantaged" lad. He took very little in the way of material goods with him when he left Laurel Hill. Nor did he stand to inherit any fortune; he would have to make it.

In the fall of 1845 having taken, and taken seriously, his oath to his mother never to touch a drop of liquor, James crossed the mountains and began more formal education at a school in Wytheville, Virginia. He had developed a reputation as a fighter within the family—he accepted challenges from people as well as hornets —and now proudly reported to an older cousin, "Contrary to the expectations of all I have been so fortunate as not to have a single fight since I have been going to school . . ." He quickly added that his pacific record resulted "Not from cowardice either (for I know you will immediately suspect that as being the reason)." He had adopted a code—"never to be imposed upon," and his classmates "saw immediately and so far from trying to do it they acted quite to the contrary." This solution to his propensity for scrapes and fights may have worked in Wytheville; but the remedy was not permanent. James would again feel the need to defend himself by asserting himself physically.

The letter in which James took such pains to speak to his fights and his courage contains more information about the thoughts and enthusiasms of the thirteen-year-old boy: He was interested in food; apparently his cousin had remarked upon the failure of cooks at his college to serve butter, and James protested, "I could not do without butter." He had recently had measles. He devoted several lines to the color and gender of a new colt. He recounted an incident in which his father had put another bullet into his already loaded rifle and "came very near shooting it off before he found out." He was no threat to win a spelling bee—"Lee is not hear [sic] now . . ." And he added a postscript about hens, a polecat, and a fighting cock.[10]

"School" really meant schoolmaster. For the next three years James studied with various teachers in or near Wytheville and at the home of some of his cousins near Danville, Virginia. He usually lived with relatives or family friends in the community and studied at the home of his mentor. He pursued a classical liberal education. In January 1847, he was "jogging away at Old Caesar." And three months later he was "still reading Caesar" while laboring in "Algebra in which I have gotten as far as Evolution of Powers." James began to read Virgil during the following academic year, but illness curtailed his study. He contracted mumps and spent four or five months under a doctor's care.

Significantly, he did not return home, but convalesced in Wytheville. He also assumed responsibility for his doctor's bill, which remained unpaid but on his mind several years later. Clearly James had crossed more than some mountains when he went to Wytheville; he had undergone a rite of passage as well.[11]

At some time during these years, he worked for a while in a law office in Wytheville and so gained a taste of his father's profession. Surely he thought about a career in law during those years, and he returned to those thoughts later. He also gave some thought to becoming a teacher; at least he wrote one of his teachers that he expected to teach. But he probably realized that he studied as a means to an end and not as an end in itself. James was bright; he worked hard; and he strove to "be perfect" in his readings and recitations. Yet an intellectual he was not. Besides, he aspired to greater things than being a schoolmaster; he would not resign himself to a dreary succession of years rapping the knuckles of recalcitrant little boys like himself.[12]

A factor that probably fed James's ambition was his growing independence. His travels to and from schools and the months he spent away from home did not exactly qualify him as a man of the world. But he had early experience in looking out for himself, and he found he could. An incident during the Christmas recess when James was thirteen is a good example. He planned to go home from school, but could not secure a horse for the journey. So he set out on foot across the mountains. The snow was "about half leg deep" and James "had to break the road nearly all the way." He encountered cousins late in the day and spent the night with them, hoping to borrow a horse the next day. However he learned that he would be unable to get a horse until after Christmas, and consequently "I stayed there enjoying myself most remarkably well, until Thursday (Jan. 5th) making a stay of just two weeks." All this he announced with some pride in a letter to an older cousin, and indeed he had every right to be proud of his self-reliance.[13]

Independence may be a euphemism for describing James's early adolescence. He left home quite early in life and really never returned. Most boys remained at or near home longer than James Stuart, and most were more anxious to return home. Surely schooling required that he leave Laurel Hill, and his many relatives throughout the region certainly mitigated the separation from his immediate family. Nevertheless, James's prolonged absences from home and his seemingly casual decision to spend Christmas of 1846 with cousins indicate that he felt less than close to his parents. And they seemed to have returned the feeling, if letters are a reliable index. During the fall of his first year away from Laurel Hill, James wrote his mother, "I can't see why you don't write to me, for you have no idea how acceptable a letter from home is to any son, but especially to one away off at a boarding school where I never hear from home or anywhere else. I have no doubt that you all have experienced this, and for that reason it appears still more astounding why you do not have mercy upon a poor, little, insignificant whelp away from his mammy." This impassioned appeal may have produced a letter or two. But, even if it did, Elizabeth and Archibald Stuart were never attentive correspondents, and James often complained of months passing without a letter from home.[14]

One reason he decided "it was not worth my while to go to Patrick until spring," was the presence of "Miss Maria L. Crockett who was as fat and pretty as ever." Like most teenaged boys, James discovered that he much enjoyed the company of girls. He became intrigued with the subtlety of courtship and tried to act as a go-between for his friends and relatives. He protested soon after he was fourteen, "I have gotten out with the girls. I believe they were just made for man's troubles." But surrounding this pronouncement were paragraphs devoted to flirtations and rivalries among suitors and comments such as "Miss Maria Crockett carried a day (or rather the night) . . ." And he did qualify his condemnation somewhat: "The[re] is no girl now that I care any thing about except Miss Mary Crockett and I do not care a great deal about her." James learned to enjoy social occasions and female companionship early in his life, and he never forgot the lesson.[15]

After three years of schools and tutors, young James was prepared for higher learning; in August of 1848, at age fifteen, he enrolled in Emory & Henry College. Founded by the Holston Conference of the Methodist Church, located about halfway between Marion and Abingdon in Washington County, the college had first enrolled students only ten years earlier; it was the first institution of higher learning in southwest Virginia. James attended Emory & Henry for almost two years. He studied mechanics, read Cicero and Livy, appreciated the "beauties as well as the 'smutties' of old Horace." He made friends and joined a literary and debating society, the Hermesians. During a speech he made before that group, he became so absorbed in his rhetoric that he forgot where he was and fell off the platform.[16]

During his first year at Emory & Henry a campus religious revival swept James into the Methodist Church. At home at Laurel Hill, James's mother had been an Episcopalian, his father was probably a Presbyterian; but apart from Elizabeth Stuart's moral strictures, James had not had much religious education or background. And even after his revival experience at Emory & Henry, his letters to family and friends contain few, if any, religious references. Later in life he would seldom write a personal letter or even publish a general order without invoking "Divine Providence" or mentioning prayers to God. During his first year at West Point, however, he wrote to at least one of his Emory & Henry chums about his conversion and commitment. "I expect that you as well as all my old friends about Emory," he wrote, "have come to the conclusion that I have renounced the cross since I came to this place usually considered at so great variance with Religion. But I rejoice to say that I still have evidence of a Savior's pardoning love. When I came here I had reason to expect that many and strong temptations would beset my path, but I relied on 'him whom to know is live [life] everlasting' to deliver me from temptation, and prayed God to guide me in the right way and 'teach' me to walk as a Christian should; I have never for a moment hesitated to persevere; indeed since I came here I have been more than ever satisfied of the absolute importance of an acquaintance with the Lord." These words penned in mid-paragraph are classic; they all but define nineteenth-century Southern evangelicalism. James professed a personal, direct relationship with God through Christ, the function of which was moral conduct now and "life everlasting" later on.

The simple credo he wrote down for his friend sounds a bit primitive, or at least immature. But at the time he wrote it, James was only seventeen years old. And as he grew older, he began to conceive of a god who was more than some cosmic streetsweeper whose major role in the world lay in clearing away potential obstacles to the righteous behavior of James Stuart. At this point in life though, he was, as one of his cadet comrades later recalled, a "Bible-class man." [17]

He wrote a revealing letter to his parents during his first year at Emory & Henry (1848–49); it was the letter of a sixteen-year-old boy attempting to cope with the expectations of manhood. James was worried about his sacred history exam. He had scuffled with one of his classmates just before the examination began and incurred a bloody nose. Consequently he lost thirty precious minutes during the exam tending to his nose, and he had to rush through his answers. It seemed he always had troubles at exam time. James recalled his bout with mumps the previous year in Wytheville and compared himself to Job. He planned to place his Bible on his desk in the hope that it would ward off the evils that seemed constantly to beset him.

His finger was healing and his hand well—perhaps injured in another fighting "scrape." He thanked his parents for twenty-five cents they had sent him and promised not to complain about the college food anymore.

James concluded his letter, "Please don't ask me any more to do better than I have done, for it makes me feel like a sheep-killing-dog." James did not enjoy an idyllic adolescence. [18]

He, of course, had enrolled at Emory & Henry to enhance his education. But within the Stuart family, and no doubt within James, was the question of what he would do once he was educated. Since he did not stand to inherit land or wealth, he would have to choose among the *"hireling* professions," as he called them—"Law, Medicine, Engineering, and Arms." It is just possible that he attended Emory & Henry to prepare himself for the United States Military Academy. At the time a West Point education was one of the best that could be had in the country, and it would provide James with training in one of the "hireling professions" and leave him the option to pursue one of the others later.[19]

Archibald Stuart ran again for Congress in 1848. He lost. But his opponent, Democrat Thomas Hamlet Averett, appointed James Stuart to West Point in what tradition holds was the first official act of his term. Perhaps there had been some sort of gentleman's agreement, spoken or unspoken, between the rival candidates. At any rate young James learned something about the value of influence and connections and began to prepare himself in earnest for West Point.[20]

He left Emory & Henry in April of 1850 and commenced his journey north in late May. This was a far more significant leave-taking than his departures for Wytheville or Emory & Henry, if for no other reason than that he would not be eligible for a furlough for more than two years. He was leaving southwest Virginia for the first time and going off to study war. If he saw his beloved hills, his family, and friends before June of 1852, it would be only because he had been "sent home" in disgrace for deficiency in studies or conduct. The trip to West Point might well have been a somber journey for young James—but it was not. Surely his romantic nature inspired a tear or two, at least a misty eye, during the trip. But if his activities and his letters describing the trip are any indication, James felt much at home in the wide, wide world, and he savored every moment of his passage.

James traveled first to Wytheville and then took a stagecoach for Lynchburg. En route he visited a sister for dinner and met some more relatives in Salem, Virginia. James remained two days in Lynchburg, visiting with an uncle and especially with two female cousins—"I had no idea what pretty cousins I had." Then he moved on to Charlottesville, where he "went all over the University and became acquainted with many of the students." James the aspiring plebe paid a call upon a family friend and secured a letter of introduction to two upper-class cadets. James the tourist visited

Thomas Jefferson's home, Monticello, and came away with a chip of Jefferson's tombstone and two roses from the yard. James the discerning observer proclaimed his dismay at "the ladies of Charlottesville, for collectively or individually they merit the rank of ugliest of the ugly." All this he did and decided during a one-day stopover.[21]

Next, James traveled to Washington, making the last portion of his trip by steamboat. In "The Great Metropolis," as he called the city, he considered himself "green as a gourd vine." Nevertheless he managed to see "Zack," President Zachary Taylor, a couple of times on the streets, and "walked all around the White House." He called upon his benefactor, Congressman Averett, and pronounced him a "very fine sensible old gentleman indeed." James visited the Senate Chamber at the Capitol, decided that Daniel Webster was the "finest looking man in the Senate," and determined "of all pleasant speakers give me Jeff. Davis of Mississippi." Henry Clay appeared "very nervous," but possessed an "air of dignity and command." Sam Houston "appears better with his mouth shut than open." Lewis Cass "is a fleshy old fellow with a very fat face." James went also to the House Chamber, but found it a "rowdy place." Following this full day of sightseeing, he packed his souvenir sprig of arbor vitae from the Capitol grounds and made ready to move on at five o'clock the next morning.[22]

He went by train to Baltimore and there boarded a steamboat for New York, where he confessed he "couldn't see the town for the houses." After a very brief stay in New York, James made an evening cruise up the Hudson to West Point. During the course of the journey he had forgotten and lost some of his belongings; but even at the time, he was able to laugh at himself. His only regret was that he steamed up the Hudson at night and so missed the scenery. And in the midst of his initiation to the Academy and the life of a lowly plebe, he announced, "Camp life is glorious."[23]

Young James put on a brave show for his correspondents when he wrote such a rosy account of his first encounter with a world wider than southwest Virginia. His response to strange places and novel circumstances was certainly a far cry from that of Ulysses Grant, to cite one example. Grant, who had journeyed to West Point eleven years earlier, admitted to "dallying" en route because of a "dread" of reaching the place and spent his most cheerful times there reading reports of a bill introduced to Congress to abolish the Academy.[24]

Surely James's blasé judgments of everything from Charlottesville women to Daniel Webster and the jolly narratives of his travels concealed some amount of insecurity. But for the most part James seemed very much at home wherever he happened to be. Indeed he had to feel at home in the world, because he did not seem to feel much at home at Laurel Hill. Elizabeth Stuart offered him very high standards of morality and conduct and Archibald Stuart provided an example of social and political success. But the youth found it difficult, if not impossible, to live up to his mother's standards, and he did not have the means to follow his father's example.

James Stuart was ready to leave home. His background, his social associations, and his youthful experiences had whetted his appetite for the many bounties available in this world. Young James was hungry.

# II

## *"Beauty"*

HE WAS NOT HANDSOME THEN. James Stuart officially became "Cadet Stuart" on July 1, 1850, after he had been at West Point about two weeks. But to his friends at West Point he was "Beauty Stuart," a nickname used to describe his "personal comeliness in inverse ratio to the term employed."[1]

One of the first known photographs of Stuart, a daguerreotype made in Washington soon after his graduation from the Academy, displays a clean-shaven, rather plain-looking young man with a high forehead, full face, and somewhat blunt features. His nose is prominent; the mouth looks slightly delicate; but his eyes are strong. Stuart expressed himself with those blue-gray eyes; they sparkled, twinkled, flashed, or pierced as his mood changed. And after a mustache and full beard concealed his mouth, cheeks, and chin, Stuart's eyes were all the more dominant. His hair was auburn-brown, and he consistently wore it combed back off his forehead and down over the top half of his ears.[2]

He grew to a little above average height—about five feet nine or ten inches. His arms and legs were long, his body relatively short. His shoulders were broad and he was barrel-chested; somewhere between plump and lean, Stuart was "sturdy." From time to time "sturdy" may have become "stout," because he did love to eat. Once when he had been ill and unable to eat with his accustomed abandon, he said, "it almost grieves me . . . when I find myself unable to do justice to a meal for which I have to pay full price, for it has always been my consolation that I always got the worth of my money in the eating line, and precious little did a hotel keeper ever make off me." He learned to carry himself erect and took on a soldier's posture at West Point. Consequently many who met him believed him taller than he actually was, and few people ever accused Stuart of being fat.[3]

"Beauty" did have a fine voice. Later in his cadet career, when he issued commands at drill and formations, at least one lower classman who was a member of an adjacent company considered a high point of any parade Stuart's musical rendering of "order arms, parade rest." And when he sang songs instead of commands, his tones were rich, full, and on key. Plebes—fourth classmen at the Academy—did not often use their voices, though. Perhaps Stuart became Beauty before the corps had heard him.[4]

Plebes did not ride horses either. When he arrived at the Academy, Stuart was already a skilled rider, and he became more so while he was there. Maybe Stuart became Beauty before anyone had seen him on a horse.[5]

It is possible that Stuart earned his nickname with black eyes, cuts, and bruises. For he continued to offer an "almost thankful acceptance of a challenge from any cadet to fight." He did so well into his first-class (fourth) year at West Point, when he was a cadet officer with seemingly no need to prove himself, physically or any other way, to anyone.[6]

Stuart was not the ugliest man in the corps. That distinction belonged to William R. Terrill, a cadet from Virginia one year Stuart's senior. But handsome Beauty was not. After he grew his beard, one of Stuart's classmates proclaimed that he was "the only man he ever saw that [a] beard improved." And the nickname stuck. Ten years later, in the midst of a very large war, West Point classmates continued to address Major General Stuart as "Dear Beauty."[7]

When the young Virginian arrived at West Point, he went, not to the barracks, but to the woods. During the summer months the entire cadet corps (then between 200 and 250 men) moved out of the Academy and into tents somewhere on the plain above the Hudson. Each year the encampment honored some military luminary with its name; Stuart reported to Camp Gaines, named for General Edmund Gaines, who served in Florida and Mexico. Very soon he exchanged his civilian clothes for some heavy high-top black shoes, white duck trousers, a short, gray coat with three rows of brass buttons and a stiff collar, and a black leather cap seven inches high adorned with a pompon. With these new clothes, Stuart moved into a tent pitched over a wooden floor platform. Under the supervision of cadet officers and Academy cadre, the new plebes drilled in infantry tactics three times each day and once in artillery. Plebes were live bodies upon whom upper classmen might practice command voices and convenient victims of pranks and hazing during the summer encampment. Stuart learned the military regimen and, somehow, how to keep those white pants clean while living in a tent.[8]

He also learned that his "free" education had plunged him into instant debt. Each cadet received $24 per month from the government. But this money went directly into his account at the Academy commissary to pay for clothes and personal essentials, and it was never enough to cover these necessary expenses; so like most of his comrades, Stuart was perennially in debt to the "company store."[9]

When he first wrote his father, within two weeks of his arrival at West Point, he complained of not hearing from home, and he promised to write every two weeks. But he was steadfast in his course—"I know that if I *try* I can go through and I am determined to *try*." Very soon, however, he recovered from his mild attack of homesickness, abandoned his promise to write every two weeks, and began to love West Point.[10]

He was enormously impressed with the place. "So far as I know of no profession more desirable than that of the soldier," he wrote. "Indeed every thing connected with the Academy has far surpassed my most sanguine expectations." He liked the "advantages afforded for intellectual culture and polish." To one of his cousins he dropped the name of one of his comrades, "Jerome Napoleon Bonaparte, who is the best looking cadet at the Point, he is Napoleon's great grand nephew." He was awed by the band, the ceremonies, and parades. And he was delighted with the stream of visitors who made a "social season" of the West Point encampment. Winfield Scott, hero of the Mexican War and ranking general in the United States Army, came with his family. His daughter was a "Belle among the Ladies' men of the Corps" and "one of the most expert riders in the Country." A "host" of congressmen and their families were also on hand, and "at evening Parade especially, the space in front of camp ground is full of smiling faces and bright eyes from every part of the Union." To the young man whose previous travel and contacts had been confined to southwest Virginia, this was heady stuff indeed. West Point seemed to be a mecca for mighty men and pretty women, and Beauty was part of it all.[11]

Once past the novelty of discipline and drill, Stuart found that he could not only survive but thrive within the military regimen. In camp, at least, he was able to use his body as well as his brain. Whatever his new friends might say about his physical appearance, Beauty found that he could make his body conform to military specifications and excel at anything active. He quickly acquired a sense of military savoir faire and set about making the system and the institution work for him.

At least one fourth classman described the encampment of his plebe summer as "slavery." "Glorious" was the word Stuart used to describe his experience in letters to two of his cousins. He went on to say to one of them, "I think I could live in Camp the remainder of my days if it remained warm enough." But Stuart knew it would not remain warm enough and he anticipated with some trepidation the next challenge of his new career at the Academy—the barracks and the classroom. On September 1 the encampment and the social season ended abruptly, and the corps marched into the barracks to begin the academic year in earnest. He saw no more "smiling faces and bright eyes" for another nine months—and he had no prospect of leaving West Point for almost two years! Only during the summer between their third- and second-class years could cadets leave the Academy (Stuart began planning the itinerary of his furlough, scheduled for June 1852, in October of 1850).

Now he moved into a room furnished with iron beds, iron tables, and little else. With him were Judson D. Bigham from Indiana and another Virginian, Charles G. Rogers, from Smyth County (between Stuart's home and Emory & Henry College). Both were "very studious and clever fellows"; indeed they both graduated with higher class rank than Stuart. For the moment Stuart counted himself fortunate to be in the company of men who set a serious tone and who were bright enough to help each other.[12]

He was quite candid with his correspondents about the academic challenge. "I used to think that I had some idea of what hard study was," he wrote, "at least my idea of it was that it was something to be avoided as much as possible which before I came here I succeeded at admirably, but on coming here I found that it was necessary to cultivate a more intimate acquaintance with it or else come out wanting at the Examination. So I turned into studying pretty hard." Stuart was particularly intrigued with the system of grading at West Point. "Here every man's grade, or 'standing,' . . . is definitely established at every Examination, it is not made out in decimals or by any complicated process of calculation, but simply his *relative* standing in his class and this is published every June in a Register to the world. So that if a man is foot everybody knows it and if he is head everybody who wants to can know it." Clearly, Stuart liked the system. It allowed him to measure himself, not against perfection as he once had or by some arbitrary standard established by a professor, but against his peers. The classroom became an arena; learning was a game. And even at the cost of hard study, Stuart wanted to play.[13]

During his first four months at the Academy, Stuart and his classmates concentrated upon only two courses, mathematics and English studies. Such a focus upon basic subjects was designed to provide the new cadets with a proper foundation for further study. It also promised to weed out young men who had come to West Point without the academic ability or background to succeed. "English studies" was English grammar and rhetoric. Stuart fared pretty well in this class; by now he could distinguish between "hear" and "here." But he never learned much about paragraphs or punctuation—to the end of his life he wrote run-on sentences (like the one about "hard study" quoted above), and his paragraphs usually contained dissimilar subjects and often covered several pages.[14]

He had to write papers during the course of the year, and upon at least one occasion, Stuart resorted to "used prose"—a speech he had written earlier at Emory & Henry. Unfortunately, when Stuart needed the speech, his cousin A. Stuart Brown had it at the University of Virginia, perhaps to use in one of his own compositions. At any rate, Stuart wrote Brown an urgent request for the return of "The Triumph of True Principles." Later, Stuart sent

Brown about a page of moralizing prose, probably copied from "The Triumph of True Principles," and it is likely that the itinerant speech received grades at both West Point and Virginia during the 1850–51 academic year.[15]

Mathematics came easier for Stuart; he achieved higher standing (sixth) in his mathematics classes than in any other course at the Academy (including cavalry tactics). He was fortunate to have had good previous training. More cadets left West Point because of poor performances in mathematics than for any other academic cause, and many Southerners and Westerners discovered that Eastern boys had received better preparation before they came to the Point. Stuart, however, had no such problem. On the contrary, in 1854 he wrote a glowing tribute to one of his mathematics instructors for the Richmond *Examiner* in an effort to help the man secure an appointment as professor of mathematics at the University of Virginia.[16]

As the January examinations approached Stuart naturally became anxious. He must have felt good about his performance in his studies; but examinations at the Academy were traumatic almost by definition. James McNeill Whistler's chemistry examination in June 1853, for example, was a thirteen-word disaster. "I am required to discuss the subject of silicon," Whistler began. "Silicon is a gas." Immediately the instructor terminated the examination and, soon after, Cadet Whistler. During the same examination season, Stuart reported that a member of the corps died from "congestion of the brain." "Mental anxiety," he wrote, caused the disease and also caused the stricken cadet to faint during his examination. In January 1851, Stuart concluded, "I came out better than I expected." He ranked sixth in mathematics and fifteenth in English; his averaged standing among the 72 members of his class (originally 102) who survived the ordeal was eighth.[17]

After the January examinations, classes resumed immediately and the plebes took on French, in addition to mathematics and English. Stuart continued his solid progress and in June stood eighth overall (mathematics, eighth; French, fifteenth; and English studies, twelfth). He accumulated forty-three demerits—far below the number for dismissal, but more than the number received by most of the cadets in the upper third of his class.[18]

By spring the novelty of life and study at West Point had worn thin for Stuart. He wrote his cousins about the "dull career of a student," and the "monstrous routine of military and college life." In fact, West Point offered cadets very little in the way of extracurricular diversions. Stuart joined the Dialectic Society, which was a debating club, not unlike the Hermesians at Emory & Henry. He subscribed to the Richmond *Examiner* and began to take some interest in national politics and current events. He checked books out of the library—travel, military history, Sir Walter Scott, Lord Byron—and later he claimed to have read Shakespeare by candlelight under his blanket after taps. There was little else to do, and Stuart, whose boredom threshold was quite low, was often bored. Even back in December he had been bored enough to spend a Saturday afternoon in the library reading thirty-three-year-old copies of *Blackwood's Magazine*.[19]

He made friends among his classmates in spite of, or perhaps because of, his propensity to take offense at insults, real and imagined, and to challenge the offending party to a fight. Most of Stuart's friends were Southerners, and perhaps he and they interpreted his conduct as defending his honor. Stuart became a Virginiaphile at West Point and had disparaging things to say about the appearance and manners of Yankee women, the ludicrous performance of Yankee cadets on horseback, and the "taint" of "free-soil-Yankeedom." He was pleased to find so many Southerners and Virginians among the faculty. He acknowledged that a sort of sectional truce prevailed at the Academy, "a sentiment of mutual forbearance." Yet this sentiment did not extend to Stuart's choice of friends—with one very significant exception.[20]

Oliver Otis Howard was one of Stuart's friends, one of the least likely. Howard was from Maine. He accepted his appointment to the Academy late and so missed the rigors of the plebe summer encampment. He was a "Sept." (enrolled September 1), who spent only four nights in camp. He was priggish, self-righteous, and opinionated. He also possessed a shrill voice, a tall silk hat, and a cane. He was reputed to be an active abolitionist, and during his entire plebe year Howard earned not one demerit. He associated with an enlisted man (an old friend stationed at West Point) and with a cadet who had been "cut"—shunned—by the corps. This combination of characteristics and conduct did not make Howard terribly popular; indeed he himself was cut by a cabal of prominent Southern cadets.

Howard recalled and recorded his early troubles at West Point when he wrote his autobiography more than a half century later. And the one cadet he remembered as befriending him in the midst of his trials was Stuart. "I never can forget the manliness of J. E. B. Stuart . . ." Howard wrote. "He spoke to me, he visited me, and we became warm friends, often, on Saturday afternoons, visiting the young ladies of the post together."[21]

Certainly, simple justice explains Stuart's friendship with Howard. The two were members of the Bible class and so shared at least something in common. But one of Stuart's other good friends was Custis Lee, the son of Robert E. Lee, who was nominally the leader of the clique bent upon ostracizing Howard. It must have been no mean feat to be a friend to both Howard and Lee. Stuart accomplished the feat, however; he did so for reasons that in his mind transcended politics, geography, manner, and demeanor. At the end of Stuart's plebe year, Howard stood first in the class; Lee was second. And throughout their careers at West Point, Howard and Lee excelled; Lee graduated number one, Howard number four. Stuart respected excellence; he admired success. He had a keen instinct for recognizing talent, and he constantly gravitated toward those people who were or would become successful. It was no accident that the classmates with whom he became friends, the ones mentioned most in his letters, all finished in the top quarter of the class of 1854—above Stuart. Such friendships were meaningful at the time, and later they might become quite valuable.[22]

Stuart began his second year at West Point with rank. He was appointed corporal of the corps, the third highest rank available to a third classman. And during his second summer encampment, he filled the place of a cadet on furlough as orderly sergeant of Company A. "I assure you," he wrote to a cousin, "there is a great difference between a third Classman and a Plebe." In addition, he continued, "Occupying a Post of so great responsibility I have been granted many privileges which are denied the rest of the Corps, so upon the whole I have had a splendid time."[23]

One cause of Stuart's "splendid time" that summer was the visit of Mary Pegram. She was the sister of one of Stuart's classmates and very good friend, John Pegram—"decidedly the best hearted fellow I ever knew." Pegram's mother and sister came from their home in Richmond to see him in August, and Stuart,

who had been "withstanding the smiles of yankeedom," immediately lost his heart to "Miss Mary." To a cousin Stuart wrote, "That
Miss Mary is intelligent, fascinating, beautiful and modest and that
she is a *Virginian* is an enumeration of by no means half of her
excellent qualities." His contact with Mary Pegram probably consisted of some chaperoned strolls about West Point, conversations
when he "happened" to meet her after parade, maybe a dinner
with the Pegrams at Roe's Hotel, and possibly some dances at
cotillion parties which the cadets gave during the encampment.
However much time Beauty spent with Mary, it was sufficient for
him to become infatuated. When she left, he was "nearly *dead*
with the 'blues.'" He found that he could not look at the flower
she gave him, preserved temporarily in a glass of water on his
table, without missing her.[24]

Stuart recovered by the following spring. His fascination with
Mary Pegram must have faded, or hers with him. He continued to
crave the company of women and attended winter band concerts,
as much to see the "smiles of the ladies" as to listen to the music.

During his third-class academic year, Stuart continued his
studies in French and mathematics and began a course in drawing.
That latter class was important, as officers had to represent terrain,
fortifications, bridges and such accurately on paper. He fared
rather well in his work and finished the year standing seventh in
his class (mathematics, seventh; drawing, twenty-first; French,
eighth, forty-nine demerits). His class also began riding during
that year. Stuart much enjoyed the exercise and soon established
himself as one of the best horsemen in his class. The riding drills
also offered amusement in "seeing what ridiculous figures these
Yankees cut on horseback."[25]

The winter of 1851–52 was extremely severe in upstate New
York. On Christmas Day Stuart had to stoke the fire in his room
against a temperature of eleven degrees below zero outside, and
snow still fell in mid-April. The cold often combined with the
tedium of the military routine to bore Stuart. Horses and "smiles
of the ladies" helped; but there were never enough band concerts
or riding classes.

He still liked the Academy; but he concluded in one letter
written on Christmas Day, 1851, "For one to succeed here, all that
is required is an ordinary mind and application, the latter is by far

the most important and desirable of the two. For men of rather obtuse intellect, by indomitable perseverance have been known to graduate with honor; while some of the greatest geniuses of the Country have been found deficient, for want of application; Edgar A. Poe for instance."

These were pretty mature reflections for an eighteen-year-old. They also reveal the secret of much of Stuart's success, at West Point and after. He was no genius, never anything like an intellectual, but he had better than an "obtuse intellect." And, though he often tried to conceal it, he all but embodied "indomitable perseverance." In the same letter he wrote that he had "always enjoyed the reputation of being pretty lazy." "But," he added, "it must be said to my credit that of all things I abhor being compelled to do *nothing most*." Stuart did "enjoy" the appearance of indolence. But even when his body was at leisure, his mind was in motion.[26]

Stuart endured the routine of his second year at the Academy and counted the days until his furlough began in mid-June of 1852. By then he had planned and dreamed about it so much that the reality of it may have been anticlimactic. But, no, Stuart enjoyed himself thoroughly with a round of visits so extensive that he spent only ten days of his ten weeks at home at Laurel Hill. The remainder of the time he spent with brothers, sisters, and cousins. His most significant visit was to a plantation called Beaver Creek, near Martinsville, Virginia. There he met sixteen-year-old Bettie Hairston, a distant cousin on his mother's side of the family. And for the second summer in a row, Stuart became infatuated. He and Bettie went walking together, hunted blackberries, and roamed the garden at Beaver Creek. When he left, Bettie gave him a drinking gourd, and he inscribed her name upon it with his knife. The gourd hung in his room for the rest of the time Stuart spent at West Point. He wrote her long letters, exchanged sprigs of flowers, and repeatedly invited her to visit the Academy.[27]

One family tradition holds that Stuart proposed marriage to Bettie Hairston and that she declined. Perhaps it is true. Stuart began his correspondence with the claim that theirs was true, as opposed to ceremonious, friendship—"friendship in its pure unvitiated and unaffected form, which comes from the heart." He certainly admired her, and he opened himself to her, telling her all his hopes and plans. But if there was love between them, it was less than torrid. She never came to see him at West Point, and he did not exactly rush to her side after his graduation. He was two months reaching Beaver Creek. Stuart wrote her long letters; but he did not write too many—perhaps a dozen over a three-year period. Still, the relationship was important to Stuart. He seemed to need a confidante, someone with whom he could share his enthusiasms, his quandaries, and his accomplishments. "I write to you my Dear Cousin," he said, "many things about West Point and myself, which I fear savor too much of egotism, but *to you* I feel disposed always to express myself freely." She (sixteen) was three years younger than he (nineteen) during a time in their lives in which three years made some difference. Maybe he confided in her because she in her youth and innocence could never threaten him. He did presume to counsel her from time to time—about boarding school when she enrolled at Salem Academy, about the relative merits of Shakespeare's plays, and more. Whether or not he proposed marriage to her, Beauty developed some intimacy with Bettie. One lonely Christmas Eve at West Point Stuart composed a poem "To Bettie," the last verse of which proclaimed:

> That gourd I'll bear where'er I go
> That name will be a charm
> To nerve my arm 'gainst ev'ry foe
> And ev'ry foe disarm.
> 'Mong those whom I can ne'er forget
> (Let none their worth gainsay)
> I'll prize thee dearest-fondest yet
> My Bettie—far away.

Certainly for a three-year period after his furlough summer of 1852, she was a factor in his life.[28]

A new Superintendent greeted the corps of cadets that September of 1852, Colonel Robert E. Lee, father of Stuart's friend Custis. During the next two years Stuart became better acquainted with Lee than did most of the cadets. He visited the Lee family often on Saturday evenings; he found Lee's daughter Mary charming and he became very fond of Mrs. Lee, who once sent him flowers, and he visited her at Arlington soon after his graduation. Another Lee came to the Academy that fall as a cadet, the Superintendent's nephew Fitzhugh Lee. Fitz Lee seemed to be as carefree as his uncle and cousin Custis were diligent. He collected 197 demerits and then got arrested for sneaking out of summer camp until 2:30 AM. It took a unanimous pledge by the members of Fitz Lee's class not to commit the offense with which he was charged to salvage his career at West Point. The unanimous pledge was a custom unique to the Academy and fortunately the precedent was well-known to Secretary of War Jefferson Davis, Academy class of 1828, who made the final decision on Fitz's fate. Stuart liked all the Lees, male and female, young and old; he cultivated their friend-ship, gravitated to their status and success. And the Lees re-sponded in kind.[29]

During his second-class (third) year Stuart continued his class in drawing and took courses in philosophy and chemistry. He ceased to visit the library on Saturday afternoons during his sec-ond-class year and engaged instead in more social activities. Often he visited at the Superintendent's home, where the Lees held court. In November one of the many Virginia women he invited to West Point while he was on furlough accepted his invitation. Eliza Meene came up from Lynchburg, and Stuart wrote Bettie Hairston that he had "enjoyed the charming society of Miss Meene" and "suffered with the Blues after her departure." The following Christmas he sent her a prune accompanied by a truly terrible bit of verse. One spring Saturday Stuart and two cadet friends es-corted Mrs. Lee and two daughters of one of the faculty members to the top of Crows Nest, a picnic spot about two and a half miles from the Academy. He complained to Bettie that he had not re-ceived even one valentine that year, "after all my devotion to the ladies during last summer." Stuart also kept current with popular music and sent Bettie the music for Stephen Foster's "Old Folks at Home" among other tunes of the time. Looking forward to the social season of his last summer encampment at West Point, he told Bettie, "after ten months toils among 'The abstruse regions of the philosopic [sic] world,' recreation is by no means unwelcome. Play is more agreeable than work at all times."[30]

During the summer encampment of 1853, Stuart did some se-rious playing. He sewed on his new chevrons as cadet captain and became "acquainted with a good many ladies." By August he was attending cotillion parties three times a week. Mary Pegram re-turned to West Point that summer; but Stuart found that he admired "Miss Mary Lee much the more both as regards beauty and sprightliness." "But I must say," he wrote Bettie, "that amid all the array of love-seekers and heartbreakers by whom we have been surrounded, I have escaped unscathed."[31]

When the Academy celebrated the Fourth of July that summer, the Dialectic Society selected Stuart to read the Declaration of Independence, a traditional part of the observance, which followed a cadet oration (given by Otis Howard). To Bettie, Stuart confessed, "I always thought I had enough brass, but when I rose before such an audience to perform the part assigned me I felt quite embarrassed, and would willingly have crawfished if it had been possible. But I had to 'stand up to the rack fodder or no fodder,' so I put on a bold face and drove ahead."[32]

Another honor came Stuart's way in his first-class (fourth) year; in addition to his appointment as second captain of the corps, he was one of eight cadets designated "cavalry officers" in recognition of their superior horsemanship. Astride Don Quixote, Stuart spent hours that winter flailing away with his saber at dummy "heads" placed on posts in the Academy riding hall.

About his academic work, Stuart informed Bettie, "Unlike other Colleges, where studies and duties become a mere trifle the last year, at West Point they are multiplied ten fold; we have a great deal to do and little time to do it in." He took a broad course in ethics that included some study of international law, a course in mineralogy and geology, and a course in engineering. In addition, first classmen had classes in infantry, artillery, and cavalry tactics. Stuart professed to his father that he found civil engineering "the most interesting study I have ever pursued." Indeed West Point was the center of civil engineering research and teaching at the time. But Stuart, hampered by his mediocre talents in drawing, fared poorly in engineering; he finished the course standing twenty-ninth (of forty-six), his worst performance at the Point. His highest standing (seventh) during his final year came in ethics. Ironically, he finished tenth in cavalry tactics.[33]

This was not all bad, for at the time West Point cavalry doctrine was based upon a Napoleonic mania for the massed saber charge. Shock action from mounted troops often worked for Napoleon; but Waterloo was a long time ago in 1854. And at Waterloo Napoleon's Old Guard made the mistake of delivering their saber-waving assault against disciplined "squares" of British infantry. The results were suicidal. Had Stuart learned his lessons in cavalry tactics any better, he would have cluttered his mind with more items to unlearn in the face of practical experience.[34]

Throughout the course of his final year at the Academy, Stuart underwent what he termed *"the important crisis* of my life"—the choice of a career. He owed his country eight years' service; however his country did not have room for all the Academy graduates in the regular army, and thus he had the option to pursue a civilian career. He wrote to "Pa" in early October and said that he had two choices, law or arms. About his father's profession he had concluded that law was "an overcrowded thoroughfare which may or may not yield a support, may possibly secure honors, but of doubtful worth." Arms promised "ample support, with a life of hardship and uncertainty, laurels if any dearly bought and leaving an empty title as a bequeathment." Stuart did not ask his father's advice; instead he said he would "rely upon the guidance of Him whose judgement cannot err." And in fact Stuart presumed to advise his politician father how he might approach President Franklin Pierce about a seat on the Board of Visitors for the Academy.[35]

Later in October he discussed his future with Bettie. Then his inclination was toward the army. "There is something in 'the pride and pomp and circumstance of glorious war,'" he said with Othello, and he asked, "Had you not rather see your Cousin or even your brother a Bold Dragoon than a petty-fogger lawyer?" He knew that she preferred the life of a farmer; but he pointed out that he had neither farm nor capital with which to purchase one. Then he discussed the *"hireling* professions," and concluded that "The officer has his toils but he has his *rewards."* [36]

In February he again broached the subject with Bettie. He was then thinking about remaining in the army "for a *while,"* and afterwards turning to law. "It is a popular sentiment that . . . a good lawyer must be a great Liar, and consummate scoundrel but I trust you will never think the less of Cousin James for being a lawyer." None of this reflects too favorably upon Archibald Stuart. But then one of the reasons Stuart confided in Bettie was the distance between him and his parents. When he wrote his father in October, he had had no letters from home since the previous May. If Stuart had become a lawyer, he would not have done so for the sake of emulating Archibald Stuart.[37]

In June Stuart graduated thirteenth in his class, now shrunk to forty-six. He left on furlough to await orders from the War Department within about two months. He still expected a cavalry assignment at Jefferson Barracks.[38] Certainly Stuart left West Point with mixed feelings. He was now free from the restrictions of the place and free to get on with his life, instead of getting ready for it. Nevertheless he loved the Academy and he was proud of his success there. Perhaps the most reliable index of Beauty's feelings for the Point, and his positive outlook on life as well, involved Academy cooking. "All of the hardships of West Point life," historian Stephen Ambrose states, "paled beside the food." Boiled potatoes, boiled meat, boiled pudding, bread, and coffee were the mainstays, and variety appeared in the form of cockroaches in the soup, rancid butter, and once a nest of three mice in the pudding. Institutional food and cooking, even at its best, has ever inspired complaints from college students. And West Point food seemed to be unappetizing and unnourishing by design. Yet never in the letters and conversations that survive did Beauty Stuart ever even once complain about the food at West Point.[39] He had adopted the place and its people and observed "that the taste of classmates for each other's society particularly West Pointers is unequalled by the strongest attachment and what is more remarkable it becomes more and more intense as time continues. A thought which makes me fear that *out of the army* I will be miserably unhappy."[40]

He still felt the need to prove himself; his reputation for fighting, even as a first classman, demonstrated that. But he had acquired sufficient social polish to allow him to relish visits and excursions with the Lees. He had mastered the requisite technical competence to enter a profession. He had sharpened and focused his ambitions for himself; he would begin his ascent to success as a soldier. West Point had proclaimed him an officer and a gentleman. And a "Bold Dragoon" is handsome by definition.

# III

## *Lieutenant Stuart*

BENJAMIN BLAKE MINOR did not usually stay in the "omnibus" room of Albert Southall's hotel in Williamsburg. On one occasion during the summer of 1854, however, Minor, who was an established Richmond lawyer, arrived in Williamsburg on business and found all the private rooms occupied. Consequently he had to settle for one of three double beds in the omnibus room and the possibility of sharing his accommodations with strangers. For a time Minor was alone in the room. Then late one afternoon in the midst of a rainstorm he saw a carriage drive up to the hotel and three young army officers scramble out and dash into the office. Minor had roommates.

After supper that night the lawyer returned to his room and crawled into bed with his law books and notes to prepare his case for the next day. He was still at work when the three young men he had seen earlier burst into the room. They were "merrier than crickets," Minor recalled, and he "soon learned what a good time they had been enjoying." The young men shed their uniforms and all three piled into the same bed. There they chattered and chuckled about the evening's visits to friends and relatives in Williamsburg. The jolly banter easily distracted Minor from logical precepts and legal precedents.

Finally one of the men exhorted his fellows to thoughtfulness. He pointed out that they had been "carrying on" for some time and disturbing their studious companion. They should "hush up and go to sleep." The lawyer thanked the young man for his consideration, but protested that he was nearly finished and could complete his work in the morning. Then Minor, who knew many of the people about whom the officers had been speaking, turned out his reading lamp and joined their party. The four of them shared stories and acquaintances long into the night.

Next morning Minor met one of his new friends on the street in front of the hotel and recognized his voice as belonging to the young officer who had called for quiet on his behalf the night before. His name was Stuart. After a few questions Minor informed the lieutenant that his wife was a Pannill and thus related to Stuart. Before they parted, Minor issued an enthusiastic invitation to visit his home in Richmond. Minor could not remember whether or not Stuart greeted him when he arrived home from Williamsburg. But Stuart did visit the Minors soon after this encounter and often thereafter. "We all took a great fancy to him," Minor recalled many years later.[1]

Minor's introduction to Lieutenant Stuart in the omnibus room of a Williamsburg hotel did not exactly cause the earth to tremble; it did provide the lawyer a charming anecdote to recount in later years, and the incident was typical of Stuart at the time. He was gregarious, and he also possessed the instincts that led him to quiet his comrades so that Minor might not be disturbed. And he pursued friendships, especially friendships with prominent and prosperous people.

The summer following Stuart's graduation from West Point appeared to be a repeat of the "furlough summer" between his third- and second-class years at the Academy. While awaiting orders to his first duty assignment, he visited old friends, relatives, and new friends in Arlington, Williamsburg, Gloucester County, Richmond, Salem, Charlottesville, Lynchburg, Wytheville, and Henry County, Virginia, and in Salem, Stokes County, Davie County, and Panther Creek, North Carolina. He probably went to other places as well; those listed above are the ones he mentioned in some of the letters he wrote that summer. As much as he enjoyed his round of visits, Stuart was impatient to get on with his life. He quickly tired of being "always going but never gone."[2]

Finally, he arrived home on one of his rare visits to Laurel Hill to find his commission as second lieutenant in the Mounted Riflemen and his orders to join a company on active duty along the Rio

Grande in southern Texas. He had expected an initial assignment at Jefferson Barracks just outside St. Louis, and it took no genius to realize that a junior officer patrolling the trackless prairie between rude frontier garrisons could become lost, in more ways than one. Once again, though, Stuart adopted a positive attitude in circumstances that were less than ideal. He confided to Bettie Hairston that he would "much rather see active service at the start than to have it deferred." Moreover he desired to serve, in the full sense of the verb, and thus he favored feeling "hard knocks" and dealing "hard blows" to a "life of inglorious ease at some delightful station on the Atlantic."[3]

Coupled with his desire to serve his country, however, was Stuart's ambition to serve conspicuously. Consequently, as he prepared to make his way in the big world, Stuart determined two things. He never wrote them down or articulated them to anyone, perhaps not even to himself. But he acted them out as surely as if he had. Stuart determined to live fully, to miss no opportunity, to experience life as richly and completely as he was able. He would accept whatever circumstances he found himself in and do his best to make the best of the situation. Actually this was a renewed determination; he had developed this approach to his life as a young boy away at school and had been refining it ever since. Stuart also determined not to get "lost." He would maintain contact with his friends and make sure that no one who could help him forgot him. In order to be promoted in a peacetime army, Stuart would have to promote himself.

Stuart's initial orders called for him to join his company at Fort McIntosh, Laredo, Texas, on October 15. Accordingly, the day after receiving his assignment, he set out for New York to outfit himself for the frontier. He went via Washington and there discovered that, because of a yellow fever scare in New Orleans, the War Department had extended his leave. Stuart went to New York anyway, made his purchases, and visited West Point, where his cousin Peter Hairston was a plebe. Then he returned home to wait.[4]

He had visited Bettie Hairston in mid-August and reached some sort of understanding with her. She remained for a time his confidante. But between the lines of his letters to her was the hint of a sense of loss. At one point he listed the cooking utensils he carried with him and with mock heroism bequeathed them to Bettie, if he should not survive. And he closed his last letter to her, "Whatever may be my fate may you be happy." Stuart also presumed to instruct his young cousin in a tone he had never used previously. It was as if by giving her a reading list (*Childe Harold* and *Ivanhoe*) and offering his critique of Shakespeare ("Hamlet is his masterpiece"), he might assert some form of mastery over her to compensate for his loss. The family tradition that Stuart asked her to marry him and she refused may indeed be true.[5]

At any rate, Stuart left home all but unencumbered. He owed at least one of his cousins $150 which he had used to support his travels and outfit himself; but the debt did not seem to trouble him. En route to Texas he had to delay his passage through New Orleans again because of yellow fever, so he tarried with friends and relatives in St. Louis. At last, about November 29, he boarded a riverboat and began his journey in earnest.[6]

New Orleans failed to impress Stuart during the one night he spent there. In the morning he embarked upon a steamer for Indianola, on the Texas coast between Galveston and Corpus Christi. No sooner had the vessel left the mouth of the Mississippi River and headed out into the Gulf of Mexico than a "norther" blew in and churned the open water of the Gulf. This was a new experience for Stuart, who had never before left the sight of land. He enjoyed it not at all and became horribly seasick. So ill was Stuart that the boat had been tied up at the dock in Galveston for twelve hours before he realized that dry land was but a step or two away. Then only did he crawl from his berth and greet Galveston. "Struck with the rusticity of the inhabitants" and buildings, Stuart pronounced a billiard hall and barroom the "most imposing" edifice in the city. His equilibrium and appetite returned as he continued his journey in calm seas to Saluria, an island off Indianola. There with some other officers Stuart awaited a small mail boat to take him to Corpus Christi. Pete Brown, the captain of the vessel, greeted his passengers in a state of extreme intoxication. When the company refused to set sail with a drunk at the helm, Brown threw himself over the side into the water. "Pete was sobered instanter." En route to Corpus Christi the boat anchored just off the deserted shore on each of two nights, and Stuart slept fitfully amid the unlikely dissonance created by screeching sea gulls and howling wolves.[7]

Stuart arrived at Corpus Christi on December 17 and remained there until the twenty-ninth, when he set out with a wagon train for Laredo. He described the region through which he traveled as "entirely uninhabited prairie . . . clothed in Cactus." He found adventure en route hunting rabbits, partridges, and wild pigs for the party to eat. On one hunting expedition Stuart and a companion experienced a tense time when they mistook some twenty or thirty "mustangers," who caught and sold wild horses, for hostile Comanches. Later he could laugh at himself in a letter to Bettie. As he traveled, Stuart kept hearing that the company to which he was assigned had moved farther and farther west. By the time he reached Laredo ("a little Mexican village of miserable 'jacals' or hovels") he learned that his company was part of an expedition of two companies and some Texas Rangers en route to Limpia. Limpia is a creek and canyon and also the site of Fort Davis, deep in the heart of West Texas, roughly midway between the Pecos River and the Rio Grande. Stuart reached Fort Davis on January 29 and found out that his company was fifty miles farther west, so he rested a day and set out again.[8]

Finally, more than two months after he left his friends in St. Louis, Stuart found his company. Major John S. Simonson commanded the expedition hunting Mescalero Apaches and Comanches through the wilds of West Texas. It was arduous and frustrating duty, involving long patrols in rough country and constant vigilance against an enemy rarely seen. Stuart wrote an account of his experiences on one expedition and sent it to the Staunton, Virginia, *Jeffersonian* for publication. He also wrote long letters about his adventures and observations to friends and relatives; he wanted to keep in touch and share his exotic travels. He revealed himself to be a keen observer and felicitous writer. The article he wrote for the *Jeffersonian* is a good example both of the sort of thing Stuart did in West Texas and of his prose style.[9]

Major Simonson had established a base camp, named Camp Stuart to honor a captain from South Carolina formerly assigned to the Mounted Riflemen. From this rendezvous Simonson dispatched one patrol south toward the Rio Grande on February 6, 1855, in search of Indians, and himself led another patrol north toward the Guadalupe Mountains near the border of New Mexico, where Indians were suspected in greater numbers. He gave Stuart charge of the artillery (one gun) belonging to the latter party. Because the trail was often rugged, the troops packed supplies on mules. On the first day out, the men, horses, and mules trudged through dust six inches deep, then zigzagged up a mountain to be greeted by a storm—"torrents of rain and hail" so thick that "we could scarcely discern the ground." As quickly as the storm had appeared, it vanished, leaving only a rainbow to cheer the shivering soldiers. "Thus you see," Stuart commented, "that in Texas . . . we can have May and December in one day in February."

Next day the trail led to "the crest of a stupendous precipice" and down a long series of switchbacks two thousand feet (Stuart's estimate) to the plain below. Stuart was awestruck with the "grandeur of the scenery." But, as he wrote in a letter to one of his brothers, one of his men rudely interrupted his awe: " 'Well, Leftenant, what you gwine to do with that cannon?' " Stuart accepted the challenge presented by the gun, and prevailed upon the detachment of Texas Rangers to help him. He sent the limber and caisson down with twenty-five men to wrestle it over the narrow trail, and himself directed the efforts of twenty-five more Rangers who lowered the gun itself with lariats. When he reached Simonson's camp with the reassembled weapon, the major was amazed; he told Stuart that he never expected to see the piece again.

The following day's adventure was the discovery of an Indian village, deserted for about ten days. The village, guarded against surprise attack by a series of outposts, consisted of lodges framed with bent spars driven into the ground and covered with brush. The lodges were in a state of "perfect preservation," and each one was large enough for a family; yet the soldiers chose to make their own camp nearby. As the men continued the march next morning, they met an infantry column from El Paso commanded by Major James Longstreet. The foot soldiers were also hunting Indians, and they reported that their Mexican guide had found some about ten days earlier. The guide had ridden ahead of the troops; they found him dead by the side of the trail amid moccasin tracks. Simonson decided to press on to Delaware Creek in hopes of finding his enemies. He hoped in vain, however, and the column made camp "in a deep and narrow valley or *arroyo*, clothed in luxuriant grass."

Weary men turned their horses out to graze and lit cooking fires in the arroyo. Then did a sudden gust of wind sweep down the hollow and "scattered our fire over the grass like a tornado, setting the whole prairie in a blaze in a few moments. It swept, apparently at one breath, over the entire camp, consuming bridles, saddles, blankets, caps, overcoats, and everything else that met its devouring grasp. Many of the horses were badly singed, nor did the men escape much better, for many lost their caps and had their beards closely singed." Stuart lost his valise and right-hand glove in the fire and had to continue his correspondence on partially scorched stationery.

In the wake of the prairie fire, Simonson decided to return his detachment to Camp Stuart. En route the soldiers found some samples of Indian art on the flat surfaces of rocks in a dry streambed. Stuart judged the artists "pretty good draughtsmen on the human figure, but [they] make very grotesque representations of horses." Two days' march brought the column back to Simonson's base camp, "which really seemed like home to us, and our floorless, chairless, and comfortless tents looked luxurious after a week's shelter beneath the broad canopy of heaven." [10]

Stuart stayed with Simonson in West Texas scouting, patrolling, and searching for just over three months. Although some Indians stole a horse tied not twenty yards from his tent one night, Stuart never saw his enemy the entire time. He did learn some things about Indians and about campaigning in rough country. He wore out a pair of thick-soled shoes, and for a time only a pair of embroidered slippers kept him from going barefooted. He also grew the beard he would wear the rest of his life and wrote to a "dear friend" that it so "altered my physique that you could not recognize me."

He found that he was "much better pleased" with army life than he expected to be. Still there were "other occupations which would be more congenial to my taste and principles." And he worried that he had been exiled—"nothing short of a resignation will ever get me back to the States." [11]

Even as Stuart wrote his lament, however, his career prospects were improving. During the spring of 1855, Secretary of War Jefferson Davis created two elite cavalry regiments (1st and 2nd U.S. Cavalry) for service on the plains. Competition for places in these units was keen; as Stuart expressed it, "Expectation is on tiptoe to see the correct list." When that list filtered down the chain of command, Stuart was on it—Second Lieutenant, 1st U.S. Cavalry, Fort Leavenworth, Kansas Territory. His former commission as Second Lieutenant was a "brevet" or temporary rank; this one was permanent. Fort Leavenworth may not have been the center of American civilization; but it was several degrees closer than West Texas.[12]

Stuart reported for duty first to Jefferson Barracks in June, traveled to Fort Leavenworth in July of 1855, and there became quartermaster of the 1st Cavalry regiment. The assignment placed a premium upon resourcefulness and called for considerable savoir faire, especially for an officer only a year out of West Point. Technically quartermasters were responsible for procuring supplies and transporting them and personnel where and when they were needed—no easy task on the frontier. Often, because of the distances involved, Stuart's responsibilities as quartermaster merged with those of commissary officer, charged with obtaining food for the troops. And Stuart also served as assistant commissary officer for all of Fort Leavenworth.[13]

An incident in May of 1856 offers some sample of the challenges involved. His regiment was in camp outside of Westport, Missouri, several miles south of Kansas City, and running very low on forage for horses and rations for men. At about noon on the day before troops and animals would consume the last of the available provisions, Stuart set out for Leavenworth. He rode thirty-four miles in ten hours and reached the fort at ten o'clock that night. Immediately, he began making arrangements for transporting the food and forage he needed, and before seven o'clock the next morning a wagon train he had ordered from "Nine-mile Camp" was loading at Leavenworth. The wagons left the fort at nine, and Stuart accompanied the train as both officer in charge and guide. When night fell, the route, as one participant described it, was "over a crooked road little traveled, much of the way through timber and mud holes, with no bridges over creeks and deep gullies. Fortunately, the moon gave a dim light. Several wagons were upset, several trees had to be cut down where the road was too narrow and crooked, and in many places limbs must be cut to give room for wagons to pass." Finally, at one o'clock in the morning the wagon train reached its destination, a campsite only two miles from Stuart's regiment. While the mules and teamsters bedded down for what was left of the night, Stuart rode on to report his arrival to his headquarters. Then only could he stumble off to his tent to sleep—after performing duties that would be described as "routine" to his assignment.[14]

Fort Leavenworth in the summer of 1855 was little more than a cluster of brick, stone, frame, and log buildings. Bachelor officers occupied a two-story frame building, appropriately named Bedlam, near the stables and the guardhouse. However primitive were Stuart's surroundings compared with posts in the East, Fort Leavenworth seemed positively cosmopolitan in comparison with Fort Davis and West Texas. And there were women there. Stuart pronounced the place "quite lively" and added, "Some seven or eight young ladies can always hoist sail for amusement."[15]

One young lady especially attracted Stuart's attention. Flora Cooke was the daughter of Lieutenant Colonel Phillip St. George Cooke, who commanded the Second Regiment of Dragoons. When Stuart first saw her, she was twenty years old and had recently finished a "finishing school." Her family wanted her to make her debut into Philadelphia society; but Flora Cooke insisted upon visiting her parents at Leavenworth during that summer of 1855.

Flora first appeared in Fort Leavenworth society as a small woman mounted on a large and very nervous horse during a review of the troops. Stuart's first response to her was a romantic fantasy; he imagined her horse bolting and himself rescuing this fair maiden before the entire garrison. Reality intrigued him even more than his imagining, though. Flora Cooke managed her skittish mount like the expert rider she was, and Stuart's admiration soared.[16]

He asked her to go for a ride with him; she accepted; and soon they were riding together almost every evening. Like the other women who had inspired Stuart's infatuation, Flora Cooke was physically active. Not only did she ride well, she could shoot. She sang and played the guitar, and even the rather formal daguerreotype that survives from this period cannot mask animation in her face. And never in her eighty-eight years of life did she feel the need to wear any sort of makeup. Stuart was more than charmed; he was smitten.[17]

Surely circumstances had something to do with Stuart's ardor;

he had been away from the company of young women for some months and he missed it. Moreover he was tired of living alone; as he wrote a cousin, "I'm bound to be married before I am 23." That Flora Cooke was a colonel's daughter and hers was a well-established Virginia family were also factors in her favor. Indeed he consistently introduced her to his correspondents as "daughter of Col. P. St. Geo. Cooke 2nd Dragoons."

But under any circumstances Stuart would probably have been attracted to Flora Cooke. She was a lively young woman who could sing, shoot, and ride horses. Their evening rides generated friendship, and friendship led to love. Stuart had found a new confidante, a person who shared his interests and to whom he wanted to open his soul. In September 1855, less than two months after their first ride together, they were engaged to be married. Stuart summarized his rapid courtship in Latin—" *'Veni, Vidi, Victus sum'* " (I came; I saw; I was conquered.) [18]

After asking blessings from their respective parents, the couple planned a gala wedding in November at Fort Riley, Kansas, to which Colonel Cooke had recently been transferred. In the interim Stuart had to accompany his regiment on an extended patrol (800–900 miles) along the Oregon Trail beyond Fort Kearny toward Laramie. He had to plan the logistics of the long march, while frantically attending to the social amenities of his wedding. Before dawn on September 20, the day his regiment was to leave Leavenworth, Stuart was writing his Cousin A. Stuart Brown in St. Louis requesting him to purchase a silver set and have the handles engraved, to have wedding cards printed, and to attend the ceremony. At this point Stuart did not know the date of his wedding; he promised to inform Brown by telegraph as soon as he returned, so that Brown could complete the printing order and make plans for his journey to Fort Riley. Stuart enclosed a draft for $150, which he hoped would cover the expense of his purchases. Beyond this harried letter Stuart could do no more; Brown and his future in-laws would just have to understand. No doubt Brown wondered at the impetuosity of his cousin, and Colonel Cooke later described his daughter's marriage as having taken place "rather suddenly." But Cooke also described his son-in-law as "a remarkably fine, promising, pure young man." [19]

When Stuart returned from the patrol he found first a letter from his father consenting to his marriage and next a more recent letter from Flora containing news of Archibald Stuart's death on September 20. Stuart reacted in more or less the way he believed he was supposed to react. In a letter to his cousin Brown, he said the proper things—"such a heart-rending occurrence ... Alas! What a shadow is life!" But Stuart's words have a pro forma sound to them, and they should, because his relationship with his father had been pretty pro forma. This was neither man's fault; they simply had spent very little time together. "I assure you," Stuart continued to Brown, "it makes me sick at heart to pursue these details of business in the midst of such melancholy tidings." But pursue them he did and concluded his letter with an urgent appeal to Brown to attend his wedding.[20]

Marriage plans continued for November 14. In deference to Archibald Stuart's death, the wedding was small and limited to family witnesses. Flora wore her graduation dress and quipped about her transformation from a cook [Cooke] to a steward [Stuart]. Ironically, whoever recorded the event in the Stuart family Bible back at Laurel Hill in Virginia omitted the *e* from Flora's name. The couple remained at Fort Riley for a few days and then moved into Stuart's "ranch" (two rooms and a kitchen) at Fort Leavenworth. They stayed there only long enough for Stuart to secure leave to take his bride to Virginia to meet his family.[21]

As usual Stuart tried to visit all his relatives and friends at once, and Flora remained in the East after her husband returned to duty at Leavenworth, perhaps to visit, more likely to rest from her whirlwind tour. Her new mother-in-law, Elizabeth Stuart, tried to give her a slave woman to take back to Kansas as a maid. Somehow Flora refused the gift. Slavery was an inflammatory issue in Kansas at the time; the Kansas-Nebraska Act (1854) had opened the territory equally to Free-Soilers and pro-slavers, and the rival factions vied for the future of Kansas. A junior officer and his wife possessed of two rooms, a kitchen, and a slave in the midst of such a situation would have been ludicrous.[22]

On December 20, 1855, Stuart became a first lieutenant, an indication that the War Department appreciated his talents and energy. Rapid promotion was rare in the peacetime army. If political influence played any part in Stuart's rise, it was not that of his father-in-law; Cooke expressed some surprise at Stuart's "extraordinary promotion." Nevertheless Stuart had not yet become lost on the frontier; his record and his friends had served him well.[23]

The death of his father, his marriage, the promotion, or his furlough journey home—one or all of these events of late 1855 seem to have inspired Stuart to reflection. He had a wife and the potential for a new family of his own, at the same time his old family was fading and fragmenting. His was now the "adult" generation. His career seemed promising enough, within the context of a small professional army; but the question remained whether the army could contain Stuart's ambitions. The sojourn home offered the time and perspective for Stuart to assess himself and his circumstance. And his subsequent actions suggest that he reached some conclusions about his future.

Stuart returned to Kansas with a renewed commitment to his career in the military. His trip home was a visit; he found nothing there that tempted him to remain. He also returned to Kansas with a renewed interest in business ventures. He had dabbled in real estate before; now he invested. He bought and sold lots in Leavenworth at a profit. He risked $105 in a projected Kansas town called Indianola and lost. He gambled on a quarter section of farmland near Leavenworth and won. These and other ventures enabled Stuart to supplement his modest military pay and to live in a more expansive style.[24]

Stuart revealed most clearly his thoughts about himself at this stage of his life in some advice to his cousin Brown. Stuart wrote to Brown from Lynchburg, Virginia, in late January 1856; ostensibly he wrote about a business transaction and about Brown's request for advice regarding his return to Virginia from St. Louis, where he was practicing law. But in the process Stuart wrote more about his own life than about Brown's. The two cousins had been corresponding for a long time; Brown was older, and always before Stuart had deferred to his age and experience, whether confessing an adolescent love or admiring Brown's initial success at law. Now, though, Stuart asserted himself.

First, he explained the details of the business deal as though he were instructing an apprentice and presumed to lecture Brown regarding legal technicality—"You have not forgotten the meaning of these distinctions in Va. Law." Then Stuart addressed Brown as "old fellow," and counseled him to return to Virginia.

"Position and influence," Stuart stated, depend upon "means" and "appearances," and in St. Louis are many men possessed of these advantages. "I may speak freely," he continued, "as I am without such advantages myself. . . . I am embittered against modern fashionable society, when I find myself elbowed in saloons by the puppies who plume themselves upon $100,000, a handsome person & a European tour." Believing himself superior in "spirit" and "mind," Stuart had decided not to "meet these gentlemen in lists, where they are *my* superiors." Stuart determined to "Gain position, information, influence, *a name* first, and *then* with the prestige of a name, go if we choose and make the denizens of fashion bow before us." Stuart advised Brown to find his success in southwestern Virginia, where he could become "a country gentleman of fortune" and then confront wider society with his "superiority acknowledged."

Having lectured Brown on the law and counseled him about life, Stuart proceeded to preach to him on "the *practice of virtue*." "Virtue" in Stuart's mind was the opposite of "the *elegant vices* of city life," and he had no good feelings for "Society" either. Invoking the parable of the Prodigal Son in language if not by name, Stuart decried Brown's "new-made city-friends," and concluded, "The voices of home & friends & patriotism & old associations cry —'come back, come back.' "

Removed from the context of his life, Stuart's letter to his cousin is curious indeed. Under the personal circumstances in which he wrote it, however, Stuart's letter makes much sense. He was declaring his independence and asserting his maturity when he presumed to tell his onetime mentor what to do. By advising Brown to return home, Stuart justified his own exile to the plains of Kansas; homecoming for Brown and leave-taking for Stuart had a common motive—make a name and win fame. And proof of name and fame, for Stuart, would be triumph on his own terms in that fashionable society he professed to despise. Eventually, he was confident he would elbow some plumed "puppies" in their own saloons.

Nor was he merely being sanctimonious in his sermon on virtue. Stuart believed himself a virtuous man, and he believed his evangelical idiom. He defined virtue to include "all the virtues which philosophy teaches us to observe"; he meant sober, diligent achievement. And he was convinced that his virtue would earn reward, not only in the next world, but in this one as well.[25]

When Stuart returned to Fort Leavenworth in early 1856, he practiced what he had preached to his cousin Brown. He worked diligently at his quartermaster tasks; he pursued his speculations in land; and he maintained his contact with people who could aid his career. He and Flora got along "swimmingly" when she rejoined him in the spring. She had had sufficient experience in a military family to accept her husband's prolonged absences without too much complaint. And he clearly treasured the time he spent with her. In December 1856, Flora became pregnant.[26]

During 1856, in addition to patrols directed against red men, the frontier army in Kansas had to try to maintain peace among whites as well. In accord with the concept of "popular sovereignty," Congress had organized Kansas and left the question of whether the territory would be open or closed to slavery unanswered. Those who actually settled in Kansas were supposed to decide the fate of slavery. However, Kansas soon became a battleground. Pro-slave and Free-Soil factions in the territory and armed bands from Missouri produced "bleeding Kansas," a small-scale civil war over slavery there in particular and elsewhere in principle.

On June 5, 1856, Stuart rode with a detachment led by his commanding officer, Colonel Edwin Sumner, into the camp of a collection of Free-Soilers led by John Brown. Acting on orders to disperse bands of armed men, Sumner insisted that Brown disband his men. Three days earlier Brown and his followers had attacked a force of militia from Missouri and captured some of the militiamen in the "Battle of Black Jack." With the prisoners was militia captain Henry Clay Pate, former student at the University of Virginia and deputy United States marshal. Sumner insisted that Brown release his prisoners, and after some wrangling Brown did so.

To Stuart the incident seemed less than earthshaking. Pate, of course, was relieved to be released. Brown became all the more convinced that the United States government was in collusion with the pro-slavery factions in Missouri and Kansas. But all Stuart had done was watch the proceedings. Later in his life, however, Stuart would again encounter Brown and Pate—under circumstances that cast him as considerably more than a spectator.[27]

While the army in Kansas was acting as peacekeeper among white settlers, members of the Cheyenne nation had been raiding and killing along the trails in western Kansas. In response to what the United States government considered violations of treaty obligations, the 1st Cavalry undertook a campaign against the Cheyenne in the summer of 1857. Designed to punish renegade Cheyenne and to reassert white authority by a show of force, the campaign began in May and lasted until August. Sumner at first divided his command into two columns, led by himself and his principal subordinate, Major John Sedgwick. Stuart began the operation as regimental quartermaster; however, he and Sumner soon disagreed over accountability procedures for governmental property, and the colonel relieved Stuart. Sumner then gave Stuart his first command, G Company of the 1st Cavalry, in exchange for his quartermaster duties.[28]

Sumner's column—four cavalry companies, a six-mule ambulance, three hundred beef cattle, and fifty wagons—left Leavenworth on May 20; by June 4 the force reached Fort Kearny. Then, reinforced by an infantry regiment, two troops of dragoons, five Pawnee scouts, and ten more wagons, the command marched for Fort Laramie. There, Sumner lost his dragoons, detached for service in Utah. The Cheyenne expedition left Laramie on June 27 and moved south to the South Platte River, where Sumner's column joined Sedgwick's. After resting and reorganizing, on July 13 Sumner led six cavalry companies, three infantry companies, and a battery of artillery to the southeast in pursuit of the Cheyenne. After sixteen days of marching, on July 29, Stuart saw his first genuinely hostile Indian in eighteen months on the frontier.[29]

The encounter occurred on Solomon's Fork of the Smoky Hill River in northwest Kansas. The six companies of cavalry confronted a force of Cheyenne warriors estimated to number three hundred men. Sumner ordered his horsemen to form a battle line and instructed two of his companies to attack the flanks of the Cheyenne line. The rest of his command was to attack the warriors head on. As Stuart deployed his troopers, he planned to advance close enough to his enemies to fire a volley into them with carbines. Then he intended to order his men to draw their pistols and charge the Indians. But as soon as the cavalry came into carbine range, Sumner ordered, "Draw sabers! Charge!"

With a wild yell, the troopers galloped down upon the Cheyenne with sabers flashing. Before the two lines collided, however, the outnumbered Indians broke their informal formation and fled. The battle quickly became a series of separate pursuits. Mounted on fresh ponies, the Cheyenne more often than not outdistanced the cavalry, and most of the warriors made good their escape. The Indians withdrew to a large village, collected women and children, hastily gathered whatever belongings they could carry, and marched south toward the Arkansas River.

Stuart and three of his fellow officers were able to continue the pursuit longer than most of the troopers. His horse, Dan, carried him at a gallop for five miles before failing. Determined to resume the chase, Stuart hailed a private whose horse seemed still fresh and commandeered the animal. Leaving the private with the exhausted Dan, Stuart returned to the chase and dashed after his companions. He caught them just in time.

When he overtook his comrades he saw that they had unhorsed and cornered a lone Indian. But the dismounted Cheyenne had a revolver and was about to shoot one of Stuart's fellow lieutenants. Instinctively Stuart charged. As he galloped past the Indian he shot him in the thigh. The wounded warrior fired at Stuart but missed. Another soldier nearby shouted, "Wait! I'll fetch him," and dismounted to steady his aim. But as he dismounted the man accidentally fired his final cartridge. He found himself afoot and defenseless; the wounded Cheyenne limped closer and leveled his pistol.

At that moment Stuart drew his saber and spurred his horse. The Indian refocused his attention as the horseman bore down upon him. In order to wield his saber Stuart had to close with his foe. The two were side by side. Stuart swung his blade at the Cheyenne's head and felt the steel strike. Simultaneously the warrior pointed his revolver and jerked the trigger. This time he could not miss. The muzzle of the weapon was only one foot from Stuart's body. The pistol roared, and the Cheyenne's last bullet crashed into the center of Stuart's chest.[30]

# IV

## The Campaign for Captain

STUART WAS STUNNED for the moment. He remained on his horse while two of his companions "dispatched" the hapless Cheyenne. Indeed the Indian proved to be the tragic figure in the incident; he had been game run to ground and had provided blood sport until he had the temerity to shoot one of his tormentors.

Gingerly Stuart dismounted and lay down. Another lieutenant fashioned shelter from the sun by sticking sabers in the ground and draping a blanket over them. A trooper rode off to find a doctor; but because the chase had extended eight miles, the doctor was slow to arrive. Meanwhile members of the command collected around Stuart, and soon Colonel Edwin Sumner rode to the scene. Sumner ordered his wounded lieutenant carried back toward the scene of the initial contact with the Cheyenne, where he proposed to make camp. The men placed Stuart on an improvised stretcher and carried him about three miles (!) before they met the doctor.

His examination revealed that Stuart had been extraordinarily lucky. The pistol ball had struck Stuart's sternum and deflected; it lodged deep beneath his left nipple. Stuart was going to be stiff and hurt some, but the ball had damaged nothing vital and, barring complications from infection, he would recover within a few weeks. After the doctor had bandaged the wound, Stuart rode into camp on some cushions attached to a two-wheel cart improvised from parts of a disabled ambulance wagon. During that five-mile trip across the plains, his pain began in earnest.[1]

Sumner rested his command for a day and buried two troopers

killed in the fight. Then on July 31 (1857), he took up pursuit of the Indians with the bulk of his force, leaving one infantry company to escort Stuart and five other wounded men and one Cheyenne prisoner to Fort Kearny. The soldiers left with the wounded built a simple field fortification and settled down to wait a few days before beginning the approximately 120-mile trek. Stuart remained supine most of the time, as his wound did not hurt unless he moved. A sure sign of his healing was the boredom that soon beset him. He had only his prayer book, a copy of Army Regulations, and a few pages from an issue of *Harper's Weekly* to read. He propped himself up enough to read and to write an account of his adventures for Flora. Otherwise he could only stare across the prairie and sweat beneath a blistering August sun.[2]

During the evening of August 4, the Cheyenne provided some diversion. About twenty or thirty warriors attacked the camp; the soldiers drove them away without injury to either side. Next morning five Pawnee guides, sent from Sumner, ran into camp with stories of having been attacked and unhorsed en route by Cheyenne. Soon after, the captain in command of the infantry company decided to begin the march to Fort Kearny on August 8. The wounded men were recovering; only three would be unable to ride. Stuart had begun to stand and walk a bit on August 5, less than a week after his wounding.[3] He was determined to ride from "this forsaken region" and did so.

The little column set out for Fort Kearny amid some ominous portents. For five days the men had been reduced to rations of fresh beef alone. A survey revealed that no one in the company had a compass, and so the troops depended upon the Pawnee guides sent by Sumner and the stars to set a course roughly supposed to be northeast. The three wounded men rode travois, two poles lashed on either side of a mule with rawhide strips woven between to form a slanted stretcher. Men walking behind the conveyance lifted the ends of the poles over the roughest spots; otherwise the poles bumped along the ground. It was very slow going. The first day the column traveled only ten miles, the second day fourteen.

Then on the morning of the sixth day the soldiers awoke in a thick fog. And into that fog had disappeared their Pawnee guides. Now the party was low on rations, which had been unbalanced from the beginning. Some of the foot soldiers had worn through their shoes and were barefoot. The wounded men needed better care, but slowed the march toward it. And they were all but lost. For a day the column was reduced to depending for directions upon their Cheyenne prisoner, whom the officers hoped might know where they wanted to go. All the while another guide, a Mexican from Fort Laramie, kept insisting that Kearny was in precisely the opposite direction from the one in which they were traveling.

As the situation of the party grew worse, Stuart grew stronger. His wound had not completely healed, of course, but he felt quite well enough to try to salvage what was beginning to look like disaster. He offered to lead a scouting party in search of Fort Kearny. Another lieutenant also volunteered, and the captain included the Mexican in the group, perhaps to prevent him from discouraging further those who remained behind. The scouting party was ready to leave on the morning of August 15; but fog settled in again and hid any hint of their course. At noon Stuart resolved to go anyhow, and navigated by making his best guess of the proper course and stationing two men along that line while the rest trotted from one point to the next. Late in the afternoon a storm blew in, and after setting out stakes along the axis of his course, Stuart and his men waited for the rain to abate. Then they continued until dark and established their stake line once more. No sooner had the men made camp than a new storm arose. The men simply sat on their grounded saddles and bowed their heads before the wind and rain. Sometime in the middle of the night someone awoke from his miserable doze long enough to notice that the "grassy ravine" in which they had picketed their horses was now a river. The water was rising and already it was halfway up the bodies of the horses. Men scrambled to their mounts and hauled them and their saddles to higher ground.

At first light on the sixteenth, wet, cold, and hungry men resumed their march. The same cloud system that had obscured the stars the night before now concealed the sun; accordingly Stuart continued to approximate his course. About seven o'clock the sun shone briefly, and Stuart discovered that he had been traveling south-southeast, instead of northeast. He corrected as best he could, and the party continued until they reached a stream they could not ford. Stuart led the way upstream, in hopes of finding a crossing. He found a trail instead, and the men followed this unknown trail in an unknown direction till dark. During the night the watch Stuart had set to look for stars awakened him, and he was able to determine from the heavens that their current course was north—the direction Stuart believed to be correct. Stuart "rejoiced"; the rest of the group hoped he was right.

Next morning (August 17) the trail led within two or three miles to another swollen stream. Stuart insisted that they attempt a crossing, and not without difficulty they swam the swift waters. Near the north bank they discovered a wagon road recently used. Now Stuart knew precisely where he was; the swollen stream had to be the Big Blue, and the wagon road connected Forts Leavenworth and Kearny. They arrived at Fort Kearny during that afternoon and the same day a rescue party set out to find those left behind.[4]

Within three weeks Stuart had seen his first combat, suffered his first wound, and led a harrowing expedition to save his comrades. He had been very fortunate. A man had fired a pistol at him at point-blank range, and he was alive. More than that, what should have been a fatal wound had merely made him very sore for several days. Then, while he recuperated, his superior officers had committed an incredible series of blunders. Sumner had left an infantry company alone and hungry with less than reliable guides and no compass to escort wounded comrades across roughly 120 miles of trackless prairie and swollen rivers. So desperate was their plight that one of the wounded, Stuart, had to take charge and lead the vital search to locate safety. Such a series of experiences surely demonstrated that Stuart possessed a robust physical constitution. During his two years on the plains, he had also acquired the knowledge and skills for survival in adverse circumstances. And he had displayed capacity for leadership—clear-headed, decisive action that inspired others to follow him.[5]

During the first week of September in 1857 Flora gave birth to a daughter. Stuart insisted that the child be named Flora to honor her mother and proclaimed "I have the prettiest and smartest baby in North America."[6]

Also during the fall of 1857, the three Stuarts moved farther

west to Fort Riley, Kansas, to which the War Department transferred the 1st Cavalry.[7] Routine duties at Fort Riley left Stuart time
to pursue his land speculations during 1857 and 1858. He wrote to
his mother to ask if she was interested in selling the southern half
of Laurel Hill. He also began tinkering, during the winter of 1858–
59, with some inventions he hoped to sell to the War Department.[8]

"Stuart's lightning horse hitcher" was a metal fixture of some
sort designed to be attached to a leather halter. The name of the
device is descriptive; but Stuart's major claim for his invention
was that it would save precious moments unhitching a horse and
thus permit a cavalryman to mount for action much faster.[9]

Stuart also designed an attachment for cavalry saber belts, "a
stout brass hook" that permitted a trooper rapidly to remove his
saber and scabbard from his belt and attach it to his saddle. The
invention promised to spare a cavalryman some clanging awk-
wardness when he dismounted and simplified the temporary use
of horsemen as foot soldiers.

The War Department was enough impressed by Stuart's inge-
nuity to grant him a six-month leave of absence during the latter
half of 1859 to come to Washington, secure a patent, and negotiate
the sale of his saber hook.[10]

Stuart also used his leave to attend as a lay delegate the General Convention of the Episcopal Church which met that year in
Richmond. He had joined the Methodist Church as a teenaged
student at Emory & Henry College. Family tradition maintains
that, because many military chaplains were Episcopalians, Stuart
gravitated toward that denomination during his career in the
United States Army. At West Point, chapel services traditionally
followed Episcopalian liturgy, so perhaps he began his Episcopal
orientation there. He did contribute substantially to the erection
of the Episcopal Church of the Covenant in Junction City, Kansas,
while he was stationed at Fort Riley. But he did not join the Episcopal Church until 1859, when he was confirmed in St. Louis
while en route to General Convention as a delegate. A sectarian
Stuart was not. He professed a staunch faith in an omnipresent
God and carried his prayer book, along with his copy of Army
Regulations, with him. Yet during his sojourn in Kansas he sent
his mother money for her to devote to the construction of "a very
respectable free church." Propriety probably had much to do with

Stuart's confirmation; he could hardly be a member of the ruling body of a church to which he did not belong.[11]

From St. Louis Stuart went to Virginia and paid his usual round of visits. He returned to Emory & Henry College and delivered a speech to the Hermesian Society in which he recalled his last speech to the group ten years earlier, when he had fallen off the platform during a flight of oratory. In Richmond he did attend meetings of the Episcopal General Convention at St. Paul's Church. And in Washington he patented his saber hook and sold the patent right to the government for $5,000. In addition Stuart would receive a dollar for each device sold by the manufacturer.[12]

On the morning of October 17, 1859, he was in the War Department offices in Washington waiting for an appointment with Secretary of War John B. Floyd, who was a fellow Virginian. While Stuart waited, he heard whispers in several offices of some trouble at a place called Harpers Ferry. The town lay at the confluence of the Shenandoah and Potomac rivers in the mountains of northern Virginia, and its principal importance stemmed from the United States Arsenal and Armory located there. Rumors were flying through the War Department that a mob had seized possession of the armory. Some said the mob contained as many as three thousand men, and most whispers agreed that most of the mob was black. A slave revolt was in progress.[13]

Stuart was on hand at the time Secretary Floyd decided to do something about the rumors. The lieutenant offered to take a summons from the War Office to Colonel Robert E. Lee. Like Stuart, Lee was on leave from duty; he had been for some time just across the Potomac from Washington at Arlington, the estate of his father-in-law, executing the complicated provisions of his will and attempting to extricate the family from financial tangles. Stuart had visited the Lees at Arlington before; but this time he came on official business. The orders from the War Department said to come immediately, so Lee left with Stuart without even changing from his civilian clothes.

Back at the War Office Lee and Secretary Floyd made arrangements to send troops to Harpers Ferry and then went to the White House to confer with President James Buchanan. Stuart tagged along. Buchanan agreed with the plans already made and endorsed a strong show of military force. The most available troops were some ninety marines stationed at the Washington Navy Yard. Four companies of Maryland militia also started for Harpers Ferry, and some Virginia militia, it happened, were already there. Buchanan and Floyd placed Lee in command of the operation; Stuart volunteered to accompany him as an aide, and Lee accepted the services of his former West Point pupil.

The colonel and his lieutenant left Washington almost immediately. Stuart was able to borrow uniform coat and saber; Lee remained in civilian clothes and unarmed. On the afternoon of the seventeenth the two men traveled by train to Relay House, a point eight miles from Baltimore, where they planned to meet the marines and a train to Harpers Ferry. There they discovered that the marines had already left; but a locomotive was available to transport the two officers in pursuit of the troops. Lee sent orders by telegraph for the marines to detrain about a mile outside Harpers Ferry and wait for his arrival. Then he and Stuart boarded the locomotive and roared away to the west.[14]

About ten o'clock that night they reached the rendezvous outside Harpers Ferry. Waiting for them were the marines and their commander, Lieutenant Israel Green, plus the four companies of militia from Maryland. Lee soon learned that the numbers involved in the attempted slave insurrection had been much exaggerated. Only a handful remained at large, and these were trapped in a small fire engine house on the armory grounds. Led by a man known only as "Smith," the insurgents, most of whom were white, had a number of hostages with them in the engine house. Private citizens from the area and Virginia militia had the place surrounded and had kept up a sporadic, free-lance fire into the building throughout most of the day. Lee ordered Green to march his marines into the town and inside the armory grounds. Then he ordered everyone else out. After surveying the scene and satisfying himself that the engine house was secure, he stationed the militia units around the armory so that they would be seen from inside the engine house. Then did he confront the challenge of subduing the insurgents with the least risk of harm to their hostages.

Stuart followed Lee around during the preliminaries. The night was very dark and cold, and a chilled drizzle increased the discomfort. At about 2:00 A.M. on October 18, Lee wrote out a message for "the persons in the armory buildings" and gave it to Stuart. Lee demanded immediate surrender, assured them escape was impossible, promised his protection if they surrendered, and warned that if he were compelled to employ force to take them he could not "answer for their safety." Lee instructed Stuart to deliver this message to those in the engine house under a white flag of truce and to make clear to the insurgents that no terms other than immediate surrender were possible. The colonel suspected that whoever was inside the engine house would reject his demand. In that event Stuart was to give a signal that would launch a storming party at the door to the engine house.

Lee hoped that the weight and speed of his projected assault would allow the insurgents no opportunity to harm their prisoners. Also for the sake of the hostages, he decided to wait until daylight to begin the showdown. He insisted that the storming party be armed only with bayonets. He did not want to risk injuring anyone innocent with stray bullets.[15]

At about six thirty in the morning, Lee assembled his subordinates to discuss the probable assault on the engine house. He offered the chore first to the commanders of the Maryland and Virginia militia units. In turn each demurred, claiming the dangerous task should devolve upon professional soldiers, not amateurs. Consequently Lee turned to Green and offered him the honor of "taking those men out." Green accepted and quickly picked a party of twelve to storm the building and another twelve men to stand by as reserves. As Green and Stuart walked toward the engine house, they agreed that Stuart would wave his broad-brimmed cavalry hat as a signal to storm the building.

By seven o'clock all was ready. Lee stood on a slight rise about forty feet from the engine house, still in civilian clothes and still unarmed. Green's marines, dressed in blue trousers, darker blue frock coats, white belts, and blue caps, stood ready with sledgehammers. Behind the principals were the militia and civilian spectators, about two thousand in all. The focus of all this attention was a relatively small building (about thirty by thirty-five feet). Two sets of heavy wooden double doors afforded the only entrance, and these the insurgents had barred and barricaded. To one of the doors strode Stuart, carrying Lee's message and waving his white flag.

He called to those inside the engine house that he had a communication for them from Colonel Lee. Soon the door opened about four inches, and Stuart looked down the barrel of a cocked cavalry carbine. Behind the weapon was "Mr. Smith," whom Stuart immediately recognized as John Brown from his Kansas encounter three years earlier. Stuart read the message, and as soon as he did, Brown began to bargain. He asked for safe passage from Harpers Ferry in exchange for the surrender of his hostages. No sooner did Stuart, in the name of Lee, refuse one proposal than Brown offered some variant of the same terms. From behind Brown came pleas from his prisoners that Stuart intercede with Lee on behalf of their safety. And amid this clamor one of the hostages shouted, "Never mind us, fire!" That speaker was Lewis W. Washington, a distant descendant of George Washington, and when Lee recognized his voice he remarked, "The old revolutionary blood does tell." Stuart realized that Brown's wrangling and the conflicting calls from the prisoners were precisely what Lee wished to avoid. Accordingly he broke off the parley and waved his hat. As he did so, he pivoted out of the line of fire.

The marines advanced with their hammers and began beating upon the doors of the engine house. Within, some of Brown's band began shooting at the sounds of the blows. Green saw that the sledgehammers were having little effect and ordered his men to stop. Then he noticed a wooden ladder lying in the yard and instructed his reserve force to use it as a battering ram. The second thrust broke a small hole in the right-hand door very near the ground. Instantly Brown fired his carbine at the intruding ladder. When the men withdrew the ladder Green crawled quickly through the hole and his men followed. In the gloom inside, Green first saw Washington, who pointed out Brown to him. The abolitionist was kneeling and reloading his carbine when Green swung his sword at Brown's head. The blow produced a deep cut on the back of his neck and knocked him down. Green followed with a thrust to Brown's body; but the light dress sword he was carrying struck something hard and bent double. In frustration mixed with fear, Green fell upon his foe and beat him about the head with the hilt of his sword until Brown was unconscious. Meanwhile other marines had entered the engine house. One of them was mortally wounded as he crawled through the opening; another was wounded less severely. Those who had reached the interior safely made short work of the assault. They bayoneted to death two of Brown's followers and captured two others. All thirteen of Brown's hostages survived the melee unharmed. They were dirty and had not eaten for sixty hours; but thanks to Lee's decisive leadership, they were alive.[16]

The entire action, from the time Stuart waved his hat, lasted only about three minutes. From the smoky gloom of the engine house the marines brought out their wounded. They also dragged out four dead insurgents, two of whom had died before the storming. Another of Brown's men was dying from a wound inflicted earlier. Two captives were unharmed; Brown was still unconscious. On first inspection most believed that Brown would soon die from Green's slash, thrust, and blows; Stuart believed he was "playing 'possum.'" Brown did regain consciousness fairly soon; but before he did, Stuart relieved him of his Bowie knife and kept it as a souvenir. Stuart also proclaimed to all assembled that "Smith" was in fact Brown, and the young lieutenant was the only person on the scene who could positively recognize the insurgent leader.

Lee gave Green charge of the prisoners; the marines carried Brown to the armory paymaster's office and stood guard on the armory grounds to prevent any disorder on the part of local civilians. In the late morning Lee dispatched Stuart with a few marines to Brown's "headquarters," a farmhouse in Maryland about four and a half miles from Harpers Ferry. Stuart took a wagon along, but himself walked with the troops. At the farmhouse he found a cache of arms and supplies and numerous incriminating documents, including a carpetbag filled with Brown's correspondence. He collected the documents, filled the wagon with a thousand to fifteen hundred pikes (poles with metal points), and returned in the afternoon to Harpers Ferry.[17]

There he found that Henry A. Wise, governor of Virginia and an old political ally of Archibald Stuart's, had arrived with other dignitaries and curiosity seekers. They all wanted to see Brown to question him, and Brown himself was more than willing to talk. For three hours he talked about slavery and his cause. He answered questions about details of his raid circumspectly and refused to implicate his coconspirators. Stuart only listened to the interrogation until Brown professed that the Golden Rule justified his deeds. Then the lieutenant exclaimed, "But don't you believe in the Bible?" Brown said he did.[18]

After the session with Brown, Lee and Stuart compiled a roster of the known raiders and attempted to account for the fate of each. And Lee sent some of the documents Stuart had discovered to Washington. Having once more made sure that the captives and the town were secure, the two men slept for the first time in at least thirty-six hours.[19]

Stuart had to leave for Kansas soon after the incident of Harpers Ferry; he resumed command of Company G, 1st Cavalry, on December 15, 1859. His six months in the East had been eventful and successful. He invested the $5,000 he received for the sale of his invention in the Bank of the State of Missouri at St. Louis at 10 percent interest. He had renewed old acquaintances and made new friends. And he had had the good fortune to be at the center of events relating to the capture of John Brown. Lee acknowledged his skill and services in his report to the War Department; everyone involved witnessed his courage before the door of the engine house; and he alone had been able to identify "old Ossawattomie Brown." Stuart was in search of his fortune and "a name" (as he phrased it); his trip east contributed to both.

But Stuart never once believed that his deeds alone would win for him the distinction he sought. He knew that he would have to orchestrate his rise to prominence, and he also knew the value of friends and influence.[20]

He had written periodically to Henry A. Wise while Wise was governor of Virginia. In the spring of 1857 he had asked Wise to help him win appointment as commissary of subsistence, an assignment that carried with it promotion to captain. In the fall of 1857, he thanked Wise for his help and asked Wise to do what he could to get him a captaincy in one of the cavalry regiments that Congress was contemplating creating. His contact with Wise during the aftermath of Harpers Ferry disillusioned Stuart somewhat. Wise, it seemed to Stuart, had attempted to snatch some credit for Brown's capture by sending a telegram to Lee to "grant no terms." By the time Lee received the message, if indeed he ever did, the entire affair was over, and Lee at the time was acting under orders from the President, not a governor. Wise, Stuart concluded, "is a queer genius." [21]

In an age when allegiance to state and state connections was extremely important in national political patronage, Stuart naturally had strong hopes for his career while fellow Virginian Floyd was secretary of war. In January of 1858 Stuart's commanding officer, Major William H. Emory, wrote to Floyd urging him to promote Stuart to captain in one of the new regiments still under consideration by Congress. In September of 1858 Emory recommended Stuart for a position as cavalry instructor at West Point. And on March 10, 1860, forty-two members of the Virginia legislature signed a petition to Floyd. In the petition, the legislators recounted Stuart's service and virtues and prayed for his promotion "whenever a suitable opportunity is offered." [22]

On January 1, 1860, Wise, the "queer genius," ceased to be governor of Virginia. The new executive, elected in May of 1859, was John Letcher, who was an uncle of Stuart's mother. Thus when Stuart wrote to his mother in January of 1860 to give her a detailed account of his actions at Harpers Ferry, it may have been no mere accident that he devoted considerable space and attention to the question of who was going to win what laurels from the event. He expressed his concern for the better part of four pages.

Lee, Stuart wrote, "deserves a gold medal from Virginia. I presume no one but myself will ever *know* the *immense* but quiet service he rendered the state and the country." The young lieutenant was proud of the fact that Lee had mentioned Stuart's name first in his report when thanking his subordinates. As for Green, Stuart pointed out that he was a "*New Yorker*," but had redeemed the stain of his birthplace somewhat by marrying a woman from Virginia. "He did his duty very handsomely . . ."

Regarding himself, Stuart declared, "I feel that I did all that my position allowed me to do, and for it, I claim—*Nothing*—but *if* a Bill passed the legislature of Va., rewarding Green and not including me, I would feel exceedingly *mortified*. . . . I shall certainly expect every friend I have in either house (if I have any) to insist upon my being included. To reduce the thing to a nutshell it is this [:] *Green* was *ordered* to do what he did. I *voluntarily* left important business in Washington and accompanied Col. Lee . . . Green is a resolute noble fellow and Va. might well vote him thanks, a sword or something, but remember what I said." Stuart claimed nothing; he wanted much. His quibble over motives, together with his cupidity over trophies, seems a bit petty.[23]

But Stuart knew that such seemingly small matters counted for much within a peacetime army. He had done the things that aspiring young officers had to do during their apprenticeships and he had done them well. He had other advantages, too. He enjoyed entrée to leading political figures and families in Virginia. He was clever enough to do some of the little extra things associated with his profession that gave his record added dimension, such as inventing accoutrements. And perhaps most important, he possessed the integrity of character required. Amid the petty detail and routine boredom of peacetime soldiering, Stuart took his tasks seriously and performed them conscientiously. He did not succumb to the artificial escapes by which other men attempted to transcend their mundane circumstances: he was faithful to his vow not to drink; he gambled only upon Kansas real estate; and although he delighted in the company of lively women, he remained faithful to Flora. He was, and knew it, a promising young officer; he was overcoming the inertia of advancement within that essentially static institution, the United States Army.

But as he did so, the United States was undergoing tensions and conflicts that threatened to make the army Stuart knew, indeed the world Stuart knew, anything but static. Stuart was an eyewitness to some of the national trauma; he had seen Bleeding Kansas, and he had had a role at Harpers Ferry. However, although he came from a political family, maintained acquaintance with politicians, and kept himself informed about the political questions of his times, Stuart was not a political person. Preoccupied as he was with the duties of his profession, the care and feeding of his career, and the obligations and amusements of his private life, he, like most Americans, had neither time nor inclination to understand the magnitude of the sectional conflict that produced civil war. Thus in 1860–61, when sectional antipathy became secession crisis, Stuart was essentially unprepared. He had to respond to circumstances he had hardly anticipated, and so his response seems at the same time confused and oversimple.

Stuart's solution to the prospect of disunion was the simple statement he repeated almost liturgically, "I go with Virginia." He said it so often that it became an article of faith, and it seemed to resolve any doubt or ambiguity about what he would do in the event some or all of the Southern states declared themselves an independent nation. He had been a Virginiaphile from the time he first left the state and at West Point found Yankee girls infinitely uglier than Virginia girls. He had strong feelings for place and identified "home" with southwestern Virginia. Everywhere else he went was exile. He left Virginia to perform deeds and win honors that would impress people whose opinion of him really mattered—his friends and family in Virginia. Hence it was only logical that he "go with Virginia." And it simplified his situation, too. He did not have to decide whether he was more Southern than American or vice versa. Virginia would decide for him.[24]

However, neither Stuart nor anyone else could reliably predict what Virginia was going to do, and for Stuart this was where the confusion began. Governor Letcher began working for some sectional compromise from the time he assumed office, and he would oppose secession even after seven Southern states left the Union. The Richmond *Examiner*, to which Stuart subscribed, favored secession editorially, and ex-Governor Wise did as well. Obviously the presidential election of 1860 would be crucial to relations among the sections. Predictably Stuart favored the candidacy of a Virginian, R. M. T. Hunter, who was a United States senator and the choice of Virginia delegates to the Democratic Convention.[25]

Yet before Stuart knew for sure the fate of Hunter's candidacy, he confronted a more immediate issue on the frontier, a campaign against Kiowa and Comanche Indians. On March 10, 1860, the War Department ordered "active operations" to commence in mid-May. Stuart commanded Company G, 1st Cavalry, in a column that included six companies under the command of Major John Sedgwick. The expedition left Fort Riley on May 15 and headed west. For three months Stuart was more or less out of touch with the presidential campaign and the fate of the Union.[26]

He was also out of touch with his family, and Flora was expecting their second child in June. He missed her whenever he was away and recorded in the diary he kept that summer, "Bless her heart. Who with my experience could live without a wife?" But he believed he had no choice. The country and his Floras would have to get along without him while he chased Kiowa.[27]

The expedition began uneventfully, and the personal diary Stuart kept recorded observations of soil, crops, water, scenery, and wildlife. He noted such things as "a fine roast of buffalo on sticks," "bird serenade at night," "fish for every meal," and "no Indians." On one occasion he volunteered to scout ahead for water. He left camp at five o'clock one morning, found water forty miles away, rested briefly, and returned to camp at one fifteen the following morning. After a brief nap, Stuart had to lead the column back to the water he had found. In thirty-five hours he traveled 120 miles and slept only one and a half hours. During the several days the troopers spent "laying by," resting in camp, Stuart read novels by Edward Bulwer-Lytton, *What Will He Do with It* and *The Disowned,* which concludes, about the death of its heroic protagonist, "But why should pity be entertained for the soul which never fell?—for the courage which never quailed?—for the majesty never humbled?—for the stormy life?—it was triumph!— for the early death?—it was immortality!"[28]

Finally on July 11, 1860, Stuart found some Indians. He led a detachment of twenty soldiers in pursuit of the Kiowa war chief Sotanko and his household. The chase began at Bent's Fort (on the Arkansas River, within the present boundaries of Colorado), and Stuart soon found the trail of his quarry leading north. He sighted the Indians in the distance and pursued at a full gallop. The troopers had covered twenty-six miles in two and a half hours when they closed upon the fleeing Kiowa.

Then did Stuart see another detachment of cavalry, returning to Bent's Fort from a patrol, riding toward him. The other detachment, commanded by Captain William Steele, mistook Stuart's dust for Indian warriors and thus charged their fellow whites. Stuart saw what was happening and ordered his bugler to blow repeated calls in order to identify his column. Finally Steele's troopers realized that they were about to engage their comrades, and the two detachments merged and continued the pursuit Stuart had begun.

The chase continued as long as the horses could run. One trooper even ran down and mortally wounded a warrior on foot after both of their horses were exhausted. Two of Sotanko's women escaped. Stuart's men killed two warriors (Sotanko's brother and son) and captured one woman. Steele's horsemen captured fifteen women and children and twenty or thirty horses. As it happened

Sotanko was not with his family. The fight at Blackwater Springs, as it became known, cost the cavalry three wounded men. The captured Kiowa women and children remained with the Indian agent at Bent's Fort as hostages for the safety of travelers on the Santa Fe Trail. After several more days at the fort, Sedgwick headed east down the valley of the Arkansas River. By August 10, 1860, the column had completed its march and Sedgwick ordered component units back to their assigned posts.[29]

The same evening Stuart made an eighteen-mile ride to Fort Larned, where he learned that he and Flora had "a fine son." The boy had been born on June 26, and he became Phillip St. George Cooke Stuart in honor of his maternal grandfather. After exactly three months on the trail, on August 15 Stuart "arrived with joyous tramp at our own doors at Fort Riley, taking our families completely by surprise." He concluded his diary and the entry for August 15, "This page need not be filled out."[30]

Stuart's reunion with Flora and their young children was relatively brief. In September he left his family at Fort Riley with his mother-in-law and sisters-in-law and again headed west. He went 387 miles west with four companies of cavalry and two of infantry to establish Fort Wise on the Arkansas River just east of Bent's Fort. It proved a difficult chore; but the promise of cold weather spurred the construction of winter quarters. On October 8 the men were still living in tents; by November 13 Stuart had "a very comfortable house nearly finished." He planned to move his family to these quarters the following spring.[31]

While not directing construction projects, Stuart spent some of his time trying to keep in touch with his contacts in the East. He sent an account of his fight at Blackwater Springs to Flora's cousin John Esten Cooke, who had begun to make a name for himself as a writer. He also expressed a desire to contribute to a volume of Southern poetry he heard Cooke was contemplating. To another friend he wrote, "I hope that during my exile in this wilderness that my civilized friends will not entirely forget me." He received a letter from Flora every week; but his letters usually took a month just to get from Fort Riley to Fort Wise. And he received his copies of the Richmond *Examiner,* but by the time they reached him the news they contained was nearly history.[32]

A week after the presidential election of 1860 Stuart inquired from the wilderness, "Who's President?" Eventually he learned of Abraham Lincoln's election. But on the same day South Carolina seceded (December 20), Stuart wrote to a friend, "I believe the north will yield what the south demands thereby avert disunion." Perhaps because he realized or sensed that the secession crisis was at hand, he applied for a leave of absence and planned to go at least as far east as Fort Riley. But the mails and the military delayed his leave orders, and so he remained at Fort Wise throughout the secession winter of 1860–61. While the country's statesmen made speeches about the fate of the Union, Stuart was composing a temperance lecture to inform the troops of the evils of John Barleycorn.[33]

Probably as much from frustration as from anything else, he began a campaign to cover all his bets, no matter what might happen. On December 5, 1860, he wrote to Governor-elect Letcher requesting his intercession with Secretary of War Floyd on behalf of Stuart's promotion to captain. In the same letter Stuart also tendered his services to Letcher in the event Virginia should leave the Union and go to war with that army in which Stuart was seeking promotion. By the time Letcher received this convoluted missive and had time to respond, Floyd had resigned as secretary of war. In January 1861, Stuart wrote to Senator Jefferson Davis of Mississippi, who had once been secretary of war. In the likely event of the "dismemberment of the Army" and of Davis's probable prominence in an "Army of the South," Stuart asked of him a position in that army. Also in January he wrote to his brother William Alexander Stuart in Wytheville and proposed to raise and command a "legion of cavalry" from the county with which to serve Virginia. On February 12 Stuart's mother personally delivered his offer of allegiance and service to the Virginia adjutant general's office; that official wrote Stuart that he would call upon him if necessary. Some time later Stuart again wrote to his brother stating that if Virginia seceded, he would go immediately to Richmond and "report in person to Governor Letcher." Should secession not provoke war, he proposed to resign from the United States Army and "practice law in Memphis." How, with no legal background, he planned to practice law, and why, after "going" with Virginia, he would choose to live in Memphis, Stuart did not explain. Stuart even corresponded with Republicans; he asked Lincoln's attorney general, Missouri Republican Edward Bates, to try to expedite his promotion to captain. Bates responded by assuring Stuart that his promotion was forthcoming and delivered a thinly veiled warning that officers who flirted with treason would be held accountable. If the pace and magnitude of events during the winter of 1860–61 baffled people who lived where the crisis was developing, it is small wonder that a lieutenant on the fringe of the American frontier seemed confused.[34]

At long last on March 4, 1861, Stuart received two months' leave. He went as soon as he could to Fort Riley; by this time seven states of the deep South were out of the Union. Their representatives, meeting in Montgomery, Alabama, had founded the government of the Confederate States of America and elected Jefferson Davis provisional president of the new nation. The crisis now focused upon possession of Fort Sumter in Charleston Harbor. While Lincoln debated whether to reinforce his garrison on Sumter and Davis debated whether to open fire upon the fort, Virginia's potential secession convention simply debated. Consequently, Stuart, like Virginia, was in limbo.[35]

He believed that Virginia would secede and that war would follow. Indeed he wrote to a friend in Richmond and reminded him of the necessity to protect the Tredegar Iron Works located there. He also said that the army's ranking general, Unionist-Virginian Winfield Scott, was "already carrying on a secret inquisition through the Army." But until someone did something at Fort Sumter, which would likely provoke some firm action for or against secession in Virginia, Stuart could only wait. And while he waited John Esten Cooke wrote him on April 4 proclaiming the time overripe to act and stating that the "plums" were being snatched up by others. Stuart did not enjoy uncertainty; soon after he reached Fort Riley, he went to St. Louis for three weeks.[36]

Upon his return to Riley, he learned that the Confederates had fired upon Sumter, Lincoln had called for 75,000 volunteers to coerce the Southern states back into the Union, and Virginia on April 17 had seceded. Immediately Stuart packed the few belongings of his family and took the two Floras and his ten-month-old son to St. Louis. From there they boarded a steamboat for Memphis. En route Stuart wrote a letter of resignation from the United States Army; he mailed it on May 3 from Cairo, Illinois. He also mailed a letter to General Samuel Cooper, who was adjutant general of the new Confederate Army, asking him for a command and appropriate rank. Meanwhile Elizabeth Stuart had written to Robert E. Lee, who was then in command of Virginia's army, requesting "a place" for her son.[37]

From Memphis the Stuarts set out by train for Virginia. On May 7 they reached Wytheville, and Stuart pressed on to Richmond. He stayed with Elizabeth Stuart, who had been living in the city for just over a year; but in the flurry of his official calls and friendly visits, he saw little of his mother. His cousin Peter W. Hairston offered to furnish him a horse and to be his volunteer aide. But it was his West Point mentor and commander at Harpers Ferry, Lee, who gave Stuart what he most wanted. On May 10 he became Lieutenant Colonel Stuart of the Provisional Army of Virginia. The commission was in the infantry, because no cavalry posts were available, but he commanded cavalry anyway.

At six o'clock on the morning of May 10, Stuart left Richmond for his first assignment. He was going back to Harpers Ferry to report to Colonel Thomas J. Jackson. Sometime during the frenzy of the week since he had mailed his resignation from Cairo, Illinois, Stuart learned that on April 22 he had been promoted to captain in the United States Army.[38] But that was not important now.

The circumstances of his military duties and his political naiveté had denied Stuart information and insight regarding the secession crisis. But in May of 1861 the uncertainty was over; the Confederacy existed; Virginia and Stuart were within the Southern fold. Moreover, this new nation was at war, and Stuart had spent more than a third of his life acquiring precisely the skills and credentials his new country needed most. He had spent four years of intense study and training at West Point. Then for the last seven years he had gained varieties of experience on active duty. Some of that experience had been frustrating—competing for small crumbs seldom offered by an army in peacetime. But now all that was behind him. He had joined a brand-new army and advanced from lieutenant to lieutenant colonel overnight. Stuart's opportunities seemed limitless. Most of his young life had been a conscious struggle to make good; here was the wonderful chance for conspicuous success.

# V

---

## *Colonel Stuart*

STUART ARRIVED AT HARPERS FERRY on May 10—only one week
after he had resigned his commission in a different army. He reported for duty to Colonel Thomas J. Jackson. Like Stuart, Jackson
had been at Harpers Ferry during the John Brown scare in 1859;
he had come with the corps of cadets from Virginia Military Institute (VMI), where he was a member of the faculty. Stuart may have
met Jackson then; but if he did, he did not know him well. To
Flora he identified his superior only as "of the institute." During
the relatively brief period during which Stuart worked directly for
Jackson, he must have noticed something special about this thirty-
seven-year-old eccentric professor because he sought Jackson's
friendship in the same way he sought the friendship of people he
considered destined for success. Stuart gravitated to Jackson at the
same time that an Alabama private judged him "a large, fat, old
fellow, looks very much like a Virginia farmer." Jackson's quirks
and Calvinism were legendary among the cadets at VMI. But
Stuart must have glimpsed something remarkable in this man apparently so unlike himself, and Jackson seemed to reciprocate.[1]

At first, Stuart posed something of a problem for his new superior. Since Stuart had professional training and experience in cavalry tactics and possessed requisite rank, Jackson determined to
ignore the fact that Stuart's commission was in infantry and to
consolidate all his cavalry companies under Stuart's command.
However, Jackson's action immediately offended Captain Turner
Ashby and his hard-riding collection of volunteer Virginians. Jack-

[ 68 ]

son resolved the crisis by dividing the cavalry companies, giving Stuart and Ashby each a regiment, and sending Ashby to cover Point of Rocks on the Potomac River. Both men kept their pride, and Jackson kept Stuart.[2]

When Joseph E. Johnston arrived at Harpers Ferry to command what had grown into a sizable army, he continued the compromise Jackson had made and kept Stuart in command of the cavalry most closely associated with his army. Neither Jackson nor Johnston nor anyone else could mediate successfully all cases of jealousy and offended dignity within this new army, and Stuart was the focus of resentment from men other than Ashby. William E. Jones, for example, arrived at Stuart's headquarters as captain of a volunteer company of cavalry looking for reason to despise his commander. Jones was older, and he, too, possessed West Point training, yet Stuart outranked him. "Grumble" Jones, as he became known, never quite forgave Stuart his superiority.[3]

Two weeks after Stuart arrived at Harpers Ferry Johnston assumed command in the name of the Confederate Army, relieving Jackson, who had commanded in the name of Virginia. Johnston began withdrawing from Harpers Ferry and eventually occupied Winchester.

Then Stuart established his camp near a little crossroads village called Bunker Hill, roughly halfway between Winchester and Martinsburg in the lower (northern) Shenandoah Valley. Tents in neat rows and picket ropes for horses covered the floor of the little valley; on the hill was a smaller group of tents over which a flag flapped in the mild breeze. To this camp came volunteer companies of cavalry to join Stuart's small command.

One such company appeared about noon on a June day. The men had been traveling for several days and had ridden twenty miles already that morning. They were tired and wanted to settle in and rest. But they were also interested in the man in charge of cavalry in this part of the war.

Colonel Stuart was young—twenty-eight—and because he was a West Pointer, citizen-soldiers were a little suspicious of his professionalism. Men who met Stuart for the first time during the spring and summer of 1861 were impressed with his ruddy complexion, full beard, and sparkling eyes. They noted his broad shoulders and powerful build, and those who remained in his

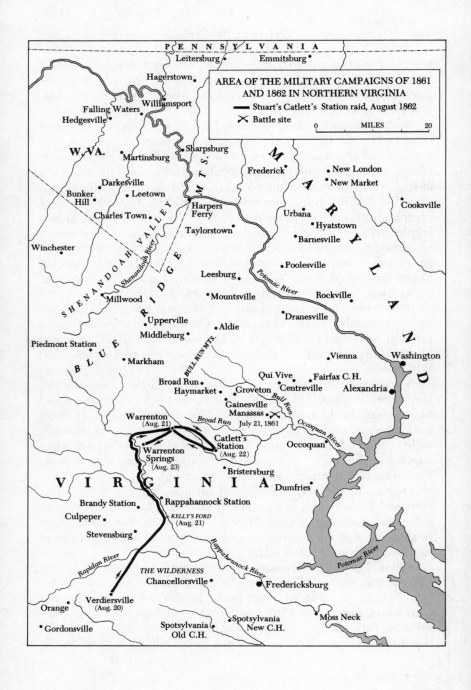

PENNSYLVANIA

Leitersburg · · Emmitsburg ·

Hagerstown ·

Falling Waters
Hedgesville ·
Williamsport ·

W. VA.
Martinsburg ·
Sharpsburg ·

Frederick ·
· New London
· New Market

Darkesville ·
· Leetown
Bunker
Hill ·
Charles Town ·
Harpers
Ferry ·
Taylorstown ·

Urbana ·
· Hyattstown
· Barnesville
· Cooksville

Winchester ·
Millwood ·
Leesburg ·
· Mountsville
· Poolesville

SHENANDOAH VALLEY

Shenandoah River

BLUE RIDGE MTS.

Upperville ·
Middleburg ·
· Aldie
· Dranesville
· Rockville

Piedmont Station ·
· Markham

BULL RUN MTS.

· Vienna
Washington

Broad Run ·
Haymarket ·
Qui Vive ·
· Fairfax C. H.
Centreville
Alexandria ·

Groveton
Gainesville
Manassas · × July 21, 1861

**AREA OF THE MILITARY CAMPAIGNS OF 1861
AND 1862 IN NORTHERN VIRGINIA**
━━━ Stuart's Catlett's Station raid, August 1862
✕ Battle site
0        MILES        20

MARYLAND

Potomac River

Occoquan River

Bull Run

Warrenton
(Aug. 21)
Broad Run
Catlett's
Station
(Aug. 22)

Warrenton
Springs
(Aug. 23)
· Bristersburg
· Occoquan
· Dumfries

VIRGINIA

Brandy Station ·
Culpeper ·
Stevensburg ·
Rappahannock Station ·

KELLY'S FORD
(Aug. 21)

Rapidan River
Rappahannock River

Potomac River

THE WILDERNESS
Chancellorsville ·
· Fredericksburg

Orange ·
· Gordonsville
Verdiersville
(Aug. 20)

Spotsylvania
Old C.H.
· Spotsylvania
New C.H.
· Moss Neck

presence for any length of time remarked upon his seemingly boundless energy. First impressions of the young colonel were not always favorable however. In fact, members of the volunteer company who joined Stuart's command on that day at Bunker Hill soon became convinced that he was some sort of damned fool.

Stuart assigned the company a campsite in the little valley he had christened Camp Jeff Davis, and ordered the captain to pitch his tents. The captain, however, objected to the mud in his designated spot and moved the site about fifty yards away to higher ground. While the men were busy setting up camp, Stuart returned and had some words with the captain. At the conclusion of this brief interview the captain turned to his men muttering something about martinets and lack of courtesy. Then he instructed the troops to undo what they had been doing and establish their camp on the site originally assigned them.

About an hour after they arrived at Bunker Hill, Stuart ordered the men of the new unit divided into three detachments, each commanded by one of the company lieutenants. By the time these detachments assembled and reported to Stuart, the men had learned several facts about their situation. The 1st Virginia Cavalry, which regiment Stuart commanded and to which the new company belonged, was the only mounted unit assigned to the army of Confederate General Johnston. That army was in Winchester, and in Martinsburg was a Federal army commanded by Union General Robert Patterson. The thirteen miles between Winchester and Martinsburg was no-man's land, and squarely between the hostile armies was Camp Jeff Davis and Stuart's little band of horsemen.

Stuart's assignment for the afternoon was for each of the three inexperienced lieutenants to take his group of amateur troopers and scout the country between Bunker Hill and Martinsburg. They were to go as close as possible to Martinsburg, and if they met any enemy cavalry, they were to give battle. With considerable trepidation but really no choice, the men trotted off to carry out Stuart's orders. Fortunately they encountered no enemy horsemen, and somehow they found their way to Martinsburg and back again. And when they returned they probably felt a little more at home in the war; but they had grave doubts about the man who had sent them so soon to find a fight.

Next morning Stuart had the company again in their saddles; he led them himself in the direction of Martinsburg. They followed this colonel into enemy lines, where he deliberately got them nearly surrounded by Union infantry on two or three occasions. Each time he warned his charges that they might have to cut their way out of the trap into which he had led them. Then each time he found a gap in the enemy lines and led them on a dash to safety. When the men returned to camp, they had learned some lessons; but they still wondered about their unorthodox schoolmaster.

Classes continued a few weeks later when Patterson's army marched forth to threaten Winchester. Stuart's men expected him to order a retreat to the protection of Johnston's army. Instead Stuart led a small body of cavalry toward the advancing enemy, ordered the men to dismount and confront the oncoming force on foot. Federal infantry skirmishers alone outnumbered Stuart's unhorsed troops, and soon they were within two hundred yards and closing fast. Then only did Stuart command his men to withdraw —marching backwards, firing as they moved. After an eternity the men reached their horses and mounted. Even though the Federal skirmishers were at this point very near, Stuart permitted no gait faster than a trot as he disengaged.

When his pupils had reached relative safety, Stuart delivered a brief lecture about what had just occurred. "Now I want to talk to you, men," he said. "You are brave fellows, and patriotic ones too, but you are ignorant of this kind of work, and I am teaching you. I want you to observe that a good man on a good horse can never be caught. Another thing: cavalry can *trot* away from anything and a gallop is a gait unbecoming a soldier, unless he is going toward the enemy. Remember that. We gallop toward the enemy, and trot away, always."

Then, noticing some activity among the Federal army, Stuart broke off his lecture and called out, "Steady now! don't break ranks!" A flat bang seemed to punctuate Stuart's words, and the men then heard an artillery shell hiss through the air over their heads.

"There," Stuart said. "I've been waiting for that, and watching those fellows. I knew they'd shoot too high, and I wanted you to learn how shells sound." [4]

By the time the men of the volunteer company had spent a couple of entire days inside enemy lines with Stuart, they were not only confident of their capacity to confront their foes, they had become convinced that Colonel Stuart was some kind of weird genius. And Stuart attended the education of his other companies in a similar manner. He ordered them into action immediately, monitored their activities, and often accompanied them.[5]

While Stuart was training his charges by experience and using his enemies as training aids in his classes, Federal cavalry units were enduring the monotony of the "School of the Trooper, dismounted." Elsewhere in the South, cavalry commanders who lacked the benefits of an inexperienced enemy army nearby tended to spend whatever time they devoted to training on formations and reviews. As a consequence combat was a novel experience for most horsemen on both sides. Stuart's 1st Virginia, however, considered themselves veterans even before the first major battle at Manassas/Bull Run. And probably because they believed they were veterans, they acted the part.[6]

At this point, Stuart was attempting to patrol a very broad front (fifty miles) between Johnston's and Patterson's armies. On June 30 Stuart had only twenty-one officers and 313 enlisted men with which to perform his mission; thus necessity, as well as his zeal for practical training, impelled him to initiate his new men to the rigors of scouting within twenty-four hours of their arrival in his camp.[7]

Stuart endeared himself to Johnston during the year the two men worked together. Later, when Johnston left the Virginia theater to command the Army of Tennessee, he wrote Stuart, "How can I eat, sleep, or rest in peace without you upon the outpost?" Certainly Stuart's performance reflected his energy, attention to training, and desire to please his superiors. It also reflected Stuart's mature understanding of the function of mounted troops within an army. The young colonel was certainly flamboyant, and he surely possessed a zeal to perform tasks that seemed to others impossible. But even at this early stage of the war, he seemed to realize the limitations of his horsemen. He once said, "All I ask of fate is that I may be killed leading a cavalry charge." But he never directed, much less led, a massive charge against organized infantry.[8]

He understood that all his training at West Point, the conventional wisdom from past wars that called for massed cavalry to break enemy lines and formations, was much outmoded. He knew that in this war the principal mission of cavalry was reconnaissance—reconnaissance in the broadest sense. Cavalry should provide a screen behind which friendly forces mass and move undetected and thus unhindered by the enemy. Mounted troops as pickets on outpost should watch enemy movements and report them; at the same time pickets should prevent the enemy from securing information about friendly forces by stopping enemy patrols and scouting expeditions. Cavalry scouting parties should control the area between armies, gather information about the country and the enemy, and prevent enemy cavalry from doing the same. Cavalry could and did have a role in major battles; but its most important tasks were performed between general engagements of large bodies of troops. And if cavalry performed those tasks well, mounted troops might determine the outcome of campaigns and battles before they ever occurred.[9]

When Patterson crossed the Potomac and began his advance to Martinsburg on July 1, Stuart was quick to discover and report the movement. Johnston dispatched Jackson and a brigade to confront the Federals and determine their strength. The result was the "Affair at Falling Waters," a brief delaying action on July 2 in which Jackson withdrew before superior numbers. Stuart's troopers were active on the Federal flank and attempted to cut off and capture some of the skirmishers who led the advance. Jackson was for a time afraid that Stuart's cavalry would be cut off instead of the enemy and recalled the horsemen. After a brief clash, Jackson, as instructed, withdrew toward Winchester; Stuart remained to watch Patterson's army occupy Martinsburg.[10]

At some time during the day Stuart was riding alone through some woods ahead of his men. As he left the woods and entered open country, he came suddenly upon a number of Federal infantry on the other side of a rail fence. The lone colonel continued riding toward the troops, and as he approached, he ordered some of them to dismantle a section of the fence. Believing Stuart to be one of their own officers, the Federals complied. Then Stuart ordered the men to throw down their arms or he would shoot them. They were his prisoners! The bluff worked, at least until Stuart's troopers rode to the scene. Then did three of the captives resist, and lost their lives so doing. By himself Stuart captured most of Company I, 15th Pennsylvania Infantry—forty-six men including a lieutenant and a surgeon.

Stuart reported this success to Jackson, and Jackson passed on the information and praise of Stuart to Johnston. To Flora, Stuart wrote, on July 4, "During the last two days this regiment has been in the midst of the enemy." In the same letter Stuart gave his address as "Before the enemy." And he remained very much before the enemy during the next two weeks.[11]

The strategic situation was this: Johnston had approximately 12,000 troops in and around Winchester; Patterson had about 18,000 men further (north) down the Valley. The Shenandoah River which flows north into the Potomac had formed this region of rolling farmland between the Blue Ridge Mountains to the east and the Allegheny Mountains to the west. In Virginia the Shenandoah Valley was, and is, the Valley, and during the war it became an important theater of operations. The two generals feinted at each other in attempts to fight on favorable terms and ground. Soon after the Affair at Falling Waters, Johnston advanced a couple of miles beyond Bunker Hill to Darkesville and for four days dared Patterson to attack him. Then Johnston withdrew again to Winchester, and soon after that on July 15 Patterson advanced to Bunker Hill. When Johnston did not attack, Patterson became concerned about his supply lines and on July 17 fell back to Charles Town. By this time Johnston was preparing to take his army elsewhere. Over the Blue Ridge Mountains to the east, two other armies confronted each other. Union General Irwin McDowell and about 35,000 men were advancing from Washington toward General P. G. T. Beauregard's 20,000 Confederates who occupied the southern bank of Bull Run near the railroad junction at Manassas. In response to Beauregard's urgent pleas for reinforcement, the Confederate War Office ordered Johnston to march most of his men to Piedmont Station and transport them by rail to Manassas. There the conglomerate force would attack McDowell. The first of several critical components in this plan was Stuart's capacity to screen Johnston's departure. If Patterson should discover Johnston's army in transit, he might attack under favorable circumstances or follow his foes to Manassas and join McDowell's attack.

Either response would produce disaster for the Confederacy in this first major campaign of the war.[12]

Stuart did his part—with some help from Patterson and Federal volunteers whose three-month enlistments were expiring. Patterson was timid and expected Winfield Scott, his superior in Washington, to tell him what to do. The volunteers with expiring enlistments composed a sizable portion of Patterson's army, and many of the men informed their general that they would not serve one hour beyond the time for which they had obligated themselves. Stuart's active outposts kept the Federals from learning of Johnston's departure until July 20, when he had reached Manassas. And even then Patterson believed that Johnston had left Winchester to try to flank Charles Town. He also believed that Johnston's 11,000 were 35,200 troops. Stuart was not content to remain in the Valley once he had completed his mission. The great battle would be somewhere else, so Stuart led a portion of his little regiment down the same road Johnston had taken in order to find the action.[13]

Leaving some of his men to watch the Federals at Charles Town, Stuart set out with four companies (about 300 men) on the morning of July 19. Before long his column encountered the wake of Johnston's army. Men and guns jammed the road through Millwood to Piedmont Station; Stuart's cavalry had to leave the road and trot through the fields. During the day fences and ditches impeded their progress and darkness compounded these impediments. Weary foot soldiers who left the road to rest also posed problems; the horsemen had to remain alert enough not to trample them. Stuart, the conscientious former commissary officer, had ordered wagons with food rations to meet his column en route; but in the backwash of Johnston's army the wagons were delayed. Consequently the troopers went hungry throughout their first day on the road. During a rest halt one of the junior officers, Lieutenant William W. Blackford, encountered a man who had just caught a large bullfrog. The man was more fastidious about his food than Blackford, so he was more than willing to surrender his catch to a good cause. Blackford quickly kindled a fire, skinned the creature, and soon feasted (?) upon broiled bullfrog. So hungry was the lieutenant that he rapidly ate, not only the legs, but the entire amphibian.

Once the troopers passed Piedmont Station they no longer had to concern themselves with the infantry, as the foot soldiers had boarded trains there for the remainder of the journey. Stuart pressed on at greater speed and arrived at Manassas on the evening of July 20. With the exception of brief rests, the men had been in their saddles for thirty-six hours.

One of them, Lieutenant Blackford, had been more than tired and sleepy. Perhaps because of the bullfrog, he had severe problems in his lower intestines. When riding his horse became insufferable, Blackford, who had just been made Stuart's adjutant (administrative assistant), had to ask his commander for permission to leave the column for a time. The lieutenant was much embarrassed at his request, lest Stuart think his malady was related to the prospect of battle. Stuart did give Blackford a searching glance; but he responded, "Yes, but remember there is going to be a battle tomorrow." In no condition to protest his determination to rejoin the regiment as soon as possible, Blackford left the line of march and took refuge in a nearby farmhouse. There he found a hospitable reception, some breakfast, and the chance to sleep for two hours. He awakened recovered and overtook Stuart's column before it reached Manassas.[14]

Stuart secured rations for his men and camped roughly halfway between Manassas and the Stone Bridge where the Warrenton Turnpike crosses Bull Run. Very early the next morning (July 21), Stuart awoke with a start. "Hello! What is that?" he asked rhetorically. He was hearing small-arms fire off to the left, where the battle was not supposed to be.

What he heard was the result of McDowell's plan to flank the Confederate army. Federal troops advancing from Centreville first threatened the Southerners at the Stone Bridge, while more Federal units were crossing Bull Run farther upstream at Sudley Springs Ford. McDowell intended to sweep down the southern bank of Bull Run and roll up Beauregard's left flank. Meanwhile Beauregard was preparing to attack McDowell at Centreville; it took him some time to realize that McDowell's army had left Centreville, that McDowell was attacking him, and that the firing on his left represented the main thrust of that attack. Throughout the morning the threat to the Confederate left grew as the relatively few Confederate troops stationed near the Stone Bridge fought for their lives. Once Beauregard realized what was happening, he hurried more troops to reinforce his flank and about noon he joined them. The battle raged across the slope of Henry House Hill and remained much in doubt as more and more units from each side reached the scene and extended the battle line. Confederate General Barnard Bee (who, likening Jackson to a stone wall, gave him his immortal nickname) rallied his own men for a charge that cost him his life. Charges, countercharges, grapeshot, and carnage swept the rolling plains, and while the battle surged over Henry House Hill, Stuart and his horsemen simply stood around and waited.[15]

Early that morning Stuart had led a short scout across Bull Run. Some of his men saw some enemy at a distance, but Stuart returned without confronting anyone. Then came an order from Jackson to divide the regiment and send two companies to another portion of the field to act in a supporting role on Jackson's right flank. Stuart dispatched Grumble Jones's company with one other under the command of a Major Robert Swann, and then he waited with his remaining two companies for a call to action. For a long time, the call did not come. Stuart could hear the battle perfectly; but with the exception of a few shells that burst in the air, trees and terrain kept him from seeing anything. He sent messages that he was available for action, and several times he rode forward, found Beauregard, and offered his services. Otherwise he waited and paced a lot.[16]

Around the Henry House, Beauregard's Confederates were confronting McDowell's Federals in a seesaw succession of combats. The Southerners had managed to stop the Federal flank attack and stabilize a battle line that ran roughly north-south. As more of McDowell's troops arrived on the scene, they deployed on the southern end of the line. Beauregard, too, had troops marching to this field from the east (Manassas Junction and positions along Bull Run downstream). Fresh Southern troops, as they arrived, countered the Federals on the southern end of the line and kept the issue much in doubt. While all this was happening, there was very little for cavalry to do.

Stuart knew that his two companies of cavalry counted for little compared to the masses of infantry and artillery engaged in that struggle beyond the woods and over the hill. He also knew that cavalry could accomplish little in such battle until the moment was ripe. Horsemen could protect a flank; they could cover a retreat; they could pursue a fleeing enemy; and *in extremis* they could sacrifice themselves in a desperate charge. Thus far this day infantry and artillery units were struggling for the flank, and none of the other circumstances yet applied. Nevertheless Stuart feared he would miss something. A great battle was raging a short way away, and all he could do was wait.

Finally, around 2:00 P.M. a rider dashed from the woods toward Stuart and his men. As the staff officer slowed his horse, Stuart strode forward and in answer to the rider's question, identified himself. "Colonel Stuart, General Beauregard directs that you bring your command into action at once and that you attack where the firing is hottest." [17]

Already the men were tightening the girths on their saddles. Stuart commanded "boots and saddles" and led them off at a trot in a column of fours toward the sounds of battle. On the way forward they had to ride through an outdoor field hospital. Blood-smeared surgeons, stripped to the waist, were busy at tables, and by this time the pile of amputated arms and legs was large. Living men screamed and moaned; only the dead were silent; and flies were everywhere. Stuart's troopers tried not to look; but the sudden horror of the scene made many of them vomit as they rode to war. Then they were past the field hospital and to the edge of some woods; beyond lay the battle.

They saw smoke and confusion. At the head of the column Stuart realized that he was entering the field on the Confederate left, and the action was indeed hot there. Closest to him was an infantry regiment with red baggy trousers, blue jackets, red caps, and white gaiters. These were Zouaves, dressed in Turkish attire. The unit seemed to be in some confusion, and Stuart, thinking it was a Louisiana Zouave regiment, Wheat's Tigers, shouted at them, "Don't run, boys; we are here." But his plea seemed to have no effect. Then he noticed their flag—the stars and stripes; these men were an amalgam of New York Fire Zouaves and the 14th New York, who also wore red trousers. They were recoiling from a bout with Jackson's Confederates. Immediately Stuart ordered a charge.

The Federals were only seventy yards away when Stuart's column of fours launched itself upon them. Stuart gave the signal with his saber, which meant for the horsemen in the rear of his column to attack in an oblique line to the left so that the column would strike the enemy over a broader front. By the time the men began carrying out Stuart's instruction, they were only about thirty yards from the enemy, and the Zouaves had faced them and were leveling their rifles.

Suddenly "a sheet of red flame" lit the field, and the attendant smoke enveloped everything near. The volley took its toll; but still Stuart and most of his men thundered forward. The Zouaves were frantically trying to reload when the horsemen hit them.

Blackford was not thinking of his lower intestines now. He only saw two men in his path. One was directly in front of him; the other just to the right. Instinctively Blackford jammed his spurs into his horse, and the animal took off as if to leap over a wall. The explosive thrust caught the first man in his chest, and he catapulted backward under the horse's hooves. Just as his horse began his lunge, Blackford leaned to his right, shoved his carbine into the other man's stomach, and fired. The Zouave had been slow to raise his bayonet, and so it fell harmlessly to the ground. Through front and back of his bright blue jacket and the human tissue between was a hole as big as an arm.

Momentum carried Stuart's cavalry once through the line of infantry. Necessity drove the Southern horsemen back through to regain friendly lines. Stuart tried to collect his men near the woods from which he had begun his charge. Blackford, as adjutant, had to chase down about half of the men, who seemed to have lost their enthusiasm for battle and were clattering down the road toward Manassas. When he returned with his catch, Stuart greeted him, "Bully for you, Blackford." But he refused to speak of discipline for those who had fled. He said that they would be more reliable next time, and they were.

The charge had cost Stuart's command nine dead men and double that number of horses. Stuart later claimed that his charge had completed the demoralization of the Zouaves and begun a general panic among all Federals. The Zouaves claimed that they had broken and scattered their foes. Surely both claims were extravagant.[18]

As soon as his men had rallied and regrouped, Stuart led them to the left, beyond the infantry battle line. On the extreme Confederate left flank Stuart found Lieutenant Robert F. Beckham and his battery of artillery. Stuart's troopers supported these guns, which maintained an effective fire upon the Federal right and rear. Because he had found ground from which he could see, Stuart hid Beckham's guns behind some trees and directed their fire from his vantage point. He also sent timely messages to commanders of infantry units whose vision was more restricted than his. From Stuart's vantage point, above the smoke and immediate confusion, the battle was simpler. He could see units march, deploy, and commit. He could watch artillery batteries dash over the field. It was as though he were watching a moving tableau; thus he shared his vision.

The most important of his messages went to Jubal A. Early, whose brigade of Southern infantry finally turned the Federal flank and began a rout of McDowell's army. Stuart informed Early of his opportunity and guided him to the crucial point from which his brigade might enter the battle on the Union flank.[19]

Stuart's two companies and Beckham's guns advanced on the left of Early's infantry at about four o'clock in the afternoon. The Federals wavered, started to retreat, and then panic overtook them. They began to run in confusion back across Bull Run toward Washington. Stuart dispatched Blackford to Beauregard to ask permission to pursue; but by the time the adjutant returned with Beauregard's encouragement, Stuart had realized that he needed no permission to undertake the obvious. He led his men upon a merry chase after the enemy. Before very long Stuart had captured so many prisoners and detailed so many men to escort them to the rear, that he had very few troopers left with him. So he halted his pursuit near Sudley Church and established his headquarters on the porch of a farmhouse. There he welcomed his returning men and laughed at their adventures in chasing frightened Federals.[20]

A few days after the event, Stuart wrote a report for Johnston of his first great battle. He emphasized his very visible charge at the expense of his more subtle service in directing Beckham's guns and guiding Early's brigade to glory—action at the expense of reflection. To Flora he reported, "I am your own Darling husband whose thoughts and affection are centered in his own Dear Flora

—and even in the fiercest fire of the battle field I thought of her and how proud she would be to see the conduct of her husband." He, too, was proud of his conduct and rightly so. "The papers have said very little about my Regt, but the Generals have said a great deal. You need not be surprised to see your hubbie a Brigadier. I have been in one real battle now and feel sure I can command better than many I saw." [21]

The day after the battle (July 22), Stuart spent collecting his men and making sure they collected what equipment and clothing they needed from items Union soldiers had abandoned or discarded on the battlefield. Overcoats and tents were in especially good supply. Then very early on the following day (July 23), Stuart left with his cavalry, plus some infantry, and advanced to Fairfax Court House. There he captured some Unionists and from them learned the magnitude of Federal disorder following the battle on Bull Run. He also was able to inform Johnston that Patterson had been replaced (only the day before) by Nathaniel P. Banks and that George B. McClellan would succeed McDowell. These things he knew after having been at Fairfax Court House only thirty minutes. [22]

When it became clear that the Confederate army at Manassas was not going to advance immediately upon Washington, Stuart made arrangements for Flora to come for a visit. She stayed in Fairfax Court House; Stuart had his headquarters about a mile or so down the Little River Turnpike toward Washington. Still he trained his troops incessantly—drill every morning and dress parade in the afternoon. Flora came to see him every day, and he probably visited her at night. Among other matters, they discussed the conduct of her father, Colonel Phillip St. George Cooke; most of his family, including Flora, his nephew John Esten Cooke, and his son John R. Cooke had embraced the new Confederacy. The elder Cooke had not, and it now seemed he never would. Indeed in June he had written a letter stating "I owe Virginia little; my country much." Stuart was not sure of his father-in-law's sentiments at this time; but if what he suspected was true, he was not about to forgive him. [23]

Peter Hairston, still acting as Stuart's volunteer aid, wrote his wife that cousin Flora "likes to stay . . . [with Stuart] as long as she can." But Stuart left the impression upon many who knew him that he spent most of his time during August and September with his men at some of his most forward positions on Munson's and Mason's hills near Bailey's Crossroad, only six miles from the Potomac River.[24]

He established a line of outposts or pickets, some of them within sight of the Capitol across the Potomac. Each outpost consisted of four to six men with a noncommissioned officer in charge. One of the men, called a vidette, remained mounted and stationed himself from one to two hundred yards in advance of the rest. The other men on outpost were supposed to have reins in their hands at all times. Each outpost was about a half mile from a company headquarters. There a reserve force rested and waited to relieve those on outpost (every four hours), and a sentinel remained alert to what was happening along the outpost line. In the event of enemy activity the vidette fired his weapon; in turn his comrades on outpost and the company reserve, roused by the sentinel, galloped forward to confront the foe. Sometimes the source of alarm was a rooting hog; on other occasions outpost duty was deadly business and men killed in this *petite-guerre* were just as dead as those who fell in the charge at Bull Run. Stuart demanded vigilance and stood no breach of his discipline. After one of his pickets was shot as he warmed himself before a fire, Stuart forbade fires on outpost and tried alleged offenders by court-martial—even when one of those charged was his former adjutant William W. Blackford.[25]

Schedules varied. Private (later Colonel) John S. Mosby recalled that his company spent twenty-four hours on picket three times per week. George Cary Eggleston, however, remembered a period during which men in his company never unsaddled their horses for ten days. Then, after those ten days of scouting expeditions, the unit took up picket duty beyond Fairfax Court House and remained on outpost for thirty-six hours without rations or even the prospect of relief. Just about this time Stuart appeared, and one of the men pointed out their plight. "Oh nonsense!" was Stuart's response. "You don't look starved. There's a cornfield over there; jump the fence and get a good breakfast. You don't want to go back to camp, I know; it's stupid there, and all the fun is out here. I never go to camp if I can help it." [26]

Certainly Stuart was attempting to inculcate among his troopers a positive attitude about the "fun" of scouting and outpost duty. At the same time he was being honest; he did enjoy the excitement of playing hide and seek between opposing armies.

One of his troopers claimed that "While we lay in advance of Fairfax Court House, after Bull Run, Stuart spent more than a month around the extreme outposts on Mason's and Munson's hills without once coming to the camp of his command . . . . he lived nearly all the time between the picket lines of the two armies." Another soldier wrote his wife, "Stuart sleeps every night on Munson's Hill without even a blanket under or over him . . . . never resting, always vigilant, always active." [27]

Eggleston later reflected: "From personal experience and observation of General Stuart, as well as from the testimony of others, I am disposed to think that he attributed to every other man qualities and tastes like his own. Insensible to fatigue himself, he seemed never to understand how a well man could want rest; and as for hardship, there was nothing, in his view, which a man ought to enjoy quite so heartily, except danger." In fact Stuart did not understand infirmity, since he had so little experience with it. He resolved this problem by removing it. He established a "cripple company," soon dubbed "Company Q," and sent tired, sick, and slightly injured men and horses along with suspected malingerers to a separate camp. It was as though he feared that weariness and wounds were contagious. In his profession men functioned at full speed; he surely did; and anything less rendered an individual worthless.[28]

Stuart did spend some time at his headquarters. John Esten Cooke found him there one day in August in a vine-covered cottage, which would have seemed tranquil in the late summer sunshine had it not been for the horses tethered to nearly every available branch in front of the house, the battle flag that flew from a staff in the yard, the bugle calls, and the noisy comings and goings of couriers and officers. Inside, the principal character in this martial drama was at work—accompanied by his own songs and laughter. He wore a blue "undress" coat from his former army, brown velveteen pants faded from service in the saddle, a gray vest, and a cravat. High cavalry boots, yellow gauntlets, French saber, Zouave cap, and revolver pistol completed his outfit. Stuart chatted with Cooke for a time, and then the two men, joined by one of Stuart's subordinate officers, shared a quick midday dinner.

After the meal Stuart suggested that the three of them ride to Fairfax Court House to interrogate an unusual prisoner. The prisoner, it happened, was a young woman captured by Stuart's pickets. She had been riding the horse of a Federal colonel, complete with all his equipment, and she had apparently been scouting Stuart's line of outposts. Stuart had lodged the lady with a local resident and requested instructions from Richmond as to what he should do with her. Now he had those instructions, and so he mounted his handsome horse Skylark and led the way to Fairfax Court House.

The "prison" Stuart had selected was quite comfortable and so was the prisoner—comfortable enough to be indignant. She had ridden from Alexandria on a pleasure excursion, she insisted. Why had she been detained? She demanded to be escorted through Stuart's pickets back to Alexandria. Stuart asked about her horse. The horse belonged to a friend. Again, she insisted that she be allowed to return to Alexandria. Stuart looked hurt and exclaimed that he would miss her company. And besides, if she went directly to Alexandria, she would miss a journey to Richmond to see the wonders of the nation's capital. She would miss a delightful boat ride down the James, up the Chesapeake Bay, and up the Potomac to Alexandria. Under no circumstances would anyone in her circumstances pass through his picket line. The woman still protested; but Stuart concluded the interrogation with a low bow and left.

Outside, he laughed when he saw in the yard an abandoned Federal drum; then he seized it, vaulted atop Skylark, and clattered down the street accompanying himself in a song. Cooke caught up with him and proposed that they call upon a female friend of his whose Southern loyalty was beyond suspicion. So they visited Antonia J. Ford (who much later married a Union officer who owned the Willard Hotel in Washington). So impressed was Stuart with her Confederate fealty that he composed a mock commission for her as his honorary aide-de-camp. Unfortunately a year or so later Antonia Ford attracted suspicion as a Southern spy, and Federal officers searched her belongings. They found her "commission" signed by Stuart, and the little parlor joke cost her some months in the Old Capital Prison in Washington.[29]

So it seemed that Stuart was everywhere at once during the late summer of 1861. He was drilling his troops and viewing parades. He was entertaining his wife. He was constantly among his outposts sleeping on the ground. He was at his headquarters. He was crossing verbal sabers with a suspected spy. He was riding down a street beating a drum. He was commissioning honorary aides. And he even found time to fight a minor battle.

On September 11 the Federals made a reconnaissance in force (nearly 2,000) to Lewinsville, a little town about four miles west of the Chain Bridge over the Potomac. Stuart learned of the activity from his pickets and by noon had started for Lewinsville with 305 infantrymen, a section of artillery, and two cavalry companies. When he reached the scene the Federals were in the process of withdrawing. Stuart sent his foot soldiers into a patch of woods and ordered them to open fire upon the nearest piece of enemy artillery. He instructed his artillery to fire at concentrations of Union infantry and held his cavalry in reserve to cover a retreat should retreat be necessary. The Federals chose not to confront Stuart's force save with some artillery shelling, but hastened their withdrawal. And as they withdrew, Stuart's infantry and artillery fire produced some confusion and several casualties. In the confusion Stuart restrained John Mosby from firing upon a Federal colonel for fear that the officer might be a Confederate. Mosby regretted his missed opportunity, but did enjoy watching artillery shells scatter the enemy. Although Union artillery shells often fell very near, Stuart's command lost neither man nor horse.[30]

Once the Federals had departed, Stuart reestablished his line of outposts. As he did so he discovered on a tree a message from a friend on the other side in this war. Orlando W. Poe, whom Stuart had known since West Point, addressed the note to "My Dear Beauty," expressed his sorrow at not having seen his old friend, and invited him to dinner at Willard's Hotel in Washington on the following Saturday. Stuart laughed at the note and kept it; but he wrote an answer on the bottom anyway. Poe might have seen him, Stuart said, if he had stopped his flight long enough to look back. Perhaps the haste of his leave-taking had something to do with preparations for the dinner.[31]

That evening Stuart returned to Munson's Hill and wrote his report of the day's work. He addressed the report to James Longstreet, his immediate superior. Next day when Longstreet forwarded the report to Generals Johnston and Beauregard, he added high praise for Stuart. "Colonel Stuart," he wrote, "has been at Munson's Hill since its occupation by our troops. He has been most untiring in the discharge of his duties at that and other advanced positions. . . . Colonel Stuart has, I think, fairly won his claim to brigadier, and I hope the commanding generals will unite with me in recommending him for that promotion." They did indeed. Johnston and Beauregard added their endorsement: "We think with Brigadier-General Longstreet that Colonel Stuart's laborious and valuable services, unintermitted since the war began on this frontier, entitle him to a brigadier generalcy. His calm and daring courage, sagacity, zeal, and activity qualify him admirably for the command of our three regiments of cavalry, by which the outpost duty of the Army is performed. The Government would gain greatly by promoting him." [32]

Virginia had made Stuart a full colonel of cavalry on July 16 and he had held a cavalry captain's commission in the Confederate army since May 24. Johnston was urging Stuart's promotion in conjunction with his campaign for more cavalry in his army. He wanted a brigade of horsemen, and he wanted Stuart to command it. On August 10, Johnston made his plea to Jefferson Davis himself and concluded his letter with strong words for Stuart: "He is a rare man, wonderfully endowed by nature with the qualities necessary for an officer of light cavalry. Calm, firm, acute, active, and enterprising, I know of no one more competent than he to estimate the occurrences before him at their true value. If you add to this army a real brigade of cavalry, you can find no better brigadier-general to command it." [33]

Beyond the army Stuart's name was beginning to circulate in Southern newspapers at last—thanks to his cousin-in-law John Esten Cooke. As "Our Virginia Correspondent" for the Charleston *Courier,* Cooke wrote of Stuart, "Probably no man in the South is more hated and more feared by the Yankees." He compared Stuart in appearance to "the Italian hero, Garibaldi" and overestimated his height at six feet one or two inches. Cooke concluded his paean with the prophecy that Stuart would "find a niche in two places— first with his trusty sabre upon some flying Yankee's caput [head], and second with his proud untainted name in the temple of Southern freedom." [34]

On September 24 (1861), the Confederacy responded to Stuart.

He became a brigadier general. And in response to Johnston, the Southern War Office reorganized the cavalry so as to give Stuart command of a brigade of six regiments of horsemen. Johnston himself sent a note to Flora addressed to "Mrs. Brigadier-General J. E. B. Stuart" and asked if he might carry any messages from her to her newly celebrated husband.[35]

Only a year ago, Stuart had been a first lieutenant whose principal enthusiasm was the patenting of his saber hook. That had been another army and a long time ago. Now there was a war, and although propriety forbade him to say so, General Stuart was having a wonderful time.

# VI

## General Stuart

WITH STUART'S STAR came additional responsibilities. He commanded a consolidated brigade of cavalry: six regiments—more than 1,500 horsemen—the entire mounted component of Johnston's army. Military hindsight has pronounced this arrangement wise. Stuart had sufficient troops to be formidable when he concentrated them, and if he efficiently coordinated his expanded system of outposts and scouts, he could provide Johnston's army with a very effective screen as well as reliable reconnaissance. At the same time the Confederates were consolidating cavalry, their enemies were scattering small units of horsemen throughout their armies. And for some time the Southern combination of structure and Stuart proved superior.[1]

During the fall and winter of 1861–62, Stuart's new brigade was "the advance" of Johnston's army. While that army, the Confederacy's principal force in the emerging eastern theater of the war, remained around Manassas, Stuart's troopers picketed the most forward positions and patrolled northern Virginia. Johnston would attempt no fall campaign, and his men settled into winter quarters. On the other side, George B. McClellan devoted his energy and attention to retraining and reinforcing his Federal army; he would not venture from the vicinity of Washington until the following spring. But Stuart could not anticipate the history in which he lived. He had to assume that McClellan might march at any moment, and even in late November, in the midst of a snowstorm, he wrote Flora that he was "still expecting the enemy." He pronounced his new line "impregnable" to attack by that enemy and asked, *"Why don't he come?"* [2]

Stuart called his new camp Qui Vive—French for the sentinel challenge, "Who goes there?" Otherwise it was "the Mellon place," a farmhouse located roughly halfway between Fairfax Court House and Centreville. Because the farmer had removed himself and his furnishings to the relative safety of Warrenton, the house was all but empty. In keeping with the name Qui Vive, the headquarters was physically stark, adorned only by military things and by General Stuart. But if Qui Vive was stark and bare because it was a forward command post, it was also stark and bare like a medieval keep. At Qui Vive, Stuart's camp was also his court. [3]

The young general began collecting musicians—minstrels in the nineteenth-century sense because they were often black men, but minstrels in the medieval sense that they played and sang popular songs of the day at Stuart's bidding. Stuart's cavalry scouts were also his talent scouts, and men with musical skills often found themselves detailed to headquarters to serve as the general's couriers. Stuart also collected "freaks," men possessed of unique physical traits. One such individual was Corporal Hagan, whom an observer described as having "grotesque fierceness . . . a very giant in frame, with an abnormal tendency to develop hair. His face was heavily bearded almost to his eyes, and his voice was as hoarse as distant thunder, which indeed it closely resembled." [4]

Of course Stuart collected skillful soldiers as well as Qui Vive. He constantly evaluated his staff and subordinates and sought talent throughout his ranks. John S. Mosby was a private and "as roughly dressed as any common soldier" when Stuart encountered him on some errand to Qui Vive. He was nine months younger than Stuart and looked younger still. Mosby had been a lawyer in southwestern Virginia before the war. He was quiet, slender to the point of appearing frail; but once, at the University of Virginia, he pursued a quarrel to the point of shooting a fellow student. For no reason Mosby could ever discern, Stuart invited Mosby to remain at headquarters overnight and insisted that the then undistinguished private dine with the general and several officers. Mosby became Stuart's protégé and soon proved himself quite worthy of Stuart's favor. [5]

At this juncture Stuart was shuffling his staff almost constantly.

Everyone who served him was handsome, and the general insisted that members of his court be well dressed and well mounted. Then, from among a jolly company of relatives, friends of friends, and men who displayed promise, Stuart picked and chose those who could also work at his pace.

During this period many men served at Stuart's court as members of his staff or favored subordinates. Captain Tiernan Brien, "that politest of Marylanders," was a fixture. Young—seventeen— Chiswell Dabney was the "Adonis of the staff . . . remarkably handsome." The Rev. Major Dabney Ball was Stuart's "fighting bishop" at this stage. At First Manassas (Bull Run) an observer saw Ball "sit on his horse ten paces from the line of the New York Zouaves and empty every barrel of his pistol as deliberately as if he was [sic] practicing at a target." John Pelham was organizing the Stuart Horse Artillery; he became the "boy major," "as brave as Julius Caesar," "innocent looking . . . but as grand a flirt as ever lived." Born (well) in Alabama, Pelham had resigned from West Point during his final year to join the Southern army. Pelham won command of the Stuart Horse Artillery over his classmate Thomas L. Rosser, with whom he shared Stuart's favor. William W. Blackford was under arrest as a result of a quarrel with Grumble Jones; but Stuart's first adjutant would return to the staff. Redmond Burke usually had "a wonderful set of yarns to tell," of his exploits as one of Stuart's most active scouts. Colonel Fitzhugh Lee, nephew of Robert E. Lee, was fast becoming Stuart's most trusted subordinate. Stuart had liked him at West Point, where Lee had come as close as possible to dismissal for excessive demerits, and he liked him now, too. The two men shared a love of song and laughter, and Fitz Lee was demonstrably competent. As commander of a farflung brigade of cavalry, Stuart could never pay equal attention to all his regiments. Consequently he chose to spend time with subordinate commanders he liked and to send officers he did not like to distant sectors of his picket line. As always, Stuart gravitated toward successful people, and to the end of his life he would seek the company and use the talents of Fitz Lee.[6]

Stuart's court at Qui Vive did not lack a certain amount of intrigue. While the new general was establishing himself, he tested those about him. At this point Stuart found "Bev Robertson by far the most troublesome man I have to deal with." Colonel Beverly

H. Robertson would continue to trouble Stuart, and one of the troubles was that he had been an old beau of Flora Stuart's. Robertson was also a protégé of Flora's father and remained in the U.S. Army until August of 1861. Stuart seemed to associate Robertson with his father-in-law, and that association sealed Robertson's guilt.

The young general realized that he had both friends and enemies within the Confederate high command. Johnston, he thought, was "as good a friend as I have," and he counted upon Custis Lee, Robert E. Lee's son and Stuart's close friend at West Point, to exert his growing influence as military aide to Jefferson Davis in Stuart's behalf. However Stuart sensed that Gustavus Woodson Smith, who commanded a corps of Johnston's army, was not his friend, and he advised Flora to avoid "Mrs. G.W." He also wrote Flora, "I have some enemy in the War Dept. or A.G.O. [Adjutant General's Office]. Ask Dr. Brewer to find out who it is."[7]

Most people who possess power generate an aura about themselves that reflects their individual tastes and quirks. Stuart was no exception. Indeed his headquarters, his court, not only reflected him, it revealed him.

One bright, crisp December day John Esten Cooke, Stuart's novelist cousin-in-law, came to call at Qui Vive. As had been the case when Cooke had visited Stuart two months earlier, the headquarters "looked like work." Horses were everywhere and men moved among them and atop them on various missions. Near the flagstaff was a Blakely gun, a rifled cannon imported from England, and guarding the prized weapon was a huge raccoon tethered to the gun carriage. The raccoon snarled at all who passed his post, and Cooke approached the house hoping the rope would restrain the beast. Inside he found Stuart at work at his desk surrounded by staff and subordinates. He wore a gray uniform now and he had adorned his brown felt hat with a black feather. The general worked hard; at this point he wrote reports promptly, and his correspondence was voluminous. But even as he wrote, he was the center of attention; he periodically broke into song or turned in his chair to banter with his staff. Stuart greeted Cooke warmly, took him outside to see his Blakely gun and his raccoon, and then invited him to return to the house for supper.

The staff set a table in the bare room and then to Cooke's great surprise Captain Brien escorted two women to the supper. For Cooke it was déjà vu times two. The last time he had visited, Stuart had had one female prisoner, captured while trying to evade Stuart's pickets. This time there were two, caught while attempting to slip through Stuart's lines to Alexandria. One of the women was young and friendly; the other old and indignant. They insisted they were not hungry, but Stuart bade them eat. After the meal Stuart returned to work at his desk, but called for entertainers to amuse his "guests."

Almost immediately three black men appeared and began to fill the room with music. Bob, who was Stuart's servant, borrowed from Laurel Hill, played the guitar and sang, and one of the others accompanied each song with birdcall imitations. Stuart sat with his back to the show, writing at his desk, and Cooke observed that the music seemed to fuel his pen: he wrote in time with the tunes. After "The Mocking-Bird" and several other popular songs, Stuart turned from his desk and requested a breakdown. The third performer proved to be "a mighty master of the backstep, viz. an old Virginia 'breakdown.' " As the music swelled, the dancer slowly built to a crescendo of motion. The staff stood and smiled; couriers crowded the doorway; the women sat before the fire. When the breakdown concluded, Stuart rose and asked the women if they were amused.

"You rebels *do* seem to enjoy yourselves!"

The general asked if they would like to see something else of interest. They would indeed. Stuart's smile faded, and he pointed out a coat and vest that hung like trophies on the bare wall before them. The garments were torn and bore dark stains.

"What is that, General?"

"It is the coat and waistcoat of a poor boy of my command, madam," replied Stuart, "who was shot and killed on picket the other day—young Chichester, from just below Fairfax Court House. He was a brave fellow, and I am keeping these clothes to send to his mother."

Then Stuart spoke of the short, sharp fight and described Chichester's death. When he finished his story, Stuart ended the audience; he escorted the two women to the door and wished them a good night. Next morning the general procured a carriage and dispatched his prisoners to army headquarters. Before they left

Qui Vive, Stuart said farewell and kissed the hand of the younger woman.

Cooke, too, was about to leave, but remained long enough to ask Stuart two questions. First, why had he put on such an elaborate show for the captives? Stuart responded that the women had been furious when first brought before him, so furious that he became determined to charm them. And charm them he had. Cooke agreed and posed his second question—why had he kissed the young woman's hand and not the hand of the older woman? Stuart turned conspiratorial and stepped closer to Cooke. "Would you like me to tell you?" he asked in a low tone. Cooke said that he would. Stuart whispered, "The old lady's hand had a glove upon it!" Then did the general explode into laughter.[8]

This was several years after Stuart's revealing letter to his cousin, A. Stuart Brown, about fame and fashion. He had counseled Brown to "gain position, information, influence, a *name* first and *then* . . . make the denizens of fashion bow . . ." and he had taken his own advice. Bowing and adulation, especially from women, were an index to Stuart of his importance.[9]

There is considerable irony in the fact that John Esten Cooke wrote so much about Stuart and so lionized him both during his life and after his death. Cooke fancied himself a "gentleman" and once confessed, "I never liked the business of war." In his diary he recorded, "My philosophy is to give myself as little trouble as possible." Highlights of his military life included dressing himself, smoking, and eating. Certainly Cooke was much unlike his cousin-in-law Stuart; yet Cooke appreciated Stuart. And he used Stuart in his writing, fiction and nonfiction, over and over again. For his part, Stuart tried to like Cooke. But he confessed to Flora, "Jno Esten is a case & I am afraid I can't like him." Cooke did not improve his standing with Stuart by telling Flora that Stuart had shaved his beard—a little joke the general did not consider funny. For the sake of family loyalty Stuart never let Cooke learn his true feelings, and he used his influence several times to try to get Cooke promotion and choice assignments. But Stuart considered Cooke a colossal bore and later made sure that his duties kept him away from headquarters as much as possible.[10]

About Flora's cousin Stuart kept his feelings quiet; he could display no such restraint regarding her father. His father-in-law's

decision to remain with the Union caused Stuart intense mortifi-
cation. Phillip St. George Cooke's conduct was a stain on the family honor, and Stuart counseled Flora, "For our own & our
children's sake let us determine to act well *our* parts & bear with
the mistakes & errors of others . . . but by no means attempt justi-
fication of what must be condemned . . . . Be consoled . . . by the
reflection that your husband & brothers will atone for the father's
conduct." To Flora's brother, Confederate officer John R. Cooke,
Stuart wrote of his father's decision, "he will regret it but once,
and that will be continually." [11]

Cold fury probably best described Stuart's feelings about the
elder Cooke. And after ample reflection, he determined to change
the name of his son; he would not have his son's name honor a
man he considered dishonorable. Phillip St. George Cooke Stuart
would cease to exist; the name would be an "irreparable injury"
to the boy and would *"embitter"* his father. "I am willing he
should be called Jno: Alexander, or Chapman Johnson after him
who was such a Dear friend to my boyhood—but never that he
should keep any part of his previous christian name." Flora should
choose the child's new name; Stuart even suggested Stuart Stuart,
but seemed to prefer James Ewell Brown Stuart. He was adamant
about the change itself and requested Flora never to refer to
his son by his former name. Flora acquiesced. The boy became
J. E. B. Stuart, Jr.—Jimmy. And Stuart began hoping for an im-
probable coincidence; he wanted to meet his father-in-law personally on the field of battle. It would be almost too perfect, the
combination of a medieval combat between good and evil and the
wild plot twist of a Victorian novel. Still, the elder Cooke was a
cavalry officer, and he had been made a brigadier general about
the same time as his son-in-law. Perhaps the encounter might
occur. Late in November a captive captain bragged to Stuart about
the improvements wrought by General Cooke in the Union cavalry. Stuart responded, "I know he has command, and I propose to
take him prisoner. I married his daughter, and I want to present
her with her father; so let him come on." For the present Stuart
confined his hopes to a mischievous scheme to have a note from
Flora to her mother secretly placed beneath Mrs. Cooke's breakfast plate in Washington.[12]

The one Cooke who was a constant in his life was Flora; she

was the reason he cared so much about the others. They were seldom together, and when she did come to Qui Vive, Stuart seemed to make a point of not allowing her presence to interfere with the work of war. "I can't promise you that you will see much of your husband when you come." Sometimes Stuart even seemed to discourage her visits; if the weather and roads were favorable, then there might be fighting and danger, and if there was no danger, then the roads and weather rendered her travel impossible. If young Flora or Jimmy was sick, Flora must remain with them, and Stuart was careful to monitor scarlet fever, mumps, and whooping cough in the vicinity of Qui Vive. As for Stuart visiting his family in Richmond, he wrote, "I don't care what other Genl's do, all I have to say is that while this war lasts I will not *leave* the *van* [the most forward units] of our Army unless compelled to. Let that answer put to rest any hope of seeing me in Richmond." [13]

Stuart seemed to hold his wife at arm's length during the war. Maybe while he held court at his headquarters, he practiced some form of courtly love—his love was the more ardent because its object was far away, beyond the dirty work of war. Perhaps her presence inhibited him and detracted from his calculated charisma. Certainly Stuart believed that his duty demanded his full attention, and he was the greater patriot for sacrificing the company of his wife. Stuart's aide and cousin, Peter Hairston, wrote his own wife, in response to her complaints about his absence, "Genl. Stuart directs me to say to you *If I neglect the higher duties of the Patriot to be a daily companion to you I would make you a husband to be ashamed of in after life.*" [14]

Yet Stuart remained close to Flora, and the bond between them transcended mere physical proximity. She was still his confidante, and in his letters to her at this time he shared his thoughts and feelings without restraint. He told her she was his "second self." To Flora, General J. E. B. Stuart was "Hubbie." He wanted to know if she thought "of her old stove on these cold nights."

Sometimes Stuart belied any pretense of platonic, courtly love and engaged in genteel fantasies with Flora. He longed for the time she "could get a little home of your own some where to have birds & flowers & books, the very best Society in the world. When 'war's dread commotion is over,' I would step quietly into such a home and xxxxxxxxxxxx." He dreamed of time in which he and

Flora might enjoy each other in "abandon." For the present, however, he feared that their meetings would have to be "unsatisfactory" and their partings "abrupt." Their relationship, he never said but seemed to mean, would have to be less complete than he would like—a sort of prolonged coitus interruptus.[15]

If Stuart dreamed and fantasized about the future in letters to his wife, he also tried to prepare her and himself for the possibility that he might not have a future. "Bear in mind that if I fall I leave in the sacrifice thus made a legacy more to be prized by my children & you Dearest than 10 years of longer life." He asked her to tell Jimmy about his father if he should die. In November he made his will and the following spring he purchased a $10,000 life insurance policy. Stuart, the grand romantic, seemed to have few illusions about his life and the outcome of the war. He told George Cary Eggleston, "I regard it as a foregone conclusion . . . that we shall ultimately whip the Yankees. We are bound to believe that, anyhow; but the war is going to be a long and terrible one, first. We've only just begun it, and very few of us will see the end." Significant in this statement was Stuart's clear-eyed realism about his likely death and most revealing was his comment, "we are bound to believe that, anyhow." Stuart was aware that victory might be a matter of believing in victory and even if his cause were doomed, he knew that he had to believe otherwise in order to function.[16]

While the armies occupied winter quarters, Stuart was learning how to be a general. He supervised scouts and pickets and delegated most of the fieldwork to subordinates. At Qui Vive he collected reports and information and relayed them to Johnston's headquarters. Constantly he prodded his commanders in the field to discover what they could about the enemy. He advised his officers to enlist the aid of females whenever they could. And he promised that "funds will be placed at your disposal" with which to purchase intelligence if necessary.[17]

Ironically, Stuart's only combat experience during the first winter of the war occurred in command, not of cavalry, but of infantry. It began as a mundane assignment; on December 20 Stuart assumed command of an expedition to protect a foraging operation near Dranesville. Every available wagon in Johnston's army was just west of the place, collecting hay from the countryside, and

Stuart's force was supposed to prevent any interference from the enemy. Stuart took with him 150 cavalrymen, four pieces of artillery, and four regiments of infantry (about 1,600 men). He knew that there were Federal outposts on the Leesburg-Georgetown and Leesburg-Alexandria turnpikes to the east of Dranesville, so he dispatched his cavalry ahead of the foot soldiers to seize the two roads near the point of their intersection. He planned to form a solid north-south line across the turnpikes to block any advance of the enemy. At dawn on the twentieth when the expedition set out, the operation seemed simple enough.[18]

What Stuart did not know was that a Federal force of nearly 4,000 men, complete with cavalry and artillery, had set out for Dranesville the same morning. The Federals intended to capture the Confederate cavalry picket at Dranesville and to engage in some foraging of their own "from the farms of some of the rank secessionists" in the neighborhood between the Leesburg-Alexandria Turnpike and the Potomac. General E. O. C. Ord, commanding the expedition, was in the process of posting his troops on high ground in roughly an east-west line parallel to the Leesburg-Alexandria Turnpike when Stuart's cavalry detachment rode onto the scene. The horsemen realized that large numbers of enemy troops were deploying where none were anticipated and sent word to the commander.[19]

Stuart came at a gallop. His first fear was for the foraging party, and thus he sent his cavalry off to the west to warn the wagon train and escort the foragers safely back to Southern lines. Actually both Stuart and Ord feared for their respective foragers, and the commanders decided to attack each other in order to divert attention from the wagons. Having dispatched his cavalry, Stuart sent for his infantry and artillery. He attempted to deploy two regiments on each side of the road leading into Dranesville from the south and have his guns fire from the road itself.

This makeshift plan had flaws. The artillery on the road was exposed to enemy fire, and that fire took its toll upon men and horses. As Stuart admitted in his report, ". . . every shot of the enemy was dealing destruction on either man, limber, or horse." Although the infantry managed to drive in Federal skirmishers, the ground was so thickly wooded that two of Stuart's regiments fired at each other in the undergrowth. They realized their mistake only after taking casualties. Stuart did not learn of this mishap until later; at the time, he admitted, the "thicket . . . was so dense that it was impossible to see either [their] exact position or their progress in the fight." After two hours of an uneven artillery duel and uncoordinated infantry action Stuart decided to disengage. So many artillery horses were down that Stuart had to call upon foot soldiers to drag his guns to safety. Nevertheless the Confederates withdrew in generally good order under fire. One regiment, however, returned to the road beyond the point at which they had deposited their knapsacks and had to abandon their baggage. Stuart withdrew his force about three miles, rested the men, retreated another two miles, and made camp for the night.

Next morning (December 21), having been reinforced with two more infantry regiments and some cavalry, Stuart again advanced to Dranesville and found that the Federals had withdrawn. He collected his dead and wounded and returned south to Centreville.[20]

Dranesville was not Stuart's finest hour. He did respond quickly to an unforeseen circumstance and counter a threat to his vulnerable wagon train. But Federal General Ord could make the same claim. The Federal force did outnumber Stuart's, but not by the three-to-one ratio Stuart claimed in his report of the action. Stuart's enemies did occupy more favorable ground from the beginning of the engagement; Stuart accepted battle essentially on Ord's terms. And the casualty figures indicate that the Southerners had the worst of it. Ord's Federals lost 7 men killed and 61 wounded; Stuart's Confederates lost 43 killed, 143 wounded, and 8 missing.[21]

Some years after the war a man who had been with Stuart at Dranesville told Stuart's last adjutant and first biographer, H. B. McClellan, a small story about the day's action. As Stuart was attempting to extricate his infantry from engagement, he encountered Captain J. Desha still leading his company down the road despite the effects of a serious wound. Stuart rode over to the stricken officer and began insisting that the man take his horse. McClellan's informant remembered that Stuart had draped his mount with artillery harness, which he had removed from dead horses. Desha thanked the general profusely, but declined his offer. Stuart satisfied himself that the captain's refusal was genuine and kept his horse.[22]

Certainly Stuart's action in this anecdote was instinctively noble and characteristically thoughtful. But it is worth asking why Stuart, the general commanding, was carrying off that artillery harness. Surely he had more important things to do. Could he not delegate the chore of stripping harness from dead animals to someone else? Were there no other live horses but his left to bear the army's belongings from the field? Perhaps out of habit Stuart the former quartermaster was salvaging government property. Maybe Stuart the cavalry commander was accustomed to his subordinate commanders' acting semi-independently and did not acknowledge the need to do more than chores once he committed his men to combat. That harness hanging from Stuart's horse certainly bore witness to his energy and attention to detail. But it was also evidence that Stuart had lost control of events. He lost contact with his infantry and watched his artillery absorb significant punishment, and he responded by collecting harness—literally picking up the pieces of a shattered day.

Back at Qui Vive, Stuart wrote his report of the action at Dranesville. He admitted that his infantry regiments had shot at each other and that his artillery had suffered. Still, he emphasized the danger to the wagons, the disparity of numbers, and labeled the affair a "glorious success." Then he returned to the work of commanding cavalry.[23]

Rival armies were in winter quarters; no major campaigning was possible until the roads dried in the spring. But cavalry picket lines remained alert and active, and scouting forays continued. Stuart's task was no less than controlling the ground between the armies and collecting sufficient intelligence from which to predict the Federals' every move. His brigade, by the first of the year, numbered 185 officers and 2,200 enlisted men. But the six regiments that composed Stuart's command had to cover a front between forty and fifty miles wide, from the Blue Ridge Mountains to the Potomac River.[24]

Stuart, acting through his dispersed pickets, assorted informants, and spies, was able to know a great deal about his enemies. On January 9, 1862, for example, he knew that Union General McClellan was still suffering the effects of an attack of typhoid fever. He knew about an expeditionary force commanded by Ambrose E. Burnside forming at Annapolis to strike via water at some point along the Southern coast. By contrast, Allen Pinkerton, who later founded the detective-security agency bearing his name and who was McClellan's trusted intelligence gatherer during 1862, was overestimating Confederate strength about two and a half times.[25]

Nevertheless, Stuart could never know enough, and his pickets could never be everywhere. As a consequence, he was open to criticism for not being omniscient and for every Federal foray that breached his picket lines. Some of this criticism reached the president of the Confederate States. On February 6 President Davis wrote to Johnston, "The letter of General [Daniel Harvey] Hill painfully impresses me with that which has heretofore been indicated—a want of vigilance and intelligent observation on the part of General Stuart. The officers commanding his pickets should be notified of all roads in their neighborhoods, and sleepless watchfulness should be required of them. The failure to secure either of these two things renders them worse than useless to the commands which rely upon them for timely notice of the approach of an enemy." Johnston sustained Stuart in this and other matters and never lost confidence in his cavalry commander. And Stuart learned a bit more about the political implications of being a general. He remained close to Johnston; for a time he took up residence across the hall from Johnston in Centreville, and he asked Flora to send him another hat like his own so that he might present it to the commanding general.[26]

Throughout the long winter, Stuart, along with everyone else in North America, speculated about the campaign or campaigns upcoming in the spring. Like many people, both in and out of the military, Stuart looked for one final campaign and one grand, climactic battle. As it happened, he was wrong in this expectation. Yet about the more specific prospect of the war between Johnston and McClellan in Virginia, Stuart had some pretty accurate instincts.[27]

McClellan believed Pinkerton's reports about Confederate strength along the Bull Run line; he believed that Johnston had 80,000 troops on hand and another 70,000 readily available, to bring his total to 150,000. Of course Johnston did not have such strength; but the belief that he did made McClellan seek victory through maneuver. The Union general planned to move his huge army (105,000 men) by water to some point behind Johnston's line in eastern Virginia and then move on Richmond. McClellan planned to use an additional 45,000 troops from Washington to strike over land once Johnston abandoned his position in northern Virginia. McClellan's plans for what became his Peninsula Campaign were quite sound. And as the campaign began to develop, uncertainty about McClellan's intentions placed Johnston in a serious quandary. The Confederates knew all about McClellan's capacity to move his army by water, and the Federals could hardly hide the large number of ships plying the Potomac. But was this combined army-navy force the primary threat, or was it merely a ruse to conceal some other invasion route? Johnston could not know. He did decide, rather suddenly, to withdraw from his position before Bull Run and move his army about thirty-five miles south to Culpeper Court House. From that point, Johnston believed, he could best discover and counter any move McClellan might make.[28]

The evacuation, which began on March 9, was much less than efficient. Casualties in the movement were tons of supplies the Confederate army had accumulated at Manassas but could not carry off. Johnston blamed "the miserable performance of the railroad"; many, including President Davis, blamed Johnston. To Stuart's troopers who covered the Confederate rear fell the unhappy task of destroying everything the army could not remove. The men burned "huge piles of bacon . . . as high as a house," and the smell of frying bacon carried twenty miles.[29]

Even as the evacuation was taking place McClellan ordered his army to march on Manassas. The Federal commander wanted to give his troops marching experience and to give the Southerners fresh doubts about his intentions in the coming campaign. Stuart's cavalry, still acting as Johnston's rear guard, skirmished occasionally with Federal horsemen and withdrew. Stuart wrote Johnston on March 12 that the enemy had occupied Manassas.[30]

Stuart's letters to Flora after abandoning Qui Vive and winter quarters seem to take on a brighter tone. The weather was horrible —sleet and snow—but Stuart never mentioned it; perhaps he was happy to be active again. On March 24 he predicted correctly that McClellan would not come "this way"; he believed that the Federals would land at Belle Plain (on the Potomac near Fredericksburg), at Urbanna (on the Rappahannock about fifteen miles from

the mouth of the river), or on the peninsula between the York and
James rivers. Actually McClellan had indeed planned to land his
troops at Urbanna, until Johnston withdrew to Culpeper. Then he
decided to land at Fort Monroe on the tip of the peninsula and
advance on Richmond from there. So Stuart's prediction, even in
the face of the Federal feint to Manassas, proved accurate.[31]

Johnston remained at Culpeper and Stuart remained in front of
the army (near Warrenton Junction, roughly halfway between Culpeper and Manassas) until McClellan's peninsular strategy became clear. Even then, Johnston was reluctant to march his army
down the peninsula and fight there on what he felt were Mc-
Clellan's terms. All the while Stuart remained active scouting and
skirmishing in the rolling country around Warrenton Junction.
One such series of encounters during the final days of March
yielded fifty prisoners and some rare words of praise from Stuart
for Grumble Jones. After spending some time with Jones, Stuart
reported his "great vigor" and "excellent service."[32]

By early April McClellan had 105,000 men on the peninsula,
and the Confederates had a defense line from Yorktown to the
Warwick River manned by only about 10,000 soldiers. The Federal general overestimated the strength of the Yorktown line and
chose to undertake siege operations against it. On April 14 Johnston journeyed to Richmond for a council of war with Davis,
Davis's military adviser Robert E. Lee, and Secretary of War
George W. Randolph. After fourteen hours of discussion Davis
exercised his prerogative as constitutional commander in chief and
instructed Johnston to confront McClellan on the peninsula. With
serious reservations, Johnston left Richmond to set his army in
motion again.[33]

Stuart wasted no time. By nine o'clock on the morning of April
18, he was on the lower peninsula near Yorktown. En route the
cavalry passed through Richmond, and Stuart paraded his command down principal streets to give residents of the capital the
chance to cheer and wave at his horsemen. He camped near the
city and allowed liberal absences from camp that evening. Next
morning, however, he resumed the march and arrived on the eighteenth ready for action. He still expected a major battle that would
decide the war and compared the Yorktown line to the siege of
Sebastopol in the Crimean War. But Stuart determined that his

cavalry would have to be content with a minor role on the peninsula because of the wooded ground and the deep ravines that
intersected otherwise flat terrain. This was no country for the deployment of massed cavalry. Nevertheless, Stuart soon found work
to do.[34]

By the time Johnston's army took up the defensive position at
Yorktown, McClellan's siege tactics were well developed. The
Federals had their own series fortifications before Yorktown, and
McClellan had almost enough heavy artillery in place to blast his
way through the Southern army. Accordingly Johnston, who did
not want to occupy the Yorktown line in the first place, determined
to abandon what he considered a death trap and withdrew toward
Richmond. On May 3, very near the eve of McClellan's projected
grand assault, the Confederates left their works and began marching west. Recent rains (twenty of the last thirty days) slowed the
pace of the retreat; yet the muddy roads churned by Johnston's
army promised to slow Federal pursuit.

Stuart's cavalry was once more Johnston's rear guard. Stuart
kept his horsemen active along the empty line to disguise the fact
that the army was retreating. Then on May 4 Stuart ordered Fitz
Lee's regiment (1st Virginia) to a place called Eltham's Landing
on the Pamunkey River, a tributary of the York. Lee was to support
a Confederate infantry division sent in anticipation that McClellan
would try to move troops by water to intercept the Confederate
withdrawal. Stuart dispatched other units commanded by Williams C. Wickham toward Williamsburg along the Telegraph
Road, which was the most direct route from Yorktown to Williamsburg. With a somewhat smaller force, Stuart himself undertook to
cover the only other road leading up the peninsula. Under the best
of circumstances Stuart and Wickham might have maintained contact with each other as they withdrew before the enemy along
parallel roads that were often only a mile apart. But the thick
woods of the peninsula did not offer the best of circumstances, and
Stuart lost communication with Wickham.

Union pursuit up the Telegraph Road was vigorous; Wickham's
command had to withdraw at a faster rate than Stuart was moving.
Indeed Wickham suffered a saber wound in the process of holding
the Federals at bay before Fort Magruder, a rude series of earthen
redoubts just east of Williamsburg. Meanwhile Stuart was falling

back toward Williamsburg at leisure. As he withdrew Stuart sent
periodic messages to Johnston regarding the strength and position
of the enemy. In the afternoon one of Stuart's couriers returned in
haste with very bad news: Federal artillery and cavalry were on
the road behind Stuart. When Wickham fell back to Fort Magruder, he had exposed the road on which Stuart was operating to the
Federals. Stuart hoped the courier was wrong and sent some companies of horsemen to investigate. This force soon returned after a
sharp fight had emptied four saddles and confirmed the courier's
report. Stuart was cut off from his friends with foes pressing upon
him from two directions. He was essentially unfamiliar with the
region; but he knew the James River was less than a mile to the
south. And along the bank of the river was a beach which he might
use as a sandy road. Thus Stuart led his column down to the river,
up the beach, and into Williamsburg by dark.[35]

By the time he arrived, Johnston had surveyed the situation
before Fort Magruder and decided that he would have to make a
stand there the next day with two full divisions. While the infantry
and artillery prepared to hold back Federal pursuit, the cavalry
moved to the rear of Fort Magruder to act as the reserve force in
the impending battle. Eschewing inaction, Stuart attached himself
to James Longstreet and ran Longstreet's errands during the fight;
he reported to Flora that he was never out of range of the firing all
day. The Battle of Williamsburg on May 5 was a bloody draw,
although Stuart claimed a Confederate victory. The oversized rear
guard action did permit Johnston to make good his escape up the
peninsula, and McClellan elected not to force the Confederate
rear further.

Still in search of action, Stuart rode from Williamsburg toward
Eltham's Landing to join Fitz Lee. He arrived too late for the brief
battle in which the Confederates drove off McClellan's force, sent
in ships to cut off the Confederate retreat. Stuart did take charge
of rear guard responsibilities for the Confederate infantry division
(G. W. Smith's) involved and followed Johnston's army toward
Richmond.[36]

As the Confederate troops took up positions before the capital,
Johnston pondered his next move. Neither he nor Davis was willing to submit to a siege at Richmond; the Confederates had to
strike McClellan's force or a substantial portion of it before the

Federals came too close. McClellan moved slowly but inexorably toward the capital; Stuart skirmished with the advancing Federals and kept Johnston appraised of their movements. Finally on May 30, the heavens seemed to present Johnston with the chance to strike a counterblow. That day rain fell in torrents, washing away most of the bridges across the Chickahominy River. For the moment, at least, two Federal corps were isolated to the south of the stream, and Johnston grasped the opportunity to attack a fraction of the enemy with his entire force. The result was the Battle of Seven Pines (and Fair Oaks) on May 31.[37]

Once more the wooded ground prevented massed cavalry action, and Stuart again attached himself to Longstreet. To Flora, Stuart wrote that the Southern army won at Seven Pines. Actually the battle represented a series of lost opportunities for the Confederates and concluded as a bloody standoff. Johnston had to plan in haste, and as a consequence of this and some blunders by his subordinates, only four of the twenty-three brigades Johnston planned to employ were ever in action at one time. The Southerners had shown themselves capable of fighting, but the goal of the battle had been the annihilation of one or both of the isolated Union corps. And to compound the larger failure of a frustrating day, Johnston himself was one of the 6,134 casualties sustained by his army. Late in the afternoon a shell fragment struck him in the chest and wounded the commanding general severely. Next day (June 1), even while fighting continued along a fairly static line, President Davis gave command of the army to Robert E. Lee.[38]

Lee's first order of consequence was a retreat from Seven Pines to the outskirts of Richmond. Then Lee put the troops to work on fortifications before the city. The situation looked quite grave. McClellan moved ever closer and prepared to do at Richmond what he had intended at Yorktown—use heavy artillery to blast the Confederates into submission and send in his infantry to rule the rubble. McClellan took time and care in his approach. But Federal victory at Richmond, and perhaps in the war, seemed only a matter of time.

Stuart named his new camp, just outside Richmond, Quien Sabe—Spanish for "Who knows?"[39] The question certainly applied to the outcome of the Peninsula Campaign and thus to the fate of the fledgling Confederacy. But it also might apply to General Stuart as well. Since gaining his star, it might seem to an objective observer, his service had been solid, but less than spectacular. He had established himself as a general and acted the part, and he had continued tireless pursuit of his mission as a commander of cavalry. Yet the frustration at Dranesville and criticism from Hill and Davis shaded Stuart's aura somewhat. And during the Peninsula Campaign thus far, he had been little more than a spectator at Williamsburg and Seven Pines. Acting like a general is not at all like being a general.

Stuart had no such reservations about himself, or if he did, he certainly never admitted to them. Confidence was an article of his faith. He told Flora about a dozen rumors that he had been promoted to major general. Still, it seemed a long way from Qui Vive to Quien Sabe.[40]

# VII

## *Jeb*

STUART BELIEVED he knew Robert E. Lee. After all, he had been at West Point as a cadet when Lee was Academy Superintendent and he had served Lee as an aide at Harpers Ferry. Lee's son Custis had been one of Stuart's best friends at West Point and that friendship endured; currently, Custis served on the staff of President Davis, where friendship translated "influence." Another of Lee's sons, William H. F. ("Rooney") Lee, was serving under Stuart as commander of the 9th Virginia Cavalry Regiment. Lee's nephew Fitzhugh Lee commanded the 1st Virginia Cavalry and continued to be one of Stuart's most trusted subordinates. Lee's daughter Mary had been Stuart's friend since West Point, and Lee's wife Mary, Stuart once stated, "was like a mother to me." Thus when Lee assumed command of the Army of Northern Virginia on June 1, 1862, Stuart had good reason to believe that he would have the commanding general's ear.[1]

Stuart also believed that Lee needed his help. When Joseph E. Johnston suffered the wound at Seven Pines that necessitated his replacement, the Confederate army before Richmond was in the process of botching its best chance to strike an effective blow against McClellan's Federal host. And when Lee withdrew the army to the fringes of Richmond, the situation seemed grave indeed. Approximately 65,000 Confederate troops stood between Richmond and McClellan's 100,000-plus. Although McClellan did not realize his numerical superiority, he was at work improving his favorable odds by expanding his front and bringing up heavy artillery with which to blast the Southern army (and perhaps the Confederacy itself) into submission.[2]

Lee's experience as a Confederate thus far seemed only to compound the crisis. He had commanded an ill-fated expedition in western Virginia and so presided over the loss of that region in a campaign that brought McClellan to prominence. He then had commanded a military department that included the coast of South Carolina and Georgia, and had had to withdraw his forces from the coast and so expose rich sea island plantations to Federal occupation. Finally he had returned to Richmond as military adviser to Davis and endured the frustration of being part of the high command without a command. Now because of Johnston's wound, Lee had an army—a command in crisis in mid-campaign.[3]

Stuart wanted to help his country and help Lee; he also wanted to impress his old mentor with the lessons he had learned. So on June 4, only three days after Lee assumed command, Stuart wrote a letter to him in which he offered his ideas on McClellan's battle plan, the nature of the Southern fighting men, and grand strategy that would lead to victory—all the while disclaiming any presumption on his part. Specifically Stuart asserted that McClellan would establish himself south of the Chickahominy before advancing further upon Richmond. Hence the proper course for the Confederates would be to hold their left (north) with concentrated artillery and attack on their right, south of the Chickahominy. Such strategic thinking was all the more valid because "we have an army far better adapted to attack than defense. Let us fight at advantage before we are forced to fight at disadvantage."[4]

Lee did not respond to Stuart's proposal, and Stuart returned his attention to matters less momentous, but more in accord with the mission of the cavalry. Specifically he sought reliable, precise information about Federal troop dispositions on the enemy right flank, north of the Chickahominy.

On June 6 Stuart moved his headquarters to a farmhouse just north of Richmond, and on the evening of June 8 Stuart went for a ride. Ostensibly he rode out to acquaint himself, some couriers, and his newest volunteer aide with the surrounding country; he often took such excursions. On this particular evening, however, Stuart inspected outposts in the vicinity, then dismissed the couriers and continued his ride accompanied only by the volunteer aide. His companion was a formidable man indeed, a huge Prussian officer turned soldier-of-fortune named Heros Von Borcke, recently arrived to serve the Southern cause. Von Borcke stood six feet two inches tall, weighed 250 pounds, and spoke English with difficulty. Stuart liked him, perhaps because Von Borcke complemented his retinue of "freaks," but also because the aristocratic Prussian shared his love of laughter and disdain for danger.

As darkness deepened, the two riders passed into enemy country, and Von Borcke examined his pistol. Stuart smiled and informed the huge Prussian that they would use their revolvers only *in extremis;* for the sake of silence they must first try to extricate themselves from danger with sabers and speed. They encountered no Federal patrols, and after about five miles the pair arrived at a small farmhouse where Stuart had arranged to meet one of his spies. The general dismounted, knocked on the door in code, and the two men went inside. The spy had not arrived, so Stuart and Von Borcke waited with the family who lived in the house for his arrival. They waited for quite some time.

Finally, near dawn, Stuart and Von Borcke left the house and rode off in the rain toward the home of the spy. They rode for another two miles deeper into enemy country and halted at a house only a quarter of a mile from a Union camp. As a Federal bugler sounded reveille, the Southern general entered the house. He found his informant very ill, which explained his failure to appear at the rendezvous the previous evening. Stuart questioned the man at his bedside and thanked him for the information. Then he rejoined Von Borcke outside, remounted his horse, and led the way back to his headquarters at a gallop.

Von Borcke sensed that Stuart was pleased with the intelligence he had taken such risk and pain to acquire. When the two returned from their night-long excursion, Stuart's staff was more than a little happy to see him. Characteristically Stuart had told no one where he was going, and his return relieved the anxiety that had been growing throughout the night.[5]

Although he had been awake all night, Stuart went again to work on the morning of June 9. He sent for John Mosby to join him for breakfast and dismissed his staff. As he and Mosby ate— probably bacon and cornbread—Stuart gave his scout an assignment. He asked Mosby to ride north-northeast to examine Federal

activity in the vicinity of Totopotomoy Creek, a tributary of the
Pamunkey River that flows roughly east-west about ten miles from
Richmond. Specifically, Stuart wanted to know if McClellan had
troops and field fortifications on Totopotomoy, which was the logical limit of his right flank.

Mosby hurried off to his camp, collected three companions,
and set out immediately. Circumstances dictated that the scouting
party take a wide detour, and Mosby never actually saw much of
Totopotomoy Creek. He did scout the south bank of the Pamunkey
River, however, and ask questions of a number of local residents.
Mosby discovered that for several miles Federal infantry did not
cover the Union supply line, which ran from White House on the
Pamunkey toward Richmond along the Richmond and York River
Railroad. He also learned that the entire region south of the Pamunkey had only some cavalry outposts to protect McClellan's
right flank. Both the Federal right and the Federal supply line
were quite vulnerable. Mosby realized the importance of this
news and hastened back to inform Stuart.

The scout arrived back at headquarters on June 10 and found
Stuart sitting in the yard of the house under the trees. Exhausted
from his long ride and loss of a night's sleep, Mosby flopped down
in the grass before Stuart and began to relate his findings. At the
time Mosby was without a commission as any kind of officer; not
many generals listened to reports given by men lounging on the
ground. But Stuart listened with interest and instructed Mosby to
write out an account of his mission. When he had done so, Stuart
had him sign the document, and then Stuart put the statement in
his pocket and galloped off to Lee's headquarters.[6]

At the Dabbs' farm where Lee had established himself, Stuart
met with his new commander. The war seemed to have aged Lee.
His hair and his stiff beard were quite white. Yet despite the June
heat, Lee regularly wore his high boots over his dark blue uniform
pants and his regulation coat of gray wool. Nevertheless, next to
Stuart, the commanding general looked almost plain.[7] Stuart
shared Mosby's news as well as the information he had acquired
from his bedridden spy. Lee was interested—interested enough
to ask Stuart to undertake a reconnaissance in force to confirm the
reports of the exposed Union right flank. The two men settled
upon a plan: Stuart would lead a sizable force north and east into

the Federal rear to learn for certain McClellan's troop dispositions and strength north of the Chickahominy and also to raid and disrupt his supply and communication lines south of the Pamunkey. Stuart then suggested that he might ride completely around the Federal army and return to Southern lines from the south. Lee demurred, but gave Stuart sufficient latitude so as not to rule out a complete circuit of the Union army. When the men believed they had reached an understanding of what Lee wanted and what Stuart was to do, they adjourned their meeting and went to work. Lee began to put his instructions in writing, and Stuart dashed back to his own headquarters to prepare for his expedition.[8]

Among other thoughts that no doubt raced through Stuart's busy mind was the prospect of matching wits, if not sabers, with his father-in-law. Cooke now commanded McClellan's cavalry reserve—a full division of horsemen behind Federal front lines— cavalry Stuart might logically anticipate encountering when scouting in enemy country.[9]

Lee's written orders arrived the following day (June 11). They said essentially what Lee had said to Stuart the day before. And because Lee knew something of Stuart's exuberance, his instructions emphasized prudence: "... you must bear constantly in mind while endeavoring to execute the general purpose of your mission not to hazard your command or to attempt what your judgement may not approve; but be content to accomplish all the good you can, without feeling it necessary to obtain all that might be desired." Lee probably knew Stuart better than Stuart knew Lee.[10]

Meanwhile Stuart had selected approximately 1,200 companions for his raid and ordered them to cook rations for three days and to be ready to ride at a moment's notice. Stuart chose Fitz Lee's 1st Virginia and Rooney Lee's 9th Virginia, and reinforced each of these two regiments with half of the men composing the 4th Virginia. He also included two squadrons of the Jeff Davis Legion commanded by W. T. Martin and a section (two guns) of artillery commanded by James Breathed. All these officers and men knew they were soon going somewhere; no one except Stuart knew where or when. Such was the circumstance at 2:00 A.M. on June 12 when Stuart awakened his staff with the tidings, "Gentlemen, in ten minutes every man must be in his saddle!"[11]

While his staff officers scrambled out of their beds, into their clothes, and onto their horses, Stuart attended some final details. He left his headquarters in charge of his adjutant, and as he informed the officer of his departure, the man asked how long he would be gone. Stuart responded, "It may be for years and it may be forever." [12]

Then he led the way north up the Brook Turnpike. Elements of his chosen force joined the column as it moved; some of the troopers from the extreme left of the Confederate line did not become part of the expedition till just after noon. The day was bright and sunny and the men were in generally high spirits. Throughout the column ran speculation as to their destination and mission. A consensus emerged that they were headed for the Shenandoah Valley to join Stonewall Jackson's Valley Army, which had been providing about the only cheerful war news the Confederates heard. Even as one unit left camp, one of the troopers shouted to his comrades who remained behind, "Good-bye, boys; we are going to help old Jack drive the Yanks into the Potomac." Stuart seemed to confirm the rumor when just beyond a little place called Yellow Tavern, he turned left off the Brook Turnpike and headed northwest. But after a few miles, he turned back toward the northeast, then north again, and finally in the late afternoon Stuart directed his column east and made camp on a farm a few miles north of Ashland. The first day's march had covered about twenty-two miles, and still no one but Stuart knew precisely where the expedition was going. [13]

Stuart did not remain in camp during the night of June 12–13. Even though he had stayed awake all night only a few nights before (June 8–9) and had worked very hard preparing for this expedition ever since, Stuart remained restless and seemingly tireless. On this evening he left his camp and rode three or four miles to a plantation named Hickory Hill; there he visited his wounded subordinate Williams C. Wickham. Had it not been for his saber wound, sustained at Williamsburg, Wickham would have been commanding the 4th Virginia (which Stuart had divided and integrated into the 1st and 9th Virginia regiments). Stuart visited Wickham's bedside and wished him a speedy recovery. What if anything else Stuart did at Hickory Hill is open to question. One story has him dozing in a chair during the night; another claims he ate breakfast with the family; and still another family member insists that he visited only briefly with Wickham and left. As was often the case, Stuart was everywhere and nowhere, and he seemed to cultivate an air of elusiveness.[14]

Before light on June 13, Stuart ordered flares sent up as a signal to resume the march; bugles would have attracted more attention, and the expedition was very near enemy country. The column continued the route east, and by now most of the men realized that their mission involved McClellan's Federals instead of Jackson's Confederates. As the horsemen took up the march, Stuart summoned Mosby and requested him to gather a few men, ride ahead of the column, and scout the village of Hanover Court House. At this point Mosby, at least, knew for sure the purpose of the expedition; this was the same route over which he had traveled four days earlier.[15]

Mosby rode forward, and as he came in sight of Hanover Court House, he also sighted a squadron (about 150 men) of Federal cavalry. Mosby and his companions halted, but did not flee; Mosby sent one man back to report the Federals' presence to Stuart. This action alerted the blue squadron to the probability that more gray horsemen were following these few. The Federals wheeled about and disappeared. When Stuart heard about the enemy cavalry ahead of him, he dispatched Fitz Lee and the 1st Virginia on a detour around Hanover Court House, hoping to cut off the Federals and prevent them from giving the alarm. However, Lee's dash became more like a splash, when the horseman plunged into a swamp, and the Federals escaped the trap and fled south.[16]

Lee's regiment rejoined the column and the march resumed along a route roughly parallel with the Pamunkey River deeper into enemy country. Another Lee (Rooney) led the way, and troopers from his 9th Virginia took up the task of running over Federal outposts stationed in the little settlements along the way. A picket force was no match for a reinforced regiment, so Stuart lost no time in these encounters. This was one reason Stuart was traveling in such strength; he knew he could overwhelm any mounted force he might logically expect to be in the area, and he could deal with small units of infantry as well. He hoped he could outrun any force he could not outfight.[17]

Participants in the charges against Union outposts in places like Enan Church and Hawes Shop likened the activity to a fox chase. But as the Federals ran from the Southern column, they spread the news. If there were enemy infantry or perhaps Phillip St. George Cooke's Cavalry Reserve in the vicinity, Stuart might soon expect the foxes to turn upon their pursuers. Stuart approached the bridge over Totopotomoy Creek especially warily. At this point in its course the creek was pretty wide; the Confederates would have to control the bridge in order to cross safely and swiftly. A determined stand here by a Federal force even a third the size of Stuart's might produce a delay in the march that would prove fatal to his mission. Consequently, when the blue horsemen merely observed the Confederates from a distance while they crossed the Totopotomoy bridge, Stuart realized that his enemy was small, or stupid, or both.

Just about a mile from Totopotomoy Creek, near a place called Linney's Corner, the Federals made a stand. Woods lined the road on both sides and so confined the battleground. Approximately one hundred Union cavalrymen formed in the road on the crest of a hill; they displayed no apparent intention to give ground. Immediately Stuart passed the order, "Form fours, draw sabers, charge!"

A squadron of Southern horsemen, four abreast, spurred up the road, yelling and waving sabers. Leading the charge was Captain William Latané commanding the Essex Light Dragoons. Latané was twenty-nine years old; before the war he had practiced medicine and managed his prosperous family plantation in the Virginia Tidewater. Now he was screaming, "On to them, boys!" and riding his half-Arabian horse, The Colonel, about fifteen yards ahead of his men. Latané galloped straight at his counterpart, Captain William Royall, who commanded the Federal cavalry. Royall was yelling, "Cut and thrust!" to his men; but he himself drew two pistols as Latané bore down upon him. The Colonel dashed to within an arm's length of Royall, and Latané flailed at the enemy with his saber. A saber slash found its mark and wounded Royall severely. But Royall responded to Latané's blade with two pistol shots. The young physician tumbled from The Colonel, and by the time he struck the roadbed he was dead.[18]

Elsewhere the clash of mounted troops favored the Confeder-

ates; there were many more of them, and they were armed more
sensibly—with carbines and rifles in addition to the standard pistol and saber. The "fox chase" resumed as Stuart's men scattered
their foes and pressed forward.[19]

In the wake of the conflict at Linney's Corner, about a half
dozen of Latané's comrades gathered around his body. Sergeant
S. W. Mitchell from the Essex Light Dragoons mounted his horse,
and the dead man's younger brother John helped lift the corpse
and drape it in front of Mitchell. Then Mitchell and John Latané
left the column, which was re-forming to resume the march. They
soon encountered a black man driving an ox-drawn cart which
they commandeered as a makeshift hearse. At this point young
Latané dismissed Mitchell, gave him his horse, and followed the
ox cart on foot to a nearby plantation called Westwood. There Mrs.
Catherine Brockenbrough and her friend Mrs. Willoughby Newton promised John Latané a proper burial for his brother. Then
they gave him a horse and sent him off to rejoin Stuart.[20]

By this time Stuart had reached the little village of Old Church,
where the 5th United States Cavalry Regiment had been en-
camped. The Southern troopers swept down upon the camp, captured or scattered its remaining inhabitants, and then burned
everything they chose not to carry off. Presiding over this legitimate looting and burning was Fitz Lee, who enjoyed the scene all
the more because the 5th Cavalry was the reorganized version of
the 2nd Cavalry, in which Lee had served before this war. While
his men were at work wrecking the camp, Colonel Lee was questioning prisoners (who addressed him as "Lieutenant") about the
health and whereabouts of his former comrades.[21]

Meanwhile Stuart's mind was racing. He knew what he had
come to find out; the Federal right flank was essentially untended.
Now all he had to do was report his findings to Lee. But between
Old Church and Richmond was McClellan's entire Union army.
Should he retrace his hoofprints, or should he do what he had
suggested to Lee he might do—ride completely around the Federal army? The issue was never really in doubt; Stuart resolved to
complete his circuit. In this case Stuart's instinct for boldness and
taste for glory coincided with prudence. If he returned to Lee's
lines by the way he had come, Stuart might expect to collide with
any of his enemies who were chasing him. Such a course would

also call more attention to the purpose of his expedition and the exposed Union right flank. On the other hand, the route around McClellan's army might disguise his purpose somewhat, and it would allow Stuart to retain the initiative. Finally, the circuit promised more chances to generate some havoc with Federal supply lines, which in turn would conceal further Stuart's primary interest in the enemy right.[22]

Stuart called his subordinates to him, explained the situation, and announced his inclination. Rooney Lee agreed with some enthusiasm; Fitz Lee simply assented. Then Stuart called for Mosby and asked him to "ride on some distance ahead" to scout the route deeper into enemy country. Mosby replied that he would need guides in this unfamiliar territory, and Stuart quickly produced two men whose homes were in the vicinity. He had taken the care to include in his raiding force troop units whose members lived in the region over which the expedition might pass.[23]

The next segment of the ride would take the column to Tunstall's Station on the Richmond and York River Railroad, which was McClellan's principal supply artery. Having dispatched Mosby and his guides ahead, Stuart made earnest inquiries of local civilians about the route back to Hanover Court House. He was doing his very best to confound his pursuers, while he prepared to press on toward Tunstall's Station.[24]

Then Stuart called to John Esten Cooke, who was riding with his staff, "Tell Fitz Lee to come along, I'm going to move on with my column." Cooke realized the significance of the direction Stuart was taking and replied, "I think the quicker we move now the better." "Right," said Stuart, "tell the column to move on at a trot."[25]

The first few miles from Old Church passed uneventfully. Mosby came upon a sutler's wagon and seized it as a "prize of war." Sutlers were essentially peddlers who sold to soldiers items unavailable (mostly food and drink) as rations or government issue. Then where the road passed quite close to the Pamunkey River at a place called Putney's Ferry, Mosby saw the masts of Union supply ships and relayed this information to Stuart. Two squadrons of troopers dashed down upon the landing at Putney's Ferry, burned two ships and some supply wagons, and returned to

the column with prisoners, horses, and mules. As they neared Tunstall's Station, the troopers increased their vigilance. There should
be troops on McClellan's primary supply line, and the railroad
might bring more Federals in a hurry.[26]

Then at the worst of times, one of Lieutenant Breathed's two
pieces of artillery became stuck in a mud hole. The men thrashed
the horses, and Breathed shouted encouragement; but the gun
remained stuck fast. A sergeant called Breathed aside and made a
suggestion. The lieutenant nodded and ordered a small barrel of
whiskey, recently liberated from the sutler's wagon, to be placed
on the gun carriage. He promised the contents of the barrel to his
men when the gun was again mobile. Instantly the men waded
into the mud hole, wrenched the gun out of the ooze, and fell to
lapping up their reward.[27]

Meanwhile Mosby was trotting down the road into Tunstall's
Station. About a half mile from the village he encountered a Federal cavalry outpost. No sooner had he reined his horse to a halt
than he heard a bugle and saw a company of Pennsylvania cavalry
a few hundred yards away. Mosby knew his horse was slow and
tired; he determined he would be safer standing still than attempting to run. So he resorted to a desperate bluff. He drew his saber,
turned in his saddle, and waved imaginary followers forward. The
tactic made the Federals pause and for a long moment nothing
happened. Then, as though in answer to Mosby's prayer if not his
gesture, the lead elements of Stuart's column came into view advancing at a rapid trot. The Pennsylvanians wheeled and scattered.[28]

Southern horsemen swept into Tunstall's Station and overwhelmed the small contingent of Federal infantry posted there.
Even as the Confederates were seizing the village, some of their
number cut the telegraph wires to prevent precise information
about their strength and intentions from reaching McClellan's
headquarters. Then did the troopers hear a rumble on the railroad
tracks and the whistle of an approaching train. Lieutenant W. T.
Robbins, who commanded the first unit of cavalry on the scene,
had only time to fashion a makeshift barricade before the train
loomed into view.

By this time Stuart and many more horsemen were on hand,
but the combination of mud and whiskey still detained Breathed's

artillery pieces. The engineer could see the rude barricade and the Southern cavalry as he approached the station. Consequently he put on more steam and opened his throttle. The engine smashed through the obstruction and the train roared past the station. The Confederates fired small arms at Federal troops aboard the cars; but without artillery there was no chance to stop the train. One of Stuart's more aggressive scouts, Captain Will Farley, grabbed a shotgun and spurred his horse. Farley rode alongside the engine and blasted the unfortunate engineer just as the man probably believed he had made good his escape. Most of those aboard the train survived the gauntlet of Southern fire, thanks to the bold engineer who did not. And Stuart speculated with some glee about the fate of the speeding train with a dead engineer arriving at White House, the major Federal supply base, only five or six miles down the tracks.[29]

By now the daylight of June 13 was fast fading. Still there was much for the raiders to do in and around Tunstall's Station. They burned a railroad bridge nearby, and plundered a wagon train, and burned what they could not carry off with them. Having lit the sky with flames from the burning wagons, Stuart dispatched his weary column down the road toward Talleysville, about five and a half miles away.[30]

In his published account of this first great cavalry raid, John Esten Cooke wrote that after Old Church, "The gayest portion of the raid now began." Perhaps—well after the fact—it all seemed "gay" to Cooke. Certainly Stuart appeared to witnesses to be out for a grand time and nothing more. Stuart's companions usually saw no more than Stuart wanted them to see, and no one knew more about Stuart than he wanted them to know. Beneath his jolly facade, however, Stuart's mind was churning.

As the Southern horsemen left Tunstall's Station and the blazing wagon train, Cooke fell into the rear of the column. Suddenly he heard a voice from the darkness around him, "Who is here?"

Cooke recognized the voice as Stuart's and responded, "I am."

In turn Stuart recognized Cooke and was happy to hear the voice of a staff officer. "Good! Where is Rooney Lee?"

"I think he has moved on, General."

"Do you *know* it?"

"No, but I believe it."

"Will you *swear* to it? I must know! He may take the wrong road, and the column will get separated!"

"I will ascertain if he is in front."

"Well, do so; but take care—you will get captured!"

Cooke assured Stuart he would find Lee, and galloped forward. He had barely started when he heard a rider approaching. Cooke commanded the horseman to halt and identify himself; he was a courier from Rooney Lee.

"Is he in front?" Cooke asked.

"About a mile, sir."

The next thing Cooke heard was Stuart's voice from the darkness behind him: "Good!" Stuart rarely revealed his anxiety or even concern; he took care to seem carefree. Not even Cooke, who recorded Stuart's anxious moments about Rooney Lee's command, seemed to understand. Cooke wrote about "the fun, the frolic, the romance—and the peril too—of that fine journey [around McClellan's army]." Neither Cooke nor anyone else seemed to grasp the fact that only Stuart's careful planning and hard work made possible "the fun, the frolic, the romance . . ."[31]

Men and horses did straggle some on the road between Tunstall's Station and Talleysville. Consequently when Stuart reached Talleysville, he called a halt to allow his column to close up. The Confederates found a Union hospital near Talleysville which they did not disturb. They also found sutlers' stores, well stocked with unmilitary delicacies, and these the hungry troopers disturbed quite a bit. Heros Von Borcke, who was certainly no stranger to the fruit of the grape, later said of the bottle of champagne he drank that night, "Never in my life have I enjoyed a bottle of wine so much." And Cooke while at Talleysville consumed figs, beef tongue, pickle, candy, catsup, preserves, lemons, cakes, sausages, molasses, crackers, and canned meats. Somehow, Cooke and the rest of the men survived their feeding frenzy and rode out of Talleysville when Stuart re-formed his column at midnight.[32]

During these first few hours of June 14, the third day of the expedition, Stuart had to focus his attention upon the Chickahominy River. He had crossed the Chickahominy before dawn on the first day of this ride about twelve miles north of Richmond, where the river was a small creek. At this point on Stuart's route, the Chickahominy was more formidable, and crossing it required a bridge or a ford. Stuart's preselected guide for this portion of the route, Lieutenant Jones Christian, knew of a ford on property belonging to his family. But upon reaching the ford, the Confederates discovered the river quite high.

Rooney Lee plunged into the swirling water and with difficulty swam to the far bank. Lee pronounced the ford definitely unfordable and, again in clear danger of drowning, swam back. Next Lee directed his troopers to fell trees across the stream for a bridge. The trees, however, were slightly short, and as they crashed into the river, the current swept them downstream. At this juncture, Stuart arrived on the scene and listened to Lee's less than cheerful report of the situation.

This was tense. On this morning of his second day in enemy country, Stuart knew that Federals had to be on his trail. The fact that the Confederate column had encountered no significant threat thus far seemed to indicate that the enemy would come in strength when he came. Stuart was in danger if caught between a formidable force and an unfordable river. And what if he were overtaken and overwhelmed by his father-in-law? That humiliation would be worse than losing his command or life. The young general sat straight in his saddle and calmly stroked his beard. His staff soon realized that Stuart's beard stroking betrayed full attention and a racing mind.

He conferred with Christian, had a look at the ruins of a bridge about a mile downstream, and decided to have a try at repairing the structure. The abutments and some of the piers were intact; an old warehouse nearby offered planks; and two members of the staff, Redmond Burke and Corporal Hagan (the hairy giant), had had some experience constructing bridges. Stuart posted one of his regiments as a rear guard and put the rest of the men to work on the bridge. He dispatched a courier on the road to Richmond with messages for Lee about the Federal right flank. Then Stuart could do no more than wait.[33]

He stretched out on the bank of the river and munched on the feast that Mosby prepared from some of the sutlers' stores "liberated" the night before at Talleysville. Involved in a race against time, defeat, and death, Stuart impressed Mosby as being "in the gayest humor I ever saw."[34]

In three hours the Confederates had a bridge, and by one

o'clock in the afternoon the entire column was across. Then did some of the horsemen have to burn the structure they had worked so hard so recently to construct. Only as the burning timbers were falling sizzling into the river did a small contingent of Federal cavalry arrive on the opposite bank. They fired a shot or two, but otherwise could only watch the raiders disappear into the woods on the far bank.[35]

Stuart led his weary band to Charles City Court House, about seven miles from the Chickahominy, and there called a halt to permit men and horses to rest. He and his staff went to a nearby plantation house, where the residents provided them with food and drink. Having eaten something, Stuart lay down in the grass under the trees that shaded the yard and slept a few hours.

When he awakened Stuart returned to work. He placed Fitz Lee in command of the expedition and instructed him to resume the march at eleven o'clock that night. Then, about dusk, Stuart with two couriers pressed on toward Richmond, about twenty-eight miles away.

He stopped en route only once, for coffee and a fifteen-minute rest. Slightly before sunrise on the Sunday morning of June 15, the three riders clattered into the Confederate capital from the south. Fitz Lee led the rest of the column into the city later the same day. In three days Stuart had ridden a hundred miles around the entire Union army. He had learned what Lee needed to know and raised considerable hell in the process. He had inflicted some damage upon the Federal supply line, and he had fed McClellan's fears that he, not Lee, was in grave danger. Stuart also had shored up Southern morale at a time when the war seemed to be going quite badly. And militarily he had introduced cavalry raiding to this war and added the conduct of raids like this one to the mission of the mounted arm.[36]

Stuart sent one of his companions to find Flora, who had arrived in Richmond for a visit on Friday, June 13, the day her husband entered enemy lines at Hanover Court House and rode on to Linney's Corner, Old Church, Tunstall's Station, and Talleysville. Told at Lee's headquarters that Stuart's whereabouts were unknown, Flora Stuart could only wait and wonder till the courier arrived on Sunday morning.[37]

His other courier, Richard E. Frayser, Stuart dispatched to Virginia Governor John Letcher. Frayser encountered some difficulty gaining audience with Letcher; the hour was early and the governor was in bed. After explaining the nature of his errand, Frayser was allowed inside the mansion and ushered into Letcher's bedroom. Then Frayser had trouble leaving. Governor Letcher was so interested in every detail of the adventure that Frayser had all but to reenact the raid.[38]

Stuart himself rode directly to the Dabbs' farm and Lee's headquarters. Naturally Lee was delighted at Stuart's success and intensely interested in the condition of the Union right flank. Stuart's information was absolutely crucial to the campaign Lee was planning. Lee intended to do precisely the opposite of what Stuart had advised in his June 4 letter. The Army of Northern Virginia would attempt to hold the bulk of McClellan's army at bay with few troops and strong fortifications. Meanwhile Lee would deliver what he hoped would be a decisive blow to the Federal right and rear. Having fulfilled his duty and received congratulations from Lee, Stuart went in search of Flora and some rest.[39]

Amid the joy of their reunion, the couple certainly speculated upon the conduct of her father, his foe, during the great raid. Encountering Phillip St. George Cooke in combat was about the only goal Stuart had not achieved in his expedition. As it happened Cooke had spent many frustrating hours during his son-in-law's caper. His troubles began, appropriately enough, on the afternoon of Friday, the thirteenth, when he began receiving fairly garbled reports of Stuart's presence and action at Linney's Corner and Old Church. These reports stated that Stuart had many more cavalry troops than he actually had and that he had five regiments (5,000 men!) of infantry, as well as artillery. Cooke began to get a series of conflicting orders and messages from his higher headquarters about what he should do next. What he did was wait until he could collect sufficient cavalry units and secure supporting infantry. Then he took up Stuart's cold trail and pursued the Confederates cautiously. Cooke remained awake for thirty-six consecutive hours and sweated considerably in the June heat; but he never came anywhere near Stuart's column. General Cooke was a very prudent soldier; he wrote a manual about cavalry tactics and died in bed at age eighty-three.[40]

While Cooke and other Federal officers were still trying to

reconstruct the events of June 12–15 and find some one of themselves upon whom to affix blame for their fiasco, the "Ride Around McClellan" or "Chickahominy Raid" or "Pamunkey Expedition," as it was variously called, became in the Confederate mind much larger than life. It was an epic event. On Monday morning (June 16), the day after Stuart's return, Richmond newspapers announced the news with such headlines as A MAGNIFICENT ACHIEVEMENT, BRILLIANT RECONNAISSANCE, and UNPARALLELED MANEUVER. As one of Stuart's subordinates recalled, "The Southern papers were filled with accounts of the expedition, none accurate and most of them marvelous." In addition to reporting the facts of the expedition, the Richmond *Examiner* substituted Stuart for Rooney Lee at the unfordable ford across the Chickahominy. According to the *Examiner,* Stuart was "first to plunge his horse into the Chickahominy." And as he spurred into the swirling water, Stuart supposedly said, "There may be danger ahead, men, but I will see, follow me." Stuart's feat was fast becoming a legend.[41]

Stuart did little to discourage the adulation. On Monday afternoon he took a stroll to Capitol Square in Richmond, ostensibly to relax and watch a routine military drill. Instantly members of the military unit, observers, and passersby recognized him. "Hurrah for Stuart," came the repeated cheer. According to one witness, "The people, citizens and soldiers, were pretty near crazy to hear the gallant General speak." In response to calls for a speech, Stuart mounted the steps of the Governor's Mansion and modestly thanked his hearers for their tribute. Then he said stirring things about "the spirit of the people, the grand object of Southern deliverance, and the determined and heroic character of our army." Stuart spoke briefly and left the scene "amidst the ring of deafening cheers."[42]

The glamour of the raid continued to grow on Tuesday (June 17) when Stuart composed his General Orders No. 11, a public statement of his "high appreciation of the bravery and cheerful endurance of his command." Members of his force, the general proclaimed, could depend upon "History" to "record in imperishable characters" and "a grateful country" to "remember with gratitude" their participation in the expedition. A few days later, Lee added his judgment via general order and pronounced the raid a "brilliant exploit."[43]

Stuart's narrative report of the expedition, also written on June

17, was a classic. It began routinely enough: "General: In compliance with your written instructions I undertook an expedition to the vicinity of the enemy's lines on the Pamunkey with about 1200 cavalry and a section of the Stuart Horse Artillery." But as Stuart reconstructed the events of his raid, his prose became more colorful. As his leading squadron chased Federal horsemen between Totopotomoy Creek and Linney's Corner, "on, on dashed [Lieutenant W. T.] Robins, here skirting a field, there leaping a fence or ditch, and clearing the woods beyond . . ." During the fight at Linney's Corner, William Latané did not simply die; "the gallant captain . . . sealed his devotion to his native soil with his blood." When at Old Church Stuart decided to continue his circuit instead of withdrawing the way he had come, one factor influencing his decision was "the hope of striking a serious blow at a boastful and insolent foe, which would make him tremble in his shoes . . ." And when the column continued the march deeper into enemy country, "There was something of the sublime in the implicit confidence and unquestioning trust of the rank and file in a leader guiding them straight . . . into the very jaws of the enemy." Stuart included such mundane matters as numbers—165 prisoners, 260 captured horses and mules, and millions of dollars' worth of property destroyed. But he also described his men standing "unappalled before the rushing torrent of the Chickahominy, with the probability of an enemy at their heels armed with the fury of a tigress robbed of her whelps." This was no ordinary reconnaissance.[44]

Latané was the only man Stuart lost during the grand raid. And because he was, his death and burial became part of the mystique associated with the expedition. Catherine Brockenbrough and Mrs. Willoughby Newton made good their promise to John Latané that they would give his brother a proper burial. Nineteenth-century women were accustomed to preparing bodies for burial, and these women had slaves to construct a coffin and dig a grave. But because they were in "enemy country," the women were unable to find a clergyman to perform the burial service. So Mrs. Newton took charge and read the service at the family graveyard while women and children from the neighborhood looked on.[45]

A poignant scene it must have been. It became one familiar to an entire generation of Southerners. About two weeks after the burial, a woman, probably Latané's fiancée Martha Davis, wrote a letter to John R. Thompson, who was a poet and former editor of the *Southern Literary Messenger* (once edited by Edgar Allan Poe). She requested Thompson to compose a poem to commemorate Latané, and Thompson responded with "The Burial of Latané." The work is a trifle maudlin, but not mawkish, and Tennyson pronounced it the "most classical poem written on either side during the war." Some of it read:

> A little child strewed roses on his bier,
>     Pale roses not more stainless than his soul,
> Nor yet more fragrant than his life sincere
>     That blossomed with good actions, brief but whole;
> The aged matron and the faithful slave
> Approached with reverent feet the hero's lowly grave.
>
> No man of God might say the burial rite
>     Above the "rebel"—thus declared the foe
> That blanched before him in the deadly fight.
>     But woman's voice, in accents soft and low,
> Trembling with pity, touched with pathos, read
> Over his hallowed dust the ritual for the dead.[46]

The *Southern Literary Messenger* published Thompson's poem in the summer of 1862, and it became an instant favorite. Two years later, Latané's interment again evoked artistic response. William D. Washington, a painter who specialized in historical subjects as well as portraits, set up a studio in Richmond to present *The Burial of Latané* on canvas. Using members of a local literary circle and some of the city's leading society maids and matrons as models, Washington worked on the painting for several months. When completed, Washington's *The Burial of Latané* drew "throngs of visitors" to its display. And soon prints of the work spread throughout the South. When the Lost Cause was indeed lost, the painting became downright sacred, a symbol of sacrifice and devotion to the Cause, and copies hung in innumerable Southern parlors during the late nineteenth century. Latané, who faced two pistols with one saber, became a cult figure because he was killed with Stuart. Latané's death became decor; his burial *objet d'art*.[47]

The Ride Around McClellan made Latané a martyr. The adven-

ture made Stuart a bona fide Southern hero. Lee had not yet
emerged as great Gray Knight; Johnston was wounded; and Beauregard, the "hero of Sumter," was mired somewhere in Mississippi. The Richmond *Enquirer* pronounced, "This achievement of
General Stuart stands alone in the history of the war and eclipses
the most brilliant achievements of the lamented and glorious
[Turner] Ashby, of the invincible [John Hunt] Morgan and we will
venture to say of the gallant and dashing [Stonewall] Jackson."[48]

Certainly he looked the part. John Esten Cooke remembered
Stuart at the time of his first great raid as "a gallant figure to look
at. The gray coat buttoned to the chin; the light French sabre
balanced by the pistol in its black holster; the cavalry boots above
the knee, and the brown hat with its black plume floating above
the bearded features, the brilliant eyes, and the huge moustache,
which curled with laughter at the slightest provocation—these
made Stuart the perfect picture of a gay cavalier." Heros Von
Borcke was impressed that Stuart "delighted in the neighing of
the charger and the clangour of the bugle, and he had something
of Murat's weakness for the vanities of military parade." But
Stuart, Von Borcke observed, "did not fail to attract the notice and
admiration of all who saw him ride along."[49]

Beneath this pomp and beyond his growing mythology, Stuart
fashioned his heroics from very hard work. His Ride Around
McClellan offers a good case in point. Before he ever spoke with
Lee about the expedition, Stuart had sent Mosby to scout the region, and he had learned more from the nocturnal visit with Von
Borcke to his spy. Stuart had a pretty good idea what he would
find before he began his reconnaissance. He could praise the endurance and skill of his men because he had devoted long hours
to their training. He had trained and tested his subordinate commanders and his staff as well; he had bold and resourceful aides
because he identified such men and drew them to him. Thus when
his column required a scout, Mosby was present, and when the
command needed a bridge, Hagan and Burke directed its building.
To guide the troopers through unfamiliar country, Stuart made
certain he took with him men who knew every footpath, and he
saw to it that they came to the head of the column at the proper
moment. The general sang and joked as he rode, but as Cooke
related, he also attended to critical details, such as the where-

abouts of Rooney Lee's regiment on a night march, with a passion.
Stuart's success was no accident. Beneath his black plume was a
military mind at work.

But Stuart seldom revealed the "ordinary" origins of his success. People believed he was a wizard, a knight of Arthur's Round
Table reincarnate—and Stuart encouraged their belief. A year ago
he had been an essentially obscure lieutenant colonel training 334
Southern horsemen. A year before that he had been First Lieutenant Stuart preparing to chase Comanche across Kansas. Now he
was Brigadier General Stuart in command of the cavalry of the
Army of Northern Virginia. But what was more important, as a
result of the ride, Stuart was a hero. He had a "name" at last.
Throughout his nation, he was "Jeb." [50]

# VIII

## Major General Jeb

FOR A PRECIOUS FEW DAYS Stuart could savor the moment. Because of the ride he was a hero, hailed and cheered wherever he went. And he went often to Richmond because Flora and the children were there. Daughter Flora, "La Pet," was approaching five; Jimmy was very nearly two. They were old enough to frolic on the floor with their father, and Flora still sang for him. He had much of what he wanted from life—fame, friends, family, and a respite in which to enjoy them. Beyond his camp and the capital lay George B. McClellan's Federal host; the war continued and the Confederacy's fate still hung in precarious balance. But this circumstance served only to excite Stuart. There were laurels left; more missions remained; the quest continued.[1]

At the same time Robert E. Lee was composing his general order congratulating Stuart's command for the ride, the commanding general was formulating his plan to act upon the intelligence Stuart had brought him on June 15. Accordingly, on June 24, Lee released his battle order. General Orders, No. 75 called for four divisions, those commanded by James Longstreet, D. H. Hill, A. P. Hill, and Stonewall Jackson (following a rapid march from the Shenandoah Valley), to attack the vulnerable Federal right flank. Meanwhile only two Confederate divisions, those of Benjamin Huger and John B. Magruder, would hold the line directly between the bulk of McClellan's army and Richmond. If McClellan realized Lee's troop dispositions, he would be in a position to storm into Richmond and then destroy elements of Lee's army at his leisure. But if Lee's gamble paid off, the Army of Northern Virginia would have the opportunity to fight the Federals outside their formidable fieldworks with favorable numerical odds.

Initially at least, Stuart's cavalry was to play a supporting role in Lee's bold play. Three regiments of his cavalry would patrol the Confederate right flank; another remained in reserve. Stuart and five more regiments of horsemen (his best) were to join Jackson's command on the left and cover the extreme Confederate left flank.[2]

In obedience to Lee's orders, Stuart led his column out of camp on June 25 and bivouacked for the night near the town of Ashland. Next morning he set out in search of Jackson and his fabled Valley Army.[3]

At the same time Stuart sent out units of his command to secure the projected route of Jackson's advance. Having only two weeks earlier passed through this region on his ride, Stuart was well acquainted with critical passages along Jackson's line of march. For example, he dispatched troopers to hold the bridge over Totopotomoy Creek. The Southerners discovered the bridge torn up and the opposite bank in possession of a small body of Federals. After Stuart's men drove off the enemy, Stuart sent W. W. Blackford, his bullfrog-eating adjutant at Manassas/Bull Run who had recently rejoined the staff as chief engineer (captain), to repair the span. Within thirty minutes the bridge was ready for traffic.[4]

Stuart found Jackson at the head of his troops as they marched past Ashland, and the two chieftains conferred by the side of the road while the Valley Army continued the march. The foot soldiers had heard of Stuart's exploits, and they cheered him and their own commander as they strode toward battle. The conference between the two Confederate generals was a bizarre scene indeed. Stuart was mounted on a blooded steed; Jackson rode a "dun cob of rather sorry appearance." As usual, Stuart was impeccably dressed —gray coat, yellow sash, highly polished cavalry boots, pistol, and saber. Jackson wore a "threadbare, faded, semi-military suit" covered with dust. In contrast to Stuart's brown felt hat and black plume, Jackson wore an old cap from Virginia Military Institute pulled down over his forehead. Just about the only common feature of their physical appearance was the eyes; both men possessed eyes that flashed on occasion and ever seemed to flame.[5]

Stuart told Jackson of his work in securing the route and of the nature of the country and roads. And when the generals believed they understood their concert, Stuart rode away to continue his scouting in front of Jackson and his screening on Jackson's left. Although the Federals had not occupied this region in any strength since the ride, Fitz Lee's 1st Virginia, leading the column, encountered enemy pickets, and Stuart reported "constant skirmishing" for long segments of the route.[6]

Naturally horsemen could move faster than Jackson's foot soldiers, and Stuart had to wait for the infantry at various points along the route. Nevertheless Jackson's famed "foot cavalry," fresh from the brilliant Valley Campaign distinguished by rapid marching and aggressive action, was unaccountably slow on June 26. On this day the Valley Army was supposed to be tearing into the rear of the Federal left flank; this was the day of battle. Jackson's arrival was supposed to unleash Lee's desperate assault upon the Union right; nothing was supposed to happen until Jackson reached the field.

As it happened Jackson led his men about fifteen miles down the road from Ashland, and at five o'clock in the afternoon, he settled down for the night at a place called Hundley's Corner. Jackson the aggressive fighter was less than three miles from a furious battle, which would last another four hours, and he made camp instead of haste.

The rest of the Confederates who were poised to strike the Federal right waited for Jackson until after three o'clock in the afternoon. Then, assuming that Jackson must be nearby, A. P. Hill launched the attack upon Union General Fitz John Porter's exposed 5th Corps at Mechanicsville. Porter fell back to the east bank of Beaver Dam Creek and held until dark against a series of Southern assaults. And all the while Jackson had 18,000 troops in camp three miles in the rear of Porter's battle line.[7]

And ever since June 26, 1862, people have been asking why. Why was Jackson so uncharacteristically slow? Knowing he was supposed to march his men into battle that day, why did Jackson stop short of the battlefield? The most plausible answer to these questions is that Jackson suffered from the "fog of war" or "stress fatigue," too many sleepless days and nights of marching, fighting, and responsibility. Perhaps Stuart should have tried to penetrate

Jackson's "fog" and guide the Valley Army into combat. Yet that
was not his role in Lee's plan; he was supposed to protect Jackson's flank, and that he was doing. Nor did it likely occur to Stuart
to question, much less interrupt, the actions of his senior. Stuart
had worked for Jackson before; he knew and liked him. Moreover
he respected Jackson and continued to do so even after this and
subsequent failings during this campaign. So Stuart's horsemen
spent the night of June 26 on picket duty around Jackson's camp.[8]

During that night Porter's Federals fell back to another defensive position, behind Powhite Creek near Gaines's Mill. Next
morning Lee determined to continue the attack and so advanced
again toward the Federal flank. Jackson set out to find the battle,
and Stuart still rode on Jackson's left. Once again Jackson seemed
confused, and he consumed much of June 27 trying to reach the
scene of the action. When he did arrive at the Battle of Gaines's
Mill, the hour was late and the Confederate circumstance desperate. But he did arrive, and he responded to the situation when
explained to him by Lee. Jackson announced to his command,
"This affair must hang in suspense no longer; sweep the field with
the bayonet."[9]

As the general assault commenced, about seven o'clock in the
evening, Stuart and his cavalry were still on Jackson's left, still in
reserve. Stuart himself and his staff, however, were exposed to
enemy fire nearly all day. On one occasion an artillery shell passed
screaming over the heads of the horsemen, and everyone instinctively ducked. Indeed John Esten Cooke ducked so low as to fall
off his horse. Stuart asked if he was hurt, and Cooke replied, "Oh,
no, General; I only dodged too far." Stuart roared with laughter
and weeks later still chided Cooke for "dodging too far." In the
event of a general rout, Stuart was ready to pursue a beaten foe
and enhance the victory. He also watched the infantry assaults
quite carefully, seeking some opportunity to be useful.[10]

One opportunity presented itself in the form of Federal artillery fire directed against the Confederate left. He sent John Pelham and the only two guns available to the Stuart Horse Artillery
to counter the threat. Almost immediately Stuart's prized Blakely
went out of action, and Pelham was left with one Napoleon gun
against eight of the enemy's. He held his ground and his nerve
and blasted away in what Stuart later called "one of the most

gallant and heroic feats of the war." Finally Jackson sent Pelham some reinforcement, and the Confederate artillery drove the Federal guns from the field. A little later Stuart received word that the enemy was in full retreat, and he hastened to pursue. He led a dash down a likely road for three miles and encountered no retreat.[11]

Because of his preoccupation with Pelham's performance on the Confederate left and his search for fleeing Federals, Stuart missed the breakthrough near the center of the battle line. Finally Porter's line gave way, and Confederates poured into the breech. Amid confusion, Stuart's father-in-law, Phillip St. George Cooke, made a decision that transformed confusion into chaos for the Federals. Cooke ordered a cavalry charge—intending perhaps to save the Union all by himself. The charge was a fiasco. Confederate infantrymen who had faced an entrenched enemy all day made short work of shooting down men on horseback. And Federal artillery, attempting to stem the Southern advance, instead poured shrapnel into the ranks of their own horsemen. What began as a cavalry charge degenerated into a stampede of horses, ridden and riderless, into the Union rear. Cooke's charge was a noble gesture perhaps; but it was also an object lesson in how not to employ cavalry in the mid-nineteenth century. No doubt Stuart would have relished the chance to witness his father-in-law's debacle. But he did not need the lesson; he already knew more than his onetime mentor. And he would never again have the chance to encounter Cooke in battle. Gaines's Mill was Cooke's last combat; thereafter the Union War Department found other duties for him. Next evening John Esten Cooke had dinner in his uncle's abandoned headquarters.[12]

On the night of Gaines's Mill, Stuart returned from his abortive pursuit very late and soon thereafter sought some sleep. No sooner had he lain down than Jackson appeared and stretched out between Stuart and Cooke. Stuart asked Jackson where his staff was, and Jackson responded that he was roaming alone. Then the two generals discussed the heat of the day's battle—Jackson thought it "the *most terrific fire* of musketry I ever heard." And they decided that McClellan would retreat toward his supplies and determined to cut him off from the Pamunkey or the James. Stuart's camp, on the edge of a very gory battlefield under nothing more than a tree, was hardly a proper or probable setting for discussions of grand strategy. Yet McClellan that night had indeed decided to retreat. The Federal commander, still convinced he was outnumbered and feeling betrayed by his own government, hoped only to save his army from destruction. Stuart and his solitary guest had guessed correctly everything but the direction of McClellan's withdrawal.[13]

Next morning (June 28) Stuart received a summons from Lee to come to his headquarters and there received orders to assail Union supply lines on the Pamunkey. As it happened, McClellan had decided to retire the other way, toward the James, and Stuart's troopers encountered no opposition on their march toward the Richmond and York River Railroad line. Near Tunstall's Station Stuart found that the bridge over Black Creek he had destroyed fifteen days earlier had been rebuilt and destroyed again. He also found some few Federals on the far bank, and it was dark by the time the Confederates had dispersed their enemies and repaired the bridge. During the night reports circulated in Stuart's camp that no fewer than 5,000 Federals held their main supply base on the Pamunkey at White House about four miles away.[14]

White House was not only the primary landing for Federal supply ships on the Pamunkey and thus a formidable depot, it was also the home of Rooney Lee. Throughout the night of June 28–29, Lee and Stuart watched the glow of flames and flashes of exploding shells. When daylight came on the twenty-ninth, Stuart himself led a small band of dismounted men to White House. He found that the white house at White House was no more. The Federals had burned it, along with huge quantities of supplies, and departed. One Union gunboat remained in the river; but accurate fire from Stuart's artillery soon drove it downstream. Then could Rooney Lee survey the shambles of his plantation, and the rest of Stuart's troopers scavenge among the smoldering piles of Union supplies.[15]

From White House Stuart was able to send a message to Lee confirming that McClellan was en route to the James. The Federal commander termed his movement, not a withdrawal, but a "change of base," and so added that phrase to the military lexicon as perhaps the ultimate euphemism for retreat.

Lee probed Union lines for most of the day on June 28 and on the twenty-ninth attempted to organize a pursuit to destroy the

Federal columns as they moved. For various reasons, however, the fighting continued to be inconclusive though constant on June 29 and 30 as McClellan marched toward his new base at Harrison's Landing on the James.

Stuart spent June 29 at White House. Men and horses rested and resupplied themselves from the bounty accumulated there by their enemies. Stuart ordered some railroad locomotives to be disabled by an artillery round into their boilers and destroyed other military goods in the event the Federals should return in strength. Next morning (June 30) he assigned a portion of one regiment (Cobb's Legion) the duty of guarding White House and set out with the rest of his command to find the war. The Southern cavalry followed the same route used during the ride from White House to Forge Bridge over the Chickahominy. There, where he had spent some anxious moments two weeks earlier, Stuart camped for the night.[16]

At 3:30 A.M. on July 1, a courier brought orders from Lee to rejoin Jackson. Stuart spent all day trying to find Jackson, never did, but camped for the night near a place called Malvern Hill. Jackson had once again been slow and seemingly unaggressive. But he had joined the rest of Lee's army in time for a series of desperate infantry charges at Malvern Hill. Lee sensed that this was his last chance to strike a serious blow at the retreating Federals, and so he let the battle happen. As it happened the Federals held Malvern Hill in significant strength; Union artillery decimated the Southern infantry; and D. H. Hill described the battle as "not war—it was murder."[17]

Stuart missed the Battle of Malvern Hill, the last of the Seven Days Campaign. On July 2 he did locate Jackson and reassumed his position on the left flank of Lee's army. Then when the Federals abandoned Malvern Hill, Stuart harassed their rear guard as best he could and took numerous stragglers prisoner. During that night (July 2–3) Pelham, whom Stuart had sent toward the river, sent word that he had found the Federal army at Harrison's Landing. Pelham had also found Evelington Heights, a plateau overlooking the Union camp from which his artillery might shell the Federals. Stuart relayed Pelham's news to Lee via Jackson and set out for Evelington Heights.

The Confederate horsemen arrived about nine o'clock on the

morning of July 3 and quickly dispersed the squadron of blue cavalry stationed on Evelington Heights. Then Stuart directed Pelham to commence firing upon McClellan's immense camp below. At this point the Stuart Horse Artillery was one gun, and Pelham had little ammunition left for it. Nevertheless, Stuart watched with some glee as his shells generated general consternation in the Federal camp. He believed that the divisions of Jackson and Longstreet were en route to reinforce him. The Federals responded to the shelling by advancing upon Stuart's position with infantry and artillery. Only when Pelham had only two rounds left did Stuart learn that Longstreet was nearly ten miles away and Jackson was not that close. Thus at about two o'clock in the afternoon Pelham fired his final round, the troopers posted as sharpshooters spent their last cartridges, and Stuart withdrew to safety.

Longstreet's troops arrived during the night, and Jackson himself accompanied Stuart the next day (July 4) to have a look at Evelington Heights. The Federal army was there in force. Stuart still favored an attack, which if successful would again place this critical piece of ground in Confederate hands. Ultimately Lee decided against Stuart's plan. Already McClellan's position was quite strong, and the Army of Northern Virginia badly needed an opportunity to rest and recover from the fearsome Seven Days. Accordingly Stuart's men did picket duty for a few days, then screened the withdrawal of Lee's army toward Richmond, and at last (with the exception of those on outpost) returned to camp outside Richmond.[18]

On July 5 Stuart finally had time to dash off a note to Flora. He wrote from "the Advance" and told her that he had remained in contact with the enemy for an entire week. There was no time for details; but he did recount his success against the Union gunboat at White House and mention his chance to shoot at the Federal camp from Evelington Heights. Had the entire army been present, he asserted, McClellan would have been destroyed instead of defeated.[19]

Certainly Stuart enjoyed confronting an enemy army numbering nearly 100,000 men with one howitzer. More reflective men, however, have questioned the wisdom of firing into the Union camp from Evelington Heights on July 3. By so doing, the critique contends, Stuart prematurely revealed to the Federals the necessity of holding this crucial terrain feature. By the time Lee's infantry was able to take advantage of Pelham's discovery, Stuart's rash gesture had prompted the enemy to seize the plateau and hold it in strength. Thus Stuart's precipitate action cost the Confederates an opportunity to force McClellan's surrender. All this ignores Stuart's belief that Longstreet and Jackson were close behind him. And the critique presupposes that no one on the Union side would have recognized the need to hold the high ground commanding the concentration at Harrison's Landing. In truth, Stuart was probably not too quick to commit to action on July 3; his comrades (for good reasons, no doubt) were too slow.[20]

The Seven Days was a brilliant campaign which saved Richmond, probably the Army of Northern Virginia, and perhaps the Confederacy. With justice did Lee issue a congratulation order terming the campaign a "signal success" and describing "brilliant results." Privately, however, Lee wrote to his wife, "Our success has not been as great or complete as I could have desired." And he later concluded his full report of the campaign with the judgment, "Under ordinary circumstances the Federal Army should have been destroyed."[21]

Lee had some ideas about the reasons for the limited nature of his success. He gave McClellan and his subordinates some credit, blamed the nature of the terrain, and decried the "want of correct and timely information." He also reached some conclusions about his subordinates based upon their performance during the Seven Days. For example, John Bankhead Magruder, who had failed to pursue actively and attack aggressively while the Federal army was marching to the James, received orders on July 3 to report to the secretary of war and thereafter found himself en route to Houston to command the Department of Texas, New Mexico, and Arizona. Benjamin Huger, like Magruder a major general who had been lethargic and late, became inspector of artillery and ordnance as of July 12. Jackson retained Lee's instinctive trust, although the hero of the Valley had certainly not covered himself with glory in the Seven Days. Amid the ferment within Lee's mind during July of 1862, Stuart found favor. Well aware was Lee that his cavalry commander dealt "in flowering style"; but Lee had earlier concluded that Stuart was "a good soldier," and he had found no reason to change his mind.[22]

Stuart was also certain that he was a good soldier, and he used the respite following the Seven Days to display himself and the fruits of his hard riding and training. When he returned from the James he first (July 12) established his headquarters north of Richmond at the farm of a man named Timberlake near Atlee Station. On the twenty-first he moved to Hanover Court House and from there on July 23 led 2,000 troopers toward Fredericksburg to meet a threatened Federal advance which failed to materialize. He held gala reviews of his troops and entertained visitors at his headquarters. Flora was now nearby, and she led the throng of admiring women who viewed the reviews.[23]

Then on July 25 Stuart received his second star; he was a major general. And three days later Lee's reorganization of the Army of Northern Virginia reached the cavalry. Stuart, in accord with his new rank, now commanded a division of horsemen. Fitz Lee, his favored subordinate, became a brigadier general and would command one of Stuart's two brigades. Lee's brigade contained five regiments, mostly commanded by familiar faces. Rooney Lee remained with the 9th Virginia and stood in Stuart's eyes next in line for promotion to general. Williams C. Wickham, now recovered from his wound, commanded the 4th Virginia, and Tiernan Brien, the courtly Marylander who had served long as Stuart's adjutant, earned a colonelcy and inherited Fitz Lee's 1st Virginia. Thomas L. Rosser, who had commanded artillery to Stuart's satisfaction, also won promotion to colonel and commanded the 5th Virginia.[24]

To command Stuart's other brigade came South Carolina's Wade Hampton, forty-four years old and one of the wealthiest men in the South. Hampton made a habit of going directly to the president when he wanted something. He had had no military experience before raising a "legion" for the Confederacy. He was quite consciously South Carolinian and concerned himself about the prominence of Virginians in the army. Hampton's presence offered Stuart a challenge, if only because he was fifteen years Hampton's junior and very much a Virginian. Hampton's brigade included the cavalry components (regiment-size) of three "legions"—Cobb, Hampton, and Jeff Davis. The 1st North Carolina and 10th Virginia regiments completed Hampton's command.[25]

The reorganization of Lee's army and Stuart's cavalry soon added a third brigade to Stuart's division. Turner Ashby, who had been Stuart's first rival in the Confederate army and who had commanded the cavalry of Jackson's Valley Army, had been killed on June 6, 1862, on a raid in Pennsylvania. The Valley troopers were a fiercely independent lot, and they had all but worshiped their leader. Ashby's death opened the way to bring his semiautonomous command under Stuart's control. Stuart urged Lee to entrust these potentially unruly horsemen to Fitz Lee, but President Davis selected Beverly Robertson to command Ashby's men. In any event Stuart added five more regiments to his division; but this blessing was decidedly mixed. In addition to some of the same soldiers who had rejected his leadership in favor of the dashing Ashby in 1861, Stuart inherited Robertson (whom he once called "the most troublesome man I have to deal with") and Grumble Jones, whose resentment of Stuart dated to their meeting in May of 1861.[26]

At the same time Stuart was attempting to establish his place (a prominent place) in the high command of the army, he had to maintain his influence and authority with that varied group of individuals who were his subordinates. The essential structure of military organization requires subordinates to respect and obey the authority of their seniors in command and rank. Veterans of the officer corps of the "old" (pre-1861) United States Army were most sensitive to such strictures. But the mass of men who composed the Confederate army included officers like Georgian Thomas R. R. Cobb, who possessed neither military experience nor instincts. Because he had recruited a "legion" for the army and had important political connections, Cobb was a colonel and destined to become a general. The cavalry contingent in Cobb's Legion did not accompany Stuart on the Ride Around McClellan; Cobb informed his wife, "In other words we were doing the dirty work and the *gentlemen* doing nothing were placed ... where éclat or honor were to be obtained." Cobb did ride with Stuart during the Seven Days; afterward he told his wife, "I was left to do all the dirty and hard work on the way, while his old West Point friends (the two Lees) were assigned every desirable position along the route." Stuart desired more than perfunctory compliance with his instructions; he wanted respect, if not love, from the men he led. To the extent that his life was a romantic quest, Stuart wanted to lead his fellow knights as first among equals, the acknowledged champion. He had scant chance of realizing his goal with Cobb.[27]

The nature of cavalry operations generally tended to ease Stuart's relations with men like Cobb, Jones, and Robertson. Although components of a central command, individual units of horsemen were most often widely dispersed across a broad front. And Stuart had already learned to post potentially difficult subordinates some distance from his headquarters. Clearly the division commander could not be everywhere at once; consequently Stuart usually pitched his tent near Fitz Lee and left Hampton to his own devices. This should not suggest that Stuart abrogated his responsibility as commander. On the contrary, he was swift to discover incompetence among his subordinates and relentless in removing an offender from his command. Stuart pursued a quest; he did so with zest and good fun; but at this stage he seldom lost sight of the mundane matters involved in his mission.

To manage and coordinate a command that had essentially tripled in size within a month in the midst of a campaigning season, Stuart required ever more of his headquarters staff. He lost Brien to a command position in the reorganization and would soon lose Mosby to an independent command as a quasi-guerrilla. Blackford remained; Pelham still graced the headquarters, though he commanded the Stuart Horse Artillery; Von Borcke continued as an aide. New to the staff was Norman R. Fitzhugh, who served as assistant adjutant general and chief of staff; Fitzhugh had risen from the ranks and impressed Stuart with his efficiency. The "military family" still included Stuart's relatives—Cooke, two of his Hairston kin, and cousin J. Hardeman Stuart. But Stuart was ever separating men, even among his relatives, who were merely ornamental from those who could contribute, and he did not suffer failure lightly. Dabney Ball's career with Stuart is a case in point. Ball, the brave clergyman, earned Stuart's praise during the first year of the war. However, while acting as commissary during the Seven Days, Ball received a stinging rebuke from Stuart for not having rations in the same place as the soldiers. In consequence, the good reverend resigned in a huff, and Stuart let him go. Ball served thereafter as a chaplain.[28]

Many people would have been overwhelmed with the contemplation of these increased responsibilities and new challenges. But Stuart was not a contemplative man; he simply acted. He believed Ball had failed, so he told him so. He held reviews of his troopers and had Sam Sweeney perform magic on his banjo for his friends. He was too busy to reflect upon the enormities of the tasks that confronted him; he simply plunged into his new role and performed.

Meanwhile infantry began to move again on the Virginia front. McClellan remained at Harrison's Landing for almost six weeks talking about renewing his campaign for Richmond but doing little or nothing about it. Then to northern Virginia came a new Northern hero, John Pope, who began building a new invading army with McClellan's troops. Transferred from the peninsula, Pope promised offensive action and reportedly proclaimed that he would make his "headquarters in the saddle." Some Confederate remarked that Pope's headquarters were where his hindquarters should be. Even while the bulk of his promised force was still with McClellan or en route to northern Virginia, Pope began menacing central Virginia and the Virginia Central Railroad as well.[29]

On August 13 Lee ordered Stuart to report with the main body of his cavalry to Longstreet at Gordonsville. On the sixteenth Stuart and some of his staff took the train to Orange Court House to meet briefly with Lee and then join Fitz Lee as the cavalry came forward. Because the train was already crowded with troops by the time it reached Hanover Court House, Stuart and his staff rode all night in the tender of the locomotive. When they arrived at daybreak the next morning, they were covered with soot. Following some heavy scrubbing, they pressed on to Orange Court House and Lee's headquarters. There Lee explained his plan.

Stuart, with Fitz Lee's and Robertson's brigades, was to ride east around Clark's Mountain and then into Pope's rear to Rappahannock Station, where he would wreck the railroad bridge. Lee and the infantry would also use Clark's Mountain as a screen, march west, and attack Pope's army from the left rear. With Stuart on his lines of supply and retreat, Pope would be ripe for destruction. Lee wrote all this down, and Stuart said he would commence his ride the next day. Stuart left Hampton's brigade to picket the Chickahominy and mapped a rendezvous of Fitz Lee's troopers and Robertson's brigade in central Virginia.[30]

After an hour with Lee, Stuart and his retinue visited Jackson's camp, where they enjoyed a three o'clock dinner. Then Stuart sent his adjutant Norman Fitzhugh and an aide, Chiswell Dabney, to a place called Verdiersville on the far right flank of the army to await

Fitz Lee. With Von Borcke, Stuart rode off to survey the rolling countryside from Clark's Mountain. They found Mosby and a companion named Gibson on the way, and these two joined the sightseers. From Clark's Mountain they could see Pope's army to the northwest, and the four scouts agreed that the Federals seemed to be getting ready to move. Very late on the evening of August 17, Stuart, Von Borcke, Mosby and his friend Gibson reached Verdiersville and found only Fitzhugh and Dabney. Fitz Lee and the rest of the cavalry had not yet arrived. Stuart was annoyed.[31]

He dispatched Major Fitzhugh and a courier down the road to look for the tardy troopers. Then Stuart slipped the bridle off his mount Skylark, left the saddle on his back, and tied the horse to a picket fence which enclosed the yard of a house in the village. On the porch of the house he spread his cloak, removed his sash, gloves, and hat, and lay down to catch a short sleep. Von Borcke and Dabney did the same.

Meanwhile Fitzhugh and his courier rode a mile or so down the road and stopped at an intersection. They took advantage of a deserted house; Fitzhugh napped on the floor, while the courier was supposed to remain on watch. Both men awakened near dawn to the sound of hoofbeats—Federal hoofbeats. Blue-coated troopers burst into the house and captured Fitzhugh and his companion. The Federals were quite impressed that they had captured a Confederate major; but Fitzhugh realized that his captors were very close to a much bigger prize. And his heart sank when the column turned up the road toward Verdiersville.

Mosby first heard the approaching column and roused Stuart. The general had the remarkable capacity to awaken instantly and become immediately alert. As he rose Stuart asked Mosby to go with Gibson and summon Fitz Lee. Lee was late and there was much to do; he had to begin the ride to Rappahannock Station as soon as feasible. As Mosby and Gibson trotted off to meet Lee, Stuart strolled into the yard.

The advancing horsemen were still shrouded in the mist of early day as Mosby rode toward them. Suddenly men emerged, pistol shots cracked, and Mosby and friend returned to the village much faster than they had left. Stuart, Dabney, and Von Borcke scrambled for their horses. With Stuart barely aboard, Skylark lived up to his name and jumped the picket fence. Dabney's horse followed. Von Borcke vaulted onto his mount and spurred through a gate held open by the woman who owned the house. The big Prussian never had an opportunity to take hold of the reins; he simply hung on and hoped his horse would outdistance his pursuers. After about a mile the Federals abandoned the chase, and the five Confederates found each other in some woods.[32]

Stuart had escaped capture or worse. But he had lost Fitzhugh, and with Fitzhugh were Lee's instructions for the trap he was laying for Pope. In response to the captured instructions, Pope withdrew across the Rappahannock River and foiled Lee's plan. Fitz Lee had not comprehended the urgency of his own instructions and had made a detour to secure provisions for his men; he did not reach Verdiersville until the night of August 18, one full day behind schedule and in no condition immediately to undertake a forced march. At fault for allowing the Federal cavalry to cross the Rapidan was Robert Toombs, who withdrew the regiments of his brigade that had been guarding the roads south of the stream. Toombs insisted that his men needed an opportunity to cook their rations, and so he removed them and opened the way for the Federal column to surprise Stuart. Stuart sent a message to Lee explaining his delay, and the commanding general directed him to rest men and horses on the nineteenth and commence his march to Pope's rear, two days late, on August 20.[33]

Stuart coordinated his proposed sweep with Fitz Lee and Robertson and gathered his massed horsemen near Mitchell's Ford on the Rapidan. While he did, news spread throughout the cavalry division of the general's narrow escape. So hasty was Stuart's flight that he had left his cloak, sash, gloves, haversack, and plumed hat on the porch in Verdiersville. When last seen by Southern eyes, Stuart's hat was being held aloft on the saber of an enemy horseman. Stuart soon acquired replacements; major generals had little difficulty securing hats and gloves. But wherever he went within the army Stuart heard the same catcall, "Where's your hat?" He had to laugh, because the taunt echoed his own brand of rough humor. To Flora he wrote that he would make the "Yanks" pay dearly for his embarrassment.[34]

He went in search of revenge when the moon rose on August 20, at four o'clock in the morning. At that time both brigades of cavalry crossed the Rapidan: Fitz Lee was on the right (east), and Robertson, with whom Stuart rode (to watch him) was to the left (west). Lee found a few cavalry units south of the Rappahannock, drove them across the river, and stopped near Kelly's Ford. Robertson's men encountered more determined resistance. Five regiments of horsemen raised too much dust to move in secret and the leading elements of the column found Federals just beyond Stevensburg, a village four miles east of Culpeper Court House. The Federals fell back until they reached open ground just north of Brandy Station; there they seemed ready for decisive action. The Southerners charged with sabers flashing; Von Borcke led some reserve troopers into action and claimed he literally cut an enemy's head off; but really the conflict concerned skirmishers. A general confrontation never occurred, and the Federals withdrew across the Rappahannock. The Union cavalry was a rear guard for Pope's army, which by this time had escaped Lee's flanking movement and was safely across the Rappahannock.[35]

Next day (August 21) Stuart hatched a plan. Stuart proposed a raid into the rear of Pope's army. He wanted to do essentially what Lee had planned for him a few days earlier—ride to the rear of the enemy and wreck Pope's supply and communications lines. This time he proposed to sweep west of the Federals, then descend upon Catlett's Station, and destroy the railroad bridge over Cedar Run. If successful, the raid would significantly disrupt Pope's direct rail line to Washington (the Orange and Alexandria Railroad). Stuart submitted his scheme to Lee over breakfast at Lee's headquarters and awaited a reply.[36]

Pope's presence still represented a threat and an opportunity for Lee's army. Here was an enemy force on Southern soil in the process of being reinforced massively by units from McClellan's army. Lee could not know how strong Pope was already; he did know that each passing day was likely to increase Federal strength. Lee's obvious course of action was to attack Pope's force before reinforcements from the peninsula rendered Pope too strong to assail. The question was how. Maybe Lee was hoping that Stuart's projected raid would help him answer that question and perhaps slow the pace of Pope's reinforcement at the same time. Whatever the reason, Lee sent Stuart a note on the morning of August 22 directing him to proceed with his raid.

Stuart was ready. By ten o'clock that morning he had 1,500

---

For map of Catlett's Station Raid see p. 70.

troopers (Lee's and Robertson's brigades, minus one regiment each) and two artillery pieces in motion. The column moved swiftly up the friendly (west) side of the Rappahannock and crossed the river at Waterloo Bridge and Hart's Mill. Then Stuart led the way to Warrenton, where he stopped briefly to allow the troopers to close up. Federals had been in Warrenton, but not for several days.[37]

The townspeople greeted Stuart's men as deliverers and Stuart questioned them about the locations of nearby enemy troops. In the course of conversation he mentioned his intention to ride as far as Catlett's Station. At that a young woman burst out laughing and expressed the hope that Stuart would capture a certain Federal quartermaster officer; if so she would happily lose a bet with the man. Why would she be so joyous about losing a bet, and who was this man? The young woman explained that the quartermaster officer, Major Charles Goulding, had boarded at her home during the period when Federals occupied Warrenton. Amid discussions about the war the officer had bet her a bottle of wine that he would be in Richmond within thirty days. She accepted the bet. If Stuart were to capture the man, he would win, though not in the way he had assumed he would. Goulding would enter Richmond as a prisoner of war, instead of as a member of a victorious army. The story appealed to Stuart's sense of humor, and he had Blackford write down Goulding's name in the unlikely event that he should encounter him.[38]

The Confederates clattered out of Warrenton about midafternoon and rode east toward Catlett's Station. As they rode, the sky darkened ominously, and soon the rains came along with lightning and thunder. The head of the column (Rosser's regiment of Fitz Lee's brigade) reached Catlett's Station after dark in what Stuart later called "the darkest night I ever knew." Rosser's men overwhelmed the Federal picket; but then the Southerners found themselves within a Federal camp in the dark in the midst of a violent thunderstorm. This was Pope's headquarters as well as the heart of supply operations for the Union army.

Then Stuart encountered an incredible stroke of luck. Coming straight toward Stuart and his staff was a man singing "Carry Me Back to Old Virginia" to the accompaniment of a tin bucket he used as a drum. The Confederates were stunned—but not half as stunned as the singer when he found himself surrounded by Stuart's staff. He was a black man who had more or less been impressed to serve one of Pope's staff officers. And he knew Stuart from some prewar connection. The black man readily agreed to guide the raiders to Pope's headquarters; he also pointed out the location of the supply depot and the quarters of the infantry regiment guarding it. Stuart confirmed this information by questioning his prisoners (from the picket force) and by sending Blackford on a short scout into the camp. Then he assigned objectives to his subordinate commanders and called for his bugler.

Inside one of the tents near Pope's headquarters a group of officers were relaxing at the close of a long day. They sat around a table listening to the rain on the tent roof and enjoyed their nighttime toddies. "Now this is something like comfort," one of the Federals remarked. "I hope Jeb Stuart won't disturb us tonight." At that precise moment Stuart ordered the bugler to blow the charge and launch his wild men upon the camp. The Federal officers heard the yelling and the host pounded the table with his fist. "There he is, by God!"

Stuart was indeed there; the Southerners were everywhere. They cut telegraph wires. They fell among the Union troops and took ample advantage of the element of surprise. Soon flames from burning supply centers illuminated the entire camp. Blackford managed to duplicate Will Farley's feat at Tunstall's Station; he rode down a departing railroad engine and shot the engineer. Von Borcke claimed he found Pope's tent but found the Union commander absent. The Confederates did capture Pope's uniform and personal baggage, along with his dispatch book and money chests containing $500,000 in greenbacks and $20,000 in gold. Officers and men acquired canteens, field glasses, pistols, and watches. Blackford tried to seize a buffalo robe; but a large Newfoundland dog guarded his master's possessions, and Blackford decided that he did not want his prize badly enough to kill the dog. In addition to booty, the Confederates carried off more than 300 prisoners. Most of the stores collected at Catlett's Station they had to burn. Tom Rosser spoke for more men than himself when he rode up to Stuart and screamed, "General, I have been giving them hell. . . ."

One of Rosser's troopers attempted to take full advantage of the plunder about him. He first found another horse which he

mounted and led his own animal by a halter strap. Next he slashed
the cover off a covered wagon and hurled a handsome trunk to the
ground to break it open. Inside was everything from "superb un-
derwear" to a pint flask containing good whiskey. The trooper
sampled the whiskey and refilled the flask from a five-gallon barrel which a comrade had just broken open. Then he strapped as
much booty as he could to himself and his saddle and hung a pair
of field glasses around his neck. But then as he was screwing the
top onto his new flask, a body of Federal troops returned to
the scene and opened fire. The trooper's new horse bolted into the
dark and ran wildly for some distance through the woods. Before
the man could regain his composure and control of his mount, he
had lost all his plunder, save the field glasses, and his own horse
as well. Eventually he found his way back to his regiment and
even recovered his horse; but, excepting the field glasses, he rode
out of Catlett's Station no richer than he was when he arrived.
From this experience the trooper learned no lessons about the
effects of whiskey or greed; he blamed his misfortune entirely
upon the "Yankee horse."

The party assigned to destroy the railroad bridge over Cedar
Creek had much less good fortune than their comrades in the Federal camp. Because of the rain, which still fell in torrents as thun-
derstorms passed through the region, the raiders could not burn
the bridge. Some Federals still maintained their stations near the
bridge and "annoyed" any prolonged attempts to hack down the
span with axes. Thus Stuart called off the futile effort and made
ready to leave Catlett's Station.

Many prisoners and most all of the mules and horses managed
to escape into the dark. Among those captives who did not slip
away was a woman dressed in a Federal uniform who demanded
to see Stuart. She demanded her release because of her sex; but
Stuart judged that she would have to accept the consequences of
her enlistment and sent her away with the other prisoners. When
Stuart's re-formed column halted a few miles from Catlett's Station
in the early morning daylight, Blackford rode among the prisoners
and inquired if any of them was Major Charles Goulding. By coincidence Goulding was indeed among Stuart's captives, and he
cheerfully agreed to receive his bottle of wine when the column
passed through Warrenton. Stuart himself guided the prisoners to

the young woman's home, supervised the ceremony, and led cheers. The weary horsemen camped that night (August 23) on the east bank of the Rappahannock near Warrenton Springs and crossed the river the following morning.[39]

Stuart sent a hurried message to Lee regarding his raid; he also sent Pope's dispatch book, which contained copies of his military correspondence. On August 23 Lee responded first to Stuart's inability to destroy the railroad bridge; he informed President Davis of the raid, the failure to burn the bridge, and concluded, "He accomplished some minor advantages." Later however, when Lee had read and digested the correspondence in Pope's dispatch book, he may have amplified his estimate of the raid on Catlett's Station. On August 29 Lee wrote Davis that a recent letter from Pope to Washington established his strength at 45,000 men and revealed his intention to wait until McClellan's troops joined his own before assuming the offensive. Lee had speculated about these facts before; now he was certain of them, and he redoubled his resolve to act upon them. He would compel Pope to fight before he could be reinforced. The intelligence produced by Stuart's raid was more than a "minor advantage."[40]

When Stuart "reported" to Flora on August 25, his emphasis was upon his capture of Pope's clothing. Here was revenge for Verdiersville and his lost hat. Indeed the capture created quite a stir. In all probability W. Keith Armistead of the 6th Virginia actually seized Pope's uniform from his tent; then somehow Fitz Lee got possession of the items. Perhaps it was only proper that Fitz Lee, whose tardiness had cost Stuart his own hat and cloak, should present Pope's apparel to Stuart. Stuart showed the items to Jackson and sent a message to Pope offering to trade the captured cloak for his famous hat. Then he sent Pope's clothes to Richmond as a present to Governor John Letcher. The governor had the cloak hung in the State Library, which was then in the capitol. Richmond newspapers reported the entire story, describing the cloak in great detail, and citizens of the capital flocked to see Stuart's spoil of war.[41]

Catlett's Station, Stuart's second great raid, rivaled his first, the Ride Around McClellan. Both revealed Stuart at work, finding new uses for his cavalry and driving his body and mind to make success seem easy. Both raids revealed Stuart at play too. Lee might launch a momentous campaign based upon the information Stuart brought back; Stuart cared a great deal about the coup of capturing an enemy cloak. And he was delighted with the public attention he received for his feat.

# IX

## Knight of the Golden Spurs

LEE WANTED TO FIGHT. He believed he had to fight now if he was to prevent the union of two Union armies whose combined strength would overwhelm him. Materials in General John Pope's dispatch book confirmed Lee's assumptions; Pope's army across the Rappahannock now was approximately equal in size to the Confederate force; but Pope was about to receive massive reinforcement by George B. McClellan's troops fresh from the peninsula. Fighting Pope before McClellan's troops arrived involved risk, but the alternative seemed to be disaster. Accordingly Lee decided to dispatch Stonewall Jackson and half his army behind the Federals, between Pope and Washington. As was the case in the Seven Days plan, Stuart had recently demonstrated (by the Catlett's Station raid) that the route to the Union rear was clear. Once Jackson was astride Pope's supply lines, Lee reasoned that the Federals would have to give battle in the open. So Lee planned to send the other half of his army under James Longstreet to join Jackson's force. The Confederate commander was gambling that Jackson and Longstreet would be able to unite in time for the showdown with Pope. Otherwise Pope would have a wonderful opportunity to destroy Jackson's and Longstreet's fragments separately. If it worked, Lee's plan was bold genius; if not, it was suicide on a grand scale.[1]

Jackson's men began moving up the Rappahannock on August 25; that night Lee summoned Stuart to his headquarters. Lee instructed Stuart to overtake Jackson with the bulk of his cavalry; he was to begin his march at two o'clock on the morning of August 26. By the time Stuart returned to his own headquarters, it was 1:00 A.M., so he remained in the saddle all night and made ready to march. Following Jackson's "foot cavalry" was no easy feat. By the time Stuart's horsemen took up the trail, Jackson had already traveled about twenty-four miles and was in camp for the night of August 25–26 at Salem. And on August 26 Jackson marched another twenty-four miles to Bristoe Station. Stuart rode hard to Salem and there encountered Jackson's artillery and wagon train clogging the road. So, just as he had done the last time he followed this route toward Manassas, Stuart left the main road and found a series of paths that took him to Jackson.

The cavalry caught the head of Jackson's column at a place called Gainesville and took up the duty of guarding the flanks of the infantry units. The troopers dashed first into Bristoe Station and captured the place. This was Jackson's objective; when his men occupied Bristoe Station that evening, the Confederates were squarely between Pope's army and Washington.[2]

Jackson was also astride the Orange and Alexandria Railroad, Pope's primary line of supply. As if to emphasize this fact, soon after the Southerners arrived a train roared through the station heading north toward Washington. A hastily built barricade and small-arms fire failed to stop the train; but Stuart and Jackson resolved to be prepared for the next one. They ordered a switch on the track thrown open so as to derail the next train. Then the two generals climbed a nearby hill to watch the train wreck. On cue a train came chugging up the tracks toward the open switch. Then did Stuart turn to Jackson and ask if he was absolutely sure the switch was positioned correctly. Jackson responded that he thought so. Stuart wanted more certainty than that, so he called out, "Blackford, gallop down there and see if it is all right." Blackford spurred his horse Comet down the hill; but when he reached a point just above the switch, it had grown too dark for him to see the device. So he dismounted and hurried down the bank to inspect the switch. He found it properly set to derail the engine and send the train tumbling off down the embankment into a ravine. By this time the train was almost on top of him, and Southern troops had begun to fire into the boxcars. Blackford realized that if he tried to scramble back to his horse he would almost certainly be shot by mistake by one of his own men. He did the only thing possible under the circumstances: he sprinted across the tracks just in front of the engine and then up the tracks far enough to be clear of the impending wreck.

Blackford had the best view of the crash. When the engineer realized that Confederates were firing on his train, he opened the throttle and so roared into the open switch (at about fifty miles per hour). The engine left the tracks and plunged into the ravine followed by many boxcars. Only when the pile of cars reached the level of the tracks did the crashing cease. Then only could Blackford recross the tracks and look for his horse. Comet was nowhere to be seen, however, and Blackford trudged back up the hill to the point at which he had left Stuart. But Stuart was gone, too; Jackson had sent him and his cavalry to Manassas to capture a huge Federal depot there. Blackford learned from members of Jackson's staff that Comet had returned without his rider and that Stuart had dispatched a search party to find him. When the searchers found nothing, Stuart presumed him dead and took Comet on the expedition to Manassas. Blackford had no choice but to spend the night at Bristoe Station and follow Stuart to Manassas the following day. In so doing he had the chance to plan more train wrecks. The portion of the Federal train that remained on the tracks had red lanterns attached to the rear car to signal an approaching train of its existence. The Confederates simply smashed these lanterns and watched the next train slam into the first. Blackford then smashed the lanterns on the rear of that train; but by this time a message must have reached the engineer of the following train, for he stopped and backed down the tracks in the direction from which he had come.[3]

While Blackford was enjoying his train demolition, Stuart approached Manassas. He sent Wickham's 4th Virginia to the other side of the town and advanced on the place with only a portion of Robertson's brigade. The rest of the cavalry Stuart had already assigned picket duty or had sent off on other missions. Jackson reinforced Stuart with Isaac R. Trimble's brigade of infantry. Stuart's troopers reached Manassas well after dark and encountered enemy artillery fire as they approached. Then Stuart and Trimble supposedly agreed to postpone any concerted assault until daylight. And next morning (August 27) Stuart claimed to have captured the place after overwhelming a small Federal garrison. But Trimble also claimed to have captured Manassas "some hours" before the cavalry arrived, and a minor controversy ensued which served primarily to enliven some hours the following winter when Stuart and Trimble wrote their reports of the action of August 27.[4]

Manassas was a prize; there the Federals had stored vast quantities of supplies and had not had the chance to destroy them before capture as they had at White House in June. Von Borcke recalled, "It was exceedingly amusing to see here a ragged fellow regaling himself with a box of pickled oysters or potted lobster; there another cutting into a cheese of enormous size, or emptying a bottle of champagne; while hundreds were engaged in opening the packages of boots and shoes and other clothing, and fitting themselves with articles of apparel to replace their own tattered garments."[5]

Stuart was delighted with his capture and probably even more delighted when Jackson arrived; he, not Stuart, would have to see the confiscation of the liquor on hand and reimpose some order upon the massed looters which the army had become. Then Blackford appeared, as though risen from the dead. Stuart hugged him, and other members of the staff told him that they were about to send a wagon back to Bristoe Station to retrieve his body for burial.[6]

Stuart spent most of this day (August 27) organizing others. He sent Fitz Lee and three regiments toward Fairfax Court House to harass enemy communication. He sent two more regiments (Mumford's and Rosser's) with Richard Ewell's infantry division. He had other regiments picketing the broad front between Jackson's troops and Pope's army. And as a consequence of these dispersions, he had very few horsemen left with him. He used these troopers to help burn whatever Federal stores the Confederates could not move and to protect Jackson's rear when he left Manassas very late in the day. Whether Stuart planned it or did it instinctively, he found that his cavalry could best serve the army in this campaign by dispersing among the various infantry elements involved. Stuart's challenge was to coordinate his units on picket, his regiments guarding flanks and rear, and his raiding expedition (Fitz Lee). At the same time he retained with him sufficient men to employ in special tasks, and the special task that most concerned him now was the junction of Longstreet's force with Jackson's.

Thus early on the morning of August 28, Stuart sought and received Jackson's permission to take those troopers who remained with him and ride west to investigate reports of enemy along Longstreet's projected route. Stuart went as far as the village of Haymarket, approximately halfway between Jackson's position at Groveton and Thoroughfare Gap, where Longstreet was meeting some Federal resistance on his way across Bull Run Mountain. Stuart was able to send word of Jackson's circumstance to Longstreet and Lee, who was with him. His cavalry spent most of the day skirmishing with enemy troops near Haymarket, and returned to Jackson after dark that night. Pope knew that a large body of Confederates (Jackson's men) threatened him and his supply line, so he decided to fight them. He also knew that more Confederates (Longstreet's men) were on the march somewhere; but in his zeal to strike an enemy nearby, Pope dismissed, or seemed to, the possibility that he might be entering a trap.[7]

Next morning (August 29) while Pope massed his men to attack Jackson, Stuart again set out to find Longstreet. This time he found Lee and Longstreet between Haymarket and Gainesville, and behind their commanders the Confederate troops raised a dust cloud that was visible for miles. Stuart, Longstreet, and Lee rode well ahead of the infantry column, while Stuart described the situation in front of Jackson; then Lee and Stuart dismounted and sat in the grass beside the road to continue the conference. Stuart took out a map and pointed out the best route to Jackson's relief. Lee ordered Stuart to take up a position on Longstreet's right flank, and the infantry column enjoyed a brief rest while the horsemen passed through the line of march.[8]

Not long after resuming the march Robertson brought word to Stuart of a sizable body of Federal infantry ahead. Stuart spurred to the front and found Rosser's men skirmishing with the enemy. As Stuart watched, he counted and soon realized that there was an entire army corps marching up a road system that would lead the Federals onto Longstreet's flank. This was Fitz John Porter's corps, and it threatened disaster. Thus far Lee had had everything his way. Pope had had the opportunity to impose his army between Jackson and Longstreet and had failed to take advantage of his good fortune. Instead the Federal general had ignored Longstreet and become preoccupied with Jackson. Even now Pope was committing his forces against Jackson, while Longstreet approached his flank. Porter's corps, however, might wreck Lee's splendid chance for a decisive victory. Longstreet could not very well crush Pope's flank if his own flank was being crushed by Porter.

Stuart knew enough of the Southern circumstance to know the threat Porter posed. His first response was to direct large numbers of his men to cut pine boughs and drag them up and down the dusty roads. The dust cloud raised by the horsemen made Porter believe that many of his enemies were just over the next hill. Thus Porter paused. Next Stuart rode rapidly to Lee and reported Porter's presence. Longstreet then sent three infantry brigades and some artillery to the ridge from which Stuart had made his observations. The Southern artillery exchanged fire with the Federals; but Porter did not press the issue.[9]

At some point during the tense afternoon Stuart delivered some report to Lee and then waited for directions from the commanding general. Lee had no orders for Stuart just then, but asked him to remain nearby. Almost immediately Stuart lay down in some grass, rolled a large rock into place as a pillow, and went to sleep. Lee seemed to forget about him and rode off on some errand. After an hour Lee returned with instructions for Stuart. No sooner did he mention Stuart's name than Stuart rose from his nap, instantly awake as usual. "Here I am, General." Lee wanted some of the cavalry shifted from one portion of the field to another. Stuart announced that he would deliver the necessary messages personally; he mounted immediately and rode off at a gallop singing "Jine the Cavalry" at the top of his lungs. Longstreet knew Stuart pretty well by this time. Nevertheless he was once more amazed at the cavalry commander's capacity to sleep and awaken almost mechanically.[10]

During the afternoon of August 29 Longstreet's men moved into position at a right angle to Jackson's line. Still Pope seemed oblivious of Longstreet and hurled assaults at Jackson's position. Porter remained in place on Longstreet's flank until dark. Then amid a confusion in orders, Porter withdrew and marched to join

Pope's line. Still Pope ignored the 25,000 Confederates who threatened his flank and concentrated only upon Jackson's position to his front.[11]

Next morning (August 30) Stuart probed what had been Porter's front and found the Federals gone. He pressed forward and sent a scout up a large walnut tree to survey the scene. The scout reported no Federals of consequence in front of Longstreet; in the distance were three lines of Union infantry slowly forming again to attack Jackson's position. Stuart quickly informed Lee of what his scout had seen and made ready to join the fun (later known as the Second Battle of Manassas/Bull Run).

About three o'clock in the afternoon Longstreet launched his attack and began to roll up Pope's exposed flank. Stuart had with him Rosser's regiment and Robertson with most of his brigade; the horsemen advanced on the far right of Longstreet's battle line. Stuart collected some artillery pieces and let Rosser exercise his old skills as an artillery commander. While artillery shells crashed into the Federal ranks, the Southern infantry advanced. By dark Pope's army held a desperate perimeter around the stone bridge over Bull Run, and during the night the Federals crossed the stream. As the Southern cavalry advanced, Federal horsemen offered battle. Stuart later claimed that his men (Robertson's) were outnumbered but "put the enemy, under [John] Buford, to ignominious flight across Bull Run" and rendered 300 Federal horsemen *hors de combat*.[12]

Lee had beaten Pope very badly; now he wanted to destroy his army. But although the Confederates pursued aggressively, Pope extricated his army from potential disaster, and on September 2 began to cross the Potomac to the safety of the defensive works around Washington.

Stuart had spent an active several days; certainly he and his cavalry had contributed to the Southern victory. He had managed to detach his horsemen to picket fronts and protect flanks and still retain enough troopers with him to operate in strength. He clearly understood the campaign as it unfolded and anticipated the need to communicate between dispersed elements of the army. He was tireless at collecting information and surely creative in generating the great dust cloud that made Porter halt his march toward Longstreet's flank. For all his personal flamboyance, Stuart seemed to be blending extremely well into the command organization of the Army of Northern Virginia—in Lee's words, performing "most important and valuable service." [13]

However much Stuart served the organization that was Lee's army and made the actions of his horse soldiers mesh with the larger mission of that army, war was still an intensely personal matter for the cavalry chieftain. On August 31, the day after the climax of the Second Manassas (Bull Run) campaign Stuart was across Bull Run pressing the enemy rear guard with a moving artillery duel. Pelham and the Stuart Horse Artillery were shelling enemy guns and gunners and moving forward as the Federals withdrew. Stuart was sitting on his horse watching his gun crews work when a rider arrived and reported the capture of a deserter. It seemed that Stuart's skirmishers had overrun an enemy artillery unit and captured some of the men. And one of the cavalry troopers recognized one of the prisoners as having once belonged to his company of Confederates. Stuart heard the story and said, "Bring him up."

The prisoner soon appeared with some of his captors. He was quite young and inexplicably nonchalant; indeed he seemed to regard the entire proceeding as something of a bore. Stuart, on the other hand, was quite intent. He equated desertion with treachery and his romantic soul abhorred treachery above most sins.

Stuart questioned the captors first, and they confirmed the original report. Moreover they said that the prisoner acknowledged his crime. "Acknowledges it!" Stuart exclaimed in disbelief. Then he turned to the young man, who continued to seem calmly detached, almost as though he had not understood the language his accusers spoke. Stuart asked his name; he answered. Stuart asked his place of birth; he told him. Stuart asked if he had once belonged to the Southern army; "Yes, sir." Stuart inquired if he indeed had been a member of the Union artillery unit that had until recently been firing upon the Southerners; he had. The prisoner answered each question politely, but matter-of-factly, as though his answers were academic instead of incriminating.

The interrogation over, the young man convicted out of his own mouth, Stuart could only stare in disbelief at this apparently brazen turncoat. Then Stuart's stare turned into a glare; desertion was heinous, and this young man's casual demeanor compounded his

crime. Good and evil were at stake here, and the prisoner's attitude was an affront—to good and to Stuart as the agent of good.

One final time Stuart reconfirmed the facts of the case. "So you
were in our ranks, and you went over to the enemy?"

"Yes, sir."

"You were a private in that battery yonder?"

"Yes, sir."

Stuart looked about him quickly and then addressed an officer
who stood by. He spoke an order and a sentence. "Hang him on
that tree!"

Quite suddenly the young man's demeanor changed; now he
realized the consequence of his actions. He was instantly pale; his
eyes were red. For a moment he was silent. Then he tried to speak
and merely gasped. Finally words formed, and he spoke weakly,
thickly, as though he had just awakened. "I didn't know . . . I
never meant—when I went over to Maryland—to fight against the
South. They made me; I had nothing to eat—I told them I was a
Southerner—and so help me God I never fired a shot. I was with
the wagons. Oh! General, spare me; I never—" His voice failed
him again. The young man could only stand and tremble before
Stuart.

The general stroked his beard; he was weighing the balance.
His adversary was literally quaking before him; he delivered a
reprieve. "Take him back to General Lee, and report the circumstances." [14]

Stuart had learned and practiced a lot about his profession; he
could be a good soldier within a large army in a big war. But he
remained a knight with a quest as well as a general with a mission.
His natural inclination was to reduce complex matters to their
simplest terms. He wanted to perceive this war as combat between
individuals; at base his orientation was personal, not corporate or
institutional. The young deserter had challenged Stuart with his
unconcern; his callous attitude about his actions called into question Stuart's values. So Stuart reacted by ordering the young man
hanged immediately. Then when the deserter had seen graphi-
cally the error of his ways, Stuart could be magnanimous; he and
his values had prevailed. The story of the young deserter is about
Stuart's attitude toward desertion, to be sure. But it is also about
the way Stuart perceived himself and responded to the world in

which he lived—simply, directly, personally—"Hang him on that tree."

Stuart dealt with the young deserter in less time than this narration and exegesis of the story has consumed. He and his cavalry continued to press at the heels of the retreating Federals. By September 2 Stuart was back at his old headquarters, Qui Vive, near Fairfax Court House. From there he wrote Flora that recent days had produced "victory upon victory" and that he had been part of every fight. He also broke the news of the death of his cousin and staff officer Hardeman Stuart. The young signal officer had lost his horse on the eve of Second Manassas/Bull Run and had marched into battle with Longstreet's infantry on August 30. He was killed in action later in the day.[15]

On September 4 Stuart was at Dranesville, the scene of his battle the previous December. He described the action for Von Borcke and pointed out some actions he would now have taken differently. From there he announced to Flora that "long before this reaches you I will be in Md." Lee had decided to retain the initiative and invade western Maryland; Stuart was to screen the movement of the Southern army as it moved north. Momentum and morale seemed certainly on the Confederate side. As Stuart pointed out to Flora, "Our present position on the banks of the Potomac will tell you volumes." And Lieutenant Channing Price, one of Stuart's new (since July) staff officers, wrote his mother, "I don't believe there is a Yankee in Virginia, this side of Alexandria." The Federals were indeed in Washington and very much on the defensive, as Lee prepared for his first invasion of enemy country.[16]

At long last Stuart would have his entire cavalry division with him for the Maryland campaign. Hampton's brigade came up to join Fitz Lee's and Beverly Robertson's. Robertson, however, would not be traveling north; instead, on September 5, he was relieved and sent south. The order stated that "his services are indispensably necessary for the organization and instruction of cavalry troops from North Carolina."

Stuart was delighted. He had neither said nor done anything officially to injure Robertson; but he didn't like the man, and he believed him less than competent to command his brigade. Ostensibly Jackson seemed to have had the most influence in Robertson's fate; he had complained about him to Lee. Yet Stuart, too, must have had a voice in the matter.

Ever since the middle of August, Stuart had been making his headquarters with Robertson and spending time with his brigade. Hampton and Fitz Lee received the quasi-independent assignments, while Stuart stuck with Robertson. Most likely Stuart did so because he did not trust Robertson to function independently and because he wanted to evaluate the man firsthand. Very clearly someone or something convinced Lee, who convinced Jefferson Davis that Robertson would be a liability in the coming Maryland campaign. For the time being Thomas T. Munford, senior regimental commander, took charge of the brigade.[17]

Stuart could work with men with whom he could not be friends; he usually gave them quasi-independent assignments and directed them from afar. He seemed to try to avoid unpleasantness and confrontation, and when he did occasionally explode at someone, he often sought the person out later, hugged him, told him that he loved him, made light of his outburst.[18]

It was not always that easy. In the midst of the Maryland campaign, Stuart became perturbed at the conduct of a company commanded by Elijah V. White, who had spent his youth near Poolesville, a town that lay in the path of the invading Confederate army. "Lige" White and his "Comanches" were part of Turner Ashby's legacy, hard-riding but unruly men who possessed their own ideas about conducting this war. White himself said it best on an occasion when some Southern pickets fired on his company as it approached friendly lines. Understandably White was much annoyed at having been shot at and vented considerable rage at the men of the picket post. One of them snapped, "If you wasn't a Captain you shouldn't talk that way." White responded, "No I ain't; I'm no Captain; I'm Lige White, and can whip you any way! Come on! I dare you!" Like the rest of his men, White was more fighter than soldier.[19]

On the march into Maryland, the Comanches ran afoul of Stuart in some way or other, and Stuart determined to send the unit back to Virginia. White protested and insisted that he be permitted to help liberate his native state. The two argued; Stuart ordered White to leave the army; White refused and vowed to take his case to Lee. "Come on," said Stuart, "I'll go with you." So the general and the captain went to see Lee. Stuart went first to speak to the commanding general, then returned to White. "Capt. White, did you say you was a Marylander?"

"Yes, sir."

"Ah! . . . I didn't know that. Gen. Lee wants you. Go in and see him."

Lee resolved the matter by sending the Comanches off to scout for him, thus releasing the company from Stuart's direct command. Once more Stuart, with Lee's help, had avoided confrontation by avoiding an adversary.[20]

Stuart assembled his division at Dranesville and declared September 4 a day of rest. Next morning the massed horsemen rode west to Leesburg, where Stuart conferred with Lee, Jackson, and Longstreet. The immediate task of the cavalry was to form a curtain of outposts across Maryland twenty miles long, east of Lee's army. When the Federals approached from Washington, as sooner or later they would, the cavalry was to fend them off as long as possible and provide Lee with timely intelligence about their strength, location, and likely intent. Lee's adversary in this campaign would again be George B. McClellan. On the same day Lee met with his principal subordinates at Leesburg, John Pope received a summons from Federal General-in-Chief Henry Halleck; soon after he was bound for the Department of the Platte to fight rebellious Sioux instead of Southern rebels.[21]

In the afternoon (September 5) the cavalry crossed the Potomac at White's Ford and entered Maryland. The Confederates came as liberators to Maryland, expecting to find a people sympathetic with the Southern cause and tired of the "tyrant's heel." Stuart's report of the campaign speaks of "the greatest demonstrations of joy" among Marylanders. Yet the initial reception did not impress Von Borcke, and on the whole inhabitants of the western part of the state tended more toward Unionist sympathies. Nevertheless Stuart and his comrades did encounter Southern enthusiasm as they rode into enemy country. After camping for the night near Poolesville, Stuart the next day (September 6) continued north to Urbana, where he decided to make his headquarters. He left the chore of establishing the headquarters with Von Borcke and rode on to Frederick, where Jackson had gone. Von Borcke was to follow Stuart to Frederick; he did so, but never found him amid

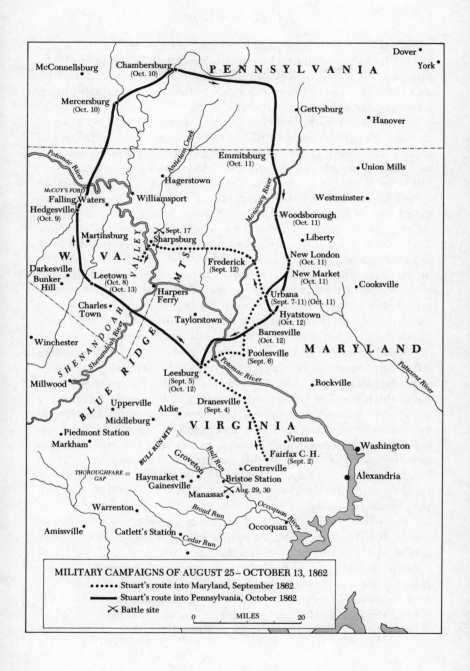

McConnellsburg

Chambersburg
(Oct. 10)

PENNSYLVANIA

Dover
York

Mercersburg
(Oct. 10)

Gettysburg

Hanover

*Anthem Creek*

*Potomac River*

Emmitsburg
(Oct. 11)

Union Mills

Hagerstown

*Monocacy River*

Westminster

*McCOY'S FORD*
Falling Waters

Williamsport

Woodsborough
(Oct. 11)

Hedgesville
(Oct. 9)

Sept. 17
Sharpsburg

Liberty

W.    VA.

Martinsburg

*VALLEY*

New London
(Oct. 11)

Darkesville

Leetown
(Oct. 8)
(Oct. 13)

Frederick
(Sept. 12)

New Market
(Oct. 11)

Bunker
Hill

*S. MTS.*

Cooksville

Charles
Town

Harpers
Ferry

Urbana
(Sept. 7-11) (Oct. 11)

Winchester

Taylorstown

Hyatstown
(Oct. 12)

*SHENANDOAH*

*Shenandoah River*

Barnesville
(Oct. 12)

MARYLAND

Millwood

*BLUE   RIDGE*

Leesburg
(Sept. 5)
(Oct. 12)

Poolesville
(Sept. 6)

*Potomac River*

Rockville

*Patuxent River*

Upperville

Aldie

Dranesville
(Sept. 4)

Middleburg

VIRGINIA

Vienna

Washington

Piedmont Station

*BULL RUN MTS.*

Groveton

*Bull Run*

Fairfax C. H.
(Sept. 2)

Markham

*THOROUGHFARE*
*GAP*

Haymarket
Gainesville

Centreville

Alexandria

Bristoe Station

Manassas

Aug. 29, 30

Warrenton

*Broad Run*

*Occoquan River*

Amissville

Catlett's Station

*Cedar Run*

Occoquan

MILITARY CAMPAIGNS OF AUGUST 25 – OCTOBER 13, 1862
••••••  Stuart's route into Maryland, September 1862
———  Stuart's route into Pennsylvania, October 1862
✕  Battle site

0          MILES          20

admiring crowds of local people who mistook every Southern officer for Jackson or Stuart. Once again Stuart had "disappeared." In
this case he was probably purchasing shoes and gloves for Flora
and the children and bestowing his buttons and autograph upon
admirers. He soon reappeared at Urbana.[22]

Once Stuart had dispersed his brigades and satisfied himself
that his picket line was in place, the general and his staff could
relax a bit. Headquarters was in a "nice grassy yard in the village"
near the home of a man named Cockey; the officers went there
often for their meals. Several "very charming and pretty young
ladies" were visiting there and others from the vicinity congregated wherever Stuart and his staff went. Stuart's favorite female
among many admirers seemed to be a young woman from New
York who was visiting the Cockey house. He dubbed her the New
York Rebel because of her especially vehement Southern sentiments. The officers, Stuart included, kept their horses saddled and
slept on the ground in their uniforms, boots, and spurs with weapons at hand. Stuart was prepared for action and vigilant in seeing
that his duty got done. But for a few precious days very little duty
needed doing, and the men took full advantage of the respite.

Stuart led a small, brief social season at Urbana. Following an
afternoon dinner, conversation still sparkled and music broke forth
until dark. Then the company became couples for evening strolls
about the town. The promenades most often led to a large building
which had housed an academy but which was empty because of
the war. From wide verandas that circled each story of the structure, the young men and women gazed into the distance and
enjoyed moonlit vistas of the countryside. As one participant
recalled, "One hour's acquaintance in war times goes further towards good feeling and acquaintanceship than months in the dull,
slow period of peace."

The officers who described in letters and memoirs their brief
peace in Urbana took pains to protest their readiness for military
action in the midst of all this social activity. And at Urbana and
elsewhere members of Stuart's staff affirmed that Stuart indulged
in none but the most innocent pleasures. He continued rigidly to
eschew alcohol himself and actively to discourage others from im-
bibing too freely. He still enjoyed the company of women, especially young, witty, and attractive women; but although Stuart was

free with his quips, his buttons, and his kisses, he apparently offered no more of himself in his relationships with his "sweethearts." The officers who surrounded Stuart were by nature high-spirited, virile young men; he attracted such followers and encouraged their liveliness. Certainly all of the members of Stuart's staff were neither so abstemious nor so innocent as their leader. Stuart's coterie was no Sunday school class, after all. Yet Stuart set the tone at his "court," and neither was his retinue a collection of drunken rowdies. In fact, during the Urbana interlude, one of Stuart's guests at his headquarters was the Rev. Charles Minnigerode, rector of St. Paul's Episcopal Church in Richmond.[23]

During the evening of September 7, while young men and women were enjoying each others' company at the abandoned Urbana academy building, Stuart broke the softness of the moment and called to Von Borcke, "Major, what a capital place for us to give a ball in honour of our arrival in Maryland! Don't you think we could manage it?" From many private places in the building came encouraging cries, and at once the ball was set for the following evening. Von Borcke decorated the hall with regimental battle flags and sent invitations to local civilians and the officers of nearby regiments. Stuart himself secured a band from the 18th Mississippi Infantry and invited that regiment's colonel and his staff.

The New York Rebel reigned as the queen of the occasion, and Von Borcke asked her to dance the first dance with him. Appropriately the Prussian had selected a polka. Great was his chagrin when his intended partner informed him that she and other "proper ladies" never danced polkas or waltzes with men to whom they were not related. Quickly, however, Von Borcke resolved his dilemma: he ordered the band to alter the tempo and announced a quadrille. Despite the makeshift circumstances, or perhaps because of them, the ball began perfectly. But just as the revelers relaxed and began to enjoy the moment, the war intruded.

Artillery boomed nearby, and as though to quash wishful thoughts that the crashing noise was thunder, the sound of small-arms fire rattled as well. Then came a courier to Stuart reporting a Federal attack upon one of the outposts. Rapidly the officers buckled on their sabers and sought their horses. The cavalrymen dashed toward the battle sounds and found indeed an outpost under attack. However, Pelham's artillery broke up the assault, and Stuart ordered a regiment to charge the Federals. The charge soon became a chase and when the Confederates had galloped a few miles in pursuit of their foes, they returned. It had been a small, sharp fight, but it was over. And because it was just after midnight, many of the officers returned to Urbana to resume the ball.

Stuart ordered the music to begin again, and the women who had remained on the scene fawned over men just back from battle. About the time Stuart's party returned to life, Blackford heard heavy footsteps outside the hall. His dancing partner peered out the door and let out a "piercing scream." The skirmish at the outpost had been a minor affair; still, men had been wounded and now their comrades were carrying the casualties into the academy for care. The ball was instantly over as the women became "ministering angels" to the wounded soldiers. The New York Rebel worked to cleanse the shoulder wound of one young man until she fainted. Blackford and Von Borcke revived her and tried to persuade her to go home; but she refused to leave until she had finished mopping the man's blood and dressing his wound. Only when the injured man himself begged her would she leave.

During the next two days (September 9 and 10) Federal pressure upon Stuart's chain of outposts increased. Finally, on the morning of September 11, Stuart began to withdraw before advancing columns of Federal infantry. Stuart remained on Mr. Cockey's veranda chatting with the women until the last possible moment. He and his staff waved good-bye—farewell to "Urbannaties," as one officer punned—shortly after two o'clock in the afternoon and galloped away. Urbana fell to the Federals ten minutes later.[24]

Stuart rode next to Frederick. He attempted to coordinate the actions and movements of his brigades and regiments so as to delay the enemy as long as possible. He also sought to show enough force to compel the Federals to reveal their total strength in order that he might inform Lee. Lee's instructions to Stuart on September 12 were to send him information about the enemy and deny the enemy knowledge of the whereabouts and movement of Southern forces. The commanding general needed this information desperately, because he had once again dispersed his army quite widely. Jackson's corps was investing Harpers Ferry, while Longstreet's divisions were scattered about western Maryland. Lee knew and Stuart realized that the Army of Northern Virginia would have to concentrate in order to fight McClellan under any circumstances. And this was especially true in this circumstance, because McClellan's army outnumbered Lee's by approximately 84,000 to 55,000.[25]

Crucial to the campaign at this point (September 12) were the passes through the mountains west of Frederick. Because of those gaps and because of increased Federal strength, Stuart did not remain long in Frederick. He was there long enough to greet admirers, however, and to impress one young man who had come there to serve Federal wounded. Dwight Dudley was a hospital attendant who remained in Frederick after the Federals evacuated the place and observed the Confederate occupation. He encountered Stuart while walking down the street and looking at a group of Southern officers gathered on a porch. One of them called to Dudley and advanced to the yard to speak with him. The officer pointed out that his army had not harmed Unionist civilians in Frederick and then asked a favor. "I want you to tell your commanding general when he comes, that we have treated his friends here with great kindness, that we expect the same treatment for ours, and unless they receive it, I will doubly retaliate at each and every opportunity . . . I am General Stuart."[26]

Dudley's commanding general did soon reach Frederick—on September 13—and when McClellan arrived, his subordinates had a rare treat for him. A Federal soldier had found at Frederick a copy of Lee's Special Order No. 191, which revealed the entire Confederate invasion plan, including the projected locations of the scattered Southern troop units. If McClellan acted quickly he could destroy the Southern army piecemeal. McClellan delayed. He waited until he could confirm the information contained in Lee's order, and a Southern sympathizer in Frederick was able to send word to Lee of McClellan's find.

Still, McClellan did order a general advance, and Lee had to reassemble his army in haste while massed columns of infantry converged upon Sharpsburg and the banks of Antietam Creek. The Battle of Antietam that followed on September 17 was the bloodi-

est single day in the entire gory war. McClellan that day commanded 70,000 troops, Lee about 39,000, and some of these
arrived barely in time for the fight. The action began early on the
Confederate left and during the day rolled down the long battle
line in front of Sharpsburg. The Federals assaulted one corps at a
time, and Lee was able (frantically at times) to shift his limited
numbers to meet each threat in turn. McClellan never seemed to
realize his enemy's peril. Military analysts usually agree that the
Federals should have crushed the Confederates, driven them
through the town and into the Potomac River. But McClellan
never mounted a decisive attack against the trembling Southern
line, although he had ample chances to do so. So more than 26,000
men (13,700 Confederates, 12,350 Union) became casualties in
what was tactically a drawn battle. On September 18 McClellan
received reinforcements and still another opportunity to destroy
Lee's weakened force. Yet the Federal commander did not renew
the combat, and during the night (September 18) Lee managed to
cross the Potomac and extricate his army from potential disaster.[27]

Cavalry could be of little consequence during such a battle.
Stuart assisted the infantry in holding the gaps in the mountains
against the Federals. He then rode to the vicinity of Harpers Ferry
(Maryland Heights) to share what he knew of the area with Lafayette McLaws, who commanded Confederate infantry on the Maryland side of the Potomac. He rode to Crampton's Gap and tried to
help Howell Cobb impose some order upon a shattered command.
He returned to Harpers Ferry, conferred with Jackson, and then
rode to Sharpsburg to report Jackson's situation to Lee. Finally,
Stuart assembled what he could of his cavalry division and took
up a position on the extreme left (north) of the Confederate battle
line along Antietam Creek before Sharpsburg. The troopers, especially Pelham's artillery, took some part in the resultant battle and
then undertook the task of protecting Lee's retreat back into Virginia.

The great invasion of the North had come to grief. The Army of
Northern Virginia licked its wounds on its home turf, and Mc-
Clellan seemed again reticent to follow his foes. For the present
Lee's army rested along Opequan Creek in the lower (northern)
Shenandoah Valley. Stuart's horsemen established their line of
pickets before the army, and Stuart himself made his headquarters
at the Bower, the home of A. Stephen Dandridge.

The Bower was about ten miles west of Charles Town, about eight miles south of Martinsburg, not far from the village of Leetown. The Dandridge family was extended; at the time it included "a house full of daughters and nieces, all grown and all attractive." And to augment the household came visitors and relatives from the region. The large house crowned a hill overlooking Opequan Creek. Huge old oaks shaded the grounds and the headquarters encampment a few hundred yards from the house. Stuart's staff, assorted hangers-on, and slaves belonging to the officers totaled almost a hundred men. Outside the cluster of tents that sheltered the people, two hundred horses grazed at their picket ropes. The Dandridges definitely had lots of company, and the company remained at the Bower for a full month. Yet Stuart's hosts continued to be delighted to have their guests, and Blackford spoke for the entire company when he later proclaimed, "The month passed at the Bower was the most remarkable combination of romance and real life that it had ever been my fortune to encounter." This was the best headquarters Stuart ever had; at least that seems the consensus among those who were there.[28]

As was the case during the sojourn in Urbana, Maryland, the men had work to do and did it. Yet because of the duties, dispersion, and mobility of the cavalry, Stuart's subordinate units (brigades, regiments, even companies) were more independent, logistically and administratively, than were comparable units of infantry. Consequently Stuart and his staff had less work to do than their counterparts in other branches of the army. Stuart probably could have been an excellent administrator—he had proven that in the "old army"; but the fact was that in the Confederate army he never quite had to be. He had to communicate unceasingly with his far-flung outposts and with his superiors. But he seldom had to worry from day to day about rations, forage, and the like. These chores, by necessity, he delegated. During this period Stuart did allow himself to get behind in his formal reports. He wrote his report of the Seven Days Campaign (June 25–July 1, 1862), for example, on July 14, 1862; Stuart did not write his report on Antietam (September 1862) until February 13, 1864.[29]

When their abbreviated workday ended at the Bower, officers usually assembled at the Dandridge home to meet their hosts and the young women of the family and neighborhood. They rode, strolled, and fished until time for tea, to which they were all in-

vited. Music, dancing, singing, and parlor games followed tea.
Moonlit walks and boating on the Opequan often concluded the
evening. Stuart made such frivolity possible and was himself "the
life of the party." He provided the principal musicians, Sam Sweeney with his banjo and Bob on the bones and sometimes the violin.
Stuart often chose the tune and led the singing and dancing. If the
group had an anthem, it was the exuberant, driving rhythm of
"Jine the Cavalry," which always closed the performance.

> If you want to smell hell—
> Jine the Cavalry—

Tiernan Brien and Von Borcke provided dramatic entertain-
ment during some evenings at the Bower. On one occasion they
stretched a sheet across a hall and arranged the lighting so that the
two men performed as shadows to the audience. Von Borcke lay
on his back wearing a huge nightshirt stuffed about the stomach
with pillows. He groaned in obvious agony from having overeaten.
Brien played the physician in a stovepipe hat, swallow-tailed coat,
and oversized spectacles. After speaking considerable medical
gibberish, Brien relieved the suffering of his patient by pretending
to reach down Von Borcke's throat and extracting all manner of
foreign objects—deer antlers, whole cabbages, oyster shells, and
boots. The cure concluded, patient and doctor took swigs from a
bottle of "medicine" and closed the show with a mock-tipsy dance.
Another performance featured Brien dressed and made up as a
stereotypical Irishman and Von Borcke disguised as a six-foot-
three, 250-pound fair damsel. Only when the pair danced and Von
Borcke's boots appeared from beneath his skirts did the audience
realize the identities of the two players. Stuart responded by em-
bracing his Prussian aide and declaring, "My dear old Von, if I
could ever forget you as I know you on the field of battle, your
appearance as a woman would never fade from my memory."

Even the weather cooperated with Stuart and his staff. The
autumn of 1862 in northern Virginia brought bright, warm days
and cool nights, and the turning leaves transformed hillsides into
mosaics. The staff usually ate under a large dining fly in the open
air. They dined well upon freshly killed game and fruits of the
local harvest. Of course all this easy living was much easier be-

cause most of the white officers had black slaves to cook and clean and care for their personal needs.[30]

News of jolly times at the Bower spread, and Stuart often had visitors at his headquarters. Two of his more welcome guests were Francis Lawley, Richmond correspondent for the *Times* of London, and Frank Vizetelly, who sketched the American war for the *London Illustrated News*. Stuart was a colorful subject for these international journalists and for the Confederate press as well. The *Southern Illustrated News*, modeled after Vizetelly's journal, featured Stuart in its September 27, 1862, issue. A sketch of Stuart dominated page one, and a glowing prose sketch followed. Stuart's military motto was *"de l'audace, encore de l'audace, toujours de l'audace."* According to the author, "He is not less instant in prayer than watchful upon the march and fearful in fight." About Stuart a lot of what sounded like patriotic extravagance was indeed true, or nearly so. And Stuart certainly did not discourage his growing fame.[31]

The month at the Bower was not without interruption and military alarms. On October 1 Union General Alfred Pleasonton led a cavalry reconnaissance in force of about 700 troopers against the Confederate pickets outside Martinsburg. Rooney Lee, commanding a brigade in his cousin's stead (Fitz Lee was recovering from a mule kick), apparently forgot to warn Wade Hampton as he had agreed to do under such circumstances, and suddenly Hampton found Martinsburg in possession of the enemy. Then Stuart rode up and did not appreciate one bit the fact that Federals were firing at him from the town. He summoned Lee and Hampton and announced, "Gentlemen, this thing will not do; I will give you twenty minutes, within which time the town must be again in our possession." Lee and Hampton responded, and within Stuart's time limit, their horsemen were chasing Pleasonton's riders northward. Pelham and four artillery pieces joined the pursuit. The affair ended in darkness at the Potomac.[32]

Stuart the "jolly cavalier" had shown some temper. He did so, probably, for the sake of his pride; Martinsburg was his town. Furthermore he had known Pleasonton at West Point and disliked him then; he had no intention of being embarrassed by the man. But Stuart also knew that his cavalry possessed an aura of invincibility on both sides of the battle line. As a Union clergyman observed in print, "Wherever Stuart rides, he carries terror with him. His victories are half won before he strikes a blow. Our soldiers feel that he may pounce on them at any minute, and that he is as resistless as a hawk in a fowlyard." Stuart wanted his men to believe in themselves; he wanted his enemy to become accustomed to defeat at his hands and get used to running from his horsemen. Stuart often retired before Federal infantry; he respected Federal artillery; but when he faced something like an equal number of Federal cavalry, he expected victory. And he knew that confidence in victory made victory that much easier to achieve.[33]

The relaxed regimen of most of October in 1862 also allowed Stuart chances for visiting. Excursions to Lee's headquarters near Winchester usually involved official duties. However, on one occasion Stuart took with him a present for the commanding general. Lee, it seemed, had injured his hand while attempting to hold his horse Traveller during some heavy action at Second Manassas (Bull Run). Stuart took it upon himself to find Lee a steadier steed. He discovered Lucy Long, a quiet sorrel mare, at the Bower and acquired her for Lee. Lee not only appreciated Stuart's thoughtfulness, he liked Lucy Long, too, and rode her regularly along with Traveller.[34]

Jackson's headquarters were closer—at Bunker Hill, where Stuart himself had made his first headquarters in May of 1861— and Stuart appeared there several times. He and Jackson continued to be friends, although their personalities were all but polar opposites. Moreover Stuart seemed to bring out whatever humor Jackson possessed, and the stern Calvinist attempted some of his few recorded comic remarks when in Stuart's company. One evening when Stuart and Pelham arrived at Bunker Hill very late, Stuart entered Jackson's tent and found him asleep. Undaunted, Stuart removed his saber, crawled into Jackson's bed with him, and during the cool night apparently wrestled Jackson for a greater share of the covers. In the morning Jackson and some of his staff were standing before a campfire when Stuart emerged from the tent.

"Good morning, General Jackson," said Stuart, "how are you?"

"General Stuart, I'm always glad to see you here. You might select better hours sometimes, but I'm always glad to have you. But, General"—as he stooped and rubbed himself along the legs

—"you must not get into my bed with your boots and spurs on and ride me around like a cavalry horse all night." [35]

Once when Stuart could not go himself to visit Jackson, he sent Von Borcke with a present, a gorgeous new uniform coat complete with gilt buttons and gold lace. Jackson was touched. After some coaxing from Von Borcke, he put on the coat, and soldiers reportedly ran by the hundreds to see the spectacle of Jackson in new finery. [36]

The reason Stuart was unable to deliver Jackson's coat himself was that its arrival at the Bower coincided with plans for an extensive raid into enemy country. Stuart had been speaking of another raid with Lee, and on October 8, Lee ordered the expedition. This was to be a raid of some consequence; Lee suggested 1,200–1,500 troopers. The destination was Chambersburg, Pennsylvania, and one goal was the destruction of a railroad bridge over Conococheague Creek just beyond the town. This was also a reconnaissance mission. Lee wanted "all information of the position, force, and probable intention of the enemy." And finally Lee wanted some tangible results from the raid—government officials from Pennsylvania to use as hostages or to exchange for Southern hostages and Pennsylvania horses to replenish the supply of Southern cavalry, artillery, and draft animals. [37]

Stuart decided to take with him 600 men from each of his three brigades. Hampton would accompany his contingent; Rooney Lee took his cousin's place, because Fitz Lee was still recovering from his mule kick; and the Robertson/Munford brigade had a new commander, Grumble Jones  Stuart and Jones were hardly friends; Stuart did not believe Jones would work for him. But for the time being Jones had the command and a general's commission on the way. Pelham would bring four guns and join the expedition. Preparations at headquarters included an address from Stuart to be read to the men. He asked for their "coolness, decision, and bravery," as well as "implicit obedience to orders without question or cavil, and the strictest order and sobriety on the march and in bivouac." Their destination for the moment "had better be kept to myself." He promised them success "which will reflect credit in the highest degree upon your arms." Stuart also wrote and distributed an order prescribing standards of conduct when dealing with enemy civilians and seizing property. He gave specific instructions about transporting captured horses and emphasized his desire to carry off as many animals as possible. He even included in his order some military wisdom: "The attack when made, must be vigorous and overwhelming, giving the enemy no time to collect, reconnoiter or consider anything except his best means of flight."[38]

Order No. 13 was a stream-of-consciousness piece of prose, somewhat resembling Stuart's letters. One reason it was so was R. Channing Price, who had become Stuart's newest adjutant. Price was quite young—in his early twenties—but he was bright and eager. And he possessed a remarkable facility for taking dictation. For some time he had served as secretary to his father, who was blind. The elder Price was a merchant in Richmond and dictated a copious correspondence to his son. This experience sharpened Price's capacity to reproduce verbatim Stuart's spoken words on paper. At the conclusion of the Chambersburg raid, Price also wrote a six-page letter to his mother that is a splendid first-person account of the adventure.[39]

On October 8 Stuart asked Price to assemble all the letters and reports requiring his attention, and he worked for some time at his desk. That evening there was a ball at the Bower, and many merrymakers sensed that this might be their last dance for some time, maybe forever. At eleven o'clock Stuart returned to his tent and completed his work; then at one o'clock in the morning he assembled his staff to offer a farewell serenade to the women of the Bower. Next morning (October 9) Stuart wrote a hurried note to Flora and completed his address to the men and his Order No. 13. Then it was time to leave.[40]

The raiders rode to Darkesville to rendezvous at noon and thence to a place called Hedgesville to camp for the night. At dawn on October 10 Stuart crossed the Potomac at McCoy's Ford and started north. The Southerners just missed a Federal infantry brigade as they rode through western Maryland and about ten o'clock that morning entered Pennsylvania.

Then did the designated horse hunters go to work; 200 of the 600 men in each brigade visited farms and houses along the route and seized horses. In return for the animals the Confederates offered receipts that said the horses were being taken in payment of damages on the part of the United States against the Confederate States. "It was ludicrous in the extreme," Price recalled, "to see the old Dutchmen as their horses were taken in every variety of circumstances." Wade Hampton was also amused: "It was very funny to see the conduct of the Yankees: some took us for Federals; some ran and some gazed at us in perfect bewilderment." Blackford, the engineer officer, went looking for a map before he indulged in any legitimate horse stealing. He found a county map at a home in Mercersburg and cut it from the wall. In the process, however, he suffered considerable verbal abuse from the women who lived there. He used maps to supplement the knowledge of local guides whom Stuart had brought along.[41]

The day was intermittently dark with clouds and showers, and as evening approached the rain became steady. Stuart's column reached the outskirts of Chambersburg about 7:00 P.M.; it was pitch black and raining quite hard. Stuart sent an officer from Hampton's brigade to demand surrender from some official in town. If refused, Stuart threatened to begin artillery shelling within three minutes. Hampton's aide found no one on hand to surrender Chambersburg at first, but finally located some prominent burghers with whom to negotiate. Stuart was soon sitting his horse in the center of town, while Hampton's troopers patrolled the place. He had come forty miles and was once again squarely in the rear of McClellan's army.

Next morning (October 11) the rain still fell while the Southerners surveyed their prize. They found stores of arms and ammunition, as well as military clothing. From these they helped themselves and destroyed whatever they could not carry. They also destroyed railroad machine shops and some loaded trains. While all this destruction was taking place, Grumble Jones confronted the railroad bridge over Conococheague Creek. Unfortunately for Jones, the bridge was built of iron and resisted any attempt to destroy it. Meanwhile the weather cleared and Stuart pondered his escape route.[42]

He knew his enemy was alert, active, and numerous; the principal advantage Stuart possessed was initiative. He decided to make the most of his initiative and attempt once more to ride around McClellan's army. So on the morning of October 11 he directed the column east out of Chambersburg along the road toward Gettysburg. As the march began, Stuart called Blackford to him and rode out a bit ahead. "Blackford, I want to explain my motives to you for taking this lower route [vis-à-vis the Potomac] and if I should fall before reaching Virginia, I want you to vindicate my memory." Then he explained that he expected that infantry would be behind him on the roads over which he had passed en route to Chambersburg. That terrain, too, had been hilly and thus more easily defended; their new route led through open, rolling country where cavalry might operate to better advantage. The distance this way was much greater; but they would march rapidly and try to prevent word of their whereabouts from spreading. Perhaps the most significant advantage of the route around the enemy was its boldness; Stuart was going where the Federals least expected him.

The column eventually stretched over five miles of road. Three scouts rode about 150 yards ahead of the column followed by one squadron as advance guard. Two hundred yards behind the advance guard were 600 massed troopers and an artillery section. Then came 600 more men leading perhaps 1,200 captured horses. Another 600 troopers followed the horse leaders; behind them was another section of artillery, a rear guard squadron, and three lonely scouts. Stuart usually rode just behind the advance guard squadron, and he kept his staff roaming up and down the road carrying messages and encouraging the men to keep the column closed up. If Federals should appear on either flank, the nearest regiment had standing orders to charge them immediately. Stuart forbade the initial use of firearms in any combat to prevent the noise from attracting more attention. The men were to fight with sabers alone until instructed otherwise.[43]

As long as the raiders remained in Pennsylvania, horse collecting continued. At some time during the day several members of the 9th Virginia approached a house in search of food as well. Only women and babies were at home, and one of the women responded indignantly that they had not a crumb in the house. An especially lean-looking soldier then began examining the babies. He said that he did not make a habit of eating humans; but he was just about starved and might have to make an exception in this case. The mothers then discovered that they did indeed have a few morsels about, and very soon the troopers had some dinner.[44]

Stuart turned south about ten miles from Gettysburg and crossed back into Maryland near Emmitsburg. At Emmitsburg the raiders found pro-Confederate crowds to welcome them with cheers, flowers, and food. But Stuart could not linger and pressed ahead toward Frederick. He was astonished not to have encountered any Federals thus far. Even though this day had been sunny, the rain of the previous day had kept the ground moist and prevented the raiders from raising a dust cloud. Nevertheless, Stuart expected some action before he reached Virginia.[45]

Near dark on October 11, Stuart turned off the road to Frederick and began to take full advantage of his guides. The route to the Potomac led through Woodsborough, Liberty, New London, New Market, Hyattstown, and Barnesville, mostly over little-known roads. The troopers rode all night, and most of them had slept very little during the previous two nights. In the moonlight Blackford began seeing things that were not there. "Over and over again I made sure I could not be mistaken; there was the lawn, there the towers, and bay windows as plain as could be, and yet in a moment it was nothing but a clump of trees . . ." To forestall his hallucinations, Blackford periodically dismounted, led his horse, and listened to the snores of his comrades as they rode.

Blackford's walks rested his horse as well as cleared his head. He rode the same horse throughout the raid; most of the men changed horses at least once. Stuart began the expedition with three horses; he returned with only one. Bob, his servant, drank a bit too much captured whiskey, dropped out of the line of march, and succumbed to sleep. He awakened to discover himself and the general's horses, Skylark and Lady Margrave, captives of the Federals.

At New Market Stuart rode near Blackford and asked "How would you like to see the 'New York Rebel' tonight?" Blackford said that he would like that very much. "Come on then." About a dozen riders took a detour through Urbana and around midnight reached the Cockey house. Stuart roused the sleepers inside and everyone present enjoyed a half-hour interlude. Then Stuart galloped away to rejoin the column.[46]

At dawn on October 12 the Confederates were entering Hyattstown. Now they had to be especially wary. The entire Federal army must be looking for them. Stuart's guide led the raiders down byroads and cart tracks on the way to White's Ford on the Potomac. They heard rumors of 4,000 to 5,000 Federal cavalry guarding the fords of the Potomac. Finally, near Barnesville, the Confederates encountered a company of Union horses; the advance guard squadron charged and scattered the Federals.

Soon after this action the raiders reached White's Ford. There they discovered infantry in place, no one knew precisely how many, on the far bank of the Chesapeake and Ohio Canal, which ran very near the river. Rooney Lee called up his artillery and dismounted some men to attack the Federals. The situation did not appear sanguine, however. So close to safety, the raiders had found well-positioned infantry, capable of denying them passage to the ford. Rooney Lee knew he could not dislodge the Federals swiftly in combat; consequently he tried a gigantic bluff. He sent a message to the enemy commander under a flag of truce demanding surrender. Rooney Lee asserted that he had sufficient strength to destroy the Federals and planned to do so within fifteen minutes. The Confederates did have the means to defeat the regiment of infantry—but not without delay, and at this point delay might be fatal. To Rooney Lee's amazed gratification, the Federals withdrew from their strong position. His bluff had worked.

Stuart stationed troopers above and below White's Ford and ordered Blackford to direct traffic across the river. No one was to allow his horse to stop and drink, the column was to keep moving at all costs. Meanwhile Pelham's guns kept in check the Federals who yet lingered on both flanks. And the rear guard, too, was withdrawing before considerable pressure from pursuing Federal cavalry.

At the ford all seemed well. Pelham got some of his guns across and began firing from the Virginia side. The horsemen were filing across as though they were on parade. Then Stuart rode up to Blackford, who was still relaying instructions about not stopping to let the horses drink, and called out, "Blackford, we are going to lose our rear guard."

"How is that, General?"

"I have sent four couriers to Butler [Colonel M.C., who commanded] to call him in, and he is not here, and you can see the enemy is closing in upon us from above and below."

Blackford volunteered to try to get the message to Butler. Perhaps the couriers had become confused about the road system. Stuart assented. He said to tell Butler to circle back through Pennsylvania, if he could not get through. "Tell him to come at a gallop."

Then Blackford dashed away over the labyrinth of trails through the woods. He passed the couriers who had been unable to find Butler and who were now trying to save themselves. At last, after three miles, Blackford found the rear of the column and delivered Stuart's message. They started for the river at a trot, and Blackford repeated Stuart's last instructions. Galloping toward the river, the Confederates urged their horses to expend the last of their energies.

Eventually they saw Pelham and one gun holding a corridor to the ford. The rear guard splashed across the river, and Pelham with his gun followed rapidly on their heels. They were still in the water when the Maryland bank was "swarming with enemy." But guns from the southern side opened and kept the Federals at bay. Stuart was safe. He had started his raid with 1,800 men, and he led 1,800 into Leesburg that afternoon.[47]

The Chambersburg Raid was a remarkable feat. Stuart had ridden around McClellan's army once more. He had traveled 126 miles and covered the final 80 miles without a stop in less than thirty-six hours. En route he had captured about 1,200 horses and destroyed enemy property. He had taken the war to enemy civilians and made fools of their military establishment. To Flora, Stuart wrote that Chambersburg was as great an accomplishment as his first Ride Around McClellan and the Catlett's Station Raid. One authority has said of Chambersburg, "I know of no equal exploit in the cavalry annals."[48]

On the morning of October 11, as Stuart was leaving Chambersburg, McClellan was reassuring General-in-Chief Halleck, "I have given every order necessary to insure the capture or destruction of these forces [Stuart's], and I hope we may be able to teach them a lesson they will not soon forget." Of course the Federals failed, and Stuart continued to teach them lessons. McClellan and his subordinates had excuses. Pleasonton's force was too small, his horses crippled in the pursuit, and his command was "not well closed up" when he approached White's Ford. George Stoneman had a "small force" to guard thirty miles of river; he asked that a court of inquiry be convened to fix any blame. McClellan complained that he was "deficient in cavalry" and that his instructions had gone unheeded. Certainly Stuart's raid embarrassed the Union army command and probably contributed to President Lincoln's decision to replace McClellan as army commander.[49]

Still the question remains about the practical results of Stuart's exertions. One military analyst later contended, "the results were hardly worth the risk; Stuart ought to have lost his whole command." Another concluded, "As a military operation, this [the raid] was rather pointless: Stuart's only tangible objective—a railroad bridge north of Chambersburg which Lee wanted destroyed —was left undamaged." These are indeed valid points from hindsight. Even in October of 1862, the raid provoked comments that were less than flattering toward Stuart. One of Stuart's old friends from West Point, Dorsey Pender, wrote his wife, "Beaut is after a Lieut. Generalcy." Wade Hampton remarked that "the whole affair was well managed." But, he added, "I suppose Stuart will as usual give all the credit to his Va. Brigades. He praises them on all occasions, but does not give us any credit." And one of Stuart's troopers who participated in the raid characterized it as "horse stealing" and "abuse of old folks."[50]

The Confederate commanding general seemed well enough pleased, however. Lee, writing to the secretary of war, called Stuart's expedition "eminently successful" and added, "He obtained many remounts for his cavalry and artillery, and deserves much credit for his prudence and enterprise." Newspapers in Richmond, too, were loud in their praise. The *Examiner* began a lead editorial, "The country is once more cheered by Stuart's cavalry." The *Dispatch* concluded a favorable comparison of Stuart with heroes of the American Revolution. "All honor to General Stuart and the brave boys that assist in upholding his banner." If nothing else the raid was a morale victory of some magnitude.[51]

Meanwhile, back at the Bower, the civilians and those soldiers left behind spent several days of anxious waiting. Then on the morning of October 13 came a distant sound of a single bugle mingled with the strumming of Sweeney's banjo. Much whooping followed, as Stuart and his staff galloped into the yard. On hand to greet the raiders was Norman Fitzhugh, the adjutant captured at Verdiersville and only recently exchanged. He and Von Borcke, the Dandridges and friends listened to the stories and rejoiced at Stuart's great feat. Two days later they all commemorated the raid officially by holding a large ball.[52]

During the celebrations Flora arrived and joined the party. Also delivered about this time was a pair of golden spurs. Some woman living in Baltimore had purchased the spurs and smuggled them to Stuart. He was delighted. From this time, Stuart signed some of his personal letters with a sobriquet he fashioned for himself—"The knight of the Golden Spurs" or "K.G.S."

Stuart had a friend in nearby Shepherdstown, Lily Parran Lee, who was the war widow of a former comrade. He visited her and her household a couple of times during his stay at the Bower, and later he wrote to her, "Did you know a lady in Baltimore (anonymous) had sent me a pair of elegant gold spurs? They came while Flora was here and *she* buckled them on." That is an interesting underline; did Flora trespass upon her husband's fame?[53]

Stuart had every right to be impressed with himself. However, he seemed to be letting it show. Fame and fun were going to his head.

# X

## *Fame*

ONLY TWO YEARS BEFORE he had been a lieutenant in the wilderness, attempting to complete construction of Fort Wise before the snows came. Now in the fall of 1862 Stuart was a major general commanding a division of cavalry. And he was a bona fide hero as well.

Soldiers talked about him, and rumors of him flew through the army. Along with true accounts of his exploits, one story had Stuart capturing Abraham Lincoln and his entire cabinet.[1]

Civilians talked about him, read about him, and on occasion attacked him. On October 31, 1862, Stuart was screening a maneuver through northern Virginia and reached the outskirts of Middleburg about dusk. He sent Von Borcke ahead to prepare a bivouac, and as Von Borcke rode through the town, he met "a group of very pretty young girls" who badly wanted a glimpse of Stuart. The Prussian promised them fifteen minutes with his general, and by the time Stuart arrived, fifty or sixty females of all ages had gathered in the street. Stuart agreed to visit with them, and before long women were kissing his hand and the skirt of his uniform. "Ladies, your kisses would be more acceptable to me if given upon the cheek," Stuart announced. Then the women "charged," and according to Von Borcke, "The kisses now popped in rapid succession like musketry, and at last became volleys." With difficulty did Stuart extricate himself from the clutches of his admirers and continue the war.[2]

His enemies took ample notice of his deeds, too. In the wake of the Chambersburg Raid, NEMO, a correspondent of the *New York Times,* termed Stuart that "bold and indefatigable marauder," "the Flying-Dutchman of the rebels," and suggested it proper for "indignation and hatred to be—for the moment—lost in admiration." NEMO concluded, "Let us bear the truth with the best temper we can. That shrewd gambler, Stuart, has euchered us again." And President Lincoln delivered much the same verdict on Chambersburg to McClellan: "Stuart's cavalry out-marched ours, having certainly done more marked service on the Peninsula and everywhere since."[3]

Poets honored him. Paul Hamilton Hayne, for example, wrote "Stuart!" for the *Southern Illustrated News* in December 1862. The ballad begins and ends with this stanza:

> A cup of your potent 'mountain dew,'
> By the camp-fires ruddy light!—
> Let us drink to a spirit as leal and true
> As ever drew blade in fight,
> And dashed on the Tyrant's lines of steel,
> For God, and a Nation's Right!

Stuart's "very name" provokes "a thought of fire" and inspires "wild desire" among the troopers. They listen for the command to "launch us forth, / Like bolts from the mountain cloud." Finally the order comes; beware, those who live in "the pleasant land of Penn." "The Southern Murat" is on his way; "Stuart rides again." The men ride hard and travel far for the sake of "A night of feasting, and wit and song" in "yon Yankee town." They knock at the mayor's door, and the old man is too scared to speak. His wife, however, wails for her daughters and "their virgin fame." Enough —the raiders leave this "churlish brood" to "war with the strong," for they belong to a "courtly race" and are "bound by a knightly vow."[4]

Hayne's ballad projected Stuart in terms perhaps even more romantic than Stuart himself would have used. But even while Hayne's romantic fantasy was being set into print, John Esten Cooke was at work on another. Completed at Stuart's camp in December 1862, Cooke's "The Song of the Rebel" is about "our band of heroes"—Lee, Jackson, Longstreet, and many more. Of course Stuart holds a prominent place in the pantheon. "And

*Stuart* with his sabre keen / And floating plume appears, / Surrounded by his gallant band / Of Southern cavaliers." After extolling Stuart's virtues and victories, Cooke has the ghost of dead Turner Ashby ride to Stuart's side. The two ride together, although Ashby's "brave soul stays behind." But his heart, even though it is "cold," nevertheless "beats in the breast of *Stuart* / And strikes with his heavy arm!" There is a certain irony that Cooke (whom Stuart roundly disliked) should invoke a vision of Ashby (who was Stuart's rival) and mystically link the two—"The Chief of the Virginia Line / Beside the Cavalier."[5]

Southerners also sang about Stuart. "Riding a Raid (A Tribute to J. E. B. Stuart)," sung to the tune of "The Bonnie Dundee," invokes "old Stonewall" and has him say " 'Now each cavalier that loves honor and right, Let him follow the feather of Stuart tonight.' " A portrait of Stuart graces the cover of the sheet music and the song celebrates his raid "on the line of Penn":

> There's a man in the white house with blood on his mouth!
> If there's knaves in the North, there are braves in the South.
> We are three thousand horses, and not one afraid;
> We are three thousand sabres and not a dull blade.
> Come tighten your girth and slacken your rein;
> Come buckle your blanket and holster again.
> Try the click of your trigger and balance your blade.
> For he must ride sure that goes Riding a Raid.

It is also fairly safe to say that when Confederates sang "Jine the Cavalry," they sang to Stuart and a vision of his merry band.[6]

Of course Stuart's contemporaries hailed other heroes during the fall of 1862. Soldiers spoke of other generals and exchanged stories about other feats of derring-do. Women read about and talked about other Confederate idols. On one occasion some little girls refused to kiss Stuart because they had just kissed Robert E. Lee and did not want to sully their lips on a lesser god. The Southern press certainly lauded soldiers other than Stuart, and early in the coverage of the Chambersburg Raid, Northern papers misspelled his name ("Stewart"). Poets praised other warriors, and Southerners played "Beauregard's March" and sang "Stonewall Jackson's Way," as well as "Riding the Raid." Stuart was aware of all this.[7]

Still, he very much enjoyed his acclaim. As the object of considerable adulation, Stuart could not avoid acknowleding that adulation. Other people might read a newspaper or magazine and give equal emphasis to several items. Stuart quite naturally focused his attention upon items relating to himself, and naturally his admirers were eager to show them to him and tell him incidents of praise. To some extent Stuart lived in a world of unreality. If his subordinates and his troopers disliked him, they rarely let him know it. His staff, in the course of normal duty, treated him like some Eastern potentate. Much of his unofficial reading matter resembled a clipping file about himself. When he encountered civilians, they fawned over him and even threatened to mob him as in Middleburg. No one could experience what Stuart was experiencing without being affected.

He was not yet thirty years old and a national hero. Once upon a time he had had to fight with his schoolmates and even with his fellow cadets at West Point to assert himself. When he ventured first from southwest Virginia, he was "as green as a gourd vine," and he marveled when he first glimpsed "great men" in Washington—Zachary Taylor, Henry Clay, Daniel Webster, and the rest. Now he was himself a "great man." He had long known that he would have to make his own way in the world; he could not rely upon inheritance or family sinecure. He was not wealthy; he simply lived as though he were. He had made it.

At age thirteen he wrote his mother, perhaps in jest but perhaps not, that he was "a poor, little, insignificant whelp." Now he described those he despised as "puppies." Once he spoke his mind when he counseled cousin A. Stuart Brown to "gain position, information, influence, a *name* . . . and *then* . . . make the denizens of fashion bow before us." Now, an awful lot of denizens were bowing to Stuart. He had name and fame; if anyone has ever been a "legend in his own time," Stuart was. And if Flora was following his instructions, she was keeping a scrapbook for him.[8]

Back at the Bower following the Chambersburg Raid, Stuart flexed his increasing fame. He flirted with "the girls." He bantered with his staff officers. He accepted compliments on his recent feat. Von Borcke by now spoke English quite well, but still stumbled over an occasional idiom. Once he intended to pay tribute to Stonewall Jackson by saying, "It warms my heart when he talks to me." But the Prussian used the words, "It makes my heart burn," and Stuart told Jackson that Von Borcke had said, "It gave me heart burn to hear Jackson talk." Von Borcke, and even Jackson, endured Stuart's barbs in good spirits. But he repeated the punch lines over and over, and not every target of the general's humor thought him so funny.[9]

Anticipating another reorganization of the cavalry within the Army of Northern Virginia, Stuart tested his influence in the matter. He wrote to Lee's chief of staff and urged the creation of a fourth brigade in his division to augment the brigades currently commanded by Wade Hampton, Fitz Lee, and Grumble Jones. To command the new unit and be brigadier general, he recommended Thomas L. Rosser. The artillerist—turned—regimental commander was young—barely twenty-six—and he had been known to drink to excess. But Stuart liked him, considered him a disciple, and pronounced Rosser "older than his years."

In the same letter Stuart recommended another promotion to brigadier general. Thomas T. Munford—Richmond-born, VMI 1852, Lynchburg planter—had led Beverly Robertson's old brigade during the Maryland campaign, and Stuart stated that Munford was "thoroughly identified with the brigade." This was the remnant of Ashby's command of "fox hunters" and Stuart added about Munford, "As a partisan, he has no superior."

Stuart well knew that if his recommendations were adopted, he would have five brigadiers and only four brigades. Indeed, if he counted his previous recommendation of Rooney Lee's promotion, Stuart would have six brigadiers. He had a ready solution for some of the problem: get rid of Grumble Jones. About his old enemy Stuart asserted, "I feel sure of opposition, insubordination, and inefficiency to an extent that would in a short time ruin discipline and subvert authority in that [Jones's] brigade." Heroes did not have to mince their words.[10]

Having spoken his mind about his subordinates, Stuart returned his attention to the Bower and the precious interlude his respite there provided. He wrote to Flora at Lynchburg about his staff—Channing Price was a wonderful scribe; Cousin Hairston could not spell; Von Borcke was noble and devoted. He missed Flora and in the midst of a rainy Sunday afternoon longed to awaken her from her nap. He wrote of his new horse Lily of the

Valley. And he shared Flora's concern for the health of her namesake, who was ill.[11]

Then, as Stuart expected, his enemies forced him to abandon
the Bower and return to service in the field. McClellan began
crossing the Potomac on October 26 and moving most of his army
east of the Blue Ridge Mountains to Warrenton. Lee decided to
counter this move with Longstreet's corps and leave Jackson's half
of his army in the Valley near Winchester. Cavalry would have to
screen Longstreet's march and provide outpost protection for Jackson, too. Stuart left this latter task to Jones. He summoned Hampton from Martinsburg, but could not count upon much help from
the South Carolinian's troopers for several days. Fitz Lee's brigade
was available, but Fitz Lee was not. (He was still recovering from
the mule kick.) Rooney Lee, too, was unwell, feeling the effects of
an old wound from the Maryland campaign. Stuart placed Williams C. Wickham in command of Fitz Lee's men, but essentially
led them himself. His force was under strength (1,000) for the task
at hand, and many of the horses, too, were victims of maladies
described as " 'greased heel' and sore tongue."

Stuart and his staff bade farewell to the Bower on October 29.
On November 6 Stuart's cavalry (Lee's and Hampton's brigades)
resumed picket duties in front of Longstreet's corps near Culpeper
Court House. During the interim week Stuart was daily in contact
with his enemies and almost constantly in motion. At Mountsville,
Union, Upperville, Markham's Station, and Barbee's Cross Roads,
Stuart usually faced heavier battalions, often cavalry augmented
by infantry. Each day wisdom dictated that he fight and fall back.
At Barbee's Cross Roads Stuart finally had Hampton's and Lee's
brigades together; but a rumor of Federals in his rear caused him
to disengage again. Stuart's screen was successful; Longstreet's
march to Culpeper Court House was unopposed. But the Southern
horsemen had had their hands quite full, and Federal generals
boasted in their reports of having roughly handled the Confederates. With reason did Stuart probably worry that his troopers were
becoming too used to retreating.[12]

Even after Stuart established his headquarters near Lee's and
Longstreet's outside of Culpeper Court House, he had to contend
with his enemies on the disputed ground between Warrenton and
Culpeper. On November 10, for example, he planned an attack

upon some Federal infantry and cavalry near Amissville, a small village about fourteen miles north of Culpeper. Stuart's orders to Hampton miscarried; nevertheless he advanced with Fitz Lee's brigade and two regiments of infantry. His attack was at first successful; then the Federals brought up artillery and a substantial body of infantry. Stuart ordered a withdrawal; Union troops advanced close upon the Confederates' heels—too close for Stuart. He determined to chastise the "impudence of the Yankees," and positioned about two dozen sharpshooters at the edge of some woods to administer his punishment. He remained near the men to see the deed done and even rode out of the trees into the open. Von Borcke became very concerned for his general's safety and not incidentally for his own. He told Stuart that he was "not in his proper place" and about to become a tempting target. Stuart was already upset. He snapped at Von Borcke and told him to leave if he chose. Von Borcke's pride would not allow him to flee; it did permit him to step behind a tree. Almost immediately Federal small-arms fire peppered the woods; three minié balls struck Von Borcke's tree. Stuart finally withdrew to safety, but as he did so, he lost some hair. A ball trimmed off half his prized mustache quite close to his skin. Not only did Von Borcke laugh at Stuart then; he also amused General Lee and his staff with the story later that evening.[13]

Barely had he embarked upon this grim duty screening Longstreet's march than Stuart began to receive messages from Lynchburg about his daughter. Five-year-old Flora was now gravely ill. Stuart wrote a letter on November 2 and tried to explain to Flora why he could not leave the war and come to Lynchburg. If young Flora should die, he pointed out, he would arrive too late, and if she should live, then there was no reason to come at all. After all she had been sick for nine days before Stuart was aware of the gravity of the situation. All he could do was pray and counsel Flora to trust God's will. He told his comrades, "I shall have to leave my child in the hands of God; my duty requires me here."[14]

During the darkness of November 5–6 a telegram reached Stuart's headquarters near Waterloo Bridge (over the Rappahannock, near Warrenton). Von Borcke first read the sad news; little Flora was dead. She had died on November 3 and was buried the following day. The Prussian awakened Stuart and handed him the fateful missive. Stuart read it, reached for Von Borcke, and fell into tears.[15]

Stuart's grief was genuine, heightened perhaps because he had been unable to be with his child in her suffering. When he wrote to Flora later that day, he emphasized that he first learned of the seriousness of the little girl's illness on November 2; she died on November 3; and he only learned of that on November 6. Months later Stuart spoke of his child's death to John Esten Cooke: "I will never get over it—never." And tears "gushed" to his eyes. Von Borcke recalled that light blue flowers made Stuart remember little Flora's eyes, and sunbeams reminded him of her hair. He sent a telegram to Flora asking her to come to Culpeper, so they might share their grief. She arrived on November 10, and brought Jimmy, who was not yet three years old and seemingly oblivious to the sadness. General Lee visited, too, and presented his sympathy to Flora.[16]

Even in the midst of mourning Stuart could not forget the war. When he wrote to Flora on the day he learned his daughter was dead, he said what he felt about the tragedy and probably some of what he thought proper for the occasion. He explained why he had not been able to come to Lynchburg—"I have been harassing and checking a heavy force." Then, as though his mention of combat triggered the transition, he wrote Flora what a fine officer Tom Rosser had become and how much help he was in battle.[17]

As he mourned, Stuart seemed absorbed not only with his duty, but also with himself. Ten days after he learned of the tragedy, he wrote to his friend Lily Lee to share the terrible news. He wrote that he still wept "like a child" when he thought of his little girl. He wrote that his wife was still "not herself." He also wrote that he wanted a new pair of "*very* high top Russian leather boots" and asked Lily to try to find them for him.[18]

As usual Stuart's letters revealed his thoughts. To Flora, to friends, and to relatives he wrote a lot of proper prose and said what he thought he ought to say. But as he wrote, he slipped into his own stream of consciousness, and one thought flowed into another as rapidly as his mind rushed from death to duty to Rosser to Russian boots. In the wake of young Flora's death, Stuart displayed himself to be noble and selfless; at the same time he sounded small and self-centered. Perhaps, then, his only constant was his humanity, which encompassed these extremes of mind and heart.

The same day Stuart lost half his mustache in a field near Amissville (November 10), he gained his fourth brigade of cavalry. Army of Northern Virginia Headquarters reorganized the cavalry division so as to give the additional brigade and promotion of Rooney Lee to brigadier general. Stuart's roster of units now looked like this:

### First Brigade.

#### Brig. Gen. WADE HAMPTON.

1st North Carolina, Col. L. S. Baker.
1st South Carolina, Col. J. L. Black.
2d South Carolina, Col. M. C. Butler.
Cobb (Georgia) Legion, Lieut. Col. P. M. B. Young.
Phillips' (Georgia) Legion, Lieut. Col. William W. Rich.

### Second Brigade.

#### Brig. Gen. FITZHUGH LEE.

1st Virginia, Col. James H. Drake.
2d Virginia, Col. Thomas T. Munford.
3d Virginia, Col. T. H. Owen.
4th Virginia, Col. Williams C. Wickham.
5th Virginia, Col. Thomas Rosser.

### Third Brigade.

#### Brig. Gen. W. H. F. LEE.

2d North Carolina, Col. S. Williams.
9th Virginia, Col. R. L. T. Beale.
10th Virginia, Col. J. Lucius Davis.
13th Virginia, Col. J. R. Chambliss, Jr.
15th Virginia, Col. William B. Ball.

### Fourth Brigade.

#### Brig. Gen. W. E. JONES.

6th Virginia, Col. John S. Green.
7th Virginia, Col. R. H. Dulany.

12th Virginia, Col. A. W. Harman.
17th Virginia Battalion, Lieut. Col. O. R. Funsten.
White's (Virginia) battalion, Maj. E. V. White.

Artillery.

Maj. JOHN PELHAM.

Breathed's (Virginia) battery, Capt. J. Breathed.
Chew's (Virginia) battery, Capt. R. P. Chew.
Hart's (South Carolina) battery, Capt. J. F. Hart.
Henry's (Virginia) battery, Capt. M. W. Henry.
Moorman's (Virginia) battery, Capt. M. N. Moorman.

The entire command numbered 603 officers and 8,551 enlisted men (present for duty on November 20); Stuart listed 30 men on his staff. These numbers did not change significantly during the next few months.[19]

To Stuart's chagrin, after the reorganization Rosser and Munford remained colonels, although Rosser now commanded Fitz Lee's brigade in Lee's absence. Stuart had wanted Pelham promoted to colonel, but his artillerist remained a major. And Grumble Jones remained. Fortunately for Stuart (and Jones) the 4th Brigade continued in the Valley where Stuart had left it with Jackson. And after Jackson crossed the Blue Ridge to join Longstreet, Jones and his troopers stayed in the Valley to provide a military presence there and to harass the Federals with raids into Maryland.[20]

On November 7 the Federal Army of the Potomac also reorganized; Lincoln replaced McClellan with Ambrose E. Burnside. The new commander determined to make the most of what little of the campaigning season was left in 1862. Burnside decided to move east to Fredericksburg, cross the Rappahannock on pontoon bridges, and threaten a drive on Richmond. He began the move on November 15; three days later Stuart led a reconnaissance foray toward Warrenton and discovered that the Federals had indeed left. Based upon Stuart's intelligence, Lee shifted Longstreet's corps to Fredericksburg and ordered Jackson to march from the Valley to join him. Then for about two weeks the rival armies faced

each other across the Rappahannock while Burnside awaited a
tardy delivery of his pontoons.[21]

Stuart moved his headquarters to the Fredericksburg area; he
established "Camp No Camp" on the Telegraph Road, about five
miles south of the town. From this point he attempted to coordinate the activities of his much dispersed command. Stuart's three
brigades spread for fifty miles along the Rappahannock, thirty
miles above Fredericksburg and twenty miles below. Life at Camp
No Camp, however, was quite comfortable. Stuart reported to
Flora that he and his staff were sleeping and eating as though they
had no other tasks to do. His tent boasted, not one, but two fire-
places to dispel the cold, and there he held court with his vassals.
Sweeney was with him as usual, and Bob returned from captivity,
although as yet minus Stuart's two horses. Francis Lawley and
Frank Vizetelly were there to report the war in words and draw-
ings to London, and Stuart furnished them a yellow buggy he had
captured in Pennsylvania to enable the correspondents to follow
him around. Stuart kept on the move. Von Borcke and Stuart's staff
surgeon, Talcott Eliason, managed to lose their way en route to
him at Port Royal, but managed to find a wine merchant in Fredericksburg and returned to camp with two demijohns of fine Madeira. Stuart was still at Port Royal watching Pelham make targets
of Federal ships, so the Madeira party produced several officers in
altered states of consciousness. Stuart returned just in time to witness a massive snowball brawl between infantry divisions (5,000-
plus men!) commanded by Lafayette McLaws and John Bell Hood.
Von Borcke raised a white flag over the headquarters; he and
Stuart climbed atop a large wooden box to watch the melee and
dodge stray snowballs.[22]

As if to remind Stuart and his staff that war was indeed deadly
business not normally prosecuted with snowballs, news came that
Redmond Burke was dead. He had been Stuart's friend and one of
his most trusted scouts; he was killed near Shepherdstown in a
surprise attack. The general published a general order praising
Burke and relayed the news to Virginia Governor John Letcher.
Stuart wrote to Lily Lee, asking her to mark Burke's grave so that
he might later erect a monument there. Then, in a way similar to
his response to little Flora's death, he shifted quickly to more
pleasant topics. He hoped to visit Lily to secure a kiss from her.

He complained that someone had stolen his picture of "Miss Folly" and said that he suspected "Mrs. Stuart."[23]

To Flora he had been writing since December 3 that a great battle appeared imminent. On December 10 Stuart even declined an invitation to a large party about ten miles away, because he believed Burnside about to advance. He did allow members of his staff to attend as long as they promised to return by daylight. As it happened, somewhat before daylight on the eleventh the Federals began shelling Fredericksburg at the rate of a hundred rounds per minute. Before dawn Stuart, Lee, and Longstreet stood on a high hill overlooking Fredericksburg and the valley of the Rappahannock attempting to peer through the dark and fog to see the battle begin.[24]

All day the firing continued. The Federals trained their guns on the town, where one Confederate regiment threatened the construction of their pontoon bridges. By the end of the day Fredericksburg was largely rubble, and Union infantry were crossing the river. The Confederates waited on the ridge line beyond the town and watched. Lee had arranged his troops along Marye's Heights above the plain about a half mile from Fredericksburg. On December 12 Stuart sent for Fitz Lee's brigade and united it with Rooney Lee's troopers on the extreme right of the Southern line. He had Pelham's artillery there, too, and Rosser was ready to command some guns as well. The battle, when it came, would belong essentially to infantry and artillery. Stuart's horsemen guarded the Confederate right flank; his artillery stood ready for more active service.[25]

The Federals attacked Marye's Heights on December 13. Burnside seemed determined to take what quickly and clearly proved to be an impregnable position, and he seemed oblivious to any alternative to futile, frontal assaults. Twelve times the Union lines surged forward, and twelve times the Confederates held firm. The Battle of Fredericksburg was, in Stuart's words, "tremendous slaughter."

During the long day Stuart remained on the right flank of the Southern battle line, directing his artillery batteries. Once more Pelham confirmed the sobriquet "Gallant" by moving and shooting from one advanced position to another. Stuart, too, spent most of the day exposed to Federal fire; to Flora he telegraphed, "I got shot through my fur collar but am unhurt." Flora's brother, Confederate General John R. Cooke, suffered a head wound in the battle, but seemed in no danger.

Altogether the Southern army absorbed 5,000 casualties; the Federals lost 10,000. On the day following the battle (December 14) neither army renewed the fighting, although Burnside wanted to compound his blunders and again attack Marye's Heights. On December 15 a truce permitted burial of the dead, and during that night Burnside recrossed the Rappahannock.[26]

Then the weather, which had been cold and damp, turned miserable. Although Burnside would attempt a winter campaign in January (the abortive "mud march"), no further combat on any scale seemed possible until spring. Stuart remained at Camp No Camp near Fredericksburg, and his staff and their slaves transformed the place into winter quarters.[27]

Nearby were Jackson's headquarters near Moss Neck at Corbin Hall, an estate owned by Richard Corbin, who was serving as an infantry private. Jackson declined an invitation to use part of the house, but did occupy "the office," an outbuilding that Corbin used as a library. Stuart visited Jackson there and teased him about the furnishings, which were those of a landed gentleman. He chided Jackson about the pictures of bloody fighting cocks and one of a terrier famous for the number of rats he could kill within a minute. What would Jackson's gentle lady friends say about the animal skins, bird plumage, and other evidence of interest in "blood sports"? How could so fine a man display such "low tastes"? Jackson reportedly made no response, but "blushed like a girl."

Jackson decided to entertain at "the office" on Christmas Day. He invited Lee, Stuart, and General William N. Pendleton to join him for a fine dinner of turkey, oysters, cakes, and more. Stuart was in rare form. He recoiled in mock horror at the bottle of wine on the table. Then he examined the pat of butter; it was stamped with the impression of a fighting cock. Stuart proclaimed that this was Jackson's coat-of-arms. Even Lee joined the fun and accused Jackson of "putting on airs" when he noticed the servant wore a white apron.[28]

Apparently Jackson's Christmas dinner was a men-only affair. Flora had come to spend Christmas with her husband; she arrived on December 23 and was the guest of a friend who lived only about a half mile from Stuart's headquarters. But none of the participants or witnesses at Jackson's dinner mention Flora's presence. She saw little of her husband during the Christmas season, because on December 26 he set out upon another protracted raid.[29]

When Burnside elected to remain on the north bank of the Rappahannock, he left about fifty miles of open country between his army and Washington. Most of his supplies arrived by water at Aquia Landing on the Potomac and thence the short distance to the troops by rail (Richmond, Fredericksburg and Potomac Railroad). But Federal overland supply and communications lines were vulnerable to cavalry raids, and already Wade Hampton had inflicted some damage and embarrassment upon the Union army. On November 27 Hampton led a small force behind Federal lines and returned with a hundred horses and 92 prisoners. On December 10, Hampton and 520 troopers swooped down upon the town of Dumfries and captured a wagon train and 50 prisoners. And on December 17–18, Hampton revisited the Federal rear and returned with 150 prisoners and twenty wagons. Now it was Stuart's turn.[30]

He went in force—1,800 men and four guns. Once again he took approximately 600 men from each of three brigades (Hampton's and the two Lees'). His original plan was to sweep the Telegraph Road (roughly the current U.S. Route 1) for more than ten miles between the towns of Dumfries and Occoquan and to wreak some havoc in those towns as well. Fitz Lee was to reach the road south of Dumfries and then ride north to the town. Rooney Lee was to approach Dumfries from the west and join his cousin there. Hampton was supposed to move upon Occoquan and then presumably march south on the Telegraph Road to meet the rest of the expedition. Apparently Stuart appointed a rendezvous at Cole's Store (west of Occoquan and Dumfries and roughly equidistant from both points) in the event any one of his three detachments failed to join the others.[31]

Stuart commenced the raid as suddenly and secretly as possible. Von Borcke claimed that he knew nothing of the expedition until one hour before the start. Stuart met his men and led them across the Rappahannock at Kelly's Ford (about twenty-five miles above Fredericksburg). They camped on the night of December

26 near a place called Bristersburg and separated to embark on their various missions on the morning of the twenty-seventh.[32]

Stuart elected to ride with Rooney Lee, perhaps because he was his newest brigadier, maybe because Lee's assignment held the best promise of a fight. The column followed the valley of Quantico Creek toward the Telegraph Road, but encountered no Federals en route. Upon reaching the Telegraph Road, the Confederates found an infantry outpost about a mile south of Dumfries. There were only a dozen men, and a squadron of horsemen soon ran them down and captured them. When the leading elements of Lee's force approached Dumfries, however, they found two infantry regiments ready for them. The troopers retreated, followed by a squadron of Federal cavalry, which in turn retreated when fired upon by Lee's column. At this juncture Stuart reached the front and ordered an artillery battery forward to fire. Then the Federals brought up artillery and a long-range duel commenced. Stuart then dispatched units of horsemen to the left, to the Brentsville Road, in an effort to flank the enemy. The Federals, estimated correctly by Stuart to be a brigade of infantry, moved from Dumfries to a wooded ridge that commanded the little town.

Fitz Lee then reached the scene with his contingent, and Stuart began maneuvering the expanded force in preparation for an attack. Even on horseback all this motion took time; Channing Price estimated that two or three hours elapsed between the time the Confederates first challenged the Federals and the moment Stuart's troopers were in position for a general assault. And when that moment arrived, Stuart called off his attack. In his report he explained, "The capture of the place would not have compensated for the loss of life which must have attended the movement, there being evidently no stores in the place." This sounds quite reasonable, indeed prudent. However, there were no stores in Dumfries because the Federals had removed them, and Stuart knew this, because he had watched the Federals move them while he was preparing his attack. Stuart did not write reports to make himself look bad.

After he decided not to attack at Dumfries, Stuart ordered Fitz Lee to leave some dismounted skirmishers and artillery there until dark. Then he led the rest of his command up the Brentsville Road to Cole's Store.[33]

Meanwhile Hampton had had no better fortune in his advance
to Occoquan. As he approached the town, he ordered most of his
men to attack the several hundred Federal cavalrymen stationed
there. Hampton himself led a smaller number of troopers around
to the other side of Occoquan to be prepared to intercept an enemy
retreat. But before Hampton's force reached its destination, the
rest of his horsemen had galloped into Occoquan and chased the
Federals away. The Confederates came away with only nineteen
prisoners and eight wagons. Hampton apparently expected Stuart
to join him at Occoquan and waited for him until dark. Then he
withdrew to Cole's Store, where he found Stuart and the rest of
the raiders.[34]

To this point Stuart's raid had been less than glorious. He had
some prisoners and a few wagons, but little else; he had not
mounted this expedition for such meager results. Accordingly he
sent his captives and captures back to friendly lines across the
Rappahannock and determined to remain a bit longer in enemy
country.

On the morning of December 28, Stuart retraced Hampton's
hoofprints and headed toward Occoquan. On the way he encountered two regiments of Federal cavalry near Greenwood Church.
Immediately he ordered Fitz Lee's brigade to charge. The Southern charge broke Federal ranks and in the running fight that followed the Confederates inflicted a number of casualties and
captured 100 Federals. Once unleashed, the Confederate troopers
followed their foes all the way to Occoquan, where they dashed
into Federal camps and captured significant booty. By the time the
Southerners had burned everything they could not transport, it
was nearly dark. Stuart, though, was determined to keep moving.

In the winter darkness, Stuart led his column north! The raiders rode to Burke's Station on the Orange and Alexandria Railroad.
As they approached, Stuart sent a small party to seize the telegraph
office. This they did before the operator could spread the alarm.
Stuart had his own telegraph operator with him and quickly substituted him for the Union man. Very soon messages began arriving from Washington concerning Federal plans to catch the
Confederates. Stuart took note of his enemies' orders and then sent
a message of his own.

To Union Quartermaster General Montgomery Meigs Stuart

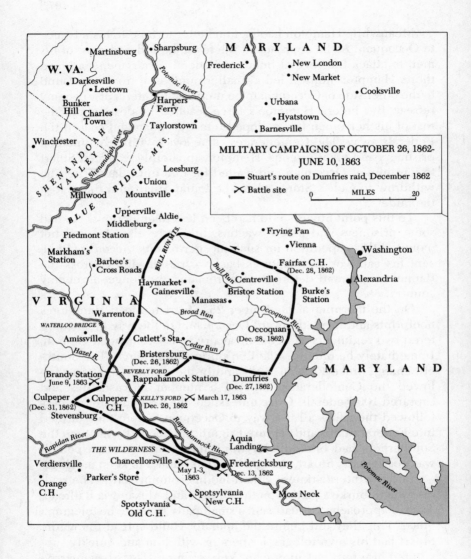

MILITARY CAMPAIGNS OF OCTOBER 26, 1862–
JUNE 10, 1863

━━━ Stuart's route on Dumfries raid, December 1862

✕ Battle site

0          MILES          20

MARYLAND

W. VA.

• Martinsburg      • Sharpsburg

• Darkesville      Frederick
• Leetown                    • New London
Bunker                         • New Market
Hill  Charles
      Town    Harpers                              • Cooksville
            Ferry
                  • Urbana
Winchester   Taylorstown
                        • Hyatstown
                  • Barnesville

SHENANDOAH VALLEY

Shenandoah River

Leesburg •

• Union
Millwood   Mountsville •

BLUE RIDGE MTS.

• Upperville  Aldie •
Middleburg •
• Piedmont Station

Markham's      Barbee's
Station        Cross Roads

VIRGINIA

• Frying Pan
      • Vienna

• Fairfax C.H.
(Dec. 28, 1862)

Haymarket •   Centreville •   • Washington
Gainesville •   Bristoe Station •   • Alexandria
• Warrenton   Manassas •   Burke's
                              Station

Broad Run

Occoquan River

WATERLOO BRIDGE
• Amissville        Catlett's Sta. •   Cedar Run   Occoquan
                                                   (Dec. 28, 1862)
Hazel R.        Bristersburg •
                (Dec. 26, 1862)
Brandy Station                BEVERLY FORD
June 9, 1863 ✕   Rappahannock Station •   Dumfries
                                          (Dec. 27, 1862)   MARYLAND
Culpeper         KELLY'S FORD ✕ March 17, 1863
(Dec. 31, 1862)  • Culpeper   Dec. 26, 1862
Stevensburg •    C.H.

Rapidan River                Aquia
                             Landing •
THE WILDERNESS
Verdiersville •  Chancellorsville •   Fredericksburg
                                      Dec. 13, 1862
• Orange         Parker's Store •   May 1-3,
C.H.                                1863
                 • Spotsylvania   • Moss Neck
                 New C.H.
Spotsylvania •
Old C.H.

Potomac River

dispatched a formal complaint. Federal mules were of uniformly poor quality, Stuart said. And this made moving the wagons he had captured significantly more difficult.

As he prepared to leave Burke's Station, Stuart sent Fitz Lee and a dozen men to burn the railroad bridge over Accotink Creek. Then Stuart led Lee's brigade and the rest of his command north to the Little River Turnpike and then west to Fairfax Court House. He flirted with the possibility of attacking the garrison there; but as he approached he found breastworks and "a heavy volley from the enemy's infantry." The Federals at Fairfax Court House were uncertain about just who was out there in the cold dark. So they suspended firing and sent a message via a flag of truce requesting the strangers to identify themselves. A Confederate responded that he would answer in the morning, and now the Federals were even more puzzled. Meanwhile the Southerners built huge campfires, as though they were going to remain, and Stuart led the expedition north to Vienna and then west to a place called Frying Pan.

At dawn on December 29 near Frying Pan, the raiders rested a few hours and then trotted on toward Middleburg. An uneventful march via Warrenton brought the column to Culpeper Court House on New Year's Eve. And on January 1, 1863, Stuart arrived at his headquarters near Fredericksburg.

Once more as he had on the peninsula, at Catlett's Station, and at Chambersburg, Stuart had confounded his foes. This time he returned with about 200 prisoners, as many horses, and about twenty wagonloads of equipment; en route he left a trail of confusion and embarrassment. The cost to his command had seen one killed, thirteen wounded, and thirteen missing.[35]

Channing Price wrote his sister that the Dumfries Raid was the "longest, most dangerous and most brilliant Expedition that the Cavalry has yet given to an admiring public." Price may well have been correct in his assessment. But if newspapers be any index, the Dumfries Raid attracted less attention than Stuart's earlier raids. The Richmond *Examiner* noted STUART AGAIN IN ENEMY'S REAR; the Richmond *Dispatch* reported the latest "dash of Gen. Stuart"; and both papers told with some glee the story of Stuart's telegram to Meigs about the quality of Federal mules. A correspondent of the *New York Times* reported that Stuart led 6,000 horsemen, but termed the raid a "failure." The writer did credit the Confederates with the successful looting of several sutlers' wagons and described the Little River Turnpike as littered with "old boots and empty bottles." Both Southern and Northern newspapers were too preoccupied with the major battle at Murfreesboro, Lincoln's Emancipation Proclamation, and the openings of congressional sessions to give much emphasis to Dumfries.[36]

Stuart himself returned from the raid "in buoyant spirits" and recounted his recent exploits in detail for those of his retinue he had left behind. He returned to "winter quarters," a circumstance that permitted some rest for the rest of the army. The cavalry, however, remained on picket duty throughout seasons in which bad weather all but precluded active campaigning.

Much of his time during this winter Stuart spent doing the same sorts of things he did at other times of the year. But the cessation of massed hostilities permitted him time to write formal reports of his activities during the previous year. Except for his account of the Chambersburg Raid, which he wrote soon after the fact, Stuart reached only Second Manassas (Bull Run) in reports written during this winter.

Stuart was also able to spend some time with Flora, who seemed to alternate her time between Richmond and her friend's home near Fredericksburg. Indeed the Stuarts conceived their third child sometime during January.[37]

Army politics especially occupied Stuart during this winter. He had time to devote to the care and feeding of his career. And of necessity he became involved in the careers of others. At stake were power and influence—the chance for further fame.

As ever, Stuart was anxious to impress his superiors. He was certainly Jackson's friend, and Jackson thought highly of Stuart's military skills as well. But Stuart was friendly with A. P. Hill, too, and Hill and Jackson were not friendly. Back in November of 1862, Hill had referred to Jackson as that "crazy old Presbyterian fool" in a letter to Stuart. Hill added, "The Almighty will get tired of helping Jackson after a while, and then he'll get the damndest thrashing—and the shoe pinches, for I shall get my share and probably all the blame, for the people will never blame Stonewall for any disaster." Somehow, Stuart got along with both men.[38]

He took greater advantage of his old friendship with Custis

Lee, who served on the staff of President Davis. In December 1862, Stuart invited Lee to visit him—"I will share my blanket with you." Lee did spend some time at Stuart's headquarters soon after, and the two West Point classmates corresponded fairly often thereafter. In Richmond Lee tried to assist those officers whom Stuart favored for promotion. And Lee actively promoted Stuart's promotion to lieutenant general. For his part, Stuart did what he could to secure a field command for Lee in his father's army.[39]

The elder Lee, the commanding general, remained something of an enigma to Stuart. Lee seemed to like Stuart and enjoy his company. He also seemed to appreciate Stuart's hard work and hard riding. But did Lee think of Stuart as anything more than a capable cavalryman? Did he really appreciate Stuart's talents, take him seriously as a senior soldier? Stuart could not know. He did confide to Flora that Joe Johnston was still the best friend he had in the Confederate army.[40]

Among Stuart's subordinates, Hampton continued to present problems. The South Carolinian complained that Stuart favored his fellow Virginians. In late January Hampton wrote his sister, "All my time and correspondence of late have been taken up in quarrelling with Stuart, who keeps me here doing all the hard work, while the Va. Brigades are quietly doing nothing. His partiality towards these Brigades is as marked as it is disgusting and it constantly makes me indignant. I do not object to the work, but I do object to seeing my command broken down by positive starvation. . . . Unless Genl. Lee, to whom I have appealed, interferes, Stuart will certainly have my Brigade out of the field before very long." When Stuart did withdraw Hampton's men from their pickets, Hampton wrote his friend Senator Louis Wigfall of Texas, "My Brigade is at last ordered to rest after it is so broken down that it can do nothing more to keep the Va. Brigades off duty." From Wigfall Hampton asked support in his campaign to command a division of "Southern," as opposed to "Virginia," cavalry. He closed his appeal sarcastically, "The Va. Cavalry being, according to the Va. papers, the best in the service, should be kept by itself, and Stuart could thus use his Division composed altogether of troops from his own State (which would be a great matter for him *if he ever runs for Gov. of Va.*) while the Southern Cavalry could form another division." As it happened, of course, Hampton was later able to use his military record to augment a successful gubernatorial campaign in South Carolina.[41]

Stuart renewed his efforts to secure promotion and command of a brigade for Rosser. On January 13 he wrote to Adjutant and Inspector General of the Confederate Army Samuel Cooper and proposed that he rearrange a number of regiments in order to create another brigade for Rosser. On February 4 Stuart wrote Cooper that Grumble Jones was incapable and proposed his transfer elsewhere. To command Jones's brigade he suggested Rosser, Munford, or Wickham. Custis Lee used his influence on behalf of Stuart's recommendations, but he admitted little success.[42]

Support of Rosser embroiled Stuart in a general court-martial during this winter. The defendant was Henry Clay Pate, whom Stuart had first met in Kansas in 1856, when Pate was John Brown's prisoner. Pate had later been most instrumental in raising a cavalry battalion (which became the nucleus of the 5th Virginia Regiment) and secured a commission as lieutenant colonel. Then Stuart gave the 5th Virginia to Rosser; Pate claimed Stuart did so because Rosser had attended West Point and he had not. During the fall of 1862 Pate accused Rosser of "intemperance" and submitted a written report to Stuart. The only thing Stuart did with Pate's report was give it to Rosser. Then Rosser found many minor charges to bring against Pate. The court-martial convened several times, but for various reasons had to be postponed until March. Stuart was a witness, and in his testimony he continued to sustain Rosser.[43]

For one who abstained from alcohol in any form and who discouraged its use in his presence, Stuart could be quite lenient with intemperate officers. Rosser's personal correspondence reveals that although he fought the tendency, he did periodically engage in drinking bouts. Another colonel, L. S. Baker of the 1st North Carolina, came to Stuart's attention during this winter because one of his subordinates had accused him of drunkenness. From Baker, Stuart secured a written pledge that he would drink no more during the war. And based on Baker's pledge, Stuart recommended that no action be taken on the charges. A few months later Stuart recommended Baker for promotion. Since his pledge, Stuart observed, Baker's conduct had been better; however, he no longer seemed as "dashing" as he had before.[44]

Stuart was quick to form pretty definite opinions of his brother officers. To his brother-in-law John R. Cooke, who recovered rapidly from his wound at Fredericksburg, Stuart wrote, "I don't see how you can avoid either [Robert] Ransom or D. H. Hill who is worse—but [Johnston] Pettigrew I thought well of on slight acquaintance." Then he offered Cooke counsel which he himself tried to heed: "Be sure Dear John to keep out of snarls of every kind, they are perfectly abominable."[45]

Stuart did try to avoid "snarls," and once involved, he did not usually hold grudges. Following his confrontation with Lige White during the Maryland campaign, for example, he seemed to go out of his way to praise White. On January 27 he forwarded White's report of a raid on Poolesville, Maryland, and added, "Major White has thus given early evidence of the essential characteristic of a successful cavalry leader—prudent boldness. His command accomplished a hard march and successful expedition, and deserves great praise for it."[46]

But because he was who he was, Stuart could not endear himself to every one of his peers. Lafayette McLaws, for instance, wrote to Richard S. Ewell in February, "Stuart carries around with him a banjo player and a special correspondent [Lawley?]. This claptrap is noticed and lauded as a peculiarity of genius when, in fact, it is nothing else but the act of a buffoon to attract attention."[47]

Politics involves power relationships, and the politics of military command was sometimes volatile within the Army of Northern Virginia. Supposedly there were rules and limits that applied to politics within the army. When Stuart heard that Minnie Ransom had written a letter to Lee's headquarters complaining about her husband's promotion, or lack of it rather, he responded, "Now if Mrs. Jeb ever takes it upon herself to write any official a letter of that kind in my behalf, she will have an account to settle with the aforesaid Jeb. It is *far better* to be neglected than to be promoted by such means."[48]

However adamant Stuart was about the impropriety of a wife's attempting to intercede on paper for her husband, he employed some questionable tactics himself for the sake of impressing his superiors. On January 10 Stuart scheduled a review of Fitz Lee's entire brigade. He planned to make a social gathering of the event and invited a number of women to come and watch the show.

Unfortunately the day was dark and dreary. Around nine o'clock in the morning, it began to rain, and it seemed certain that the rain would fall all day. Still he refused to postpone the exercise. Fitz Lee's troopers had to rise before daylight, ride fifteen miles in the cold rain, go through their paces at the review, and then ride fifteen miles back to their camps. The downpour limited visibility to fifty yards, and some of the troopers feared frostbite from the cold. Stuart's staff shivered through the show. Naturally the women did not attend; the only people watching the "grand review" who did not have to be present were Blackford's younger brother and a wagon driver. Why then did Stuart insist upon subjecting men and animals to such discomfort and perhaps debilitation for the sake of an empty exercise? There were two other spectators at the review whose presence may have had some influence upon Stuart's insistence—Longstreet and Lee.[49]

Stuart, at thirty, was a bit young to act the part of mentor to younger officers. He did, however, tend to favor men younger than himself: Fitz Lee at this time was twenty-seven; Rooney Lee was twenty-five; and Rosser was twenty-six. If Stuart had a genuine protégé, that man was twenty-four-year-old John Pelham. He complimented Pelham in just about every report he wrote and all but hounded Richmond to promote him. He also enjoyed Pelham's company, perhaps to the point of obsession.

During early March, Pelham tried several times to secure Stuart's permission to visit some friends at Orange Court House. Finally during the evening of March 14 Stuart relented and authorized Pelham to make an inspection visit to some unit of the Horse Artillery. Pelham had Stuart's adjutant Norman Fitzhugh write out the order that night, and before light the next morning, Pelham was gone. He told Fitzhugh that he planned to eat breakfast at the camp of one of his batteries. When Stuart sat down to breakfast that morning, he asked where Pelham was. When he learned Pelham had already left, he told Fitzhugh to send a courier after him; he had reconsidered permitting Pelham to go. Presumably Pelham had anticipated Stuart's change of heart and rode toward Orange Court House as though he were a fugitive. He did not stop long enough to eat breakfast; he only gulped some coffee and sped away. Fitzhugh's courier with Stuart's summons could not overtake the major before he reached Orange Court House and by then it was night. Pelham determined to spend one night, at least, away from headquarters.[50]

Next day (March 16), as Pelham prepared to leave Orange Court House, a train arrived from Culpeper Court House bearing news of a projected advance of Federal cavalry on the upper Rappahannock. Union General William W. Averell with 3,000 troopers intended to cross the river, confront Fitz Lee's brigade, and "rout or destroy him." Intelligence regarding Averell's intentions reached Confederate headquarters, and Fitz Lee received a warning via telegraph at 11:00 A.M. on the sixteenth. Pelham decided to return with the train to Culpeper Court House; he would then be near the likely scene of action, and he probably knew Stuart would be there for a session of Pate's court-martial. Pelham met Stuart at Culpeper Court House and both men remained there that night.

Very early on the morning of March 17 Averell's column appeared at Kelly's Ford, about fourteen miles by road from Culpeper Court House. In response to the warning from headquarters, Fitz Lee had reinforced his picket at the ford; but sixty men were no match for the 2,100 with which Averell overwhelmed the outpost. At seven thirty that morning Lee learned of Averell's presence at Kelly's Ford, and soon thereafter the news reached Stuart. With his usual haste he collected Pelham and prepared to ride to Kelly's Ford. Harry Gilmor, a captain on leave from Jones's brigade, joined them, and the trio galloped out of Culpeper Court House while Bessie Shackelford, one of Pelham's friends, waved her handkerchief.[51]

By the time Lee's 800 troopers confronted Averell's 2,100, the Federals were about a half mile south of the ford, nearer the village of Kellysville. The Confederates charged almost at once. Then both sides commenced a series of charges and countercharges which lasted most of the day. Gilmor recalled that *"the sabre was 'the order of the day' "*; however, dismounted troopers and artillery probably did more damage than blades. Averell's command was able to seize the first series of fields that the Southerners contested and advance perhaps a mile to a second stretch of open ground. There Lee's troopers and artillerists stood firm. At five thirty in the afternoon Averell decided to withdraw back across the Rappahannock. He claimed he had been "successful thus far," but faced "intrenched positions" with "very much exhausted horses," and he heard reports of Confederate infantry in the neighborhood with more en route by rail. Stuart interpreted the day somewhat differently. He telegraphed army headquarters at 7:00 P.M. that the enemy was retiring and badly hurt—"His dead men and boxes strew the roads." Next day Stuart prepared a congratulatory order in which he mocked the Federals for being afraid to "contest the palm as Cavalry" and relying instead upon artillery and dismounted riflemen to defend themselves. Lee's horsemen, Stuart announced, had met the "insolent foe" and "driven, broken, and discomfited" him.[52]

Stuart left the conduct of the battle to Fitz Lee. But as usual he remained visible on the field during the combat. Early in the action Lee ordered a regiment to charge some Federals who were on foot behind a formidable stone wall. He sent first a dismounted squadron as skirmishers. The Southerners advanced until they were within 200 yards of the wall and then met a volley from the carbines behind the wall and artillery fire from some guns concealed in the woods. The men slowed, stopped, and began to fall back; still the Federal fire poured into them. Suddenly Stuart was among them, waving his hat and screaming. "Confound it, men, come back! Don't leave me alone here." And the troopers rallied to him.[53]

For his part, Pelham watched his guns join the action and urged the battery commander, "Captain, do not let your fire cease; drive them from their position." Later he and Gilmor were sitting their horses with a cavalry regiment. The concentration attracted Federal artillery and just as the horsemen were wheeling their mounts to move the column, a shell burst nearby. Gilmor next saw Pelham lying on the ground, his eyes open, face relaxed. He dismounted and found blood pouring from a small hole in the back of Pelham's head. Gilmor scooped up the limp body, draped Pelham over his horse, and left his friend in the care of two troopers. Then Gilmor galloped away to find Stuart. Initially Stuart believed Gilmor, who was spattered with Pelham's blood, was wounded; when he learned the truth, he stared at Gilmor in pain and horror.

Pelham never completely regained consciousness. Gilmor took him to Bessie Shackelford's house in Culpeper and watched the surgeons attempt to repair his skull. Pelham died early the next afternoon. Stuart came to look at his body and cried. He leaned down, and one of his tears fell on Pelham's cheek while he snipped a lock of Pelham's hair and kissed the smooth forehead. Then, as he made himself turn away, he spoke—quietly—"Farewell."[54]

Stuart did all he was able to honor Pelham. He wrote a general order in his praise and had the Horse Artillery wear a badge of mourning for thirty days. He sent a telegram to Pelham's Alabama congressman. He wrote Flora, "I want Jimmy to be just like him." And he insisted upon giving Pelham's name to the child Flora was carrying. Elsewhere three young women put on mourning dresses in Pelham's memory.[55]

The fight at Kellysville (Kelly's Ford) cost Stuart's force 132 casualties besides Pelham (11 killed, 88 wounded, and 34 captured or missing). The Federals lost 78 (6 killed, 50 wounded, and 22 captured or missing). Averell's division surely outnumbered Fitz Lee's brigade (2,100 to 800), and, true, it was the Federal cavalry who withdrew. But the battle seemed to serve notice. The Federal cavalry was now operating in strength instead of being dispersed throughout the army. And the Federal troopers were gaining confidence in their capacity to fight. Stuart's reference to the "insolent foe" was a kind of compliment.[56]

During the rest of March and all of April, Federal cavalry continued to threaten on the Rappahannock. With Jones still in the Valley and Hampton's command resting and recruiting after its arduous season on picket duty, Stuart had only the Lees' brigades available—perhaps 2,000 troopers. Federal General George Stoneman, who commanded a consolidated corps of cavalry, had perhaps 11,000 horsemen on the north bank of the Rappahannock. Stoneman's massed cavalry figured prominently in the plans of Joseph Hooker, who had replaced Burnside as commander of the Army of the Potomac on January 25.

Hooker had concentrated his cavalry and worked quite hard to improve the efficiency and morale of his army. As the campaigning season of 1863 loomed, he announced that he commanded the "finest army on the planet." Hooker now intended to unleash most of his mounted horde and dispatch them into Lee's rear to wreck Confederate communications and supply lines. With his infantry he planned to march up the Rappahannock, cross the river, and then fall upon Lee's flank at Fredericksburg.[57]

Stuart knew Stoneman's strength and petitioned Lee for more cavalry; he wanted to bring Jones's brigade east of the Blue Ridge. But Lee decided otherwise; he ordered Jones to mount an expedition into western Virginia and wrote Stuart to "be prepared for non-cooperation on that side of the [Blue] Ridge." Lee continued his counsel, "I am aware that from the superior strength of the enemy he will be able to overpower you at any one point, but believe, by your good management, boldness, and discretion, you will be able to baffle his designs." The vigilant Southern horsemen who guarded the Rappahannock fords did baffle one design of Stoneman's cavalry to break through the Southern screen in mid-April.[58]

But on April 28 the Federals came in overwhelming strength to Kelly's Ford—three army corps plus cavalry. In accord with Hooker's plan, Stoneman's cavalry corps crossed the Rappahannock on April 29 and broke into the hinterland behind Confederate lines. To oppose these blue columns, Lee (not Stuart) decided to send Rooney Lee and only two regiments. Stuart and the rest of his command (essentially Fitz Lee's brigade) remained near the river and attempted to harry Hooker's advance as much as possible. Meanwhile, Lee advanced from Fredericksburg and marched westward to confront the Federal infantry.

Stuart could do little to slow the blue mass as Hooker moved east to the little village of Chancellorsville. Indeed Stuart, staff, and many of Fitz Lee's troopers spent a harrowing night of April 30–May 1 playing a deadly game of hide and seek with the Federal cavalry who screened the Federal right. When Stuart joined Lee on the morning of May 1, the commanding general stationed two regiments of Southern cavalry on the right of his emerging battle line and kept the rest of Fitz Lee's brigade on his left. On that day (May 1) Stuart elected to remain near Fitz Lee's contingent, but spent most of his time with Jackson.[59]

Union and Confederate infantry collided near Chancellorsville in some very thickly wooded country. As was often the case when armies en masse confronted each other, the cavalry had no specific assignment other than guarding the flanks of the lines of foot soldiers. And since in this case most of Hooker's cavalry was raiding in the Virginia interior, Confederate horsemen had few people to fight on the flanks. Nevertheless Stuart attempted to make himself useful on May 1. On one occasion in the late afternoon he ordered some guns from the Horse Artillery forward to challenge some Federal artillery. During the duel that followed, a shell fragment struck one of Channing Price's arteries. The young adjutant with the capacity for near total recall of Stuart's spoken words bled to death that evening while his friends and comrades stood helplessly around his bed.[60]

On the evening of May 1, Lee and Jackson held their famous conversation about Jackson's flank march. Scouts reported that Hooker's right was unsecured, and Jackson proposed to strike a telling blow. At that moment Lee and 43,000 Confederates were facing west and confronting their enemies in heavily wooded country. They faced Hooker's 73,000 Federals, who had marched east down the southern bank of the Rappahannock. Thick woods curtailed the weight of numbers; but now Jackson was suggesting that he detach 26,000 men from an already smaller force and leave Lee with only 17,000 with which to hold off Hooker. Really, it was Lee's plan; he simply let Jackson say what both men were thinking. If adopted, the strategy demanded that the Confederates move rapidly and strike with authority. If the Southerners did so and maintained the initiative, they might crush Hooker's army between divided elements of an inferior force. But if Hooker realized what was happening, he could easily turn upon one or the other Southern fragment, destroy it, and then dispatch the other. Lee determined to dare. The reward was worth the risk, and so he blessed Jackson's intention and instructed his cavalry to lead Jackson's corps into the Federal right rear.

Fitz Lee led the way on May 2, as Jackson's corps marched essentially undetected into Hooker's rear. Stuart rode with Jackson and at six o'clock that evening watched as three divisions of Confederate infantry crashed down upon the camps of the enemy. Initially the Federals fled in disorder; Jackson pressed his advantage.[61]

While the battle raged, Jackson determined to render his victory as complete as possible. Thus he sent an infantry regiment north from the front to seize Ely's Ford on the Rappahannock, a possible route of escape for the Federals. Stuart learned that some Union cavalry was advancing toward the ford and offered to follow the infantry with a regiment of cavalry. Jackson assented, and

Stuart rode off into the night. He found a Federal camp near the
ford and prepared to attack. But as he did so, Captain R. H. T.
Adams of A. P. Hill's staff found Stuart and delivered a message.
After a few hurried words in hushed tones, Stuart summoned the
commander of the infantry regiment, ordered him to take charge,
fire briefly into the enemy camp, and return south to the larger
conflict. Then Stuart wheeled his mount and spurred away.

Jackson was wounded, seriously. Hill had been wounded,
slightly. Stuart rode to assume command.[62]

Under other circumstances, the next senior division commander (Robert E. Rodes) might have stepped forward when Jackson and Hill fell. However Major General Stuart outranked
Brigadier General Rodes, and circumstances were extremely
tense. Jackson's corps was poised on the brink—either of glorious
victory or of disastrous defeat. Lee had divided a numerically inferior force in the face of his enemy. Jackson's troops were isolated
from the rest of the army, and all Hooker had to do was realize that
fact and act upon his realization to destroy one or both halves of
Lee's army. Someone had to restore the momentum of Jackson's
assault and in the process reunite the separate elements of the
Southern army. Rodes later reported that he thought at the time
Jackson or Hill had sent for Stuart. He explained that he yielded
to Stuart for the sake of morale among the troops. "General Stuart's
name was well and very favorably known to the army, and would
tend, I hoped, to re-establish confidence."[63]

It was after midnight when Stuart arrived. Members of his staff
had carried Jackson to the rear. Rodes and Hill were on hand, and
Hill officially turned over the command to Stuart. Now what?
Stuart had no precise grasp of the situation and not many people
around who could help him. Most of Jackson's staff had gone with
their chieftain, and Stuart's own staff was still at Ely's Ford.
The new corps commander sent to Jackson and asked his advice;
Jackson could only suggest that Stuart use his own discretion.
Stuart also sent a message to Lee informing him of what had
transpired. He knew enough to know that he must renew the
attack at dawn. For what remained of the darkness, Stuart rode
up and down his lines attempting to impose order and organization and to discover what he could about the disposition of his
troop units.[64]

J. E. B. STUART, c. 1854.

MAJOR GENERAL J. E. B. STUART.

*(Courtesy of the Museum of the Confederacy)*

STUART'S PISTOL,
GAUNTLETS,
HAT,
AND FLAG.
GENERAL STUART
WITH HIS CAVALRY
SCOUTING
IN THE
NEIGHBORHOOD
OF CULPEPPER
COURTHOUSE.
SKETCH BY
FRANK VIZETELLY. ▼

*(Courtesy of the Museum of the Confederacy)*

J. E. B. STUART.

FLORA COOKE STUART
AS A YOUNG WOMAN.

◀ COLONEL JOHN S. MOSBY,
43RD BATTALION,
VIRGINIA CAVALRY, 1865.

*(Courtesy of the Virginia State Library)*

MRS. GENERAL J. E. B. STUART.

THOMAS L. ROSSER. ▲

◄ G. W. CUSTIS LEE AS A CADET.

JOHN PELHAM. ▼

WILLIAM H. F. LEE.

FITZHUGH LEE.

WADE HAMPTON.

HEROS VON BORCKE.

JOHN ESTEN COOKE. ▲
ROBERT E. LEE. ▶
THOMAS J. "STONEWALL" JACKSON. ▼

*(Courtesy of the Virginia State Library)*

At 3:00 A.M. Lee sent a message: "It is necessary that the glorious victory thus far achieved be prosecuted with the utmost vigor, and the enemy be given no time to rally . . . . they must be . pressed, so that we can unite the two wings of the army." A half hour later Lee repeated his plea: "It is all-important that you still continue pressing to the right, turning, if possible, all the fortified points, in order that we can unite both wings of the army."[65]

In preparation for his attack, Stuart ordered Jackson's artillery commander, Edward Porter Alexander, to find the best place to deploy his guns in order to support the charging infantry. Alexander informed Stuart that a "cleared ridge" known as Hazel Grove would permit Southern guns placed there to sweep Federal lines with devastating effectiveness. Since the Federals held Hazel Grove, Stuart made it his principal objective when daylight came.

Sometime during the night, in the midst of his hasty preparations for battle, Stuart made time to change his clothes. He put on a "brand new uniform of blue broadcloth, richly decorated with gold lace and gilt buttons, while a black and red plume danced from his head . . ." As if to underscore his much expanded command and to acknowledge the importance of Alexander's guns in the impending combat, he replaced his yellow cavalry sash with a bright red artillery sash.

As the rising sun of May 3 dispelled the morning mist, Stuart launched his attack. Dense undergrowth and prepared enemy positions and obstacles slowed the advance. The Southerners surged forward repeatedly, only to be repulsed. Some of them remembered Stuart riding along their lines singing, "Old Joe Hooker, Get Out of the Wilderness."

One infantryman recalled Stuart's personal example in critical moments of the battle. "He leaped his horse over the breastworks near my company, and when he had reached a point about opposite the center of the brigade, while the men were loudly cheering him, he waved his hand toward the enemy and shouted, 'Forward men! Forward! Just follow me!' "

Stuart was concentrating his attention and attack upon Hazel Grove, the ridge where he proposed to place his guns. "The men were wild with enthusiasm. The veriest coward on earth would have felt his blood thrill, and his heart leap with courage and resolution. The men poured over the breastworks after him like a wide raging torrent overcoming its barriers."

The charge Stuart inspired succeeded in chasing the Federals from their breastworks. The Southerners did not stop, however, but continued toward the critical ground of Hazel Grove. Indeed some of the Confederates advanced too fast for their own good and left themselves vulnerable to a counterattack on their flank. "To our left and rear appeared a long dark line of men that immediately opened fire on us. They were at short range, and it was impossible for us to hold our position against such a fire, or to change our front in the face of it, so that we might meet it."

Again Stuart was on hand to intervene. "He slapped spurs to his horse and sped like an arrow straight into the face of the line, and commanded it in the most peremptory manner to stop that firing!" Whether Stuart believed the Federals were friendly forces firing at other friends by mistake or whether he was attempting a bold bluff, the result was the same. His blue uniform coat and firm commands made the Federals cease their fire just long enough for the Confederates to recoil. And Stuart was able to pivot his horse and escape unscathed through a veritable hail of bullets.

He re-formed his line and again pressed the attack on the ridge. At last Southern infantry took Hazel Grove, and Stuart sent thirty big guns to begin firing from the place. These guns, later increased to fifty, supported Stuart's attacks and the assaults of Lee's wing of the army farther to the right. And one of them fired the shell that struck a pillar of a house at Chancellorsville and then dropped on Joe Hooker's head. The Union commander was for a time severely wounded; but he refused to surrender his command. Instead he ordered a withdrawal from Chancellorsville north toward the Rappahannock.

Stuart had done what had to be done; Chancellorsville was a stunning Confederate victory. In his report to Lee a few days later, Stuart was quick to point out that he had been "called to the command . . . without any knowledge of the ground, the position of our force, or the plans thus far pursued, and without an officer left in the corps above the rank of brigadier general. Under these disadvantages the attack was renewed the next morning and prosecuted to a successful issue." He believed that he had been tried and found winning.[66]

On May 5 Stuart wrote the draft of a general order congratulating his corps upon the victory at Chancellorsville. He left the number of the order blank, perhaps intending to fill it in when he issued the document. He never did issue the order. But he kept it in his pocket for as long as he lived. Corps command meant promotion to lieutenant general. It meant larger influence and greater fame—a higher order of knighthood.[67]

# XI

## *"One of Those Fops"*

AMBROSE POWELL HILL was not badly hurt. Soon after Jackson fell during the night of May 2, 1863, a piece of an artillery shell or flying debris or something struck Hill's legs near the tops of his boots. He could stand, but only with great pain, and riding his horse was out of the question. Consequently Hill, who had just succeeded Jackson in command, decided to send for Stuart to lead Jackson's corps at Chancellorsville. Stuart performed admirably in the emergency; but Hill recovered rapidly, and the emergency passed. By May 6 Joseph Hooker was leading his Federal army back across the Rappahannock River, and Hill was back in command of the corps. Stuart returned to his cavalry.[1]

Still, command of Jackson's corps remained open, and Stuart considered himself a candidate. He continued to carry around his draft general order congratulating "his" corps and wrote to Flora about the rumors that named him to succeed "Stonewall." West Point classmate Dorsey Pender told his wife, "Some think in his [Jackson's] absence Stuart will be made Lt. General, but I hope not." Pender supported Hill's claim and considered his old friend Stuart "totally deficient in dignity."[2]

Clearly Stuart wanted promotion. He had been striving to excel for most of his young life. On May 9, the day before Jackson died, Stuart wrote a note to Lee about some cavalry matters. He concluded, however, with some remarks about his role in the Battle of Chancellorsville that fairly fished for compliments from his chieftain. Lee responded that he was quite satisfied with Stuart's conduct, but had neither opportunity nor policy to be effusive in his praise. Later (May 23), when Lee had decided to divide his infantry into three corps commanded by Hill, Longstreet, and Richard S. Ewell, he wrote Stuart a letter hinting that Stuart had suggested a similar decision. "I am obliged to you for your views as to the successor of the great and good Jackson . . . . I agree with you on the subject, and have so expressed myself." Maybe Stuart was reconciling himself to Lee's reorganization. "It is rumored," Pender told his wife, "that Stuart has tendered his resignation because they will not give him this corps, but I cannot think him so foolish." Stuart was never so foolish.[3]

Perhaps he had a divided mind on the matter, however. He wanted, and believed he had earned, larger laurels; but he was also reluctant to leave the cavalry. Since his days at West Point, he had envisioned himself a "bold dragoon," and now his vision had materialized. It was almost as though Stuart had made a mold for himself and poured himself into it. He had become the jolly knight he aspired to be, the cavalier-cum-warrior figure of his imagining. Tom Rosser probably echoed Stuart's expectations when he wrote his fiancée that soon Stuart would be lieutenant general of cavalry. Could he maintain his romantic vision of himself commanding soldiers who walked?[4]

A by-product of Lee's reorganization of the Army of Northern Virginia following Chancellorsville was a greatly expanded cavalry command. Ever since Hooker had consolidated his Union cavalry, Lee had been concerned with the numbers of his own horsemen. The enemy had learned about massed cavalry from Stuart's example, and now the Army of the Potomac possessed much heavier battalions of horse. Lee wrote to Jefferson Davis urging him to do all in his power to strengthen his mounted force, and he encouraged Stuart to go to Richmond and discuss his needs with anyone of influence he knew. Lee also decided to assemble for Stuart as much cavalry as was available in the eastern theater of the war. In addition to the brigades of the two Lees, Rooney and Fitz, and Wade Hampton, Lee ordered Grumble Jones to bring his brigade from the Valley and Beverly Robertson to march with a brigade from North Carolina. Suddenly Stuart commanded almost 10,000 men, and he could not help being excited at the numbers. He happily complied with Lee's instruction to "get your cavalry together, and give them breathing time, so as when you do strike, Stoneman may feel you."[5]

During the "breathing time" following Chancellorsville, Stuart found a worthy successor to Channing Price as his adjutant. Henry B. McClellan had joined Stuart's staff in early April on the recommendation of Fitz Lee. McClellan, who was a first cousin of the Federal general and who had three brothers who fought against the Confederacy, had been a regimental adjutant before, and he proved an efficient and faithful member of Stuart's military family.[6]

Wade Hampton still sulked. He wrote his sister that Stuart was no more than a "newspaper puff." But at least one newspaper, the *Christian Index*, asked, regarding the raid of George Stoneman that coincided with the Chancellorsville battle, "Where was Gen. Stuart . . . ? We have not heard of him in the late battles at all. Yankee raids will be the order of the day now that some have been made with comparative impunity." Stuart, of course, was where Lee ordered him to be, and he was quite prominent in the late battle of Chancellorsville. But his reputation and flamboyance led men like Hampton into something close to jealousy and led the good Baptist who edited the *Christian Index* into superhuman expectations regarding the cavalry chief.[7]

As his horsemen gathered and drilled, Stuart moved his headquarters, first to Orange (May 10), and then to Culpeper (May 20). Jackson's death and the uncertainty over his successor for a time were prime topics of conversation in the camp. Tom Rosser told Stuart that Jackson had supposedly said on his deathbed that Stuart should have his corps. And Stuart reportedly replied, "I would rather know that Jackson said that than to have the appointment." Stuart did write to Jackson's widow to express his sympathy and ask about the last moments of his friend; but Mary Jackson could only refer him to newspaper accounts which she said were generally accurate.[8]

When his cavalry had assembled, rested, and drilled to his satisfaction, Stuart decided to display his strength. On May 22 he held a grand review of three brigades, Hampton's and both Lees'. The spectacle of 4,000 troopers massed before him inspired Stuart to hold an even grander review on June 5. This time he would assemble all 9,536 of his troopers—the brigades of Hampton, both

Lees, Jones, and Robertson. He would not merely display his strength; he would flaunt it. And at the same time he would display and flaunt himself.[9]

Near Culpeper Court House, Stuart's headquarters were in a hilltop grove of large hickory and tulip poplar trees which overlooked Mountain Run. The valley of the stream featured fields of clover and rich grass for the horses, and Mountain Run offered clear water and fresh fish for the men. From this command post went invitations far and wide to friends and families to come and view the review. Staff officers relayed orders to the commanders of Stuart's brigades and placed orders for new uniforms to adorn the occasion. When the visitors, mostly female, began arriving, they quickly overfilled accommodations in Culpeper, then private homes in the neighborhood. Many of the guests stayed in tents hastily pitched for them near headquarters.

On the afternoon of June 4 every train arriving in Culpeper brought more visitors, and Stuart's staff arranged for wagons and ambulances to shuttle their guests to lodgings. Former Secretary of War George Wythe Randolph rated a special train with Stuart's battle flag mounted on the locomotive. That evening the cavalry took over the town hall and held a ball. According to Von Borcke the revelers had only "a few tallow candles" to light the hall. But dim lighting no doubt heightened the romantic mood—if that was possible.[10]

Promptly at eight o'clock on the morning of June 5, Stuart assembled his staff for the ride to Brandy Station, where the review would take place. Buglers rode before the party, and women and girls strewed their path with flowers. Plumes waved, brass glittered, sabers clanked, and spurs jingled as the major general commanding rode to his command. The day was sparkling bright, still springtime, but warm.

When Stuart and his escort reached the knoll that served as a reviewing stand, twenty guns from the Stuart Horse Artillery fired off their salute. A mile and a half of horsemen cheered. Visitors thronged the knoll, and trains stopped on the tracks nearby provided a vantage point for even more spectators.

First Stuart rode at a gallop up and down the ranks of his troopers. As he did so, subordinate officers joined his entourage until perhaps a hundred vassals accompanied Stuart back to his knoll.

The artillery passed in review; then the cavalry rode by at a fast walk. Three bands played, while the horses pranced in time. All the while Stuart was being "familiarly polite" to his ladies. Once past the reviewing stand, the artillery batteries dispersed over the large field and unlimbered their guns. The cavalry wheeled for another ride by the reviewing stand and broke into a trot. One hundred yards from Stuart the horsemen spurred into a gallop, lifted their sabers, and raised a spirited yell. After they dashed by Stuart, the columns peeled off and "charged" assigned artillery pieces, which were firing blank charges with rapid precision from all parts of the field.

The effect of so much grandeur and pageantry was all but overwhelming. Stuart's staff officers, who might have been by now immune to pomp and ceremony, confessed that they were genuinely moved—the spectacle made "the heart swell with pride" and "hair stand on end." One of the artillerists judged it a "useless expenditure of powder and horseflesh," but also confessed "it was one of the grandest scenes I ever saw." All about the hillside women clasped their hands, probably squealed, and reportedly swooned into the arms of their escorts.[11]

For Stuart himself, the scene was a confirmation. He had become his ideal, the character he had conjured for himself. He had acted his part so well that his audience believed in the character he played—and so did he. Here was Stuart at the peak of his fame.

That evening Stuart held another ball—this time in the open air near his headquarters. A series of bonfires lit the dancing area and soft moonlight was available for private strolls. All this, the splendid review and firelit ball, was nearly too perfect. It was as though Stuart had taken as his script Lord Byron's "The Night Before Waterloo" passage from *Childe Harold's Pilgrimage.*

> There was a sound of revelry by night,
> And Belgium's capital had gather'd then
> Her Beauty and her Chivalry, and bright
> The lamps shone o'er fair women and brave men;
> A thousand hearts beat happily; and when
> Music arose with its voluptuous swell,
> Soft eyes look'd love to eyes which spake again,
> And all went merry as a marriage bell;

But there was a Waterloo, and the next line portends:

> But hush! hark! a deep sound strikes
> like a rising knell!

No one heard or acknowledged the knell in Byron's poem; nor did they at Stuart's headquarters on June 5, 1863.[12]

While cavalry officers danced and promenaded, the infantry marched. Lee was shifting his army westward from Fredericksburg to Culpeper. From Culpeper he planned to move still farther west, then north down the Shenandoah Valley, and across the Potomac once more. Stuart's massed cavalry was supposed to screen this movement, to cross the Rappahannock on June 9. Meanwhile Confederate troops converged on Culpeper, and Lee came, too.

Stuart had invited the commanding general to his grand review on June 5; but Lee had had to decline. On June 7, however, Lee sent word that he would be pleased to review Stuart's horsemen the next day. So once more Stuart's orders spread through his command; the men were to prepare to pass in review before Lee on the eve of their departure on the screening mission.[13]

Troopers did not greet these directives with universal enthusiasm. Men who had dashed past the reviewing stand only two days earlier had had enough pageantry for a while. Such exercises, one man wrote, were "very pleasant to the spectators but very unpleasant to us." After all, when the review concluded, they had to return to their camps and tend their horses, while the officers attended Stuart's ball. And the review had been "a grand display to gratify the vanity of one man." They "grumbled at the useless waste of energy" on June 5, and when they heard about the repeat performance on June 8, "the grumblers were even more numerous and outspoken." Some declared themselves "worried out by the military foppery and display." One man recorded in his diary, "Stuart thinks more of lists and prancing around . . . to show off his fine figure." And another completed the two reviews "hungry and weary and needing rest."[14]

Stuart had moved his headquarters a few miles to Fleetwood Hill, which overlooks Brandy Station and the Rappahannock northeast of Culpeper. Because of the short notice given by Lee and plans to march the following day, this review was much less a social event than the one three days earlier. Nevertheless Stuart appeared on the field with his horse and himself bedecked with flowers. Lee reportedly looked askance at such display and told Stuart that John Pope (or Ambrose Burnside, depending on the storyteller) had greeted his army in just such a condition. Lee hoped that Stuart would not share Pope's fate. Fitz Lee had invited John Bell Hood to come watch the show "and bring your people," meaning Hood's staff. Hood did indeed come to Fleetwood Hill with his people—his entire infantry division, 10,000 men.

Once again Stuart rode along the lines of his division, this time accompanied by Lee. And again the horsemen walked past the reviewing party. But there was neither galloping nor artillery fire; Lee forbade wasting horses' energy and gunpowder in a mere show for him. At one point Stuart noticed that Grumble Jones's brigade was nowhere in sight and sent an aide to correct the situation. The aide found Jones and his men lounging in the grass and encountered indignation when he repeated Stuart's order. Still, Jones managed to get his men mounted and in line in time. The review was nothing like the earlier one; but it went well, and Lee had to have been impressed with his cavalry.[15]

That evening Stuart's staff and their slaves packed up the headquarters baggage and sent the wagons into Culpeper. Stuart slept under only a tent fly on Fleetwood Hill. His cavalry brigades were in position to march next day; all of them were in camps near the river on good roads. At Oak Shade Church, about seven and a half miles northwest of Fleetwood was Fitz Lee's brigade. Lee himself was ailing, rheumatism in his knee; he watched the day's review from a carriage with some "pretty girls." In Lee's stead Thomas T. Munford commanded the troopers. At Welford, about two miles north of Stuart, was Rooney Lee's brigade, and directly between Stuart and the Rappahannock, near St. James Church, was Jones's camp. The Stuart Horse Artillery, now commanded by R. F. Beckham (in place of Pelham), was between Jones and the river. Three miles behind Stuart as he faced the Rappahannock, on the farm belonging to John Minor Botts, was Robertson's brigade. Five miles south of Stuart, near Stevensburg, was Hampton's brigade. The cavalry division was well placed for marching—but not for fighting.[16]

While Stuart slept, his enemies were riding to battle. Union General Alfred Pleasonton, who had replaced Stoneman in command of Hooker's cavalry corps, was about to launch 11,000 men across the Rappahannock to "disperse and destroy" Confederate troops near Culpeper. At Beverly Ford, John Buford led a division and a brigade of cavalry and an infantry brigade, too. At Kelly's Ford, David M. Gregg led two cavalry divisions and an infantry brigade. Pleasonton had ordered Buford and Gregg to cross the river at dawn and converge on Brandy Station; then the reunited command (minus one of Gregg's divisions, which would support Pleasonton's flank from Stevensburg) would move on Culpeper. Pleasonton did not know precisely where Stuart was; but he believed that his column would find the Southern cavalry between Brandy Station and Culpeper.[17]

Buford began to cross the river at 4:30 A.M. and Confederate pickets could do very little to slow down the blue column. Chaos broke out in the Confederate camp (Jones's) near St. James Church. Men in various states of dress and undress ran for their horses, which they had turned out to graze. A hundred men (out of a regiment!) managed to mount and charge down the road toward the ford. Meanwhile artillerists struggled to hitch their teams and move their guns. Then Jones himself led another regiment into action. Two guns opened fire on the Federals, while Beckham concentrated the rest near the church. Miraculously the Southern spontaneity was sufficient to impede Buford's advance up the narrow road from the ford, and the situation stabilized temporarily.

The firing awakened Stuart on Fleetwood Hill, and he peered into the hovering fog toward the river. Soon a courier from Jones brought a report, and Stuart responded with a flurry of orders. No one knows exactly what Stuart's orders said; but from the subsequent actions of his subordinates, the effect was, "Saddle up; mount up; and find the fight." Stuart did instruct Robertson to march down the road to Kelly's Ford in the event the Federals should be coming from that direction, too.

Hampton's brigade advanced from Stevensburg and joined the conflict against Buford. Rooney Lee's brigade moved down to the river and took up a position on Buford's right flank with dismounted troopers behind a stone fence and artillery on a nearby hill. Munford led Fitz Lee's brigade down from the north and supported Rooney Lee's men. Thus four brigades of Southern cavalry (Jones, both Lees, and Hampton) managed to contain Buford's advance and force him back into the woods near the river. While all this was happening Stuart remained on Fleetwood Hill.[18]

Then about midmorning Stuart and his staff, excepting McClellan, rode down toward St. James Church to oversee the action. The situation there seemed well in hand. Buford was shifting units to bring his infantry brigade to the front, and there was a lull in the fighting. A message from Robertson to Jones warned of Gregg's column en route from Kelly's Ford. Jones relayed the news to Stuart, who told the courier, "Tell Gen. Jones to attend to the Yankees in his front, and I'll watch the flanks." When the courier complied, Jones snapped, "So he thinks they ain't coming, does he? Well, let him alone; he'll damned soon see for himself."

Stuart had been on the scene at the church for a time when, near noon, a courier from McClellan dashed up to him and reported a strong, long column of Federal cavalry advancing up the slopes of Fleetwood Hill. Stuart did not believe this and turned to an artillery captain nearby. "Ride back there, and see what this foolishness is all about!" Then another courier from McClellan galloped up. "General," the man screamed, "the Yankees are at Brandy!" And to punctuate his words came the sound of heavy firing to the rear.

It was Gregg's column, or most of it anyway, advancing via Kelly's Ford. Gregg had been quite late; he crossed the Rappahannock after 8:00 A.M., almost four hours behind Buford. Stuart, of course, had provided for the possibility of a second Federal column by sending Robertson's brigade toward Kelly's Ford. But Robertson that day seemed to confirm every negative thought Stuart had ever had about him. He led his brigade down the road, dismounted his men in some woods, and watched two divisions of enemy cavalry ride past his position. Robertson occupied the most direct road from Kelly's Ford to Brandy Station. Gregg took a more circuitous route, detached one of his divisions toward Stevensburg, and led the other division on to Brandy Station. Robertson was aware of all this; but did not know what to do, so he asked for specific instructions. By that time it was too late. As it happened, Robertson's men did very little all day. His losses from this bloody battle were four horses.[19]

One of Robertson's scouts first reported the Federal column to McClellan on Fleetwood Hill. McClellan was incredulous and told the man to go back and make sure of his message. Very soon thereafter the scout returned and suggested that McClellan look for himself. When he did, he saw the Federals about to march into Brandy Station. Once at Brandy Station the enemy would surely continue to Fleetwood Hill. And if the Federals were to seize the hill in strength with artillery, they would then be in a position to destroy Stuart's entire command.

To resist the Federal advance, which was already forming, McClellan had several couriers and one artillery piece, which the gunners had brought to headquarters in search of ammunition. The desperate adjutant quickly sent two couriers to Stuart, anticipating (correctly) that Stuart would not believe only one. Then he had his lone gun moved to the forward slope of the hill and instructed the gunners to commence a slow rate of fire upon the Federal column. This he did for two reasons: first, there were only a few rounds available; second, the deliberate firing might bluff his enemies into believing that there were more guns and troops on the hill.

McClellan's ruse was effective. Gregg had encountered virtually no opposition on his march from Kelly's Ford. The Confederates had to be somewhere, and Fleetwood Hill looked from Gregg's perspective like a likely place for them to be. Accordingly he ordered three of his guns forward to fire on the hill and prepared his horsemen for an assault.

Still, McClellan was frantic. Union shells exploded all over Fleetwood Hill. His own gun fired its final shot and withdrew. Federal cavalry had formed for the charge. And in the distance he saw a Southern regiment (12th Virginia) coming to the rescue at a trot (!). Clearly no one seemed to understand the urgency of the situation. McClellan mounted his horse and spurred down to meet the regiment; he ordered a gallop. When leading elements of the 12th Virginia reached the crest of Fleetwood Hill, the Federals were only fifty yards away. The Confederates were strung out for some distance; their adversaries were closed up. Consequently the odds were uneven at first. But there was a fight. The Federals were not able to seize the hill and consolidate their position.[20]

Stuart, even after he heard McClellan's second courier, had underestimated the danger. He sent only two regiments to McClellan's assistance. But he rode back to see for himself what the problem was and saw that it was indeed a big problem. It was perhaps at this point that he turned to Blackford and ordered him "to gallop along the line and order every commanding officer of a regiment to move on Fleetwood at a gallop." [21]

Meanwhile the contest for Fleetwood Hill continued very much in doubt. Charges and countercharges swept the slopes. Dust clouds covered the field and hid friend from foe. Cavalry units were supposed to sweep forward in unison, overwhelm their enemies, and recover together. Sometimes this happened. More often regiments rode into action in good order, and then the fighting became individual and isolated. The crest of the hill changed hands often, and for a time neither side seemed to be able to hold it. Federal artillerist J. W. Martin began the fight with thirty-six men; of these twenty-one were killed or wounded and nine were missing; at day's end he led only six survivors. Confederate artillerists resorted to using their sponge staffs (poles with sponges attached) as weapons against their mounted foes.

Then Hampton's brigade, four regiments and horse artillery, advanced in amazing order and entered the fray. The fresh troopers, attacking in concert, carried the hill and drove the Federals back to Brandy Station. Another charge by one of Jones's regiments (11th Virginia) drove them from Brandy Station. This was cavalry against cavalry in massed melee. Many of the men who fell were victims of saber slashes and thrusts. And many did fall. Of 280 troopers in the 1st New Jersey, for example, 56, including the lieutenant colonel commanding, were casualties by the time the battle concluded. [22]

Once Fleetwood Hill seemed to be his again, Stuart worked furiously to keep it. He withdrew his men to a line of battle along the forward slope of the hill which extended more than three miles. As Stuart's line began to appear more secure, one very interested observer probably expressed relief. In the cupola of the Barbour house immediately behind Fleetwood Hill, only a half mile from Stuart's battle line, was Robert E. Lee. [23]

Fighting continued on the flanks. To the north Rooney Lee led a charge that prevented Buford from flanking Stuart's line. In the midst of desperate fighting, Lee suffered a serious wound in the thigh. But the Confederates were able to drive Buford's men back toward the river.

On the other flank three Southern regiments confronted the Federal division advancing from Stevensburg. Amid some intricate maneuvers in the face of the Federals, one regiment (4th Virginia) broke and ran. But the Southerners generally gave ground grudgingly. As they did so, Colonel M. C. Butler, who commanded the 2nd South Carolina, sat on his horse talking to Will Farley, who was a volunteer aide to Stuart and one of his most trusted scouts. A Federal artillery piece opened fire on the pair; one shell struck the ground nearby and ricocheted. The flying piece of metal cut off Butler's foot just above his ankle, and drove through Butler's horse, then Farley's horse, and tore away Farley's leg at the knee. Butler eventually recovered.

When men went to help Farley, they found him in great pain, but determined to retain his composure. As they were about to carry him away, Farley pointed to his severed leg and asked to have it. He then hugged the gory stump and smiled (!)—"It is an old friend, gentlemen, and I do not wish to part from it." Farley believed that he would soon die, and he did. This was the man who had ridden alongside a Federal locomotive at Tunstall's Station a year before and blasted the engineer with a shotgun. Almost casual bloodthirst in life and grand gesture in death—Stuart wrote of Farley, "May his spirit abide with us!"[24]

Back at Fleetwood, Stuart called for help. The presence of the two Federal infantry brigades inspired him to dispatch Blackford toward Culpeper to summon Confederate foot soldiers. Actually Robert Rodes had anticipated Stuart's request and marched out to the Botts farm, about two miles from Fleetwood. Late in the day he advanced to the Barbour house, from which Lee was watching the conflict.

Rodes's men never joined the fight. But presumably Pleasonton saw them or saw some Southerners he believed were infantry reinforcements. Pleasonton realized that his troopers were exhausted, and the Confederate infantry he saw convinced the Federal commander to withdraw back across the Rappahannock. Pleasonton had failed to "disperse and destroy"; but he claimed a successful reconnaissance in force. Stuart's Confederates let their enemies withdraw at their own pace. Thus the Battle of Brandy Station wound down.[25]

Stuart claimed a great victory. He wrote a general order to his division stating that the day "tested your mettle and found it proof-steel." Confederate casualties totaled 523; the Federals lost 936. But more important than numbers and Southern mettle was the performance of Federal cavalry at Brandy Station and the legacy of that performance. McClellan, who was certainly in a position to know, later proclaimed: "One result of incalculable importance certainly did follow this battle—it *made* the Federal cavalry. Up to that time confessedly inferior to the Southern horsemen, they gained on this day that confidence in themselves and in their commanders which enabled them to contest so fiercely the subsequent battle-fields." Tom Rosser reflected later, "This engagement taught us one thing, however, and that was that the Federal cavalry was improving and fought better on this occasion than ever before. . . ." John Opie, who was closer to the common soldier than McClellan or Rosser, echoed their sentiments: "In this battle . . . they [the Federal cavalry] exhibited marked and wonderful improvement in skill, confidence, and tenacity." Even Stuart, in his report of the battle, admitted, "The contest for the hill was prolonged and spirited."[26]

Brandy Station forced a delay in Lee's plans to use his cavalry to screen his movement west and north. On the evening of June 9, Stuart insisted that he make camp precisely where he had made camp the previous night. The headquarters staff tried to comply, but found it impossible. Too many dead men and horses covered the ground. And the flies were too thick around the many bloodstains on the ground. There was no space to pitch their tents in the midst of this death and gore. So Stuart had to deny his pride and move his headquarters three or four miles to the rear. Next day (June 10) Stuart and his staff rode over the field. Turkey buzzards had arrived by hundreds to feast on the carrion of battle. Lord Byron had made it sound romantic—"Rider and horse—friend and foe—in one red burial blent!" The buzzards and flies had never read Byron.[27]

While Stuart prowled about the battlefield, the Army of Northern Virginia made up its collective mind about Brandy Station. One soldier wrote his parents, "Genl Stewart [*sic*] it is said has been paying more attention to the ladies of Culpeper than to his business as a soldier . . ." Blackford's brother, who was serving on Longstreet's staff, concluded, "The cavalry fight at Brandy Station can hardly be called a *Victory*. Stuart was certainly surprised and but for the supreme gallantry of his subordinate officers and the men in his command it would have been a day of disaster and disgrace. . . . Stuart is blamed very much, but whether or not fairly I am not sufficiently well informed to say." Dorsey Pender wrote his wife, "The cavalry affair in Culpeper was a sad one and our loss was very serious. . . . I suppose it is all right that Stuart should get all the blame, for when anything handsome is done he gets all the credit." Hampton later stated, "Stuart managed badly that day, but I would not say so publicly." Stuart did not read the words of these comrades, though he may have sensed their sentiment in the army. He did read qualified praise from Lee, whose judgment mattered most. "The dispositions made by you to meet the strong attack of the enemy appear to have been judicious and well planned. The troops were well and skillfully managed." Lee seemed to know that Stuart needed reassurance, however restrained.[28]

Civilians spread the story of Brandy Station unfettered by military discipline or etiquette. A woman from Culpeper wrote Jefferson Davis in the aftermath of the great battle, "President, allow a true Southern lady to say, General S's conduct since in Culpeper is perfectly ridiculous, having repeated reviews for the benefit of his lady friends, he riding up and down the line thronged with those ladies, he decorated with flowers, apparently a monkey show on hand and he the monkey. In fact General Stuart is nothing more or less than one of those fops, devoting his whole time to his lady friends' company." Custis Lee thought the letter very funny and forwarded it to Stuart with the advice that he either pay no attention to "the ladies" or attend them all.[29]

Newspapers throughout the South seemed to share the verdict of the woman in Culpeper. The Mobile *Daily Advertiser and Register* reported "a very unpleasant affair" and a "disastrous fight." The correspondent claimed that Stuart's entire headquarters with many confidential plans fell to the enemy. He also charged that reports of the battle were attempts to "sugar coat" a "bitter pill." The Memphis *Appeal*, which by this time had migrated to Atlanta, emphasized "surprise" on the Confederate side and termed the resultant battle "needless slaughter." And one of the paper's correspondents reported, "It is said that some of the officers had made their encampments too much of a brandy station for a long time past." In the Charleston *Mercury* Brandy Station was an "ugly surprise," and the *Mercury's* Richmond correspondent recorded the words of a supposed witness: "If anyone asks you about the cavalry fight at Culpeper, tell 'em we were whipped." Readers then "learned" that Lee had "censured Stuart severely," and that "Stuart's head has been turned by the ladies and the newspaper claquers of raids." In Richmond the *Enquirer* summarized, "Gen Stuart has suffered no little in public estimation by the late enterprises of the enemy."[30]

By far the unkindest cut of all came from the Richmond *Examiner*, the newspaper to which Stuart had been subscribing and contributing since his years as a cadet at West Point.

The more the circumstances of the late affair at Brandy Station are considered, the less pleasant do they appear. If this was an isolated case, it might be excused under the convenient head of accident or chance. But this puffed up cavalry of the Army of Northern Virginia has been twice, if not three times, surprised since the battles of December, and such repeated accidents can be regarded as nothing but the necessary consequences of negligence and bad management. If the war was a tournament, invented and supported for the pleasure of a few vain and weakheaded officers, these disasters might be dismissed with compassion. But the country pays dearly for the blunders which encourage the enemy to overrun and devastate the land, with a cavalry which is daily learning to despise the mounted troops of the Confederacy. The surprise on this occasion was the most complete that has occurred. The Confederate cavalry was carelessly strewn over the country, with the Rappahannock only between it and an enemy who has already proven his enterprise to our cost. . . . In the end the enemy retired, or was driven, it is not yet clearly known which, across the river. Nor is it certainly known whether the fortunate result was achieved by the cavalry alone or with the assistance of Confederate infantry in the neighborhood. . . . Events of this description have been lately too frequent to admit of the supposition that they are the results of hazard. They are the effects of causes which will produce like effects while they are permitted to operate, and they required the earnest attention both of the chiefs of the Government and the heads of the Army. The enemy is evidently determined to employ his cavalry extensively, and has spared no pains or cost to perfect that arm. The only effective means of preventing the mischief it may do is to reorganize our own forces, enforce a stricter discipline among the men and insist on more earnestness among the officers in the discharge of their very important duty.

The author of this rebuke never mentioned Stuart by name; he did not have to.[31]

Nor did Stuart lack defenders—not the least of whom was himself. His congratulatory order about Brandy Station, written the day after the *Enquirer* concluded that "if he is to be the 'eyes and ears of the army,' we would advise him to see more and be seen less," appeared widely in print. And his formal report of the battle not only presented his conduct in a favorable light, it also contained considerable fantasy. Here is some of Stuart's fancy about the battle, written four days after the fact.

[Several factors] determined me to make the real stand on the Fleetwood ridge. To this point I also ordered a section of artillery in reserve, and posted there my adjutant-general, Major [H. B.] McClellan, in observation, while I was absent on the Left.

On a field geographically so extensive, and much of it wooded, presenting to the enemy so many avenues of approach, I deemed it highly injudicious to separate my command into detachments to guard all the approaches. . . .

Major McClellan reported to me that the column . . . appeared to be advancing upon the Fleetwood Hill, having turned to the right from the Stevensburg road. The artillery sent to that hill unfortunately had little ammunition. Ordering more artillery to that point, and directing General Jones to send two regiments without delay to hold the heights, I repaired in person to that point, leaving General Jones with the remainder of his brigade to occupy the enemy in his front.

The force moving on Fleetwood was at first reported to be two regiments, but, as I approached, I saw that the force was larger, and then sent orders to Hampton and Robertson to move up their brigades, and to Jones to follow, notifying General W. H. F. [Rooney] Lee to join the command on the left.[32]

In Stuart's version the surprise and frantic activity occasioned by Buford at Beverly Ford became a reasoned response to an anticipated movement of the enemy. The single gun on Fleetwood Hill, there only because the crew was in search of ammunition, became a section of artillery ordered to the spot. McClellan's panic and heroics on Fleetwood when confronted by a Federal division became a mundane report to Stuart, who promptly responded to the matter. And the subsequent stampede of Confederate regiments to reach Fleetwood before the Federals could secure the height became a prudent concentration of Stuart's command. The report reads as though Stuart had orchestrated the entire day, instead of being twice surprised by enemy columns and of recovering only at the cost of desperate fighting.

Stuart partisans emerged in letters addressed to several newspapers and reprinted in still more. "A Friend of Truth and Justice," for example, insisted in a letter to the Richmond *Sentinel* that Stuart was not surprised at Brandy Station. An anonymous letter published in the Richmond *Enquirer* called the several charges being leveled at Stuart (surprise, captured baggage, et al.) "wholly unfounded" and then presented Stuart's version of the truth. The *Examiner,* too, received a long letter that "corrected" purported falsehoods. The authors of these letters were most probably officers on Stuart's staff. However it is entirely possible that Stuart assisted with the compositions of his defenders and perhaps even joined them in print.[33]

Brandy Station was indeed a large cavalry battle—the largest ever in North America. In a strictly tactical sense, it was inconclusive. Neither commander carried the day, although both Stuart and Pleasonton claimed to have done so. Stuart was surprised and embarrassed. Pleasonton certainly failed to accomplish his "disperse and destroy" mission, and even his claim of a successful reconnaissance in force is nonsense. He already knew Stuart had massed his cavalry near Culpeper. The captured documents of which he boasted were inconsequential items probably taken from artillery chief Beckham's camp desk, which had tumbled from a wagon on the day of the battle. Pleasonton, too, had managed to achieve surprise and then squander his advantage by failing to coordinate the actions of his divided forces.[34]

Brandy Station offered two strategic consequences. First, Federal cavalry was finally a potent force in the Army of the Potomac; no longer would Confederate horsemen control a field simply by being on it. And ironically, this great cavalry battle demonstrated the influence of infantry in mounted actions. Pleasonton planned for infantry participation in his expedition and made his decision to withdraw when he saw Southern foot soldiers. For his part, Stuart summoned infantry to assist him and explained his decision not to follow Federal cavalry to the river by referring to Federal infantry posted there.[35]

But what about Brandy Station and Stuart? The battle seemed to contradict the image Stuart had of himself. He had been embarrassed, surprised, and nearly defeated. Such things should not afflict heroes. Stuart responded to a sub-Stuart performance, not by attempting to improve it, but by insisting that a poor performance had been just perfect. He seemed more concerned with image than with substance because he confused the two.

# XII

---

## *Gettysburg*

LIKE MANY PEOPLE who rise rapidly from obscurity to prominence, Stuart was often insecure in his success. He had done and become everything he desired. He had defined an ideal vision of himself and acted out the fantasy. But beneath the facade he had constructed for himself, Stuart remained mortal; he was still the schoolboy trying futilely to please his parents, the young man falling off the platform while making a speech, and the second lieutenant too seasick to realize his boat was tied to a dock. Stuart let people know and see what he wanted them to know and see about himself. His friends, his staff, his family, even Flora, saw the bold facade. Living legends could not be vulnerable.[1]

Only a few weeks earlier, Stuart had written to Flora about the prospect of her and Jimmy's moving in with her sister and husband, Maria and Charles Brewer. Stuart opposed the idea, and his reason is very interesting. He liked the Brewers very much, he said; but living with them might jeopardize this affection. Familiarity might reveal things about the Brewers he would rather not know, and he did not want to risk becoming disillusioned. If such reasoning applied to the Brewers, might Stuart have believed something similar about himself? If he allowed people to get too close to him, they might find his flaws. So Stuart continued to act the part he had cast for himself and never removed his mask.[2]

Tom Price's diary is also revealing. Price, brother of Channing Price, was briefly on Stuart's staff during early 1863. His diary fell into Federal hands during the Chancellorsville campaign, and

Price transferred quite soon after Stuart read extracts from the
diary published in the *New York Times.* While Price was his assistant engineer officer, Stuart seemed intrigued by him and invited
him to dinner and breakfast on occasion. The young man, who had
just returned from university study in Europe, yearned to be in
Berlin, Paris, Athens—anywhere but in an army. He longed for
literary conversation. Stuart "called me into his tent this evening
and asked me if I had nothing better than the *Fairy Queen* to pass
my evenings—offered me thereupon the use of Jomini's *Practice
of War . . ."*

As Price recorded him, Stuart seemed always "on stage." One
evening, "Gen. Stuart came to headquarters about midnight; had
a great romp with his two aids [*sic*], and roused up the whole camp
by his singing and shouting." A few days later, "The general
tickled his Staff and threw them down in the mud. Then we had
hard-boiled eggs and stories about his different raids." Still later,
"Gen. Stuart was with us and prattled on all evening in his garru-
lous way—described how he commenced the war by capturing 50
of Patterson's advance guard on the day preceding Bull Run." All
this seems excessive—"over-acting"—on Stuart's part. His romps
and tickling and tales protested too much. This behavior was in-
appropriate for a hero. Stuart was becoming a boor.[3]

Maybe by mid-June of 1863 Stuart had reason to wonder about
his capacity to live up to his legend. He had established himself
and his cavalry against an inept enemy. Until recently Federal
cavalry had been weakly deployed, poorly trained, and timidly
led. Now the Federals had consolidated their units of horse soldiers, and the battles of Kelly's Ford and Brandy Station had
served notice of vast improvements in their confidence and performance.

Stuart still believed in himself; he knew he had to have faith
in himself or no one else would. He believed in the mold he had
cast for his life and career. But he had always been quite sensitive
to what other people said and wrote about him. He had cultivated
his public image and in turn the poems, songs, and praise seemed
to confirm his vision of himself. How could the newspapers and
gossips be so wrong?

The cavalry battle on June 9 had not altered Lee's determination to take the war into the enemy's country in order to provoke a

showdown battle and destroy the Army of the Potomac. His axis of advance was down the Shenandoah Valley, across the Potomac, through Maryland, and into Pennsylvania, via Hagerstown and Chambersburg. During the initial phase of this march, Lee again ordered Stuart to screen the infantry movement and keep the Federals east of the Blue Ridge.[4]

So on June 16, one week after Brandy Station, Stuart crossed the Rappahannock and led the march into the country between the Bull Run/Catoctin Mountains and the Blue Ridge. Next day (June 17) Stuart and his staff rode into Middleburg. He sent Fitz Lee's brigade (commanded by Thomas T. Munford) to Aldie to guard there a gap in the Bull Run mountains and Rooney Lee's brigade (now commanded by J. R. Chambliss) to Thoroughfare Gap. Beverly Robertson's brigade he stationed about halfway between the two gaps. Grumble Jones and Wade Hampton were to remain on the Rappahannock until the last of Lee's infantry departed.

Munford reached Aldie, stationed pickets about the village, and awaited the arrival of the rest of his command. Suddenly a brigade of Federal cavalry, Judson Kilpatrick and four regiments, appeared and swept through Aldie, driving Munford's troopers from their post. Thomas L. Rosser's 5th Virginia countered with a saber charge and contained Kilpatrick's advance. Then Kilpatrick charged again and the battle continued along the road west of Aldie. During the succession of charges and countercharges, neither side gained any clear advantage, and near dark Munford withdrew about a mile up the road toward Middleburg on instructions from Stuart.[5]

While the fighting raged at Aldie, Stuart and his staff were relaxing in Middleburg. Women and girls, probably some of the same ones who had mobbed Stuart during his last visit to Middleburg the previous fall, gathered around the officers, flirted with them, and listened to their tales of adventure. All at once about four o'clock in the afternoon, some of the men Stuart had stationed as pickets dashed down the street screaming, "The Yankees are coming!" The Yankees were A. N. Duffié and a regiment of Rhode Island cavalry, and they were indeed coming. Von Borcke lumbered out of the house in which he had been visiting and clambered aboard his horse. He spurred away with Stuart, who was, as Henry McClellan phrased it, making "a retreat more rapid than was consistent with dignity and comfort."[6]

Stuart rode to find Robertson's brigade and sent messages to Munford at Aldie and Chambliss at Thoroughfare Gap to converge on Middleburg. About seven o'clock that evening (June 17) Robertson attacked the lone Federal regiment in Middleburg and drove Duffié out of the place. Duffié retreated down the same road on which Chambliss was advancing, and that night and the next morning most of the Federal horsemen became prisoners. Although Stuart himself had spent his most active moments of the day charming women in Middleburg and running from Duffié's Rhode Islanders, his cavalry had had a pretty good day on June 17. Robertson and Chambliss had avenged their general's embarrassment, and Munford still barred the road leading west to the Blue Ridge.[7]

On June 18 Stuart remained near Middleburg. He wrote later in his report that he decided not to commit himself to a general engagement until joined by Jones and Hampton. He did dispatch scouts to try to determine the strength and dispositions of his enemy. That evening John Mosby, who had made this region his own in a series of partisan raids, managed to capture a Federal staff officer and the dispatches he was carrying from Joe Hooker to Alfred Pleasonton. Mosby hurried to Stuart with the news that the Federals at Aldie now included Pleasonton's entire cavalry command, just under 7,000 troopers.[8]

Next day (June 19) Pleasonton attacked with a full division of horsemen. The Confederates held the line Stuart had drawn west of Middleburg for some time and then withdrew to another position further west. As Stuart and his staff were withdrawing, Federal sharpshooters fired on them from the edge of some woods about 200 yards away. William W. Blackford heard an ominous thump "like some one had struck a barrel a violent blow with a stick." He looked first to Stuart, and then saw Von Borcke slump in his saddle and drop his reins. The huge Prussian felt a blow to the back of his neck and saw "fiery sparks" before passing out. He regained consciousness moments later, and found himself sprawled on the ground. Blackford had helped Von Borcke off his horse; but now he had a 250-pound wounded man on the ground, and the Federals were closing and firing as they came. Von Borcke's case appeared hopeless. Blood poured from the wound in his neck and ran from his mouth as he tried to breathe. Somehow the Prussian summoned strength and managed to help the men who were trying to help him. Blackford throttled Von Borcke's horse by twisting the animal's ear, a trick Von Borcke himself had taught him. The men managed to hoist the Prussian aboard his horse and support him in the saddle until they reached safety. During the struggle to remove Von Borcke from the field, Federal sharpshooters shot and killed two of the group gathered to aid the fallen giant. And it seemed that they had rescued a man soon to be a corpse. Blackford found an ambulance wagon and supervised loading Von Borcke inside. The driver, however, knew a mortal wound when he saw one and took no care for his patient's comfort as he drove at a gallop toward Upperville. Finally Von Borcke roused himself and dragged himself to the front of the vehicle. He pressed his pistol to the driver's head and told him he would cheerfully blow his brains out if he did not slow down. The slower pace permitted staff surgeon Talcott Eliason to overtake the ambulance. Eliason's examination revealed that the bullet had entered Von Borcke's neck, barely missed his spinal cord, but severed his windpipe, and then plunged into his left lung. "My dear fellow," Eliason said as gently as he could, "your wound is mortal, and I can't expect you to live till the morning."[9]

Meanwhile, back at the battle, Stuart watched his horsemen defend their new position as the battle wound down. Again the Southerners had retreated, but not far, and again they had shielded Lee's infantry columns in the Valley. Moreover, Jones arrived that evening; Hampton was en route and expected the following day. Then Stuart would have his full command on hand—the brigades of Hampton, Jones, Robertson, Munford (Fitz Lee's), and Chambliss (Rooney Lee's).[10]

During the night (of June 19) Stuart rode into Upperville to visit Von Borcke, who was now at Eliason's home on what everyone assumed was his deathbed. Other members of the staff had come to pay their respects. Von Borcke's neck and face were swollen and pale; he was coughing up small pieces of his collar, which the bullet had carried with it into his lung. Eliason had given him opium for his pain, and he lay in a trance of semisleep. Stuart bent over his comrade and kissed his forehead; two tears spilled on Von Borcke's cheek.[11]

Rain fell steadily almost all day on June 20 as Stuart posted his five brigades on a long line between Middleburg and Upperville.

Pleasonton did not venture forth in strength from Middleburg, although he did send out skirmishers to probe Stuart's flank. The Federal commander had ambitious plans for the following day, however. He wrote to Hooker and proposed with his entire corps to assault Stuart's force and "cripple it up." To assist with the crippling, Pleasonton requested infantry. Hooker complied and sent orders for a full division of foot soldiers to march at two o'clock on the morning of June 21. Pleasonton intended to do the job he had tried to do at Brandy Station.[12]

For his part, Stuart claimed in his report that he, too, was "extremely anxious now to attack the enemy as early as possible." However June 21 was a Sunday in 1863, and "I recognized my obligation to do no duty other than what was absolutely necessary." Such piety had not prevented Stuart from fighting on Sunday at First Manassas (Bull Run) and Chancellorsville, nor from raiding on Sunday during his Ride Around McClellan, Chambersburg, and Dumfries expeditions. At any rate, Pleasonton launched his attack between seven and eight o'clock on that Sunday (June 21), and Stuart soon found lots of duties that were "absolutely necessary."

Pleasonton first committed three regiments of infantry against Stuart's horsemen. Then he dispatched another infantry regiment around Stuart's right flank. Then, when the Confederates withdrew as Pleasonton knew they must, Federal cavalry charged in an effort to transform retreat into rout. Each time Stuart's troopers made another stand, Pleasonton repeated his infantry-cavalry tactics. As a result the Southerners fell steadily back toward Upperville.[13]

Some time during the morning Stuart found time to visit Von Borcke, who had surprised everyone, including himself, by remaining alive. Indeed he had rallied considerably. Stuart told Von Borcke that he might have to abandon Upperville, and if so he would send an ambulance to carry his comrade to safety.

As it happened Stuart did withdraw through Upperville and beyond to Ashby's Gap in the Blue Ridge. He said that he did not wish to make a stand at Upperville for the sake of the safety of the women and children who remained there. Nevertheless, artillery shells were crashing in the streets and rifle bullets whizzing when Von Borcke left in his ambulance. His friends carried the wounded

Prussian to a farmhouse about two miles from the village. There
Von Borcke spent an anxious evening while Union cavalrymen
swarmed the neighborhood. He did eventually recover, though
not sufficiently to return to duty in the field. Von Borcke spent an
extended recovery period in and around Richmond.[14]

Dark ended the Battle of Upperville, and Pleasonton decided
not to press the issue the following day. The Federals withdrew
to Aldie; Stuart followed and reestablished his presence on approximately the same line he had established before the Aldie-
Middleburg-Upperville fights began.

Pleasonton reported a series of victories, and historians since
have generally agreed with him in principle, if not degree. It is
true that Federal cavalry wrested the initiative from Stuart and
pressed him back. It is also true that the Federal horsemen once
more performed well; too, the combined cavalry-infantry operation at Upperville added a new tactic to mounted warfare. And
during one of the retreats on June 21, Stuart's Horse Artillery had
to abandon a gun, the first piece of artillery Stuart had ever lost.
But the fact remains that Stuart conducted a successful screening
operation against a force superior in size to his. In the fighting
from June 17 through June 21, the Federals suffered 827 casualties, the Confederates 660. The action of June 21 at Upperville
lasted from eight in the morning till dark and involved both enemy
cavalry and infantry. Yet Stuart withdrew only about six miles
across less than crucial ground that day and emerged much less
than "crippled up." Aldie, Middleburg, and Upperville might
have buoyed Stuart's confidence.[15]

Yet Stuart did some uncharacteristic things during this brief
campaign. In his report, written in August, he remembered that he
had intended to seize the initiative and attack Pleasonton's force.
Always, though, there were excuses why he had not—his entire
command was not together; it was Sunday; women and children
might have suffered. Taken together these excuses sound somewhat lame. Von Borcke's wound must have shaken Stuart. He had
lost John Pelham and Channing Price, and now Von Borcke. Moreover Stuart believed with reason that the Federal sharpshooters
had mistaken Von Borcke for himself. In fact friends as well as
enemies may have confused the two flamboyant cavalry officers,
and one of Stuart's troopers was convinced that adverse gossip

about Stuart's social habits resulted from the confusion. In any event, Stuart wrote Flora that the enemy was trying specifically to kill him.

McClellan detected another anomaly. By now the adjutant had been with Stuart long enough to know his habits, and in the aftermath of Upperville, McClellan realized that Stuart had not participated in the action. He had been on the scene, but content to watch. "I asked the reason of this unusual proceeding," McClellan recalled, "and he replied that he had given all necessary instructions to his brigade commanders, and he wished them to feel the responsibility resting upon them, and to gain whatever honor the field might bring." Certainly, this was an eminently logical explanation; but it does not sound at all like Stuart. It would seem that Stuart's faith in himself may indeed have wavered. So he chose to rest upon his past laurels rather then seek new ones.[16]

When Stuart established his headquarters at Rector's Cross Roads, near Middleburg, on June 22, Lee's Pennsylvania campaign was rapidly developing and the cavalry had work to do. Stuart's communications with Lee, over the next three days, together with his assumptions, assignments, and plans relating to the Pennsylvania campaign would later become more important than they seemed at the time.

The cavalry now needed to be in several places at once. While Longstreet's corps and A. P. Hill's corps advanced down the Valley, horsemen still had to hold the gaps in the Blue Ridge to prevent the enemy from detecting and interrupting the march. At the same time, Ewell's corps was already in Pennsylvania, and cavalry belonged also in the vanguard of the army. Ewell did have a brigade of horsemen commanded by Albert G. Jenkins, but these troopers, like their commander, were strangers to larger-scale operations. There was also the matter of which route to take into Pennsylvania; if Stuart marched down the Valley, west of the Blue Ridge, he might give away Lee's plans or even lead Pleasonton to Lee's army. Very early on the twenty-second, Stuart wrote a note to Longstreet asking for guidance. Longstreet passed the note on to Lee, and then both generals wrote to Stuart. Lee said nothing directly about a route, but suggested that if Stuart were satisfied that two of his brigades could hold the gaps in the Blue Ridge, he should start north to Ewell with his other three brigades. Longstreet's note urged Stuart to cross the Potomac in the rear of Hooker's army and indicated that Lee concurred with this choice of route.[17]

Next day (June 23) Mosby rode to Stuart's headquarters and said that his scouts confirmed that Stuart could indeed ride through Hooker's dispersed units and cross the Potomac between Hooker and Washington. Such a scheme might confuse the Federals and would surely alarm them. In addition Stuart might raid enemy supply lines while en route to Pennsylvania. Stuart dispatched Mosby to reconfirm his intelligence and then posed the essentials of Mosby's plan to Lee.[18]

It rained steadily on the night of June 23 at Stuart's headquarters. Stuart, however, chose to sleep outside under a tree, rather than avail himself of the shelter of a house nearby. McClellan tried to dissuade the general; but Stuart protested, "No! my men are exposed to this rain, and I will not fare any better than they." Maybe he was trying to purge himself of recent afflictions; maybe he was reimmersing himself into his noble mold; maybe he simply preferred fresh air and solitude. Whatever the reason or whim, Stuart lay down with his blanket and oilcloths and went to sleep.

Late in the night a courier from Lee rode to the house where McClellan was sleeping and gave him a letter marked "Confidential." The faithful adjutant thought about Stuart sleeping soundly nearby and opened the letter to determine whether or not he should disturb the general. He quickly discerned that Lee had written detailed instructions about Stuart's route and role in the campaign, so he took the letter at once to Stuart. Lee offered his cavalry commander wide latitude to select his route in accord with circumstances. He was to leave two brigades in the gaps of the Blue Ridge and instruct them to follow the infantry. Whether he crossed the Potomac to the west or east of the mountains, however, he should cross soon and then "move on and feel the right of Ewell's troops collecting information, provisions, etc." Stuart read Lee's instructions, told McClellan not to open any more confidential dispatches, and went back to sleep.[19]

Next morning (June 24) Stuart made ready to march. He ordered Hampton, Fitz Lee (again in command after his bout with rheumatism), and Chambliss (Rooney Lee's brigade) to rendezvous at Salem, about ten miles south of Rector's Cross Roads. Stuart also took with him six artillery pieces. Remaining behind in Ashby's and Snicker's gaps were the brigades of Jones and Robertson. Stuart exhorted Robertson, who would command this force, to observe and harass the Federals as long as they remained in Virginia. When Hooker moved north, as common sense dictated he must, Robertson was to leave strong pickets in the gaps and at Harpers Ferry and follow the army into Pennsylvania.

Stuart had decided to do what he wanted to do—march between Hooker's army and Washington and mix raiding with riding en route to Ewell in Pennsylvania. He took with him his best brigades and left behind units and commanders he believed could accomplish less ambitious tasks. These things he did because he was Jeb Stuart, and Jeb Stuart could do no less.[20]

At one o'clock on the morning of June 25 Stuart's column left Salem and rode east through a gap in the mountains toward the village of Haymarket. As the horsemen approached Haymarket, they discovered a corps of Federal infantry (Winfield Scott Hancock's troops) marching north on the road Stuart planned to use. After firing upon the Federals with his artillery, Stuart recoiled and decided to make a still wider detour. Allowing some time on the twenty-fifth for the horses to graze, Stuart set out once more on June 26. The column moved east and south through Bristoe Station and Brentsville to Butler's Fork and then north to Wolf Run Shoals on the Occoquan River. Next day (June 27) the march continued north through Fairfax Court House to Dranesville, and on to Rowser's Ford on the Potomac. Along the route Stuart encountered evidence that Hooker's army was also on the move north, and at Fairfax Court House, Hampton's horsemen clashed briefly with a squadron of Federal cavalry. Rowser's Ford, about twenty miles above Washington, was unguarded; but the Potomac was running two feet higher than normal. Cavalry could cross with difficulty; artillery posed a serious problem. Stuart investigated another ford and then wrestled the guns across at Rowser's. McClellan stated, "No more difficult achievement was accomplished by the cavalry during the war." All this took time, though, and by the time the rear guard was finally across, it was three o'clock on the morning of June 28, already the fourth day of the march.[21]

Following the arduous crossing, men and horses had to rest.

Hampton, who was leading the way, pressed on to Rockville and cleared the town of a small Federal force. Stuart and the rest of the column did not reach Rockville until after noon. There he discovered two delights—women and wagons.

The women were from a "female academy" in Rockville. According to Blackford, "flocks of the pretty maidens congregated on the front to greet us, showing strong sympathy for our cause, and cutting off all the buttons they could get hold of from our uniforms as souvenirs."

The wagons, 150 of them, composed a supply train eight miles long from Washington bound for the Federal army. The Southerners swarmed about the wagons and easily captured 125 of them. Those the cavalry did not capture their teamsters wrecked in an effort to escape. And inside the wagons were bags of grain for hungry horses and food and whiskey for cavalrymen who had packed three days' rations four days ago. The wagon chase had taken Stuart's troopers to within three or four miles of Washington. By the time Stuart paroled the 400 Federal soldiers he had captured and the column re-formed, June 28 was over and the Confederates were still in Maryland—at Cooksville, twenty miles west of Baltimore.[22]

On June 29 Stuart continued to move north with his 125 wagons. Fitz Lee's men managed to destroy a segment of track on the Baltimore and Ohio Railroad, and everywhere the Southerners cut telegraph lines. During the late afternoon the column encountered opposition at Westminster, but disposed of two stubborn companies of Delaware cavalry and pressed on to Union Mills, where Stuart called a halt for the night. And during the night he learned that substantial numbers of Federal cavalry (a division, as it happened) were seven miles ahead of him on the road to Gettysburg.

At this point Stuart had no idea where Lee's army had gone. In his report he said that he assumed that by this time Lee must have reached the Susquehanna River. Actually elements of the Army of Northern Virginia had reached the Susquehanna while Stuart was capturing wagons in Rockville on June 28. Now on June 30, the army was spread from Chambersburg to Heidlersburg and converging upon Gettysburg. And Stuart, though he did not know it, was almost in the middle of the Union army as it marched north to

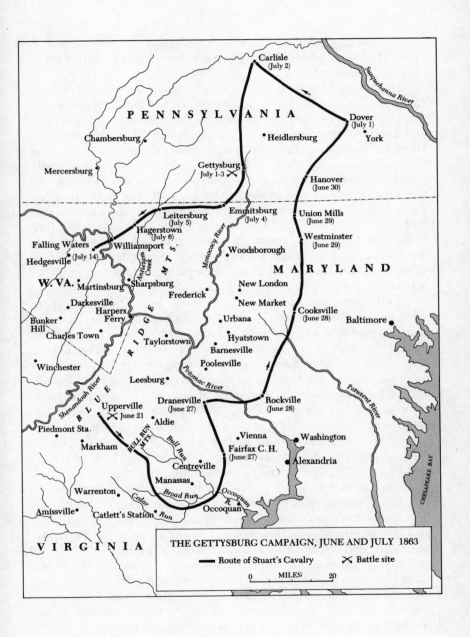

THE GETTYSBURG CAMPAIGN, JUNE AND JULY 1863

— Route of Stuart's Cavalry    ✕ Battle site

0        MILES        20

meet Lee. In round numbers, 41,000 Federal troops were ahead of
Stuart (between him and Lee), and another 41,000 Federals were
close behind him.[23]

On the morning of June 30, Stuart marched toward Hanover.
He sent Fitz Lee off to the left to screen his flank. Leading the
main column was Chambliss's brigade; then came the 125 wagons;
and finally Hampton's brigade. At ten o'clock Chambliss reached
Hanover and found there some of Judson Kilpatrick's division of
Federal horsemen. One of Chambliss's regiments (2nd North
Carolina) immediately charged and drove a Pennsylvania regiment through Hanover, as Stuart and his staff rode to the head of
the column. Then the Federals returned the favor and charged the
2nd North Carolina. The Confederates broke and ran before a full
brigade of the enemy, and as they galloped back down the road,
the Southerners passed Stuart and his staff. Seconds later the pursuing Federals thundered down upon Stuart, Blackford, and the
rest of the staff.

"Rally them, Blackford!" shouted Stuart. But as he said this, he
wheeled his mare Virginia, jumped over a hedge beside the road,
and galloped into a field. Blackford followed his leader, as did the
rest of the staff. They jumped, however, into the midst of two
dozen or more blue horsemen in the field on the flank of their
comrades who were charging up the road. Ignoring cries of "Halt!"
and pistol shots from the Federals, Stuart led the race to escape
through the tall grass. Suddenly through the grass he saw the
creek, a small stream that had cut a gully fifteen feet wide and four
feet deep. There was nothing to do but jump. Stuart and Blackford
took off together and Blackford turned his head to look to Stuart
and Virginia. "I shall never forget the glimpse I then saw of this
beautiful animal away up in mid-air over the chasm and Stuart's
fine figure sitting erect and firm in the saddle." Stuart and Blackford made the leap unscathed and, though still in danger, laughed
at their friends who landed in the water. The pursuing Federals
pulled up short of the gully and did not press the chase.[24]

Stuart regrouped on a line of hills south and east of Hanover,
called his guns from the rear of the column, and held his enemy at
bay with artillery, while he waited for Hampton to move up from
the rear and for Fitz Lee to move in from the flank. The wagons he
placed hub to hub so he could burn them efficiently if necessary.

Kilpatrick did not attack. But the presence of the wagon train and of a division of enemy cavalry forced Stuart to detour still farther in his search for the Army of Northern Virginia.

He began in the dark. Three brigades and 125 wagons headed east, then turned north. The mules who pulled the wagons had had no food and little water for three days; they, according to McClellan, "often became unmanageable." Blackford said they were a "source of unmitigated annoyance." Prisoners collected en route fared little better. And the Southern troopers and horses, too, were by now exhausted. All night they marched while riders dozed and teamsters beat their miserable animals. Still Stuart could learn nothing definite about the location of Lee's army.[25]

Daylight on July 1 found the column near Dover, and Stuart ordered a brief rest. But now he searched, not only for the Confederate army, but also for rations and fodder for his men and animals. Stuart decided to follow a rumor and ride on to Carlisle in hopes of finding friends and food. He sent Andrew Reid Venable from his staff in search of Lee's army and later sent another staff officer on a similar mission. The march to Carlisle was arduous, only slightly less so than the night march to Dover. And when the column arrived in the afternoon, the Confederates found it occupied by two brigades of Pennsylvania militia. If the troopers wanted food, they would have to fight for it. One of the junior officers remembered the situation in a letter to his mother: "It is impossible for me to give you a correct idea of the fatigue and exhaustion of the men and beasts at this time. From great exertion, constant mental excitement, want of sleep and food, the men were overcome, and so tired and stupid as almost to be ignorant of what was transpiring around them. Even in line of battle, in momentary expectation of being made to charge, they would throw themselves upon their horses' necks, and even the ground, and fall asleep."[26]

Stuart tried to convince the militia officers to surrender Carlisle. When the commander refused, Stuart ordered his artillery to shell the place and had his men burn the barracks of the cavalry school on the edge of Carlisle. Afterwards residents of the town remembered their fright and a terrible bombardment of defenseless women and children; McClellan recalled "throwing a few shells into the outskirts of the town." And within the Southern ranks the weary junior officer reported, "Most of us were kept in our saddles to fight till 12 o'clock [midnight]—though neither the prospect of a *melee,* nor the thunder of artillery, nor the bright red glare of a burning town, "in the enemy's country,' kept me awake that night." [27]

During the night Venable returned with news. Lee was at Gettysburg, thirty-three miles to the south, and Lee wanted Stuart to join him there. While Stuart had been skirmishing with Pennsylvania militia, Lee had engaged Hooker's army, which was now George G. Meade's army. The showdown battle had begun.

Between midnight and one o'clock on the morning of July 2, Stuart started his command south and marched all night. Hampton's troopers encountered Federal cavalry near Hunterstown as they approached Gettysburg and concluded their long march with a spirited but inconclusive fight. Stuart rode ahead of his column and found Lee on Seminary Ridge in the afternoon. [28]

"Well, General Stuart, you are here at last." This and no more, according to legend, was Lee's greeting. [29]

On July 1, as Stuart's weary horsemen were riding away toward Carlisle, Confederate infantry had encountered Federals at Gettysburg. A skirmish on the outskirts of town attracted reinforcements on both sides and by afternoon there was a battle. The Southerners had managed to capture the town; but the Federals had seized the high ground (Cemetery Hill) overlooking Gettysburg. During the night (July 1–2) more troops had arrived and on July 2, as Stuart was driving his men toward the scene, Lee ordered attacks upon both flanks of the Federal position. Elements of Ewell's corps assaulted Culp's Hill on the Union right; Longstreet's men assaulted Big Round Top and Little Round Top on the Union left; neither attack dislodged the Federals. Now Meade's army occupied Cemetery Ridge. The position ran north-south along the ridge, anchored at the north end by Cemetery Hill and Culp's Hill and at the south end by Big and Little Round Tops. Lee's army held Seminary Ridge to the west and coiled part of the way around the Federal position so as to resemble a very large fishhook.

During the evening of July 2, Lee decided to attack the center of Meade's lines in an attempt to break through the Federal formation. The plan was a gamble. Lee had no firm knowledge of the strength of his enemy, because he had had no cavalry support. But

Lee had not come all this way to shrink from a moment of truth, so he determined once more to dare.

Lee assigned Stuart a position on the far left flank of his army —perhaps to be the "barb" of the Southern fishhook. Besides the brigades of Hampton, Fitz Lee, and Chambliss, Stuart commanded the brigade of Albert G. Jenkins. These latter horsemen had marched north with the main army; but Jenkins and his men had had no prior experience in major campaigns, although they had served creditably in southwestern Virginia. Jones and Robertson had not yet joined the campaign as Stuart had instructed them to.

Initially, Stuart ordered his men to remain mounted all night in case the enemy should come their way. However Stuart's subordinates persuaded the general that his troopers had reached the limits of their endurance, and he permitted them to rest. Next morning (July 3), Stuart became aware that, not only were his men and horses jaded, they were also in need of ammunition. Consequently the cavalry consumed the early hours of the day resupplying themselves, and even so, Jenkins's men rode off with only ten rounds apiece.[30]

Stuart's intentions on July 3 are not at all clear. He knew that Lee intended to try to break the center of Meade's lines on Cemetery Ridge with what became Pickett's Charge. Stuart's position on the extreme left of the Confederate line, east of Gettysburg, was sound; from there he could protect the Confederate left flank and/or launch an attack upon retreating Federals in the event Pickett broke their line. It is also possible that Stuart hoped to assault the rear of the Union line at the same time that Pickett's force assailed the front. In that event, Stuart realized that he would probably have to win a battle with Federal cavalry before he could threaten Meade's rear.[31]

All four brigades left their camps during the late morning, rode down the York Turnpike, and then occupied a terrain feature known as Cress's Ridge. From the wooded summit of the ridge, the Confederates could overlook a mile of open country beyond which was Cemetery Ridge and Meade's infantry. Stuart concealed his horsemen from view in the trees and then did a strange thing. He ordered one artillery piece into the open and himself directed a series of seemingly random shots in different directions across the empty plain below. It was as though he were announcing his presence to his enemies or perhaps giving a signal to Lee. Then Stuart sent forward two regiments of Jenkins's men dismounted to hold a line of fences to his front and a barn belonging to a man named Rummel.

Federal cavalry, three brigades of it, responded to Stuart's threat. First dismounted men moved forward to contest the fence line held by Jenkins's skirmishers. Then artillery opened on the Confederate guns. Stuart had hoped to conceal the brigades of Hampton and Fitz Lee until the Federals committed against his dismounted troopers. But the men from Jenkins's brigade soon shot off their ten rounds and had to fall back. Then Hampton and Lee moved beyond the trees and gave away their position. So Stuart sent mounted regiments into the fray. And finally Stuart launched his own version of Pickett's Charge.[32]

At almost the same time as Pickett set out for immortality and slaughter a few miles to the west, Hampton's and Lee's brigades formed to attack. One of their enemies described the Confederates: "A grander spectacle than their advance has rarely been beheld. They marched with well-aligned fronts and steady reins. Their polished saber-blades dazzled in the sun. All eyes turned upon them. . . . Shell and shrapnel met the advancing Confederates and tore through their ranks. Closing the gaps as though nothing had happened, on they came. As they drew nearer, canister was substituted by our artillerymen for shell, and horse after horse staggered and fell. Still they came on."[33]

George Armstrong Custer led the Federal countercharge. "As the two columns approached each other the pace of each increased, when suddenly a crash, like the falling of timber, betokened the crisis. So sudden and violent was the collision that many of the horses were turned end over end and crushed their riders beneath them. The clashing of sabers, the firing of pistols, the demands for surrender and cries of the combatants now filled the air." The author of this account, William E. Miller, a captain in the 3rd Pennsylvania, was not given to hyperbole; after the battle he wrote his brother that he had suffered a "slight scratch," which was really a bullet through his arm.[34]

The courage and weight of the Confederate column carried it forward. But then Federal units, one of them led by Captain

Miller, began slamming into the Southern flanks and breaking up the formation. At last the leading riders faltered and the momentum of the charge dissipated. Out of the swirling melee the Confederates withdrew to their original line on the Rummel farm, and fighting continued for a time there. When Rummel returned to his home, he found thirty dead horses in his lane. He also found two dead men from opposite sides with their stiffened fingers still embedded in each other's lifeless flesh.[35]

The battle left both cavalries about where they had been before, although Confederate and Federal veterans squabbled for years over who last held Rummel's barn. Stuart lost 181 casualties (exclusive of his artillery and Jenkins's brigade); the Federals lost 254 men. Among the Confederate casualties was Hampton, who suffered a saber wound in his scalp. At dark Stuart left a regiment on picket at Cress's Ridge and withdrew up the York Turnpike a few miles with the bulk of his command. Tactically a draw, the cavalry battle was, according to Blackford, "about as bloody and hot an affair as any we had yet experienced." He added, "The cavalry of the enemy were steadily improving and it was all we could do sometimes to manage them." And Stuart had to watch his hope of thundering into the rear of Meade's army frustrated. Regardless of what he saw, though, he reported a victory.[36]

Across a couple of ridges to the west, Lee saw the frustration of his own hopes and knew he would have to retreat. Stuart knew none of this until he rode to Lee's headquarters very late that night. There he learned the worst. The attack upon the Federal center, Pickett's Charge, had been a gallant disaster. The Confederates, 12,000 of them, had marched forth in perfect order following a massive artillery barrage. But as the Southerners marched upon Cemetery Ridge, Federal guns opened fire and opened large holes in their ranks. Then Federal infantry joined the bloodletting. A remnant band of Confederates reached the top of the ridge; but Union reinforcements chased away those who survived. Pickett's Charge had failed and lived only as a legend.

Now Stuart knew also that his cavalry would have to screen the withdrawal; his worn men and mounts had still more work ahead. Lee's infantry remained in place on Seminary Ridge on July 4 while a summer rain set in and washed the battlefield. At dark they began the long march to the Potomac. Supply wagons and ambulances started south earlier, and the cavalry dispersed to escort the wagon train and columns of infantry.

Stuart rode and fought for ten more days. On July 4 he rode toward Emmitsburg, Maryland, and became lost in the dark and rain. On July 5 he fought his way through the Catoctin Mountains to Leitersburg. On July 6 he united the brigades of Jenkins, Chambliss, Jones, and Robertson and fought his way through Hagerstown toward Williamsport on the Potomac. On July 7 he began posting his horsemen to screen the infantry, which had to stop and wait for the Potomac to subside before crossing into Virginia. On July 8 he moved from his lines to assault Federal cavalry and keep the enemy from harassing Lee's infantry—to maintain "a predominance of pluck over the enemy." On July 9 he remained in front of the army at Funkstown. On July 10 he had a horse shot under him as he directed dismounted fighting nearly all day; in the night he withdrew to a more defensible line behind Antietam Creek. On July 11 he rearranged his screen some more, and on July 12, he directed a withdrawal and uncovered Lee's infantry, who by this time had had time to entrench their perimeter defense. On July 13 he watched his horsemen skirmish much of the day at various points and spent the night screening Lee's passage of the Potomac at Falling Waters. The cavalry finally crossed the river behind Lee's army at eight o'clock on the morning of July 14.[37]

During this period, perhaps for the only time in his life, Stuart became too exhausted to function from the constant riding, fighting, and responsibility. One evening, maybe July 6, Stuart and his staff arrived about nine o'clock at the home of a Southern sympathizer in Hagerstown. Stuart had eaten nothing for twenty-four hours. While a young woman prepared late supper for the hungry officers, Stuart slept on a sofa. When the food was ready, Stuart would not stir until McClellan all but dragged him to the table. Even then he only pushed his food around the plate and ate very little.

The young woman became concerned and asked, "General, perhaps you would relish a hard-boiled egg?"

"Yes," said Stuart, "I'll take *four or five*." The words were rude; but the woman hurried away and soon returned with some eggs. Stuart ate only one and left the table. McClellan and other staff members were alarmed at this uncharacteristic behavior and the adjutant tried to penetrate Stuart's fog. He went to the piano in the parlor, and encouraged everyone to sing with him. Even though no one at the time was having any fun at all, they sang "If you want to have a good time, jine the cavalry," and Stuart joined the singers. The music seemed to revive the general, and when told of his actions during supper, he apologized profusely.

A few nights later Stuart was riding with McClellan and dictating messages for Fitz Lee and the artillery about where they should move that night and the next day. So that McClellan might write out these orders, they stopped at a turnpike toll house. As McClellan wrote, Stuart put his head down on the table and went to sleep. The adjutant woke him to read the dispatches, as he always insisted upon doing. But when Stuart read the instructions to his artillery, he erased the names of two Maryland towns and scribbled "Shepherdstown" and "Aldie" (Virginia) in their place. Again, McClellan had to reawaken the nominally conscious general and correct his errors, before he could dispatch the dispatches.

McClellan later offered the eggs and erasures anecdotes as academic evidence that a person may appear to be awake and in fact be mentally asleep. At the time he was surely much less detached. He must have wondered whether Stuart was still fit to command. And maybe Stuart wondered the same thing.[38]

After crossing the Potomac on July 14, Stuart stopped at the Bower for a few days. This visit, however, was unlike the idyllic sojourn at the Dandridge estate during the previous fall. Meade threatened Lee's army, and the cavalry had to counter Federal probes on short notice. Too, the Bower could only remind Stuart of his friends and staff members who were no longer with him— Pelham, Von Borcke, Price, and Farley. After a little more than a week in the lower Shenandoah Valley, Stuart rode east before the army, resumed a picket line on the Rappahannock, and established his headquarters (Camp Von Borcke) on July 25 near Culpeper.[39]

Already gossip was spreading through the army and the nation about Stuart and Gettysburg. "General Stuart is much criticized for his part in our late campaign . . . ," wrote Blackford's brother. "In his anxiety to 'do some great thing' General Stuart carried his men beyond the range of usefulness and Lee was not thereafter kept fully informed as to the enemy's movements as he should have been, or as he would have been had Stuart been nearer at hand." In Richmond, an official at the War Office heard that Stuart had been relieved of his command because he had been absent "without orders" at Gettysburg. A newspaper correspondent in Richmond reported, "There are many wild reports in circulation today regarding Gen. J. E. B. Stuart, the Chief of Cavalry in Virginia. It is said that he will be deposed, and that Gen. Hood will be put in his place. For some time back many serious charges have been made against Stuart, reflecting severely upon him. His vanity seems to have controlled all his actions, and the cavalry was used frequently to gratify his personal pride and to the detriment of the service." The writer renewed criticism of Stuart at Brandy Station and continued, "At the Battle of Gettysburg he was not to be found, and Gen. Lee could not get enough cavalry together to carry out his plans." Stuart had admirable traits, the reporter concluded, "But that inordinate personal pride—that weak-minded vanity, so subject to flattery and praise, ruin entirely his character as an officer." [40]

Even Lee, who rarely allowed his censure to show, included in his final report of the Gettysburg campaign the statement: "The movements of the army preceding the battle of Gettysburg had been much embarrassed by the absence of cavalry." And the list of Lee's subordinates who criticized Stuart's conduct in the campaign was long indeed. Staff officer G. Moxley Sorrel later charged that Stuart's antics cost the Confederacy a victory at Gettysburg, and another member of Lee's staff, Charles G. Marshall, urged the commanding general to court-martial Stuart. Longstreet, Henry Heth, Edward Porter Alexander, Walter Taylor, C. M. Wilcox, and other Southern officers later judged Stuart in print guilty in some degree for the Confederate defeat in Pennsylvania. [41]

Stuart had his defenders in the midst of such general criticism. An anonymous newspaper pundit responded to some unflattering remarks made about Stuart and called him "the first cavalry leader on this continent." [42]

Later, when refighting the war became a consuming passion among old Southern soldiers, McClellan and Mosby were vigorous in Stuart's defense. In his biography of Stuart, McClellan suggests that his chieftain perhaps should have burned the captured wagons instead of allowing his booty to impede his movement. McClellan admits that Lee needed cavalry, but points out that Lee had available horsemen, and concludes, "It was not the want of cavalry that General Lee bewailed, for he had enough of it had it been properly used. It was the absence of Stuart himself that he felt so keenly . . ." McClellan was judicious, but firm, in making Stuart's case and, in concert with Flora Stuart, took pains not to advance Stuart's cause by attacking the reputations of other officers.[43]

Mosby was much less restrained—so much so that McClellan and Flora disapproved. Yet Mosby considered Stuart's defense something of a crusade—"He [Stuart] made me all that I was in the war, but for his friendship I would never have been heard of . . ." Consequently Mosby wrote a book on Stuart at Gettysburg, contributed frequently to newspapers and periodicals, and carried on a significant private correspondence—all on behalf of Stuart's absolution from blame for the outcome of the battle. He considered McClellan's defense unsatisfactory. Mosby accused Longstreet and Heth of trying to cover their own mistakes by attacking Stuart. He harped on the fact that Lee had authorized Stuart to choose his route and raid en route. And Mosby was especially critical of Robertson's failure to follow Lee's army into Pennsylvania in time to contribute to the campaign. The brigades of Robertson and Jones reached the scene on July 3, only in time to help cover the retreat. Mosby remarked, "Stuart had ridden around General Hooker while Robertson had ridden around General Lee." And Mosby wrote to Flora, "The only thing I blame Stuart for, was not having him [Robertson] shot."[44]

Not all of Stuart's friends and subordinates rallied to his defense with the energy of McClellan or the zeal of Mosby. Fitz Lee, for example, later acknowledged that Stuart's cavalry should have been between Meade and Lee, but insisted that the cavalry chief had had sufficient authority from Lee to conduct his raid. Tom Rosser concluded that although Stuart was "a cavalry general of great ability and of unexceptional enterprise, courage and energy . . . he was like all other men, *human* and liable to err, and did in my opinion on this campaign, *undoubtedly,* make the fatal blunder which lost us the battle of Gettysburg!" Hampton later wrote to Munford, "Lately I saw for the first time Stuart's report of the Gettysburg campaign and I never read a more erroneous—to call it no harsher name—one than it was."[45]

Charges and countercharges of the old veterans about Gettysburg continued long and shrill while Southerners contemplated the Lost Cause. And when the participants ceased their fulminations, historians took up the activity with only slightly less zest. If there be a consensus in scholarship relating to Gettysburg, it is that Stuart had some prominent part in the Confederate defeat. And perhaps the most damning piece of evidence in the case is Stuart's report of his conduct in the campaign. Ironically, Stuart has been his own worst enemy for the way in which he attempted to justify his actions. Indeed some scholars have become so indignantly absorbed in Stuart's unfortunate explanations that they have judged him more for what he wrote rather than what he did.

Clearly Stuart felt the need to defend his course of action in the campaign. He wrote Flora from Hagerstown on July 10 that "My cavalry has nobly sustained its reputation, and done better and harder fighting than it ever has since the war [began]." Three days later he wrote, "I had a grand time in Penna . . ." Then he recounted (and magnified) his accomplishments: "I . . . went close to Georgetown and Washt. cutting four important railroads and joining the army in time for the battle of Gettysburg with 900 prisoners and 200 wagons and splendid teams." Still later (July 18) he complained to Flora about the lies of his enemies and the errors of Richmond newspapers. He said he was content to do his duty and let his reputation take care of itself.[46]

But when he prepared his report of the campaign, he took near manic care for his reputation. He spent an abnormal amount of time on the report and presented the lengthy document (14,300 words!) on August 20. In addition to being a narrative of his activities, it was Stuart's apologia.

He wrote of spreading "terror and consternation to the very gates of the [enemy] capital." The 900 prisoners about whom he had written Flora became 1,000, and he had deprived Meade of "all his communications with Washington." But Stuart also insisted that he had left Lee with plenty of cavalry and remarked that, "properly handled, such a command should have done everything requisite . . ." Stuart also blamed Jubal Early for not finding him in Pennsylvania, when clearly the responsibility for finding someone lay with cavalry, not infantry. Stuart even suggested that Hill and Longstreet should have continued their advance to place the army in a more favorable location for the route and timetable of his cavalry. Had Lee "properly handled" the cavalry Stuart left with him; had Early's infantry found the cavalry column; had Hill and Longstreet acted in accord with Stuart's after-the-fact assumptions—then all would have been well.[47]

Stuart's report/apologia was indeed unfortunate; it contained even more fantasy than his account of Brandy Station. Stuart's pretension and prevarication compounded his errors in the Gettysburg campaign. In fact Lee did grant him the discretion to take the route he did and to raid enemy lines of supply and communication on his way to join the army. Had his raiding not been so successful, Stuart might have joined the army in time to contribute to the ensuing battle. But Stuart moved too slowly, even before he captured the Federal wagon train. And once he had the wagons, he refused to give up his prize. He was greedy. He clearly underestimated the need for speed, and he gravely miscalculated the effect of his tardiness upon the campaign. And as he rode through enemy country, he seemed to see only the road on which he was, when he should have been seeing a map of Pennsylvania.[48]

The standard study of the entire Gettysburg campaign concludes, "If, as Stuart's accusers insisted, the absence of cavalry permitted Lee to be surprised into an unfortunate encounter of major proportions at Gettysburg, they overlooked two important elements in the situation. Meade was just as surprised, and the initial advantage lay with Lee."[49] This is indeed a temperate judgment and perhaps fair.

But compare Stuart's actions on this expedition with his conduct of the Dumfries or Chambersburg or Catlett's Station raids. In contrast to the rare blend of prudent audacity Stuart had displayed on former occasions, this time he had been both timid and careless. The man who had all but defined the art of reconnaissance had managed to lose two very large armies, his friends and his foes, within a relatively small area (about fifty by thirty-five miles). Something was dreadfully wrong.

Stuart's critics, then and later, have erred when they accuse him of conducting his prolonged raid only in order to "do some great thing" to absolve himself for Brandy Station. He undertook this raid, not to atone for anything, but to confirm his vision of himself. And the difference is more than semantic.

Stuart had a serious problem with failure. Perhaps because he had failed so seldom at anything he deemed important, he never learned to confront failure. He feared failure perhaps more than anything else in life and certainly more than death. He dealt with failure by not dealing with it, by denying it. Stuart's reports on Brandy Station and Gettysburg, and, more so, his letters to Flora, reveal him incapable of acknowledging shortcomings, much less failure. Stuart was an ironic victim of his own success; he had so often won that he became incapable of coping with defeat.

Charles M. Blackford, younger brother of Stuart's engineer officer William, was in Martinsburg, Virginia, when the Army of Northern Virginia marched through the town on the way back from Pennsylvania. He stood beside the road and watched Robert E. Lee, A. P. Hill, Richard S. Ewell, and James Longstreet, the commanding general and his three corps commanders, pass his vantage point. Each one of these exalted officers road along quietly with only one or two companions. Blackford also saw Stuart. The young cavalry commander dashed into town with "a large cavalcade of staff and courier"; not one, but two buglers "blowing most furiously" heralded Stuart's coming. The contrast struck Blackford as most amusing. What he witnessed, though, was Stuart acting like Stuart. If he displayed the trappings of success, they became prima facie evidence that he was successful.[50]

# XIII

## *Stuart As Usual*

HENRY MCCLELLAN ONCE STATED that Stuart had only two military maxims and but one fault. His maxims: "Believe that you can whip the enemy, and you have half won the battle"; and "If you are in doubt what to do, attack." The sole fault: He never admitted "that he was worsted in an engagement." McClellan was an analytical man, and he knew Stuart pretty well.[1]

When the war was going well, Stuart's maxims rang true. And as long as he consistently won battles, Stuart had no fault; he never had to confront being "worsted." But by the latter half of the summer of 1863, Stuart's maxims seemed less appropriate. Federal cavalry had improved enormously during that summer—"come of age," as one historian has phrased it. Moreover there were more blue horsemen than before, and they moved and fought en masse. They rode better horses than the Southerners, because they possessed more horses and had more to feed them. In such circumstances belief in Confederate omnipotence might lead to folly; insistence upon attack might produce disaster; and false claims of victory might sound ludicrous to soldiers and civilians alike.[2]

After Gettysburg the war was going badly for the entire Southern nation and every element of its military. Lee offered to resign his command; government and people despaired. Yet Stuart magnified his old aura. He dashed, he laughed, he flirted, and he sang. He still responded to quandary with a cavalry charge, still expected victories, and still claimed success in the face of contrary reality. Much of what he did and most of what he said during the

---

For military activities in the fall of 1863 see map on p. 198.

late summer and fall of 1863 and the winter of 1863–64 seemed
more appropriate to the war and his cavalry in years previous. The
Confederate circumstance had changed; Stuart continued to play
the role into which he had cast himself. He expected victory, pursued it aggressively, and denied defeat. Once upon a time Stuart
had defined his role; now he seemed merely to play a role.

Stuart even confidently expected promotion in the wake of
Gettysburg. Both he and Lee knew his cavalry required reorganization, and he believed that he would emerge from the reshuffle a
lieutenant general.

At Gettysburg Stuart had commanded a division composed of
six brigades. Leaders of those brigades were Wade Hampton, Fitz
Lee, Beverly Robertson, Albert G. Jenkins, Grumble Jones, and
Rooney Lee. Since May Stuart had urged Lee to reorganize the
cavalry; he wanted three divisions of horsemen and an option
for a fourth, and he wanted Hampton, Fitz Lee, and Rooney Lee
to become major generals in command of the new divisions.
Stuart also had recommendations about promotions to brigadier
general to command the brigades that would compose the new
divisions.[3]

If Lee accepted Stuart's recommendations Stuart would then
command a cavalry corps, and by act of the Confederate Congress,
"each army corps shall be commanded by a lieutenant general." It
seemed so logical to make the cavalry brigades smaller (three or
four regiments instead of as many as six) and then create division
commands to move, maintain, and engage these brigades more
efficiently. Logic further demanded a corps command and thus
promotion for Stuart; the good of the service would also be good
for Stuart.[4]

The Gettysburg campaign only underscored Stuart's plea for
reorganization. By the late summer of 1863, here was the status of
Stuart's subordinates:

Hampton was wounded. He would soon recover, though, and even
   though he and Stuart did not always get along, his experience,
   record, and influence were strong.
Fitz Lee remained Stuart's favorite. He also had proven himself
   on many occasions to be a skilled and resourceful commander.
Jenkins was a prisoner of war; his brigade had to return to the

Shenandoah Valley. So neither the man nor the unit figured in Stuart's plan for the immediate future.

Robertson had disappointed Stuart, and his brigade had dwindled to two undersized regiments; thus Stuart was delighted when Robertson asked for assignment elsewhere. Robertson spent the remainder of the war in South Carolina.

Rooney Lee, wounded at Brandy Station, had been recuperating at Hickory Hill with his in-laws, the Wickhams. Then in late June a Federal raiding party captured Lee. But, barring the unforeseen, Lee would recover and be exchanged.

Jones and Stuart were on a collision course once more; Jones had tried to resign before the Pennsylvania campaign, and only the efforts of Lee deferred his departure from the army. Now Jones resumed his feud; the Army of Northern Virginia was not big enough for both him and Stuart.

The fates of these men and the future of cavalry organization lay in Lee's hands. While Lee pondered the situation, Stuart pondered his promotion. He informed Flora that the rumor about John Bell Hood's replacing him in command of Lee's cavalry was false. The cavalry, secretary of war, and president all supported him, he assured her. On August 28, he wrote Flora that "LG" (lieutenant general) was "still in suspense." A week later he wrote, "Rumor is quite rife that I have been actually appointed Lt. Gen'l. I think it must be so." [5]

Lee ended the rumors and suspense on September 9, 1863; the new organization looked like this.

## FIRST DIVISION

### Maj. Gen. WADE HAMPTON.

#### Jones's Brigade.

#### Brig. Gen. W. E. JONES.

6th Virginia, Lieut. Col. John Shac Green.
7th Virginia, Col. R. H. Dulany.
12th Virginia, Col. A. W. Harman.
35th Virginia Battalion, Lieut. Col. E. V. White.

Baker's Brigade.

Brig. Gen. L. S. BAKER.

1st North Carolina, Col. J. B. Gordon.
2d North Carolina, Lieut. Col. W. G. Robinson.
4th North Carolina, Col. Dennis D. Ferebee.
5th North Carolina, Col. Stephen B. Evans.

Butler's Brigade.

Brig. Gen. M. C. BUTLER.

Cobb's (Georgia) Legion, Col. P. M. B. Young.
Jeff. Davis (Mississippi) Legion, Lieut. Col. J. F. Waring.
Phillips (Georgia) Legion, Lieut. Col. W. W. Rich.
2d South Carolina, Lieut. Col. T. J. Lipscomb.

SECOND DIVISION

Maj. Gen. FITZHUGH LEE.

Lee's Brigade.

Brig. Gen. W. H. F. LEE.

1st South Carolina, Col. John L. Black.
9th Virginia, Col. R. L. T. Beale.
10th Virginia, Col. J. Lucius Davis.
18th Virginia, Col. John R. Chambliss, Jr.

Lomax's Brigade.

Brig. Gen. L. L. LOMAX.

1st Maryland Battalion, Lieut. Col. Ridgely Brown.
5th Virginia, Col. Thomas L. Rosser.
11th Virginia, Col. O. R. Funsten.
15th Virginia, Col. William B. Ball.

Wickham's Brigade.

Brig. Gen. WILLIAMS C. WICKHAM.

1st Virginia, Col. R. W. Carter.
2d Virginia, Col. Thomas T. Munford.
3d Virginia, Col. Thomas H. Owen.
4th Virginia, Lieut. Col. William H. Payne.[6]

For the time being, Gordon served for Baker (wounded), Young for Butler (wounded), and Chambliss for W. H. F. Lee (captured). Stuart now commanded a cavalry corps as he had suggested; but he remained a major general. He was surprised and disappointed. But he could not bring himself to blame Lee. For his part, Lee seemed to have used the non-promotion to chasten Stuart without injuring him. Stuart had not lost Lee's favor; yet Lee seemed increasingly to assume an avuncular tone in correspondence with his cavalry commander—as though Stuart needed more guidance and instruction.[7]

Hampton and Fitz Lee now enjoyed rank equal with Stuart, who still commanded them; and Hampton, when he returned to the army in November, enjoyed "the absence of orders from Stuart," although he found his new administrative responsibilities "irksome." The new brigadier generals (Baker, Butler, Lomax, and Wickham) had all been Stuart nominees for promotion at one time or another. Baker and Butler were Carolinians (North and South respectively), which defused charges of a Virginia bias. Stuart had served with Lomax on the frontier when both had been lieutenants; indeed Lomax had cared for Stuart immediately after the Indian shot and wounded him in 1857. Wickham had served with Stuart almost since the beginning of the war and, in addition to being a new general, Wickham was also a candidate for the Confederate Congress.

Passed over in the reorganization promotions were two men Stuart had consistently recommended, Thomas T. Munford and Thomas L. Rosser. Both remained colonels in command of regiments. Stuart, along with Munford's friends and father, appealed to Lee with no success, and Munford continued a colonel.[8]

Stuart also tried to mollify Rosser. He told him that he would be the next brigadier general, and also said that he had told Munford of his preference for Rosser. "You deserve promotion more than any Col. of a Va regt in my command," Stuart wrote, and he urged Rosser to take this endorsement to the secretary of war.[9]

Rosser, however, refused to be consoled and turned on Stuart viciously. "Stuart has been as false to *me*," Rosser wrote his new bride, Betty, "as he has ever been to his country and to his *wife*. I will leave him in his glory." Determined to secure a transfer from Stuart's command, Rosser told Betty that only she knew his true

feelings on the matter. "I don't speak of it myself. I seem cheerful
and speak of Gen. Stuart as usual. I will never give him an opportunity of deceiving me again." When Stuart tried to explain to
Rosser why he had not been promoted, Rosser wrote Betty, "His
arguments I thought quite silly. He seems to hate the way that he
has treated me, but that is too late now you know." And in addition
to accusing Stuart of being false to country and wife, Rosser became routinely critical of Stuart's performance in combat—"Gen.
Stuart is *badly* whipped . . ." Never suspecting the depth of Rosser's loathing, Stuart managed to secure a general's star for Rosser
only one month after the reorganization and later referred to him
as "a cavalier of the right stamp." [10]

Rosser's promotion, however, was the result of even more ill
feelings. The vacancy he filled came only after Grumble Jones
attacked Stuart in writing, and Stuart had him arrested and tried
by court-martial for showing disrespect for a superior officer. The
court quickly found Jones guilty, and Lee transferred him to southwestern Virginia. Rosser took Jones's place in command of the so-
called Laurel Brigade on October 10. [11]

While Rosser fumed and Jones feuded, Stuart still wondered
about his own career and hoped that Lee would offer some explanation. He held reviews of his reorganized brigades every day, so
that the troopers might become accustomed at least to riding together before they had to fight together. Since the summer of 1861,
after the first engagement at Bull Run, Stuart had banished broken-
down horses and slightly wounded men to Company Q. Now it
seemed that assignment to this motley collection of unfit men and
beasts had lost its stigma, and Company Q attracted more and more
malingerers and malcontents. So Stuart ordered, "That nonde-
script irregular body of men known as Company 'Q' which has so
long disgraced the cavalry service and degraded the individuals
resorting to it is hereby abolished." Men who were ill or injured
should go to the hospital; stragglers should live only in disgrace;
and "artful dodgers" should be shot. In effect, Stuart dealt with
morale problems by ordering them to stop.

At the same time, he learned of the death of one of his sisters.
Then Flora, who was now eight months pregnant, became ill and
begged him to come to her in Lynchburg. Meanwhile Stuart began
actively looking for a house to purchase for his family. In short,

Stuart had much both professional and private on his mind during the period McClellan described as devoted to "rest." [12]

And then the Federal army compounded Stuart's quandaries. Sometime after midnight on September 12–13, one of Stuart's staff surgeons who had been at home on leave following the death of his wife made his way to cavalry headquarters near Culpeper Court House. The man had noticed much increased enemy activity across the Rappahannock and came to warn Stuart. Quickly Stuart ordered his wagons moved to the rear and alerted the two brigades he had nearby. At dawn on September 13 the Federals crossed the Rappahannock in strength—two divisions of cavalry with infantry and artillery support. [13]

There was a reason for all this. George Meade's advance came after he learned that James Longstreet's corps had left Lee's army to reinforce Braxton Bragg's Confederate army in northern Georgia. Aware that he had a substantial numerical superiority, the Federal general moved to exploit his advantage.

Stuart could only fall back to the Rapidan River at Rapidan Station, and in the process he lost three artillery pieces near Culpeper. Rosser wrote Betty, "This I think is the finishing stroke to Stuart's declining reputation. I can't sympathize with him now." With friends like this, Stuart hardly needed the Federals. [14]

To press the issue on Lee's left flank, Meade dispatched his cavalry on a reconnaissance to the Rapidan and beyond. On September 22 John Buford's division of blue horsemen advanced from Madison Court House toward Liberty Mills on the Rapidan. Stuart rode out to meet his enemy. On the road, near a place called Jack's Shop, the two mounted forces clashed inconclusively. Meanwhile Judson Kilpatrick's division of Federal cavalry was surveying fords on the Rapidan. Kilpatrick planned to meet Buford on the road between Madison Court House and Liberty Mills near Jack's Shop. This plan placed Kilpatrick's cavalry between Stuart's force and the Rapidan. Stuart's Confederates were apparently trapped at Jack's Shop between Buford to the north and Kilpatrick to the south. [15]

All Stuart could do was place his artillery atop a small hill and order the gunners to fire in both directions. At the same time cavalry regiments charged both ways. In classic understatement, McClellan recalled, "The scene was now extremely animated."

Finally the Southerners were able to drive Kilpatrick's men off the road long enough for Stuart to extricate himself. He directed a dash back to Liberty Mills and called for help from an infantry division. Southern troops and troopers then repulsed Kilpatrick's cavalry and kept them north of the Rapidan.[16]

Stuart, who had a horse shot from under him in the melee, sent a telegram to Flora describing the fight as "successful." Lee congratulated Stuart for "arresting" the enemy's advance. Buford reported that Stuart "was whipped," and Rosser told Betty that Stuart "as usual, was whipped."[17]

When Lee wrote his congratulatory note to Stuart, he added a warning that the cavalry might expect continued enemy offensive action on the right. But that prediction changed radically. Down in Georgia on September 20, Bragg's army, augmented by Longstreet's corps, won what seemed at the time a stunning victory on Chickamauga Creek. In response, on September 24 the United States sent two corps from Meade's army to Chattanooga. And in response to that, Lee commenced offensive action of his own. He sent his army west around Meade's right flank and then north toward Manassas in hopes of getting between Meade and Washington and trapping a sizable segment of the Army of the Potomac.

What became the Bristoe Station campaign opened on October 9; Lee moved to flank Meade, and Meade warily withdrew toward Washington. While Fitz Lee's division remained temporarily on guard at the Rapidan, Stuart led Hampton's division forward on October 10 to screen the march of the Southern infantry (Hampton was still recovering from his Gettysburg wound).[18]

During the first day, Stuart encountered scattered regiments of Federal cavalry and then Kilpatrick's division plus some infantry at James City. The two bodies of horsemen confronted each other, but confined the action to skirmishing and artillery shelling. Next morning (October 11) Stuart found that the Federals had withdrawn, and so he resumed his march. At Culpeper Court House he learned that Meade's infantry had already crossed the Rappahannock. But he did find Kilpatrick at Culpeper in strength and decided not to confront the Federal horsemen there.

Instead, Stuart led his column around Culpeper by a series of farm roads, and headed for Brandy Station and Fleetwood Hill. He could hear the sound of artillery fire back on the Rapidan and thus believed that Fitz Lee was advancing. If Stuart could link his division with Lee's north of Culpeper, he would then have Federal cavalry trapped. The Confederates would be between their foes and the Rappahannock and could expect to take advantage of a Federal stampede to safety.

It was a very good idea, but the Federals refused to cooperate. Fitz Lee was indeed advancing from the Rapidan; but ahead of him was John Buford's division of Union cavalry. And Kilpatrick was not content to allow Stuart to disappear. Accordingly Kilpatrick watched the Confederates, and when he realized Stuart's scheme, he sent his own troopers to occupy the commanding ground on Fleetwood Hill.

What happened was a mass horse race to Fleetwood. Northern and Southern regiments dashed toward the high ground in a deadly game of king-of-the-hill. Whichever side arrived first in sufficient strength would likely carry the day.

Stuart ordered some of his leading units to attack the Federals on their flank and so slow them down. Kilpatrick returned the favor, and both columns slowed. Thus, some of Buford's troopers were first to Fleetwood, and enough blue horsemen arrived fast enough to hold the heights. Then Kilpatrick fought his way through Rosser's brigade to Fleetwood Hill, and Fitz Lee linked his command with Stuart.

For a time it was the Battle of Brandy Station all over again, with positions reversed. Stuart was able to push the Federals back to Fleetwood, but no farther. Then he tried to maneuver, so as to cut the Federals off from the Rappahannock River. Enemy artillery and darkness frustrated that plan, and during the night the Federals withdrew across the river.[19]

To this point in the campaign, Stuart had bagged 555 prisoners and exerted considerable pressure upon enemy horsemen. He hoped for more, however, as Meade continued his retreat; he wanted to find the rear of the Union army and strike a blow. On October 12 Stuart crossed the Rappahannock and rode north, still screening Lee's advance and alert for opportunities. On the morning of the thirteenth, Lee ordered a reconnaissance in force to Catlett's Station. By this time the Confederates had reached Warrenton, and Lee needed to know more about Meade's actions.[20]

Stuart set out with three brigades of cavalry and seven guns.

About midafternoon, he reached the crossroads village of Auburn and learned there that there were indeed Federals southeast of him. Prudently he left Lomax and his brigade at Auburn and pushed on toward Catlett's Station, about four miles away. As he rode, Stuart dispatched Blackford ahead to scout, and Blackford found Meade's rear—Federal troops and more wagons, probably, than he had ever seen in one place. In response to Blackford's note, Stuart himself came to the grove of trees where his engineer officer hid. Meade was withdrawing along the railroad, and Lee must know. Stuart sent Venable at a gallop back to Warrenton to tell the commanding general. Here was a chance to assail the Union army while it was strung out on the march.

But when Venable neared Auburn, he saw, not Lomax's Confederates, but two corps of Federal infantry marching up the road, which was roughly parallel to the rail line. The resourceful staff officer sent a courier back to Stuart with the bad news and then managed to avoid the Federal column and deliver an amended message to Lee.

Stuart was not pleased; he was in the middle of Meade's army with seemingly no place to hide. He formed his column and rode back toward Auburn in hopes of slipping past the Federals as Venable had done. Venable, however, was one man; Stuart had with him two brigades, seven guns, and five ordnance wagons. As the Confederates approached Auburn they encountered enemy pickets. And to make a bad situation worse, the rear guard had attracted the attention of Federals from Catlett's Station. Federals front and rear—the only recourse seemed to be flight. Stuart's troopers could probably cut their way through the enemy at Auburn and rejoin Lee's army; but in so doing they would empty some saddles and lose all or most of the guns and wagons.

Stuart responded to the situation as though he had planned the whole project. He saw what no one else seemed to see—a small, secluded valley north of the road in the very outskirts of Auburn. As night approached, Stuart led his horsemen into the valley and took precautions to conceal his presence. He posted guards near the entrance to the valley, but ordered them to hide. At the head of every mule was a man assigned to stifle the animal's bray. Staff officers spread the order for absolute silence among the men, and those present remembered that even the horses seemed to understand. During the long night Stuart sent six couriers to Lee with the same message—send help!

Once he had issued all the orders and taken all the precautions he could, Stuart went with Blackford to the crest of the ridge that lay between his men and the enemy. There they watched Federals march with lanterns up the road about 150 yards away. Blackford lay down, and then Stuart flopped down beside him and, with Blackford's stomach as a pillow, fell fast asleep.

As daylight approached, Stuart stirred. He hoped that Lee would send infantry to strike the enemy column and extricate his command. He ordered all seven guns to the ridge on which he and Blackford had slept and had his men mounted and ready. Actually the Federal column had almost passed Auburn, and the troops now on the other side of the ridge were its rear guard. These men, weary from their night march, halted and began to prepare breakfast, while the Southerners watched from hiding.

About a half hour after daylight (October 14), Stuart heard the sound for which he had been waiting all night. From the west rifle fire broke out; infantry had come to the rescue. Immediately Stuart's gunners pushed their pieces over the top of the ridge and began blasting the breakfast fires at a range of only 150 yards. With coffeepots flying around them, the startled Federals attempted to confront Stuart's guns. The rapid fire, however, forced them to recoil. That same fire, though, discouraged the men from Ewell's corps who were attempting to advance from the other side of the Federals, and they, too, recoiled. Consequently Stuart was not able to trap the Federal rear guard between himself and friendly infantry. Instead, the Southern cavalry had to fight its way past the blue infantry in order to open the road back toward Warrenton.[21]

For the next several days, Stuart continued to follow the Federal withdrawal and clash on occasion with enemy cavalry. All the way to Bull Run the Southerners chased Meade. But Lee was unable to threaten the Union flank seriously enough to provoke a third battle near Bull Run like the first two. The same day Stuart made his escape near Auburn, there was severe fighting at Bristoe Station, which gave the campaign its name. After that Meade withdrew to Centreville and a sound defensive position. So Lee pulled back to the Rappahannock once more, destroying the railroad as he went.[22]

Now (October 18) Stuart's task changed once more; he was to cover the withdrawal. Still with Hampton's division, Stuart maintained communication with Fitz Lee and attempted to operate in tandem. Federal cavalry followed, and on the evening of the eighteenth, attacked Stuart's pickets in strength. Stuart notified Fitz Lee and on October 19 withdrew down the Warrenton Turnpike to the south bank of a stream called Broad Run at the little village of Buckland. Kilpatrick's division followed aggressively and attempted to cross Broad Run. Stuart's troopers threw them back, and Kilpatrick then sent horsemen to cross the stream elsewhere and attack Stuart's flanks. While Stuart was thinking about his next move, a courier from Fitz Lee arrived. Lee's division was en route to Buckland, and Fitz suggested that Stuart fall back farther so that they might trap Kilpatrick between the two Southern divisions. Stuart concurred and told Lee that he would turn upon Kilpatrick when he first heard Lee's guns.[23]

After disengaging at Broad Run, Stuart led his men down the Warrenton Turnpike for a couple of miles and halted behind a ridge. As Blackford sat his horse and looked back up the turnpike, he saw Kilpatrick's Federals: "as far as the eye could reach their column of splendidly equipped cavalry came marching on with flags fluttering and arms glittering in the bright autumn sunshine. Hampton's division was formed in two columns, each heading at a gap in the ridge, and all before them was smooth, firm ground." Stuart listened intently as the Federals drew nearer. They were only two hundred yards away, beginning to ascend the other side of the ridge when Fitz Lee's guns began to boom.[24]

Stuart launched his horsemen at the head of the enemy column. After a brief fight, the Federals turned to flight. Then did the action become a chase for the sake of prisoners. Kilpatrick had prudently posted Custer's brigade at Buckland, so Fitz Lee found stiff resistance there instead of the rear of the enemy column. But when the rest of Kilpatrick's division came thundering down the road with Stuart's Confederates in hot pursuit, Custer's men, too, had to flee in order to escape being caught between Fitz Lee and Stuart.[25]

All told the chase lasted five miles and yielded 250 prisoners. Stuart called the event the "Buckland Races," and claimed to be "justified in declaring the rout of the enemy at Buckland the most signal and complete that any cavalry has suffered during the war." Kilpatrick avoided any mention of the headlong flight in his report; Custer claimed he had faced a "line of infantry more than a mile in extent." None of the Federal commanders had an easy time writing around the large number of their men who became prisoners at Buckland. And an especially embarrassing loss to young General Custer was his baggage wagons, which contained, among other things, his private correspondence. "Some of the letters to a fair, but frail, friend of Custer's were published in the Richmond papers and afforded some spicy reading," Blackford recalled, "though the most spicy parts did not appear." [26]

The Bristoe Station campaign was essentially inconclusive for Lee and Meade; two large armies marched forty miles north, fought a brief, bloody battle, and then marched forty miles south again. By November 9, Meade had forced his way across the Rappahannock, and Lee once more held the south bank of the Rapidan. Stuart performed no screening or reconnaissance wonders for the Army of Northern Virginia during the campaign. He had discovered no exposed enemy flanks; nor had he kept the enemy baffled as to Lee's whereabouts. But he had conducted a series of successful cavalry operations. He had extricated himself from probable disasters at Jack's Shop and again at Auburn. He had skillfully directed his 8,500 horsemen at Brandy Station and also at Buckland. During the campaign his cavalry collected almost 1,400 prisoners, while sustaining 390 casualties. And significantly, in almost daily fighting, Stuart had kept the massed Federal cavalry from impeding the movement and deployment of Lee's infantry. Stuart's success may have been more solid than spectacular; but he decided to celebrate Bristoe Station anyway with a review on November 5. One of his troopers was less than impressed. "Gen. Stuart," the man wrote, "purposed holding another of his 'spread eagle' grand reviews, which did no good except to give Yankee spies an opportunity to count the exact number of cavalry attached to the Army of Northern Virginia, and to display the foppishness of Stuart, who rode along his war-torn lines with a multitude of bouquets, which fair hands had presented to him, fastened in his hat and coat." Appropriately Stuart held his review at Brandy Station. Lee was present, and so were Virginia Governor John Letcher and Mrs. Letcher. Maybe Stuart was trying to act out a statement that nothing had changed since June, when his horse-men had last displayed themselves on this field. Precisely five months ago, in the aftermath of Chancellorsville on the eve of invasion, Stuart had lived his moment of unblemished glory in this place. For almost everyone present June seemed long ago and far away. Stuart, though, seemed always to live in moments of glory.[27]

Certainly he could rejoice in the birth of a daughter. Flora had had the child on October 9, while Stuart was making ready to cross the Rapidan. Flora and the baby were in Lynchburg; Stuart had not seen his daughter and on November 2 still did not know for sure what her name was. He wanted her called Virginia Pelham, and so she was.[28]

Good news, of a sort at least, came from Chattanooga in a letter from Longstreet. After spending a month with Bragg's Army of Tennessee, Longstreet took the time to write Stuart about the state of the cavalry in the Confederacy's western army. In Longstreet's judgment, the troopers commanded by Nathan Bedford Forrest and Joe Wheeler were about as well trained and as effective as Stuart's horsemen had been when Longstreet first encountered them in the summer of 1861. Now, of course, Longstreet stated, Stuart's command was "vastly improved." A few weeks later Stuart heard from London *Times* correspondent Francis Lawley, who had accompanied Longstreet. Lawley said that Longstreet's so-journ west had made him appreciate Stuart's cavalry—"You have no notion of how you have gained."[29]

But most of the news Stuart heard was bad. Or so it would have seemed to anyone else.

One very significant problem was horses; there never seemed to be enough of them. Someone wrote a letter to the editor of the Richmond *Examiner* in August complaining that the Gettysburg campaign had cost the cavalry between fourteen and fifteen hundred dead horses. The writer said that men without horses were drilling as infantry, and this did not befit the dignity of a horse soldier. The *Examiner* responded with a suggestion that troopers take better care of their animals.[30]

But care did not seem to be at issue. Confederate cavalrymen had to furnish their own mounts, for which the government paid forty cents per day. If a trooper's horse broke down, suffered a wound in combat, or in any other way became disabled, the trooper had to find another horse or walk. Only if a horse was killed in combat would the Confederate government compensate the owner, and then only at the value established when the man mustered into the cavalry. Thus it became simple good sense for cavalrymen to take good care of their horses. Indeed McClellan recalled often seeing men hacking the hooves off dead horses in order to get the shoes to use on their own mounts.[31]

This system of Southern horse supply produced a number of problems. A dismounted trooper usually had to return to his home to secure another horse. If the man was from Virginia, this meant he would be absent for a month or more. And if the man was from Mississippi, Georgia, or the Carolinas, the system seemed ludicrous in the extreme. On September 10, for example, Stuart commanded 9,530 men, and of this number 1,361—14 percent—were dismounted. Three weeks later the percentage of dismounted troopers had shrunk to 11 percent; but the number of men present for duty was down to 8,376. In all probability, most of the absentees were on leave attempting to secure remounts. Only by the end of December did the number of men in Stuart's command approach 9,500 once more.[32]

One very good reason for an increased attrition rate among Confederate horses was the shortage of food for the animals. While Federal cavalry horses were munching ten pounds of grain per day, Confederate mounts were gnawing the bark of trees. Lee wrote President Davis in August, "Some days we get a pound of corn per horse and some days more; some none. Our limit is 5 pounds per day per horse." Of course in August the horses could still graze, so long as there was no active campaigning. But in February 1864 Stuart reported that one of his regiments was receiving eight pounds of corn per day per horse and only one or two pounds of hay.[33]

Stuart's experience during late 1863 was one good index of the Confederate horse crisis. Some time after she carried Stuart over the fifteen-foot-wide gully near Hanover, Pennsylvania, the mare Virginia died of distemper. He lost a horse in combat at Jack's Shop (September 22) and another (Star of the West) to distemper in December. Maryland, one of Stuart's favorites, became very ill, and Stuart sent the animal to the farm of a friend in an attempt to save it. He also sent a chestnut horse captured at Auburn to the country to recuperate during the fall. In December he learned from a cousin that still another of his horses, Chancellor, had died from the effects of a combat wound. In one way or another, then, Stuart lost the use of six horses within six months. And although his penchant for exposing himself to enemy fire cost Stuart four horses shot while he rode them, the major general's mounts received the best of care and feeding from Bob, his personal servant. The mounts of Stuart's subordinates did not usually fare as well.[34]

Weapons posed another problem for Southern cavalry during the fall of 1863. Lee summarized the situation in a letter to Stuart. "There are many difficulties . . . in the way of arming the cavalry thoroughly, and keeping it in that condition. Few cavalry arms are imported, and those manufactured in the Confederacy are generally rejected. I fear there is great carelessness, too, in the preservation of arms . . . Where infantry arms have been issued to the cavalry, it is stated that they have either been turned in or thrown away in nine cases out of ten." Federal cavalry were using repeating carbines with increasing frequency. Confederates were often unable to find carbines and regularly refused to carry the longer, heavier infantry rifles. Consequently many of Stuart's men faced their enemies at a disadvantage in dismounted fighting. Sabers and pistols were worse than useless against an enemy on foot a couple of hundred yards away. And dismounted action was rapidly becoming routine, even in cavalry clashes.[35]

To try to make the best use of limited and dwindling resources available to the Army of Northern Virginia during the waning months of 1863, Lee counseled Stuart regarding small arms and horses. He attended Stuart's grand review on November 5, even though he did so "with fear and trembling" for his rheumatism. Lee sent officers to inspect Stuart's artillery, and sent Stuart a list of serious deficiencies. Harness in one battery was lying ungreased on the ground. Another battery had no records of its property and was short sixty-two horses. In a style peculiar to himself, Lee chastised his cavalry commander. "I know that you and the officers of your artillery will do all in your power to correct these evils, and it was only with that view that they were brought to your attention."[36]

Lee even sent Stuart an officer to serve on his staff as assistant inspector general. Lieutenant Colonel George St. Ledger Grenfell was an English soldier of fortune who Lee hoped would help Stuart by keeping him informed of conditions within his cavalry. Grenfell had served with Wheeler and John Hunt Morgan, so he was no stranger to Southern cavalry. But he remained a stranger to Stuart and his staff. Stuart complained of Grenfell to Lee and perhaps resented his imposition by the commanding general. Grenfell complained that his "want of a musical ear, and a decided antipathy to the twang of the banjo" set Stuart against him. McClellan surely despised Grenfell and retold with some glee in his biography of Stuart a story about Grenfell at Jack's Shop. Federal cavalry was in front of and behind Stuart's smaller force, and "Grenfell became demoralized on this day. The fighting was closer and hotter than he liked. He was at my side when our regiments were attempting to force Kilpatrick from the road. Seeing one of them recoil from a charge, Grenfell concluded that the day was lost. He took to the bushes, swam the river, returned to Orange Court House, and reported that Stuart, his staff, and his whole command were surrounded and captured." Needless to say, Grenfell lost whatever standing he had with Stuart at Jack's Shop, although he remained officially assigned to Stuart's staff until after Christmas.[37]

Late in October Stuart became concerned with some sort of slander being spread about him by Robert Swan. He had encountered Swan during the early months of the war when the Marylander had been a major in the 1st Virginia. Stuart led Swan into battle at First Manassas (Bull Run) and gave him charge of two companies during combat. But Swan responded timidly to battle and according to John Mosby cowered behind Confederate artillery even as the Federals were in full flight from the field. Mosby recalled that Grumble Jones witnessed this performance and ordered Swan's arrest. Swan left the 1st Virginia in April 1862, and never again held an official position in the Southern army. He remained in various headquarters as a volunteer aide, however, and Stuart became convinced that Swan was undermining him. Stuart never said what Swan was saying, but in letters to Flora called the man several kinds of dog.[38]

In November Richmond newspapers printed a debate between anonymous protagonists over Stuart's competence for command. "Investigator" (Grenfell? Swan?) on November 14 in the *Whig* delivered a scathing critique of Stuart's cavalry. The writer attacked everything from an alleged lack of bugles to Stuart's capacity to conduct combat. "Stuart's Chickahominy raid [Ride Around McClellan], like his raid into Pennsylvania [Chambersburg], was simply daring, costly and without result." "Investigator" lauded the accomplishments of Forrest and Morgan and concluded by asking whether any cavalry leader in history had ever had a command blessed with "as many men and so prodigious a number of horses, and on the whole done so little with it?"[39]

"W.W.G." responded in the *Enquirer* (November 19) by calling "Investigator" an "ignorant and bitter enemy of the cavalry of this army and its commander." The charges against Stuart and his cavalry are "*Lies*" inspired by "personal enmity." And "Investigator" was part of a "*covert plot*" in a campaign against Stuart designed "to blacken his pure fame."[40]

Several days after "W.W.G.'s" piece appeared, "Investigator" disclaimed any enmity regarding Stuart or his cavalry and claimed to wish the commander and his command well. "The real enemies of Gen. Stuart . . . it seems to the writer are over-zealous friends."[41]

One of Stuart's friends, using the pseudonym "C. Effingham, Esq.," did contribute two columns of poetry to the November 28 edition of the *Southern Illustrated News*. "The Ballad of Sir James" recounted Stuart's feats of valor and victory, beginning with his clash at Falling Waters July 2, 1861. The poem, however, stopped the story after the Chambersburg expedition in October 1862, and suggested that if the reader wanted to hear more "feats of this good Knight," he or she should

> Go ask the Yankees—they can tell
> How in full many a fight
>
> His plume has waved his voice rung out,
> His banner floated free,
> And on his soldier face has shone
> The light of victory.[42]

Engineer officer Blackford even contributed some verse to the Stuart legend during the fall of 1863. Using the tune of a song called "The Pirate's Glee" Blackford composed "The Cavalier's Glee":

> Spur on! Spur on! We love the bounding
> Of barbs that bear us to the fray;
> "The charge" our bugles now are sounding,
> And our bold Stuart leads the way.

Stuart liked the song, and so it livened his headquarters often in the winter of 1863–64. Fortunately for Stuart, Blackford's maps were much better than his scansion.[43]

Just as Lee's army was settling into winter quarters in late November, Meade made one more try at destroying the Southern army in 1863. The Federals began moving on November 26; Meade intended to cross the Rapidan rapidly and thrust his army between Hill's and Ewell's corps. His army marched too slowly, however, and once south of the Rapidan, Meade found the Confederates entrenched behind a stream flowing north-south called Mine Run. While Meade prepared to commit his men to battle on Mine Run, Lee developed a counterplan. Some of his Southerners would make maximum use of trenches to hold off their enemies; others (most of Ewell's corps) would attack the Federal flank from the south. As it happened, Meade thought better of his attack and began recrossing the Rapidan on December 1. Consequently, Ewell's flank attack struck mainly trees, and both armies went into winter quarters on opposite sides of the Rapidan.[44]

Cavalry played a very minor role in the Mine Run campaign. However, on two occasions Stuart marched off to battle with one of Hampton's brigades and left Hampton, who supposedly commanded the division, few clues about where to find his command. In his report of the campaign, Hampton recorded, "In the absence of all orders and without any intimation of the direction or destination of Rosser's brigade, which had been taken by General Stuart (except the notice given by the major-general commanding that he proposed to attack the enemy), I followed the line of march of this brigade."[45]

While Hampton had been in South Carolina recovering from the wound he suffered at Gettysburg, it seemed to make some sense that Stuart lead Hampton's division, as he had done during the Bristoe Station campaign. But now Hampton had returned to duty, and his duty was to command his division. By interrupting his own chain of command at Mine Run, Stuart cast considerable doubt upon his capacity or willingness to function as the head of the new cavalry organization. Certainly his actions did not endear him to Hampton. Yet more was at stake than bruised egos or administrative tidiness. Stuart commanded a corps of horsemen; logic dictated that he coordinate the actions of his two divisions and their component six brigades. At Mine Run he had personally led one brigade into combat and in effect lost contact with five-sixths of his command. Perhaps as he contended in his report, tactical circumstances dictated his personal intervention. But Stuart's first real experience in his reorganized command did not establish a hopeful precedent.[46]

From the heights of hindsight, it seems clear that Stuart had some serious problems during late 1863. He had too few horses. He had too little to feed the horses he had. He had too few weapons to fight the kind of fight the horseback war had become. He thought he had too many inspections and inspectors; but they uncovered too little discipline and too much waste. He believed he was the victim of slander and he saw his career and person dissected in public print. And in the last campaign of 1863, Stuart had his first test in command of a cavalry corps. He may not have failed the test, but he certainly did not pass it either.

A poem that posed Stuart as the knight "Sir James" and a camp song about "the bounding of barbs that bear us to the fray" were not going to resolve Stuart's problems. But Stuart himself responded to his new challenges in much the same way as Blackford and "C. Effingham, Esq." He continued to be the knight-cavalier cum warrior.

He once wrote Flora that the mood of the country had changed while he remained constant, and he wrote the truth. Having become the model person he had made for himself, he could be no other. He was "Stuart as usual."[47]

He established his winter headquarters, "Wigwam", at Orange Court House, and there he held court during Christmas. Flora came to him and stayed in a house nearby. Jimmy was now three and a half years old and called himself "General Jimmy J. E. B. Stuart, Junior." Stuart encouraged the boy to be rough and tumble and Jimmy responded; he loved to come to his father's camp and run among the horses. Stuart insisted that Flora's room have an outside entrance so that he could come and go at odd hours and not disturb anyone.[48]

On Christmas Eve the staff gathered in Stuart's tent at Wigwam. Frank Vizetelly of the *Illustrated London News* and Fitzgerald Ross, an English professional soldier who had served twelve years in Austria (Hussars), were special guests. The day was cold, but the fire in Stuart's tent warmed the company. The men sang to the accompaniment of Sam Sweeney, joined by his brother Dick, on banjo and violin; and Vizetelly "told some of his best stories." At bedtime Stuart let Ross have his tent and blankets and slept elsewhere himself. Christmas dinner was supposed to be turkey and ducks; but the food did not arrive in time. Ross testified that Stuart, his staff, and guests ate well anyway, and that evening they opened a huge box of oysters. Because of the cold weather the oysters were frozen, so the men tossed them onto the coals of the fire and ate them roasted when they popped open. Ross and Vizetelly were able to celebrate the season with cups of eggnog; but to do so they had to leave Stuart's camp.[49]

Stuart went to Richmond on December 31 and probably attended President Davis's reception on New Year's Day, 1864. While in the capital Stuart spent some time with his older brother William Alexander, who was managing family affairs in southwestern Virginia, including a crucial salt works in Saltville, Virginia. Stuart wanted his brother's help in purchasing a house, so the two men had much to discuss. William Alexander had his eleven-year-old son Henry with him, and Henry obviously worshiped his famous Uncle James. While the men were talking, Henry admired Stuart's sash and sword. Then Stuart interrupted the conversation with his brother: "No, before we go into that there is something I must attend to first." He turned to Henry and began a serious discussion about refreshment—what would taste good right now? Next Stuart led the way to Pizzini's, a legendary confectioner's shop in Richmond. There Uncle James bought Henry as many sweets as he could eat on the spot and more to take with him. Naturally Stuart endeared himself to his nephew, and later Henry reflected that Uncle James was the first adult to treat him as an equal and talk to him as "man to man." Certainly part of Stuart's charm was his capacity to take people seriously and consider their individual needs and concerns. It is possible, though, that Uncle James dealt with Henry as "boy to boy." In so doing and in his lavish attention, Stuart may have patched some gaps in his own boyhood.[50]

Stuart returned to Wigwam and on January 9 set out upon a round of inspections with Ross. After a visit to Young's brigade, the mayor of Fredericksburg invited them to dinner, and in the evening Stuart and Ross attended a ball. Next morning Stuart conducted Ross on a tour of the Fredericksburg battlefield and then attended church services. On January 11 they met Hampton, had a look at Gordon's brigade, and the following day returned to Richmond. On January 14 Stuart attended a charade party at the home of former Secretary of War George Wythe Randolph, and there he flirted with Hetty Cary and Constance Cary, two cousins from Baltimore who were Richmond's most popular belles. At another evening of charades Stuart agreed to support a ladder for Constance, but only if Hetty would stay "backstage" with him in a closet. Apparently he became so absorbed with Hetty that he forgot his task, and Constance fell off her perch. Fitz Lee then strode to the rescue and promised to be faithful to the ladder. Amid much laughter, Stuart took a place in the audience.[51]

Later in January Stuart went to Charlottesville. He considered renting a house ($200 per month) there. And probably on this visit to Charlottesville he attended a ball given by Fitz Lee. Local gossip reported Stuart "the gayest of the gay." And one woman "heard he told some of the ladies at the ball they must not judge his taste by his wife. She was extremely homely."[52]

This was, of course, thirdhand hearsay; it may have been gossip and nothing more. Still, Stuart seemed abnormally absorbed with women during the winter months of 1864. The day after he returned to Wigwam from Charlottesville (January 28), he wrote a poem:

> While Mars with his stentorian voice
> Chimes in with dire discordant noise,
> Sweet woman in angelic guise
> Gives hope and bids us fear despise.
>
> The Maid of Saragossa still
> Breathes in our cause her dauntless will

Beyond Potomac's rockbound shore
Her touch bids southern cannon roar . . .

And the same day he copied more poetry into an album. The verses he copied, like those he wrote, laud women as keepers of hearth and home and as keepers of pure virtues (hope, courage, will) in the crude, masculine world of war.[53]

Stuart earnestly wanted a place for Flora to settle with the children. Many of his letters during this winter contain news of his search for a house to rent or buy. In April he made an agreement with a man named Lewis M. Harbaugh to collect $5,000 he had left on deposit in the Bank of the State of Missouri in St. Louis. Harbaugh was to go to St. Louis, get the money, convert it to sterling or a bank draft on Baltimore Bank. For this service Stuart promised to pay Harbaugh a wage and the expenses of his journey. He wanted the money to purchase his first real home.[54]

At the same time he was so actively attempting to find a hearth and home for Flora to keep, Stuart became more critical of his wife. He accused her of being "never so happy as when . . . miserable" and of insisting upon "looking on the dark side in preference to the bright." He also charged, "It is strange how you seem to be ill-inclined to those who have treated me with such openhearted kindness." And he confronted a criticism made of him by Flora and others.

"As to being laughed at about your husband's fondness for Society and the ladies. All I can say is that you are better off in that than you would be if I were fonder of some other things, that excite no remark in others. The society of ladies will never injure your husband and ought to receive your encouragement. My correspondence with the ladies is that kind of correspondence which pertains to the position I hold, and which never could obtain with me were I a subordinate officer, such no doubt as you hear insinuations from."[55]

Still did Stuart use the attention of women as an index of his worth. More than most men, he treasured his flirtations and in a sense counted them as "conquests." If women were such paragons of virtue and piety, then their favors were proof, not only of his fame, but also of his knighthood. Stuart seemed to practice some nineteenth-century variant of courtly love. He idealized women, placed them upon pedestals, and strove to please them.

Flora need not have worried that her husband's associations with women were less than physically innocent. Stuart may have used women to measure his self worth. But knights of the sort Stuart believed himself to be did not deflower fair maids who inspired their gallantry. Yet Flora may indeed have suffered from Stuart's romantic convictions. She suffered in comparison with Stuart's fantasy of what a woman should be and represent. No woman could live up to such an ideal, and her very human failure to be perfect probably had something to do with Stuart's criticism of her.

During the winter within Stuart's society of men at Wigwam, the men changed somewhat; but the society remained constant. Late in January Blackford, the last member of the staff who had served with Stuart since the first year of the war, left to take a promotion and assignment with a new engineer regiment; and then Sam Sweeney died of smallpox, silencing his banjo. Von Borcke was still recuperating in Richmond. McClellan, Reid Venable, and Norman Fitzhugh were staff veterans by now, and Dabney Ball returned (after resigning in a huff as commissary officer in 1862) as chaplain. Stuart even decided to invite John Esten Cooke back into the fold, so that Cooke might help him with his tardy reports.[56]

Although faces changed, the atmosphere was much the same as it had always been in Stuart's camp. Early in February someone presented Stuart a very special turkey. The large gobbler had spent considerable time successfully dodging enemy bullets, and the Federals named the elusive bird "Jeb Stuart." Then, as Stuart phrased it, "He however made his escape alive and reported for duty at these Hdqrs." Stuart decided to make an occasion of devouring his namesake and invited Lee and some of his staff to dinner. Lee declined, protesting that he had to "work that the young men might play." Then he added, "Besides I could not bear to see 'Jeb Stuart' consumed." It may not have been a hilariously funny remark; but Stuart was one of very few people who could inspire humor from the commanding general.[57]

As constant as Stuart's laughter was his ambition; he still wanted to be a lieutenant general. Perhaps with promotion in mind, he proposed another reorganization of his cavalry. He suggested a third division of horsemen commanded by Rooney Lee, who had just returned to duty from captivity. The reorganization would make a place for Rooney Lee and might make the cavalry corps seem large enough to justify command by a lieutenant general, even though its strength remained the same. To do this, Stuart would have had to remove a brigade from Hampton's division, and the very suggestion sent Hampton in a rage to complain to Lee. Lee refused to sympathize with him; but Stuart's new plan never went into effect. Stuart also pursued his promotion through his friend Custis Lee ("Growls"). He even offered to serve in the trans-Mississippi, if the transfer involved promotion.[58]

Of all the ways in which Stuart persisted in acting out his vision of himself during the winter of 1863–64, one was almost too perfectly symbolic. It occurred on January 8 in Richmond at an elaborate charade party given by some local luminaries for other luminaries. Rules of the game required the amateur actors and actresses to pantomime a word syllable by syllable and then to present a scene depicting the entire word. On January 8 the final word was "pilgrimage." The first scene featured a quack selling a *pill;* next beggars implored the aid of a rich man who looked *grim;* and then two characters affected the look and actions of *age.* Finally came the climactic scene of the entire evening, a representation of the whole word.

One of the actors described it. "The stage became a shrine, draped and flower strewn, the Cross surmounting it. Toward it slowly moved pilgrims from every age and clime, entering from opposite sides and walking in pairs. Peasant, priest, Knight, Imam, beggar and emperor, all approached, kneeling to lay their offerings upon the Cross. Then they separated once more, grouping on either side in brilliant contrast. A little pause. The band struck up 'See! the conquering hero comes.' Forth strode grand 'Jeb' Stuart, in full uniform, his stainless sword unsheathed, his noble face luminous with inward fire. Ignoring the audience and its welcome, he advanced, his eyes fixed on the shrine until he laid the blade, so famous, upon it." Stuart stepped away, but "never raised his eyes from the floor as he stood with folded arms." Women dressed as nuns then came "to bless the sword laid there as votive offering to country: no breath now breaking the hush upon the audience."

And then came men dressed as Mecca pilgrims to touch the sword and prostrate themselves. "The music had softened to a sweet pianissimo as the sword was laid upon the altar. Now it swelled out into a solemn strain, and the Franciscans, the Paulists, the Capuchins and the nuns in the pilgrimages stood forth and chanted the 'Miserere,' as the refrain softly closed."[59]

It was a magnificent performance. And Stuart played himself.

# XIV

## *"I Had Rather Die Than Be Whipped"*

ONCE BEFORE Stuart had made an issue of mourning dress with Flora; he did not like it at all. Late in April of 1864, he absolutely forbade her to wear black—told her to take off those depressing clothes and never wear them again. Once more he tried to cheer her, in fact he commanded Flora to brighten her spirits.[1]

Stuart himself seemed brighter than usual. People were naming babies after him. He had a new toy for Jimmy. He had a dog named Beauty. And the war was about to begin again.[2]

As the weather warmed and roads dried, it took no military genius to know that the campaigning season of 1864 would soon open. Stuart was ready. He sent his winter gear—his overcoat and extra blankets, his Spencer rifle and his carbine—to Norman Fitzhugh's home in Scotsville, and at his winter headquarters near Orange Court House the staff stirred and made ready to break camp quickly. This year Stuart commanded 9,700 horsemen, and despite chronic concerns over horses, fodder, and weapons, his cavalry was experienced and as prepared for combat as it would ever be. Stuart did hope to see Flora and Jimmy one more time before the action began; they planned to come up from Richmond by train during the first few days of May.[3]

This year Lee left the initiative to his enemies. Across the Rapidan was Meade's army and in March a new Union general-in-chief, Ulysses S. Grant. Meade still commanded the Army of the Potomac; but Grant came east to command Meade. And to command Meade's cavalry Grant installed Philip Sheridan. Grant

For a map showing the Wilderness and Stuart's route to Yellow Tavern see p. 112.

wanted to match wits and armies with Lee, and Sheridan was just as eager to take on Stuart.[4]

Federal cavalry, like their Confederate counterparts, had spent the winter doing picket duty and attempting to keep themselves and their horses in shape for spring. The single exception was a major raid by Kilpatrick against Richmond (February 28–March 1). Custer led a diversionary ride toward Charlottesville and drew Stuart away. Kilpatrick then led a dash toward Richmond which reached the intermediate defense lines north of the capital on March 1. But there Kilpatrick's nerve seemed to fail him. With 3,000 troopers against only about 500 Confederate defenders, Kilpatrick withdrew and sought safety within Federal lines on the lower peninsula. Meanwhile a second, smaller Federal column commanded by Ulrich Dahlgren came to grief west of Richmond, and during Dahlgren's attempt to rejoin Kilpatrick's force, the young officer lost about 100 of his men and his own life as well.[5]

Sheridan had even more ambitious ideas and a stronger nerve than Kilpatrick. He pressed Meade to turn his cavalry loose to fight Stuart. He proposed to threaten Richmond in order to draw the Confederate horsemen away from Lee's infantry. Richmond was not Sheridan's objective; once he had Stuart's command away from the Army of Northern Virginia, he proposed to destroy it. For the time being, however, Meade insisted that his cavalry function conventionally with his infantry. Sheridan would have to screen and picket and protect flanks and supplies. The Federal cavalry commander chafed at such a subordinate role in the coming campaign. He had almost 12,500 horsemen, eight batteries of artillery, and he had many of his troopers armed with repeating Spencer carbines. Sheridan wanted to put these men and weapons to conspicuous use; he wanted Stuart.[6]

Stuart had his scouts in enemy country beyond the Rapidan, and their reports confirmed what he already knew: the enemy was on the march. On May 3 Stuart prepared to strike his Wigwam, and that night scouts rode into his headquarters with news that would set the Southern army in motion. Grant was ready to cross the Rapidan the next day.[7]

Just after the midday meal on May 4, Stuart sent Talcott Eliason to intercept and turn back Flora and Jimmy, who were en route, and himself set out for Lee's headquarters. He rode cross-country and jumped fences, while most of his staff and couriers followed the roads. After a brief conference with Lee, Stuart and his entourage headed down the Orange-Fredericksburg Plank Road toward the enemy advance. After a few miles the open, rolling country on each side of the road became the Wilderness, a thickly wooded region of which one staff member said, "a gloomier, wilder and more forbidding region can hardly be found this side of the Alleghenies." Unbroken woods laced with veritable walls of tangled vines and undergrowth spread for miles on both sides of the Plank Road.[8]

Stuart rode into the Wilderness until he received a sudden volley from the side of the road that announced the presence of the enemy. A brief exchange of fire produced no casualties, and Stuart had discovered the extent of the Federal advance. As darkness began to fall, Stuart retraced his hoofprints back along the Plank Road to meet Lee's infantry (A. P. Hill's corps) and his cavalry (most of Hampton's division).

The situation was roughly this. Grant had crossed the Rapidan and sent his army south; Lee was moving his forces east to strike the Federal flank in the Wilderness. Stuart had summoned Fitz Lee from the vicinity of Fredericksburg and Hampton from the upper reaches of the Rapidan. Southern cavalry was supposed to define and contain if possible the enemy advance to the south, while opposing infantries found and fought each other in the Wilderness. Lee hoped to stop the Federals with Ewell's and Hill's corps and then bring Longstreet's corps into battle from the south on the Federal flank. Because of the density of the Wilderness woods, cavalry could do very little more than fight on the fringe of the primary battleground. And even then most of the fighting would be dismounted.[9]

Stuart encountered the leading element of Hill's corps near where the Plank Road crosses Mine Run. A little farther back toward Orange, near Verdiersville, Stuart met his horsemen— Hampton's division (minus Rosser's brigade) coming to assume a position on the infantry flank.

Alexander R. Boteler, who was a Virginia congressman and at this time a volunteer aide to Stuart, described the scene. "Stuart himself a little in advance of us with his plumed hat in his hand, looked like an equestrian statue,—both man and horse being as

motionless as marble,—his fine soldierly figure fully revealed in
the light of the camp fires that were blazing brightly on both sides
of the road, as far as the eye could reach and lighting up the fore-
ground splendidly." Confederate horsemen rode past Stuart, "in
columns of fours at full trot, saluting the general with a shout as
they wheeled off, at a gallop, toward their designated positions
while the infantry, catching inspiration from their cheers, mingled
their loud hurrahs with theirs, in one grand chorus of twice ten
thousand voices. It was really, a grand spectacle to see these gallant horsemen coming toward us out of the gloom of night into the
glare of the fires, making the welkin ring with their Wild War cries
and the earth to tremble beneath their horses hoofs." [10]

When the excitement passed with the cavalry, Stuart and his
staff made camp at Verdiersville, where he had lost his hat and
cape during a hasty exit in August of 1862. This time Stuart slept
on the ground in greater confidence that Union cavalry would not
greet him the next morning.

Flora had had a difficult day on the train with Jimmy. A fellow
passenger remembered the boy as "the willfullest [sic] and most
unmanageable youngster that ever sprung from a military sire to
test the patience and affection of an amiable mother." When Eliason informed her that her husband had ridden off to war, Flora
cried. Then she made ready to apply patience and affection some
more on the return trip. [11]

Stuart was awake before dawn on May 5. He drank some coffee,
ate a bit of hardtack, and mounted at first light. His first chore that
day was to guide Hill's infantry down to Orange-Fredericksburg
Plank Road to the point at which he had encountered Federals the
day before. This he did in person and spent the rest of the day
attempting to maintain contact with his subordinates and with
Lee. The Wilderness became a factor as combat became general.
Thick woods and undergrowth tended to nullify Grant's numerical
advantage and channel the fighting toward roads and rare clear-
ings. The Wilderness not only broke up military formations, it
confused men on both sides about distance and directions. On two
occasions bands of lost Federal skirmishers surprised Stuart and
his staff, and in one of these instances Union troops strayed into a
conference among Stuart, Hill, and Lee. The Southern generals
made a hasty exit before the Federals realized who they were.

During the day Stuart had his uniform ripped in places by thorns and his face scratched by briers. That evening he again slept behind the infantry lines near a place called Parker's Store.[12]

On May 6 Stuart remained on the Plank Road and attempted to guide the efforts of others as Longstreet advanced. About midday Edward Porter Alexander came to Stuart with questions about locations for his (Longstreet's) artillery. Stuart escorted Alexander along his picket line in search of gun positions. At one point they came upon an open field. Across the cleared ground, about 200 yards away, Stuart suspected Federal pickets held the woodline among some pine trees. To find out for sure, he turned to one of his couriers and said matter-of-factly, "Ride out there and see if you can draw any fire." The courier-target did as he was ordered and immediately attracted several shots from the pines. None of the bullets did serious damage; but one clipped the muzzle of the courier's horse. The animal seemed to know who had been responsible for its wound; the horse went directly to Stuart and snorted blood on him.[13]

Longstreet's attack was a limited success, and in its wake Longstreet suffered a wound in the throat at the hands of his own men, who mistook him for the enemy. Lee took over direction of the attack, and if the troops had allowed him, would have led a charge himself. That evening Stuart sent a hurried note to Flora: "I am safe and well tonight."[14]

Next day (May 7) neither army renewed the fighting in the Wilderness. Grant had sustained severe losses, seemingly to no advantage. Nevertheless, he determined to continue the campaign and prepared to shift Meade's army south and east. In the course of these preparations Federal cavalry supported by infantry advanced upon the crucial road juncture at New Spotsylvania Court House. There Fitz Lee gave ground stubbornly and at dark still held Spotsylvania. Lee hurried his weary infantry to meet the new threat, and Stuart took charge of selecting routes and guiding the foot soldiers. That night he sent a telegram to Flora proclaiming himself "safe and well" once more. Then he came about as close as he ever would to disclaiming victory—"We have beaten the enemy badly but he is not yet in full retreat."[15]

Stuart spent May 8 guiding and deploying the men of Longstreet's corps, now commanded by Richard H. Anderson. For several hours he commanded both infantry and dismounted cavalry in the desperate battle to hold Spotsylvania. Meanwhile a few miles on the other side of the battle line, Sheridan and Meade were doing verbal combat at Meade's headquarters. In the course of the discussion about Sheridan's horsemen impeding the progress of the infantry en route to Spotsylvania, Stuart's name came up.

"Never mind Stuart," Meade reportedly remarked, "he will do about as he pleases anyhow."

"Damn Stuart," Sheridan supposedly replied, "I can thrash hell out of him any day."

A short while later, Meade repeated Sheridan's boast to Grant. "Did Sheridan say that? Well, he generally knows what he is talking about. Let him start right out and do it." That very night (May 8) Sheridan had his wish—orders to fight Stuart with his entire corps.[16]

The Federal column, 10,000 troopers occupying thirteen miles of road, began the march at a walk early on the morning of May 9. Sheridan moved east of the great battle still raging at Spotsylvania and then due south on the Telegraph Road. Stuart learned of Sheridan's activities very soon after the Federals began their ride. Williams Wickham spread the alarm and with his brigade began the pursuit. Stuart with one of Hampton's brigades (James Gordon's) joined Fitz Lee, who had with him Wickham's troopers and those of Lunsford Lomax. Stuart, then, had three brigades—about 4,500 men—with him when the chase began in earnest.[17]

Both cavalries rode all day on May 9, and Stuart rode all night as well. Sheridan's trail led ever south; but he left the Telegraph Road and reached Beaver Dam Station on the Virginia Central Railroad near dark. There was Lee's advance supply base, and during the night the Federals burned enormous quantities of rations and medical supplies. Before they left on the morning of May 10, the raiders also destroyed two locomotives, a hundred railroad cars, and ten miles of track. Then Sheridan reassembled his column and pressed on toward Richmond.[18]

Stuart reached Beaver Dam Station very soon after the Federals departed on the morning of the tenth. Surely the sight of so much destruction he had not caused depressed him. He was also concerned about Flora and the children, who were staying at Beaver Dam, the home of Edmund Fontaine for which the station was named. While his troopers rested briefly, Stuart and Reid Venable rode a mile and a half to the house. He never dismounted, but did speak privately to Flora for some minutes. Then he kissed her, said good-bye, and rode away. On the way back to his men, Stuart's mood turned somber. He said nothing to Venable for a time and then said that he had never expected to survive the war. He had said such things before, but seldom so seriously. He also said that he would not want to live if the Confederacy were to lose the war.[19]

Back at Beaver Dam Station, Stuart heard enough reports from enough sources to believe that Sheridan was still heading toward Richmond, although his route also threatened the tracks of the Richmond, Fredericksburg and Potomac Railroad. He decided to send Gordon's brigade after the Federals, while he and Fitz Lee led his other two brigades down an alternate route in an attempt to get ahead of the enemy column. The day was hot; both horses and men were tiring rapidly; but Stuart continued the march as fast as possible under the circumstances. He reached Hanover Junction after dark and prepared to ride on throughout the night. Fitz Lee, however, interceded and insisted that the column rest until one o'clock on the morning of May 11. Stuart agreed; but he sent McClellan with Lee, ordered the adjutant to remain awake and make sure Lee's men move promptly at 1:00 A.M. He himself rode ahead two and a half miles to Taylorsville and slept for perhaps three hours on a blanket with Venable.[20]

McClellan awakened Stuart with the news that the Southern troopers were once more riding south. As Stuart prepared to join them, McClellan fell asleep. And when the general rode off, McClellan remembered hearing Stuart answer someone's question about arousing him, "No, he has been watching while we were asleep. Leave a courier with him and tell him to come on when his nap is out." The adjutant overtook his general not too far from Ashland, where a Federal detachment had wrecked more railroad track before being driven away by one of Stuart's squadrons. As the main column continued down the Telegraph Road, McClellan rode with Stuart. Again Stuart seemed somber, and McClellan recalled, "He was more quiet than usual, softer, and more communicative."[21]

At 10:00 A.M. on May 11, Stuart reached the intersection of Telegraph and Mountain roads, a place called Yellow Tavern, less than six miles from Richmond. He had arrived ahead of Sheridan's Federals. If his intelligence and his assumptions were correct, the enemy would come down the Mountain Road to this point. Once upon a time on June 12, 1862, Stuart had led his cavalry up that same Mountain Road en route around McClellan to fame. Now Stuart had to decide what to do when the Federals arrived. He had at least two options: he could make a stand directly in Sheridan's path, or he could try to get on Sheridan's flank and attack the Federals as they rode toward Richmond. He favored the latter ploy; but it depended upon Richmond's defenses being strong enough to stop Sheridan if necessary. Accordingly, he sent McClellan into the capital to speak to Braxton Bragg, who was now the president's military adviser and ranking field commander in the city.[22]

The Federal cavalry reached Yellow Tavern before McClellan returned, however, and Stuart simply had to hope Richmond's defenses were strong enough. He deployed his 3,000 men along Mountain Road, instead of across it, and prepared to fight at odds of less than one to three. Gordon's brigade was active at the rear of the Federal column, but clearly too far away to support the fight at Yellow Tavern. And because Stuart chose to fight on the defensive dismounted, he had to remove one man among every four from the battle line to hold horses. Still, Stuart selected a strong position and had artillery in place to strengthen it further. Wickham's men occupied a ridge line more or less perpendicular to Telegraph Road facing south-southwest. Lomax's force held another ridge essentially parallel with Telegraph Road facing west.[23]

Had Sheridan's goal been Richmond, he might have brushed past Stuart's defensive position and ridden on toward the capital. Then Stuart might have assailed the rear of the Federal column with help from Gordon's brigade while Sheridan confronted Richmond's defenses. In that event the Federal cavalry might have had to fight for its very life. But Sheridan's goal was not Richmond; it was Stuart.

When the Federals came down the Mountain Road before noon (May 11) and found Stuart, they advanced immediately on his flanks. Very soon the enemy held a portion of the Telegraph

Road between the Confederates and Richmond. Then they assaulted Stuart's lines. Fighting was especially furious on the
Southern left among Lomax's troopers.

At one point it seemed that the entire day depended upon the
5th Virginia Regiment, commanded by Henry Clay Pate. Pate it
was whom Stuart had first met in Kansas when he had been part of
the party that rescued Pate from John Brown. Later Stuart had
taken Tom Rosser's side in a Pate-Rosser feud that ended in Pate's
court-martial. Now Stuart needed Pate desperately and rode over
to tell him so. Pate listened to Stuart's exhortations to hold his
position and responded firmly, "I will do it." Stuart thanked him;
Pate moved closer and extended his hand; Stuart shook it warmly.
Then Pate and his men held off the next Federal surge, and Pate
lost his life.

When McClellan tried to return to Stuart from Richmond with
assurances from Bragg that he could hold the city, the adjutant
found his way barred by enemy troops. By the time he had made
a detour cross-country and found Stuart, it was 2:00 P.M. and there
was a lull in the fighting. The earlier Federal attacks had pushed
Lomax back and straightened the angle in the Confederate line so
that Stuart's force now faced approximately south, down Telegraph Road. Stuart was sanguine as usual. Gordon would join him
shortly, and he sent a message to Bragg asking him to march out
from Richmond and attack Sheridan from the south while he attacked from the north—"I cannot see how they can escape." [24]

For more than an hour Stuart sat and talked with McClellan,
Venable, and more of his staff. Had Stuart been Sheridan, he probably would not have pressed the issue at Yellow Tavern; he would
more likely have made a dash at Richmond. But Sheridan was not
Stuart; he had not come here to dash. While Stuart chatted, Sheridan planned another attack.

About 4:00 P.M. they came again—dismounted troopers in
numbers too great for the Confederates to withstand for long, and
mounted charges as well. Stuart mounted his horse, summoned
his staff, and rode to rally his troopers. During the next minutes,
he was in many places at once. [25]

He sat his horse in the open with Reid Venable while men
behind trees around him were falling. "I don't reckon there is any
danger!"

He was on the Telegraph Road shouting to the men of Company G, 1st Virginia Cavalry. "Boys, don't stop to count fours. Shoot them! Shoot them!"

He was alone. His horse cantered behind the thin line of troopers while Stuart whistled.

Finally he joined Company K, 1st Virginia Cavalry. His horse stuck its head over a fence between Fred Pitts and J. R. Oliver. He was still alone.

Then the Federals made a mounted charge. "Bully for old K. Give it to them, boys!" Stuart bellowed and waved his saber.

He jerked his pistol and fired as the enemy horsemen swept past him. Federals on horseback and unhorsed were within the Southern lines. Those who were there remembered chaos. Somewhere to the rear some Confederates rallied and delivered a mounted charge. Amid more confusion the Federals recoiled. Again Stuart fired his pistol at the men who rode and ran near him.

One of the men on foot fired back. From ten to fifteen yards away he sent a .44-caliber pistol bullet into Stuart's right side below his ribs. Then the man resumed his running.

Stuart reeled in his saddle, but did not fall from his horse. His hat did fall off, and he clasped his side. Men soon noticed the general's difficulty and gathered around him. To one of them Stuart said, "Go and tell General [Fitz] Lee and Dr. Fontaine [Staff Surgeon John B.] to come here."

Gus Dorsey, who commanded Company K, came to him. The enemy would return. Stuart could not remain here. Dorsey tried to lead Stuart's horse toward the rear; but the animal resisted and began to rear and shy. Stuart asked to be taken down and propped against a tree. Dorsey sent for another horse; he had to get the general away from this exposed area. Stuart told Dorsey to leave him. "Dorsey, save your men!" But Dorsey replied that he must refuse that order; he would take the general to safety first. Someone led another horse to the scene, and Dorsey and his men helped Stuart mount and led him away.

When they reached a place of probable safety, Dorsey did obey Stuart's instruction and returned to his men. At some point during these events Fitz Lee appeared. Stuart informed Lee that the command was his and told him to get to work. "Go ahead, Fitz, old fellow. I know you will do what is right!" [26]

Finally the doctor, members of the staff, and an ambulance arrived. The men loaded Stuart into the vehicle and began to think about how they would avoid the enemy on the way to Richmond. As they drove away from the battle, which still raged, Stuart saw some Southern troopers leaving the field.

"Go back! go back! and do your duty, as I have done mine, and our country will be safe. Go back! Go back! I had rather die than be whipped."

For a little while the ambulance remained near the action, while the men decided on a route. Dr. Fontaine took a look at the wound, and as he did Stuart asked staff officer W. Q. Hullihen, "Honey-bun, how do I look in the face?"

"General, you are looking right well. You will be all right."

"Well, I don't know how this will turn out; but if it is God's will that I shall die, I am ready."

Fontaine could not determine much from his examination. But the prognosis did not appear good. The bullet had entered Stuart's lower abdomen and remained somewhere inside him. Many things were possible; but experience with such wounds indicated that Stuart would suffer and not survive. And at that moment he seemed most threatened by "prostration"—shock. Fontaine wanted him to drink some whiskey, which conventional wisdom agreed would act as a stimulant. Stuart demurred and spoke of the vow to his mother. Venable at length convinced him, and Stuart drank some of the whiskey.

Soon after this, the journey to Richmond commenced. They had to travel first northeast to Atlee's Station, then to Mechanicsville, and from there to the city. Had the roads been straight, the distance would have been thirteen miles. But the roads were not straight; nor were they smooth. Stuart suffered significant pain during the circuitous ride.

Well after dark he reached the home of his brother-in-law, Dr. Charles Brewer, on Grace Street in Richmond. Other doctors joined Brewer and Fontaine; they agreed that they could do nothing but apply ice to the wound. Stuart spent the night in periodic intense pain.[27]

Members of the staff attempted to send a telegram to Flora at Beaver Dam; but Sheridan's Federals had cut telegraph wires wherever they had gone. Eventually a message sent by Heros Von

Borcke traveled via Lynchburg and Gordonsville and reached
Beaver Dam Station about noon on May 12. By coincidence Flora
and the Fontaine family were at the station trying to help wounded
soldiers sent from Spotsylvania when the telegram arrived. Edmund Fontaine took the message, but did not show it to Flora until
he had hurried her back to his home. GENERAL STUART HAS BEEN
SERIOUSLY WOUNDED; COME AT ONCE. Flora, the children, and two
male escorts began the trip to Richmond just after 1:00 P.M. They
traveled by private train; Fontaine, who was president of the Virginia Central Railroad, managed to secure an engine and a car in a
hurry. It took them two hours to reach Ashland, where they had to
leave their train because Federals had torn up tracks between
there and Richmond. Some wounded cavalry officers insisted that
Flora and her party take their ambulance. So as spring storm
clouds gathered ominously, the party set out once more for Richmond.[28]

Meanwhile Stuart had been alert and lucid during the morning.
He held ice to his side and ate some of it as well when Von Borcke
visited him. McClellan came into the city on an errand for Fitz
Lee and seized the opportunity to go to Stuart's bedside. Between
spasms of pain the general instructed McClellan regarding his
military papers and charged him to deliver his personal effects to
Flora.

"I wish you to take one of my horses and Venable the other.
Which is the heavier rider?"

McClellan said that Venable was.

"Then let Venable have the gray horse, and you take the bay."

Next he told McClellan to look in his hat, find a small Confederate flag, and return it to a woman in Columbia, South Carolina.
McClellan, who had never known about the flag, promised to comply.

"My spurs which I have always worn in battle I promised to
give to Mrs Lilly [sic] Lee, of Shepherdstown, Virginia. My sword
I leave to my son."

While McClellan was with him, they heard artillery, and Stuart
asked about the military situation. McClellan explained that Sheridan was moving east down the Chickahominy; Fitz Lee and some
Confederate infantry were still trying to trap him. "God grant that
they may be successful," Stuart said, then sighed. "But I must be
prepared for another world."

When, at Stuart's prompting, McClellan was leaving, Jefferson Davis arrived. "General, how do you feel?" he asked.

"Easy, but willing to die, if God and my country think I have fulfilled my destiny and done my duty."[29]

All the while her husband was doing and saying these noble things, Flora was still trying to reach him. She traveled through a thunderstorm over a maze of roads. And every time her party met soldiers, she inquired about Stuart. Someone said his wound had not proven serious; so with renewed hope the journey continued.[30]

As afternoon wore on, Stuart was increasingly out of touch with those who watched by his bedside. In all probability he was suffering from a combination of internal hemorrhaging and peritonitis. The bullet had severed blood vessels as well as intestines, probably the large intestine, in one or more places.[31]

Every now and then he roused himself. Several times he asked about Flora. Late in the day he asked Dr. Brewer if he might be able to survive the night. Brewer said "no" as gently as he could. "I am resigned if it be God's will; but I would like to see my wife. . . . But God's will be done."

He said more about destiny, duty, and God as evening came. Just after 7:00 P.M. everyone in the house gathered by his bed. The Reverend Joshua Peterkin prayed Episcopal prayers, and the company sang Stuart's favorite hymn.

> Rock of ages, cleft for me
> Let me hide myself in thee;
> Let the water and the blood
> From thy side, a healing flood,
> Be of sin the double cure,
> Cleanse me from its guilt and power.

He tried to sing with them, but he was too weak. Soon after the hymn, he turned to Brewer. "I am going fast now. I am resigned; God's will be done."

Then he drifted into unconsciousness. And soon after that, he died. Those who watched him die believed that his breathing ceased at 7:38 P.M.[32]

At this time Flora was still north of the Chickahominy River, still hoping her husband was recovering. Her ambulance reached the Chickahominy about eight o'clock that night and the party found the bridge destroyed. They sought out a cavalry picket and the men directed them to a ford a mile or so downstream. After crossing the river they resumed the journey toward Richmond; by the time they reached the outskirts of the city it was after ten o'clock and the rainstorm continued. Suddenly a rider appeared out of the dark immediately in front of the horses. "Who's there? —stand!" They explained who they were and what they were doing. "Thank God!" The sentinel said he had actually tried to shoot them when his earlier challenges went unheard and so unanswered. Fortunately his weapon failed to fire.

Flora and the children finally drove up in front of the Brewer home at eleven thirty that night. She remembered noticing the quiet, and instinctively she knew the worst had happened. Her husband was dead; she had come too late.[33]

They held the funeral at five in the afternoon of the next day (May 13). Eight general officers bore the coffin before the altar of St. James' Church; the Reverend Mr. Peterkin read the service, which concluded with singing. Then the pallbearers returned the coffin to the hearse, and there was a procession in the rain to Hollywood Cemetery. There another Episcopal cleric (the Reverend Charles Minnigerode) read the service committing Stuart's physical remains to the ground. Flora, his child, had been reinterred here the previous fall. Many people, including President Davis, attended the funeral and burial. But there was no military display; all the available troops were still chasing Sheridan's cavalry. Those who stood in the rain at the cemetery could hear their cannon booming in the distance, and this had to suffice as a salute.[34]

He had written his will in November of 1861 and left everything he owned to Flora and his children. But Stuart owned very little, and his heirs did not bother with probate until October 1866. He left a gold pencil to his daughter Flora, who had since died. He left his class ring, diplomas, commissions, and clothes to his wife. His sword went to Jimmy. He did express the wish that his children be educated south of the Mason and Dixon line and that his family always live in the South.[35]

Stuart's estate was all but insignificant. But his intangible legacy was large. To his family, to all who ever associated with him, and indeed to many who never knew him, he left his name and his fame. And many people shaped their lives and livings from this legacy.

Robert E. Lee missed the talents of the soldier who "never brought me a piece of false information." He also grieved for his surrogate son. "I can scarcely think of him without weeping." [36]

Wade Hampton succeeded Stuart in command—"The Cavalry Corps has received me warmly." Indeed one trooper asserted, "Under Stuart stampedes were frequent, with Hampton they were unknown." [37]

John Esten Cooke used and embellished his in-law's fame in a series of stories and novels that made Cooke famous. He never knew that Stuart had thought him an enormous bore.

Heros Von Borcke wrote memoirs of Stuart in which Von Borcke is often the hero. In late life the Prussian aristocrat weighed 405 pounds and was unable to tie his own shoes for years. From a tower of his castle in Prussia he flew a Confederate flag. [38]

Henry B. McClellan became Stuart's "official" biographer. He was principal of a girls' school in Lexington, Kentucky. [39]

Virginia Pelham Stuart married and settled in Norfolk, Virginia. She died after childbirth in 1898.

James Ewell Brown Stuart II eventually joined the army of his father's enemies. He retired a captain and lived in New York City.

Flora was ever "Mrs. General J. E. B. Stuart." Her father tried to convince her to come north and even arranged for a pass and transportation; but she refused. She later became principal of a girls' school in Staunton, Virginia—Virginia Female Institute— which later still became Stuart Hall. After her daughter's death, Flora moved to Norfolk to care for her son-in-law's family and lived with the family for twenty-five years. She died on May 10, 1923, fifty years (minus two days) after her husband. For all those years, she wore the black of mourning. [40]

# Metaphor As Man:
## Some Speculations by Way of Conclusion

STUART'S APOTHEOSIS BEGAN EARLY. On the day of his funeral, John R. Thompson, who had immortalized Latané in 1862, wrote a poem about his friend and fallen hero.[1] The concluding stanzas read:

> The Spanish legend tells us of the Cid
>     That after death he rode erect, sedately
> Along his lines, even as in life he did,
>     In presence yet more stately;
>
> And thus our Stuart at this moment seems
>     To ride out of our dark and troubled story
> Into the region of romance and dreams,
>     A realm of light and glory.
>
> And sometimes, when the silver bugles blow,
>     That radiant form, in battle re-appearing
> Shall lead his horsemen headlong on the foe,
>     In victory careering!

When the Confederate cause became the Lost Cause, novels like those of John Esten Cooke and Thomas Dixon compounded the romantic image of Stuart; statues added substance, and memoirs, biographies, and histories reinforced the Stuart symbol. Eventually symbol became stereotype—the rollicking, romantic Southern centaur. And the stereotype is familiar to many who cannot quite recall who Stuart was—who thus know Stuart, but not his name.

There is a very good reason why Stuart the man became so quickly and completely Stuart the metaphor. That reason is Stuart himself. He began the metaphor-making process while he lived, and he succeeded.

He was warrior, knight, and cavalier; his life was mission, quest, and lark. This was his ideal vision of himself, the mold he made for his life, the part he cast for himself in the human drama. It was an ambitious role and a bold facade, and somewhere beneath an actor's mask was Stuart the finite human being. So he cared what people said of him and used the attention and favors of women to gauge his success. He required the reinforcement of fame and permitted very few people to glimpse beneath his mask. Only Flora his wife and confidante came close to knowing him whole.

Stuart's triumph as a person lay in his success at acting out his vision of himself. He became the cavalier-knight cum warrior he wanted to be. He was a legend even while he lived.

One of his enemies, Federal corps commander John Sedgwick, called Stuart "the greatest cavalryman ever foaled in America." And Sedgwick was correct. Stuart displayed the capacity to command both small and large numbers of horsemen, and he was able to integrate his cavalry with artillery and infantry, as well as to conduct independent operations. Nathan Bedford Forrest, Wade Hampton, John Hunt Morgan, and Joseph Wheeler, at one time or another, proved they could do one of these things. Stuart did them all and did them consistently well. On the Federal side, Philip Sheridan was effective. But by the time he emerged in the war, his Southern opponents were weak and few, and the only time he encountered Stuart (Yellow Tavern), Sheridan outnumbered him by three to one. Even after Stuart had become inordinately concerned with his name and fame and was at his worst as a cavalry commander, he still performed as well or better than his contemporaries in either army.

The tragedy in Stuart's life lay, ironically, in his success. He eventually became so absorbed in posturing and playing his role that he could not leave the stage or remove his mask. He was neither free to fail nor to feel or think anything more or less than what he believed he was supposed to feel or think. He was supposed to win; so he revealed himself thoroughly when he said, "I had rather die than be whipped." He confused fame with greatness because he lacked the depth and experience to discern the difference. So consumed was he by his vision of what he ought to be that he never quite came to terms with his humanity—until he lay dying.

There was a cruel irony in Stuart's death. He once said that all he ever wanted from life was to be killed at the head of a cavalry charge. But he died in bed, and then only after twenty-seven hours of excruciating pain and agony. He lived by the saber; he expected to die by the saber. Yet death came from internal hemorrhaging and peritonitis; he died by his own blood and feces.

But while Stuart was dying, he did and said some revealing things. He gave away his horses; he gave away his spurs; he returned a woman's favor; and he gave up his sword. In so doing Stuart stripped himself of cherished trappings that had defined his life. During his final hours, he rendered himself a naked knight.

Over and over from the time he received his wound at Yellow Tavern to his last recorded sentence, Stuart said he was resigned to the will of God. He said it so often that, within the context of Stuart's simple evangelical faith, it may indeed have been an honest prayer that he might be spared. He may have asked that God might will him to live. One thing is certain; God in this case was not the warrior god Mars. "Rock of Ages" is hardly a hymn of human triumph. Stuart confronted in death his ultimate humanity.

Among the various things people recalled that he said, he made only one request. He wanted to see Flora, his wife. In effect he was asking for intimacy and love, and this was not the request of a blasé cavalier.

While he died, Stuart did as much as he could to remove the mask he had made and worn in life. He abandoned his quest, surrendered his mission, and gave up his lark. He died free from the metaphors that had defined and driven his life.

But those who watched him die did not seem to notice. They saw noble gestures and heard pious words. And they remembered Stuart as he lived.

# Notes

## Man as Metaphor: An Epilogue
## by Way of Introduction

1. William Faulkner, *Sartoris* (New York, 1956), 8–19.

2. Stuart appears in the works of John Esten Cooke (*Surry of Eagle's-Nest* [New York, 1866]), Thomas Dixon (*The Man in Gray* [New York, 1922]), Stephen Vincent Benét (*John Brown's Body* [New York, 1928]), Michael Shaara (*The Killer Angels* [New York, 1975]), Barry Hannah (*Airships* [New York, 1978]), and others.

3. For recent examples, see James M. McPherson, *Ordeal by Fire: The Civil War and Reconstruction* (New York, 1982), 243; and Stephen Z. Starr, *The Union Cavalry in the Civil War*, Vol. II, *The War in the East from Gettysburg to Appomattox, 1863–1865* (Baton Rouge, 1981), 108–10. Stuart biographies include H. B. McClellan, *The Life and Campaigns of Major-General J. E. B. Stuart* (Boston and New York, 1885); John W. Thomason, Jr., *Jeb Stuart* (New York, 1930); and Burke Davis, *Jeb Stuart: The Last Cavalier* (New York, 1957).

## I. Young James

1. Elizabeth Stuart's ancestors were Welsh. Her great-grandfather Giles Letcher emigrated to Virginia from Ireland; his second son was William Letcher. At the time of his murder in 1780 Letcher had an infant daughter, Bethenia, who eventually married David Pannill. Elizabeth was the child of Bethenia Letcher and David Pannill. H. B. McClellan, *The Life and Campaigns of Major-General J. E. B. Stuart* (Boston and New York, 1885), 3–5; Peter W. Hairston, ed., "J. E. B. Stuart's Letters to His Hairston Kin, 1850–1855," *North Carolina Historical Review*, LI (July 1974), 261n, 262n; Stuart Family Bible, copy of Bible Record on deposit Virginia Historical Society, Richmond, Virginia.

2. Archibald Stuart descended from another Archibald Stuart, a Scottish Presbyterian, who escaped religious persecution in Londonderry, Ireland, by fleeing to western Pennsylvania in about 1726. His second son was Major Alexander Stuart. Alexander H. H. Stuart, "History of the Stuart Family" and memorandum of Stuart B. Campbell, Stuart Papers, Virginia Historical Society, Richmond, Virginia; McClellan, *Stuart*, 1–3.

3. McClellan, *Stuart*, 1–3; *Biographical Directory of the American Congress, 1774–1961* (Washington, D.C., 1961); Cynthia Miller Leonard, comp., . . . *A General Assembly of Virginia: Bicentennial Register of Members* (Richmond, 1978); see also Dickson D. Bruce, Jr., *The Rhetoric of Conservatism: The Virginia Convention of 1829–30 and the Conservative Tradition in the South* (San Marino, California, 1982).

4. Virginia G. and Lewis G. Pedigo, *History of Patrick and Henry Counties Virginia* (Baltimore, 1977), 263–64; H. B. McClellan, "Address on the Life, Campaigns, and Character of Gen'l. J. E. B. Stuart," *Southern Historical Society Papers*, VIII (1880), 435; John W. Thomason, Jr., *Jeb Stuart* (New York, 1930), 17–19; some of Elizabeth Stuart's letters are in the possession of Stuart B. Campbell, Jr., Wytheville, Virginia.

5. McClellan, "Address," 436; Stuart Family Bible, copy of Bible Record on deposit Virginia Historical Society, Richmond, Virginia; Hairston, ed., "Stuart's Letters," 288n.

6. 1830 U.S. Census; 1840 U.S. Census; 1850 U.S. Census; Burke Davis, *Jeb Stuart: The Last Cavalier* (New York, 1957), 18; Nathaniel Beverly Tucker, *The Partisan Leader: A Tale of the Future*, Intro. C. Hugh Holman (Chapel Hill, 1971); *The Official Military Atlas of the Civil War*, Intro. Richards Summers (New York, 1978), plates CXXXVII and CXLII; *State Historical Markers of Virginia*, 6th ed. (Richmond, 1948), 117, 199.

7. Hairston, ed., "Stuart's Letters," 262n; 1850 U.S. Census; 1830 U.S. Census; 1840 U.S. Census; McClellan, *Stuart*, 5.

8. "Lines Addressed to a Pressed Geranium Leaf" and other verses are in Stuart's Commonplace Book, on deposit at the Virginia Historical Society, Richmond, Virginia. On West Point, see Stuart to George Hairston, August 17, 1850 in Hairston, ed., "Stuart's Letters," 265, and Stuart to A. Stuart Brown, July 8, 1850, original in possession of Stuart B. Campbell, Jr., Wytheville, Virginia. The poem to Maryland ("I hear your old familiar neigh, / Maryland, my Maryland! /Asking for your corn and hay. /Maryland, my Maryland . . .") is in *Confederate Veteran*, July 1928, 255; Stuart to Mother, December 6, 1846, printed in *Confederate Veteran*, XXVII (March 1919), 97.

9. Thomason, *Stuart*, 19–20.

10. Stuart to A. Stuart Brown, April 11, 1846, original letter in possession of Stuart B. Campbell, Jr., Wytheville, Virginia.

11. McClellan, *Stuart*, 6; Hairston, ed., "Stuart's Letters," 269; Thomason, *Stuart*, 18–19; Stuart to A. Stuart Brown, January 17, 1847, and March 27, 1847, original letters in possession of Stuart B. Campbell, Jr., Wytheville, Virginia; Stuart to Dear Sir [former teacher], September 4, 1849, typescript in Museum of the Confederacy, Richmond, Virginia; Stuart to Alexander H.

H. Stuart, May 24, 1853, Alexander H. H. Stuart Papers, University of Virginia Library, Charlottesville, Virginia; Stuart to parents, n.d., on deposit Virginia Historical Society, Richmond, Virginia.

12. Thomason, *Stuart,* 19; Stuart to Dear Sir, September 4, 1849, typescript in Museum of the Confederacy, Richmond, Virginia. He may have been attempting to enhance his request for a favor. The "be perfect" quote is from Stuart to A. Stuart Brown, March 27, 1847, original letter in possession of Stuart B. Campbell, Jr., Wytheville, Virginia.

13. Stuart to A. Stuart Brown, January 17, 1847, original letter in possession of Stuart B. Campbell, Jr., Wytheville, Virginia.

14. Stuart to Mother, December 6, 1846, printed in *Confederate Veteran,* XXVII (March 1919), 97.

15. Stuart to A. Stuart Brown, January 17, 1847, and March 27, 1847, originals in possession of Stuart B. Campbell, Jr., Wytheville, Virginia.

16. Notes and letters in Burke Davis Papers, Swem Library, College of William and Mary; *Emory & Henry College Catalog,* 1982–83; Stuart to Dear Sir, September 4, 1849, typescript in Museum of the Confederacy, Richmond, Virginia; Stuart to John Milton Davis, January 25, 1851, Stuart Papers, Virginia Historical Society, Richmond, Virginia; Speech to Hermesians on deposit Virginia Historical Society, Richmond, Virginia.

17. McClellan, *Stuart,* 6–7; Thomason, *Stuart,* 18; Stuart to John Milton Davis, January 25, 1851, Stuart Papers, Virginia Historical Society, Richmond, Virginia. For a recent study of Southern evangelicalism, see Donald G. Mathews, *Religion in the Old South* (Chicago and London, 1977), especially xv–xvii.

18. Stuart to parents, n.d., on deposit Virginia Historical Society, Richmond, Virginia.

19. Stuart to Bettie Hairston, October 28, 1853, in Hairston, ed., "Stuart's Letters," 304.

20. McClellan, *Stuart,* 6–7; Davis, *Stuart,* 19.

21. Davis, *Stuart,* 19; Stuart to A. Stuart Brown, June 9, 1850, and July 8, 1850, original letters in possession of Stuart B. Campbell, Jr., Wytheville, Virginia.

22. Stuart to A. Stuart Brown, June 9, 1850, original letter in possession of Stuart B. Campbell, Jr., Wytheville, Virginia.

23. Stuart to A. Stuart Brown, July 8, 1850, original letter in possession of Stuart B. Campbell, Jr., Wytheville, Virginia.

24. See William S. McFeely, *Grant: A Biography* (New York, 1981), 13–16.

## II. *"Beauty"*

1. Fitzhugh Lee, "Speech at A.N.V. Banquet, October 28, 1875," in *Southern Historical Society Papers,* I (1876), 100; *Official Register of the Officers and Cadets of the United States Military Academy,* West Point, New York.

2. The photograph is in the Museum of the Confederacy, Richmond, Vir-

ginia. A lock of Stuart's hair is on deposit at the Virginia Historical Society, Richmond, Virginia. Descriptions of Stuart are in Douglas Southall Freeman, *Lee's Lieutenants: A Study in Command,* 3 vols. (New York, 1942–44), I, xlviii–xlix; John W. Thomason, Jr., *Jeb Stuart* (New York, 1930), 1–15; John Esten Cooke, *Wearing of the Gray,* ed. Philip Van Doren Stern (Bloomington, Indiana, 1959), 7–14; Burke Davis, *Jeb Stuart: The Last Cavalier* (New York, 1957), 27–28; W. W. Blackford, *War Years with Jeb Stuart* (New York, 1945), 16; Heros Von Borcke, *Memoirs of the Confederate War for Independence,* 2 vols. (New York, 1938), I, 21–22.

3. Thomason, *Jeb Stuart,* 20–21; Stuart to Bettie Hairston, September 27, 1854, in Peter W. Hairston, ed., "J. E. B. Stuart's Letters to His Hairston Kin, 1850–1855," *North Carolina Historical Review* LI (July 1974), 316.

4. Fitzhugh Lee, "Speech . . ." 100; Cooke, *Wearing of the Gray,* 14.

5. Thomason, *Jeb Stuart,* 1.

6. Fitzhugh Lee, "Speech . . ." 100; Stuart's father wrote him about his fighting in letters cited in Davis, *Jeb Stuart,* 20.

7. Stuart to George Hairston, Christmas Day, 1851, in Hairston, ed., "Stuart's Letters," 274; Stuart to My Dear Friend, April 19, 1855, typescript in the Museum of the Confederacy, Richmond, Virginia; G. W. C. Lee to Stuart, letters in possession of Mrs. Andrew J. Davis, Alexandria, Virginia.

8. Stuart to George Hairston, August 17, 1850, in Hairston, ed., "Stuart's Letters," 265–68, 265n; Stephen E. Ambrose, *Duty, Honor, Country: A History of West Point* (Baltimore, 1966), 153, and n; Oliver Otis Howard, *Autobiography,* 2 vols. (New York, 1907), 1, 46–47.

9. Stuart to Alexander H. H. Stuart [1853], Alexander H. H. Stuart Papers, University of Virginia Library; Ambrose, *Duty, Honor, Country,* 148–49.

10. Stuart to Pa, June 24, 1850, Stuart Papers, Virginia Historical Society, Richmond, Virginia.

11. Stuart to George Hairston, August 17, 1850, in Hairston, ed., "Stuart's Letters," 265–68; Stuart to A. Stuart Brown, July 8, 1850, original letter in possession of Stuart B. Campbell, Jr., Wytheville, Virginia.

12. Stuart to George Hairston, August 17, 1850 in Hairston, ed., "Stuart's Letters," 265–68; Stuart to A. Stuart Brown, July 8, 1850, original letter in possession of Stuart B. Campbell, Jr., Wytheville, Virginia; Henry A. du Pont to Mother, July 14, 1856, cited in Ambrose, *Duty, Honor, Country,* 148; Stuart to A. Stuart Brown, October 21, 1850, original letter in possession of Stuart B. Campbell, Jr., Wytheville, Virginia; Howard, *Autobiography,* I, 49.

13. Stuart to John Milton Davis, January 25, 1851, Stuart Papers, Virginia Historical Society, Richmond, Virginia; Stuart to George Hairston, March 6, 1851, in Hairston, ed., "Stuart's Letters," 268–71.

14. *Official Register . . .* ; Hairston, ed., "Stuart's Letters," 264.

15. Stuart to A. Stuart Brown, January 24, 1851, and May 12, 1851, original letters in possession of Stuart B. Campbell, Jr., Wytheville, Virginia.

16. *Official Register . . .* ; Sidney Forman, *West Point: A History of the United States Military Academy* (New York, 1950), 86; Stuart to Bettie Hairston, May 8, 1854, in Hairston, ed., "Stuart's Letters," 311–12.

17. Douglas Southall Freeman, *R. E. Lee: A Biography,* 4 vols. (New York, 1934–35), I, 334–37; Stuart to Bettie Hairston, June 29, 1853, in Hairston, ed., "Stuart's Letters," 297; Stuart to John Milton Davis, January 25, 1851, Stuart Papers, Virginia Historical Society, Richmond, Virginia.

18. *Official Register . . .*

19. Stuart to A. Stuart Brown, May 12, 1851, original letter in possession of Stuart B. Campbell, Jr., Wytheville, Virginia; Stuart to George Hairston, March 6, 1851, Stuart to Betty Hairston, January 4, 1855, in Hairston, ed., "Stuart's Letters," 268–71, 326; Ambrose, *Duty, Honor, Country,* 137–38; Marie T. Capps, Map and Manuscript Librarian, United States Military Academy, to author, January 3, 1983.

20. Lee, "Speech," 100; Stuart to George Hairston, March 6, 1851, and Christmas Day, 1851, in Hairston, ed., "Stuart's Letters," 268–71, 273–76.

21. William S. McFeely, *Yankee Stepfather: General O. O. Howard and the Freedmen,* Norton edition (New York, 1970), 31–33; Howard, *Autobiography,* I, 44–54.

22. *Official Register . . .* Stuart's friendship with Lee persisted; Lee was a firm ally in the military bureaucracy in Richmond during the war. During the same war Stuart would face Howard across a hostile battle line at Chancellorsville.

23. Stuart to George Hairston, August 13, 1851, in Hairston, ed., "Stuart's Letters," 271–73.

24. Ibid.

25. *Official Register . . .* ; Ambrose, *Duty, Honor, Country,* 94; Stuart to George Hairston, Christmas Day, 1851, in Hairston, ed., "Stuart's Letters," 273–76.

26. Stuart to George Hairston, Christmas Day, 1851, and April 13, 1852, in Hairston, ed., "Stuart's Letters," 273–78.

27. Stuart to Bettie Hairston, September 23, 1852, and November 6, 1852, in Hairston, ed., "Stuart's Letters," 278–86.

28. Stuart's letters to Bettie Hairston are in Hairston, ed., "Stuart's Letters," 278–312, 315–27.

29. Freeman, *Lee,* I, 332–34, 346; Stuart to Bettie Hairston, May 7, 1853, June 29, 1853, August 17, 1853, and May 8, 1854, in Hairston, ed., "Stuart's Letters," 292–302, 310–12.

30. Marie T. Capps, Map and Manuscript Librarian, United States Military Academy, to author, January 3, 1983; Stuart Commonplace Book, on deposit at Virginia Historical Society, Richmond, Virginia; Stuart to Bettie Hairston, December 20, 1852, March 23, 1853, and May 7, 1853, in Hairston, ed., "Stuart's Letters," 286–95.

31. Stuart to Bettie Hairston, June 29, 1853, and August 17, 1853, in Hairston, ed., "Stuart's Letters," 296–302.

32. Stuart to Bettie Hairston, June 29, 1853, in Hairston, ed., "Stuart's Letters," 296–99.

33. Stuart to Bettie Hairston, February 9, 1854, in Hairston, ed., "Stuart's Letters," 305–08; Stuart to Pa, October 7, 1853, original letter in possession

of Stuart B. Campbell, Jr., Wytheville, Virginia; *Official Register* . . . ; Forman, *West Point,* 74.

34. See Stephen Z. Starr, *The Union Cavalry in the Civil War,* 2 vols. (Baton Rouge, 1979–81), I, 50–53.

35. Stuart to Pa, October 7, 1853, original letter in possession of Stuart B. Campbell, Jr., Wytheville, Virginia.

36. Stuart to Bettie Hairston, October 28, 1853, in Hairston, ed., "Stuart's Letters," 302–05.

37. Ibid.; Stuart to Bettie Hairston, February 9, 1854, in Hairston, ed., "Stuart's Letters," 305–08.

38. *Official Register* . . .

39. Ambrose, *Duty, Honor, Country,* 154–55.

40. Stuart to Peter W. Hairston, August 3, 1854, in Hairston, ed., "Stuart's Letters," 312–15.

## III. *Lieutenant Stuart*

1. Benjamin Blake Minor, "Jeb Stuart: How He Played Sheriff in a Lawyer's Bedroom," *Southern Historical Society Papers,* XXXVI (1908), 267–70.

2. Stuart to Peter W. Hairston, August 3, 1854, and to Bettie Hairston, September 27, 1854, in Peter W. Hairston, ed., "J. E. B. Stuart's Letters to His Hairston Kin, 1850–1855," *North Carolina Historical Review* LI (July 1974), 312–19; Stuart to Dear Friend, June 19, 1854, J. E. B. Stuart Papers, Virginia Historical Society, Richmond, Virginia.

3. Stuart to Bettie Hairston, September 27, 1854, in Hairston, ed., "Stuart's Letters," 315–19.

4. Ibid.

5. Stuart to Bettie Hairston, January 4, 1855, in Hairston, ed., "Stuart's Letters," 321–27.

6. Ibid., and 317n; W. Gordon McCabe, "Major Andrew Reid Venable, Jr.," *Southern Historical Society Papers,* XXXVII (1909), 62.

7. Stuart to Bettie Hairston, January 4, 1855, in Hairston, ed., "Stuart's Letters," 319–27.

8. Ibid.; Stuart to _____, January 29, 1855, typescript in J. E. B. Stuart Papers, Museum of the Confederacy, Richmond, Virginia.

9. W. Stitt Robinson, ed., "The Kiowa and Comanche Campaign of 1860 as Recorded in the Personal Diary of Lt. J. E. B. Stuart," *Kansas Historical Quarterly,* 23 (1957), 383; Stuart to My Dear Friend, April 20, 1855, J. E. B. Stuart Papers, Museum of the Confederacy, Richmond, Virginia; J. S. Simonson to H. B. McClellan, December 27, 1880, printed in H. B. McClellan, *The Life and Campaigns of Major-General J. E. B. Stuart* (Boston and New York, 1885), 10–11.

10. Stuart to *Jeffersonian,* February 15, 1855, printed in McClellan, *Stuart,* 11–15; Stuart described his wrestle with the artillery piece in a letter to his brother, Dr. John Stuart, also printed in McClellan, *Stuart,* 16–17; he described the fire again in a letter to My Dear Friend, April 19, 1855, type-

script in the J. E. B. Stuart Papers, Museum of the Confederacy, Richmond, Virginia.

11. Stuart to My Dear Friend, April 19, 1855, typescript in the J. E. B. Stuart Papers, Museum of the Confederacy, Richmond, Virginia.

12. Ibid.; Robinson, "Personal Diary," 383.

13. Robinson, "Personal Diary," 383.

14. Percival G. Lowe, *Five Years a Dragoon*, Don Russell, ed. (Norman, Oklahoma, 1965), 167-69.

15. Ibid., 24-26; Burke Davis, *Jeb Stuart: The Last Cavalier* (New York, 1957), 36.

16. Conversation with Mrs. Andrew J. Davis, June 27, 1983. Mrs. Davis is Stuart's granddaughter and lived with Flora Stuart from 1898 until her death in 1923.

17. Ibid.; Stuart's note requesting a ride with Flora is printed in Davis, *Stuart*, 36; the daguerreotype is at the Virginia Historical Society, Richmond, Virginia.

18. Davis, *Stuart*, 36-37; the Cooke Family Papers are in the Virginia Historical Society, Richmond, Virginia; Stuart to My Dear *Dear* Friend, November 25, 1855, typescript in J. E. B. Stuart Papers, Museum of the Confederacy, Richmond, Virginia; Stuart to A. Stuart Brown, September 20, 1855, original letter in possession of Stuart B. Campbell, Jr., Wytheville, Virginia; "Mrs. J. E. B. Stuart," *Confederate Veteran*, XXXI (1923), 244.

19. Stuart to A. Stuart Brown, September 20, 1855, original letter in possession of Stuart B. Campbell, Jr., Wytheville, Virginia; Cooke to John Esten Cooke, printed in J. O. Beaty, *John Esten Cooke, Virginian* (New York, 1922), 75.

20. Stuart to A. Stuart Brown, October 28, 1855, original letter in possession of Stuart B. Campbell, Jr., Wytheville, Virginia.

21. Ibid.; conversation with Mrs. Andrew J. Davis, June 27, 1983; Stuart Family Bible, copy of Bible Record on deposit in Virginia Historical Society, Richmond, Virginia; Stuart to My Dear *Dear* Friend, November 25, 1855, typescript in J. E. B. Stuart Papers, Museum of the Confederacy, Richmond, Virginia.

22. Ibid.; Stuart to A. Stuart Brown, April 9, 1856, original letter in possession of Stuart B. Campbell, Jr., Wytheville, Virginia.

23. McClellan, *Stuart*, 19; Cooke to John Esten Cooke, printed in Beaty, *John Esten Cooke*, 75.

24. Stuart to A. Stuart Brown, April 9, 1856, original letter in possession of Stuart B. Campbell, Jr., Wytheville, Virginia; Stuart to Percival G. Lowe, March 14, 1858, April 2, 1858, and May 10, 1858, printed in Don Russell, "J. E. B. Stuart on the Frontier," *Civil War Times Illustrated*, 13 (April 1974), 15-16.

25. Stuart to A. Stuart Brown, January 28, 1856, original letter in possession of Stuart B. Campbell, Jr., Wytheville, Virginia.

26. Stuart to A. Stuart Brown, April 9, 1856, original letter in possession of Stuart B. Campbell, Jr., Wytheville, Virginia; Davis, *Stuart*, 40.

27. See Stephen B. Oates, *To Purge This Land with Blood: A Biography of John Brown* (New York, 1970), 152–56.

28. Robinson, "Personal Diary," 384–85; Lowe, *Five Years a Dragoon*, 185–87.

29. Lowe, *Five Years a Dragoon*, 186–202.

30. Stuart to My Darling Wife, July 30, 1857, printed in McClellan, *Stuart*, 20–22.

## IV. The Campaign for Captain

1. Stuart to My Darling Wife, July 30, 1857, printed in H. B. McClellan, *The Life and Campaigns of Major-General J. E. B. Stuart* (Boston and New York, 1885), 20–22.

2. Stuart to Flora, August 1, 1857, printed in McClellan, *Stuart*, 22–23; copy of Report of Col. Sumner to Commanding Officer, Fort Kearny, August 3, 1857, in possession of Mrs. Andrew J. Davis, Alexandria, Virginia.

3. Stuart to Flora, August 1, 1857, printed in McClellan, *Stuart*, 22–23.

4. Stuart to My Dearest Wife, August 19, 1857, printed in McClellan, *Stuart*, 23–27.

5. For testimony that this experience inspired Stuart to a fatalistic recklessness, see John Esten Cooke, *Wearing of the Gray*, ed. Philip Van Doren Stern (Bloomington, Indiana, 1959), 28–30.

6. Burke Davis, *Jeb Stuart: The Last Cavalier* (New York, 1957), 42; Stuart to Percival G. Lowe, February 19, 1859, printed in Don Russell, "J. E. B. Stuart on the Frontier," *Civil War Times Illustrated*, 13 (April 1974 [1]), 16.

7. W. Stitt Robinson, ed., "The Kiowa and Comanche Campaign of 1860 as Recorded in the Personal Diary of Lt. J. E. B. Stuart," *Kansas Historical Quarterly*, 23 (1957), 385.

8. Stuart to Percival G. Lowe, March 14, 1858, April 2, 1858, and May 10, 1858, printed in Russell, "Stuart on the Frontier," 15–16; Stuart to Mother, quoted in Davis, *Stuart*, 42.

9. Benjamin Blake Minor, "Jeb Stuart: How He Played Sheriff in a Lawyer's Bedroom," *Southern Historical Society Papers* XXXVI (1908), 269–70.

10. See Robinson, ed., "Personal Diary," 385. Stuart's manuscript agreement with a manufacturer with further description is in "J. E. B. Stuart items in other collections," Huntington Library, San Marino, California.

11. McClellan, *Stuart*, 6; Churchill J. Gibson, "J. E. B. Stuart," *Southern Churchman*, February 11, 1934, 9; Stuart to Mother, quoted in Davis, *Stuart*, 42.

12. Stuart's address to the Hermesians is among the Stuart papers on deposit at the Virginia Historical Society, Richmond, Virginia; Gibson, "Stuart," 9; Stuart to My Dear Mama, January 31, 1860, Stuart Papers, Virginia Historical Society, Richmond, Virginia.

13. Stuart to My Dear Mama, January 31, 1860, Stuart Papers, Virginia Historical Society, Richmond, Virginia.

14. Ibid.; Douglas S. Freeman, *R. E. Lee: A Biography*, 4 vols., (New York, 1934–35), I, 394–97.

15. Freeman, *Lee*, I, 39–97; Stephen B. Oates, *To Purge This Land with Blood: A Biography of John Brown* (New York, 1970), 298–300.

16. Israel Green, "The Capture of John Brown," *North American Review*, December 1885, 564–65; Freeman, *Lee*, I, 397–400; Oates, *Brown*, 300–302; Stuart to My Dear Mama, January 31, 1860, Stuart Papers, Virginia Historical Society, Richmond, Virginia.

17. Stuart to My Dear Mama, January 31, 1860, Stuart Papers, Virginia Historical Society, Richmond, Virginia; Freeman, *Lee*, I, 399–400.

18. Oates, *Brown*, 302–6; Louis Ruchames, ed., *A John Brown Reader* (London and New York, 1959), 120.

19. Stuart to My Dear Mama, January 31, 1860, Stuart Papers, Virginia Historical Society, Richmond, Virginia; Freeman, *Lee*, I, 401.

20. Robinson, ed., "Personal Diary," 386; Agreement between Stuart and Lewis M. Harbaugh, April 30, 1864, copy on deposit Virginia Historical Society, Richmond, Virginia; J. E. B. Stuart, Will, November 16, 1861, copy on deposit Virginia Historical Society, Richmond, Virginia; Stuart to My Dear Mama, January 31, 1860, Stuart Papers, Virginia Historical Society, Richmond, Virginia.

21. Stuart to Henry A. Wise, November 11, 1857, Murray J. Smith Collection, U.S. Army Military History Institute, Carlisle Barracks, Pennsylvania; Stuart to My Dear Mama, January 31, 1860, Stuart Papers, Virginia Historical Society, Richmond, Virginia.

22. Emory to Floyd, January 29, 1858, ms. copy in possession of Mrs. Andrew J. Davis, Alexandria, Virginia; Emory to William J. Hardee, September 14, 1858, ms. copy on deposit Virginia Historical Society, Richmond, Virginia; A. A. Chapman et al. to Floyd, March 10, 1860, ms. copy in possession of Mrs. Andrew J. Davis, Alexandria, Virginia.

23. The standard biography of Letcher is F. N. Boney, *John Letcher of Virginia* (University, Alabama, 1966); Stuart to My Dear Mama, January 31, 1860, Stuart Papers, Virginia Historical Society, Richmond, Virginia.

24. One of Stuart's "I go with Virginia" pronouncements is in Stuart to Percival G. Lowe, December 20, 1860, printed in Russell, ed., "Stuart on the Frontier," 17. He told the Hermesian Society at Emory & Henry that he loved the United States; but he loved Virginia more (address on deposit Virginia Historical Society, Richmond, Virginia).

25. Stuart to Jno. O. Steger, October 8, 1860, Stuart Papers, Museum of the Confederacy, Richmond, Virginia.

26. Robinson, ed., "Personal Diary," 386–89.

27. Ibid., 392, 399.

28. Ibid., 389–96; Edward Bulwer Lytton, *The Disowned* in *The Complete Works of Edward Bulwer Lytton*, 13 vols. (New York, n.d.), X, 416–17.

29. Stuart to Lt. Jno. A. Thompson, July 12, 1860; Sedgwick to Capt. D. R. Jones, July 24, 1860; Steele to Lt. J. A. Thompson, July 14, 1860, all printed

in Don Russell, "Jeb Stuart's Other Indian Fight," *Civil War Times Illustrated*, 12 (January 1974), 10–17.

30. Robinson, ed., "Personal Diary," 398–99.

31. Stuart to Jno. O. Steger, October 8, 1860, Stuart Papers, Museum of the Confederacy, Richmond, Virginia; Stuart to P. G. Lowe, November 13, 1860, printed in Russell, "Stuart on the Frontier," 16–17.

32. Stuart to Jno. O. Steger, October 8, 1860, Stuart Papers, Museum of the Confederacy, Richmond, Virginia.

33. Stuart to Percival G. Lowe, December 20, 1860, printed in Russell, "Stuart on the Frontier," 17; Stuart's temperance speech is on deposit Virginia Historical Society, Richmond, Virginia.

34. Letcher to Stuart, December 31, 1860, original letter in possession of Mrs. Andrew J. Davis, Alexandria, Virginia; Stuart's letter to Davis is quoted in Davis, *Stuart*, 46; Stuart's letters to his brother are also quoted in Davis, *Stuart*, 46–47; William H. Richardson to Stuart, February 12, 1860, original letter in possession of Mrs. Andrew J. Davis, Alexandria, Virginia; Bates to Stuart, April 13, 1861, "J. E. B. Stuart items in other collections," Huntington Library, San Marino, California.

35. Special Orders #12, February 2, 1861, in "J. E. B. Stuart items in other collections," Huntington Library, San Marino, California.

36. Stuart to Jno. O. Steger, March 23, 1861, Stuart Papers, Virginia Historical Society, Richmond, Virginia; John Esten Cooke to Stuart, April 4, 1861, Stuart Papers, Virginia Historical Society, Richmond, Virginia; McClellan, *Stuart*, 31.

37. Stuart's letter to Cooper and his mother's letter to Lee are quoted in Davis, *Stuart*, 48–49; McClellan, *Stuart*, 31–32.

38. McClellan, *Stuart*, 31–32; Stuart to Flora, May 9, 1861, printed in Bingham Duncan, ed., "Letters of General J. E. B. Stuart to His Wife, 1861," *Emory University Publications*, I, 1, 1943.

## V. *Colonel Stuart*

1. Stuart to Flora, May 9, 1861, printed in Bingham Duncan, ed., "Letters of General J. E. B. Stuart to His Wife, 1861," *Emory University Publications*, I, 1, 1943, 11; an example of Jackson's regard for Stuart is Jackson's report of the affair at Falling Waters, July 3, 1861, in *War of the Rebellion: A Compilation of the Official Records of the Union and Confederate Armies*, 70 vols. in 127 (Washington, D.C., 1880–1901), ser. I, II, 185–86 (hereafter cited as *O.R.*; all citations are Series I). "Colonel Stuart and his command merit high praise, and I may here remark that he has exhibited those qualities which are calculated to make him eminent in his arm of the service."

2. John D. Imboden, "Jackson at Harper's Ferry in 1861," in Robert Underwood Johnson and Clarence Clough Buel, eds., *Battles and Leaders of the Civil War*, 4 vols. (New York, 1956), I, 124–25.

3. W. W. Blackford, *War Years with Jeb Stuart* (New York, 1945), 16.

4. Ibid.; George Cary Eggleston, *A Rebel's Recollections* (Bloomington, Indiana, 1959), 111–14.

5. Charles Wells Russell, ed., *The Memoirs of Colonel John S. Mosby* (Boston, 1917), 30–32; Eggleston, *Recollections*, 114–15.

6. See Stephen Z. Starr, *The Union Cavalry in the Civil War*, 2 vols. (Baton Rouge, 1979), I, 132–43. For the South, the 7th Tennessee provides an example. The first fighting in which the regiment engaged occurred because the men established a regular route and schedule for scouting. When ambushed, the men had their weapons securely strapped to their saddles. They fled in unseemly haste before ten Federal infantrymen. J. P. Young, *The Seventh Tennessee Cavalry*, Morningside edition (Dayton, Ohio, 1976), 24–25.

7. *O.R.* II, 187; H. B. McClellan, *The Life and Campaigns of Major-General J. E. B. Stuart* (Boston and New York, 1885), 32.

8. The Johnston quote is from McClellan, *Stuart*, 32; Stuart's quote is in Eggleston, *Recollections*, 117.

9. See Russell, ed., *Mosby Memoirs*, 31.

10. Jackson's Report, *O.R.*, II, 185–86.

11. Ibid.; Stuart to Flora, July 4, 1861, in Duncan, ed., "Letters," 13; McClellan, *Stuart*, 33.

12. See William C. Davis, *Battle at Bull Run* (Garden City, New York, 1977), especially 132–43.

13. Ibid., 141; Patterson's correspondence is in *O.R.*, II, 172.

14. Russell, ed., *Mosby Memoirs*, 47–48; Blackford, *War Years*, 19–21, 23–24; Stuart's Report, *O.R.*, II, 482–84.

15. Blackford, *War Years*, 23–26.

16. Ibid., 24–25; Russell, ed., *Mosby Memoirs*, 48–49.

17. Blackford, *War Years*, 27.

18. Ibid., 27–32; Stuart's Report, *O.R.*, II, 482–84; Davis, *Bull Run*, 207–8.

19. Stuart's Report, *O.R.*, II, 482–84; McClellan, *Stuart*, 35–40; Jubal Anderson Early, *War Memoirs: Autobiographical Sketch and Narrative of the War Between the States*, Frank E. Vandiver, ed. (Bloomington, Indiana, 1960), 22–23, 25–26, 38.

20. Stuart's Report, *O.R.*, II, 482–84; Blackford, *War Years*, 33–46.

21. Stuart's Report, *O.R.*, II, 482–84; Stuart to Flora, July 27, 1861, and July 31, 1861, Stuart Papers, Manuscript Department, Duke University Library, Durham, North Carolina.

22. Blackford, *War Years*, 46; Stuart to Johnston, July 23, 1861, *O.R.*, II, 995.

23. Blackford, *War Years*, 49; John Esten Cooke, *Wearing of the Gray*, ed. Philip Van Doren Stern (Bloomington, Indiana, 1959), 203; Cooke's letter was much later published in the *Ohio State Journal*, Columbus, Ohio, November 28, 1887.

24. Hairston to Fanny, September 28, 1861, Peter Wilson Hairston Papers, Southern Historical Collection, University of North Carolina at Chapel Hill; Charles Minor Blackford III, ed., *Letters from Lee's Army* (New York, 1947), 42.

25. Blackford, *War Years*, 52–54.

26. Russell, ed., *Mosby Memoirs*, 86; Eggleston, *Recollections*, 122–23.

27. Eggleston, *Recollections*, 124; Blackford III, ed., *Letters*, 42.

28. Eggleston, *Recollections*, 122; Burke Davis, *Jeb Stuart: The Last Cavalier* (New York, 1957), 56.

29. Cooke, *Wearing of the Gray*, 202–9.

30. Stuart's Report, September 11, 1861, *O.R.*, V, 183–84; Russell, ed., *Mosby Memoirs*, 90.

31. Orlando W. Poe to My Dear Beauty, September 11, 1861, Stuart Papers, Virginia Historical Society, Richmond, Virginia.

32. Longstreet's Report and endorsement by Johnston and Beauregard, September 12, 1861, *O.R.*, V, 182–83.

33. McClellan, *Stuart*, 32; Johnston to Davis, August 10, 1861, *O.R.*, V, 777.

34. Charleston *Daily Courier*, September 21, 1861.

35. McClellan, *Stuart*, 32–33; Johnston's note to Mrs. Brigadier-General is in the Stuart Papers, Virginia Historical Society, Richmond, Virginia.

## VI. *General Stuart*

1. *War of the Rebellion: A Compilation of the Official Records of the Union and Confederate Armies*, 70 vols. in 127 (Washington, D.C., 1880–1901), Ser. I, V, 932 (hereafter cited as *O.R.;* all citations are to Series I); Stephen Z. Starr, *The Union Cavalry in the Civil War*, 2 vols. (Baton Rouge, 1979–81), I, 289–90.

2. The Richmond *Dispatch*, October 8, 1862, published an account by one of its correspondents about Stuart and "the advance, the most important part of the army." Stuart to Flora, October 18, 1861, and November 24, 1861, printed in Bingham Duncan, ed., "Letters of General J. E. B. Stuart to his Wife, 1861," *Emory University Publications*, I, 1, 1943, 14, 19–20.

3. Stuart to Flora, October 18, 1861, in Duncan, ed., "Letters," 14; John Esten Cooke, *Wearing of the Gray*, ed. Philip Van Doren Stern (Bloomington, Indiana, 1959), 185.

4. George Cary Eggleston, *A Rebel's Recollections* (Bloomington, Indiana, 1959), 120; W. W. Blackford, *War Years with Jeb Stuart* (New York, 1945), 50–51.

5. Charles Wells Russell, ed., *The Memoirs of Colonel John S. Mosby* (Boston, 1917), 100–101.

6. Blackford, *War Years*, 52–54, 89–93; Stuart to Flora, December 1, 1861, December 11, 1861, in Duncan, ed., "Letters," 21–22, 25–26; Cooke, *Wearing of the Gray*, 188.

7. Stuart to Flora, October 21, 1861, December 12, 1861, December 17, 1861, in Duncan, ed., "Letters," 16, 27–29.

8. Cooke, *Wearing of the Gray*, 185–92.

9. Stuart to A. Stuart Brown, April 9, 1856, original letter in possession of Stuart B. Campbell, Jr., Wytheville, Virginia.

10. Jay B. Hubbell, ed., "The War Diary of John Esten Cooke," *Journal of Southern History*, VII (1941), 527–29; Stuart to Flora, December 11, 1861,

NOTES TO PAGES 94–102 [ 313 ]

December 1, 1861, in Duncan, ed., "Letters," 25–26, 21–22; Stuart to Flora, March 20, 1862, Stuart Papers, on deposit Virginia Historical Society, Richmond, Virginia. The standard biography of Cooke is John O. Beaty, *John Esten Cooke, Virginian* (New York, 1922).

11. Stuart to Flora, November 24, 1861, in Duncan, ed., "Letters," 19–20; Stuart to John R. Cooke, January 18, 1862, Cooke Family Papers, Virginia Historical Society, Richmond, Virginia.

12. Stuart to Flora, December 1, 1861, December 11, 1861, in Duncan, ed., "Letters," 21–22, 25–26; Charles Minor Blackford, III, ed., *Letters from Lee's Army* (New York, 1947), 57–58.

13. Stuart to Flora, October 18, 1861, October 21, 1861, December 17, 1861, in Duncan, ed., "Letters," 14, 16, 29.

14. Peter Hairston to Fanny, October 11, 1861, Peter Wilson Hairston Papers, Southern Historical Collection, University of North Carolina at Chapel Hill.

15. Stuart to Flora, December 12, 1861, November 24, 1861, in Duncan, ed., "Letters," 27–28, 19–20; Stuart to Flora, January 16, 1862, April 29, 1862, Stuart Papers, on deposit Virginia Historical Society, Richmond, Virginia.

16. Stuart to Flora, December 4, 1861, in Duncan, ed., "Letters," 23; Stuart's will, Stuart to Flora, May 22, 1862 (Stuart's policy premium was $300), Stuart Papers, on deposit Virginia Historical Society, Richmond, Virginia; Eggleston, *Recollections*, 117.

17. Stuart to Major W. T. Martin, December 3, 1861, Stuart Papers, Manuscript Department, Duke University Library, Durham, North Carolina.

18. Reports of Stuart, December 21, 23, 1861, *O.R.*, V, 490–94.

19. Reports of Stuart, December 21, 23, 1861, *O.R.*, V, 490–94; Report of George A. McCall, December 28, 1861, *O.R.*, V, 474–76; Report of E. O. C. Ord, December 21, 1861, *O.R.*, V, 477–80; H. B. McClellan, *The Life and Campaigns of Major-General J. E. B. Stuart* (Boston and New York, 1885), 44–45.

20. Reports of Stuart, December 21, 23, 1861, *O.R.*, V, 490–94; McClellan, *Stuart*, 44–45.

21. Returns of casualties, *O.R.*, V, 489, 494.

22. McClellan, *Stuart*, 46.

23. Report of Stuart, December 23, 1861, *O.R.*, V, 490–94.

24. Abstract from return of the Department of Northern Virginia . . . December, 1861, *O.R.*, V, 1915; General Orders No. 15, October 22, 1861, *O.R.*, V, 913–14.

25. Stuart to [D. H.] Hill, January 9, 1861, *O.R.*, V, 1025; E. J. Allen [Allen Pinkerton] to McClellan, March 8, 1862 (Enclosure, January 27, 1862), *O.R.*, V, 736–38.

26. Davis to Johnston, February 6, 1862, *O.R.*, V, 1063–64; Stuart to Flora, January 16, 1862, March 2, 1862, Stuart Papers on deposit Virginia Historical Society, Richmond, Virginia.

27. Stuart to Flora, January 16, 1862, Stuart Papers on deposit Virginia Historical Society, Richmond, Virginia.

28. E. J. Allen [Allen Pinkerton] to McClellan, March 8, 1862 (Enclosure,

January 27, 1862), *O.R., V*, 736–38. The standard study of the Peninsula Campaign is Clifford Dowdey, *Seven Days: The Emergence of Lee* (Boston, 1964).

29. Report of Johnston, March 12, 1862, *O.R., V*, 526–27; Davis to Johnston, March 15, 1862, *O.R., V*, 527–28; Blackford, *War Years*, 59–60.

30. Stuart to Johnston, March 12, 1862, Stuart Papers, Manuscript Department, Duke University Library, Durham, North Carolina.

31. Stuart to Flora, March 14, 1862, March 24, 1862, Stuart Papers, on deposit Virginia Historical Society, Richmond, Virginia.

32. Report of Stuart, March 31, 1862, *O.R.*, XII, pt. 1, 415–17.

33. Emory M. Thomas, *The Confederate Nation, 1861–1865* (New York, 1979), 158–59.

34. Stuart to Flora, April 18, 1862, April 21, 1862, April 29, 1862, Stuart Papers, on deposit Virginia Historical Society, Richmond, Virginia; Blackford, *War Years*, 60–62.

35. McClellan, *Stuart*, 47–50.

36. Ibid., 50–51; Stuart to Flora, May 9, 1862, Stuart Papers on deposit Virginia Historical Society, Richmond, Virginia.

37. Thomas, *Confederate Nation*, 159–60.

38. Emory M. Thomas, "The Peninsula Campaign," Part II, *Civil War Times Illustrated*, April 1979, 28–35; Stuart to Flora, June 4, 1862, Stuart Papers, on deposit Virginia Historical Society, Richmond, Virginia.

39. Emory M. Thomas, "The Peninsula Campaign," Part III, *Civil War Times Illustrated*, May 1979, 13–14; Stuart to Flora, June 4, 1862, Stuart Papers, on deposit Virginia Historical Society, Richmond, Virginia.

40. Stuart to Flora, May 28, 1862, Stuart Papers, on deposit Virginia Historical Society, Richmond, Virginia.

## VII. *Jeb*

1. The quote is from Stuart to Bettie Hairston, May 8, 1854, printed in Peter W. Hairston, ed., "J. E. B. Stuart's Letters to His Hairston Kin, 1850–1855," *North Carolina Historical Review*, LI (July 1974), 311.

2. For a brief summary of the situation, see Emory W. Thomas, "The Peninsula Campaign," Part III, *Civil War Times Illustrated*, May 1979, 13–14.

3. Ibid.; Douglas S. Freeman, *R. E. Lee: A Biography*, 4 vols. (New York, 1934–35), I, 448–II, 74.

4. Stuart to Lee, June 4, 1862, Stuart Papers, Huntington Library, San Marino, California.

5. The description of Von Borcke is from W. W. Blackford, *War Years with Jeb Stuart* (New York, 1945), 69–70; Heros Von Borcke, *Memoirs of the Confederate War for Independence*, 2 vols. (New York, 1938), I, 34–36.

6. John S. Mosby, "The Ride Around General McClellan," *Southern Historical Society Papers*, XXVI, 246–48; the speculation about breakfast originates with Von Borcke's account of his meals at the time (*Memoirs*, I, 34).

7. Lee to Mrs. W. H. F. Lee, June 22, 1862, printed in Clifford Dowdey and Louis H. Manarin, eds., *The Wartime Papers of R. E. Lee* (New York, 1961), 196–97.

8. Mosby, "Ride," 248; Stuart's report of the expedition refers to "my favorite scheme, disclosed to you before starting, of passing around," *War of the Rebellion: A Compilation of the Official Records of the Union and Confederate Armies*, 70 vols. in 127 (Washington, D.C., 1880–1901), Ser. I, XI, pt. 1, 1038 (hereafter cited as *O.R.*; all citations are Series I).

9. Cooke's commission as brigadier general (November 12, 1861) is in Cooke Family Papers, Virginia Historical Society, Richmond, Virginia.

10. Lee to Stuart, June 11, 1862, printed in Dowdey and Manarin, eds., *Wartime Papers*, 192.

11. Stuart's Report, *O.R.*, XI, pt. 1, 1036; Von Borcke, *Memoirs*, I, 37.

12. Mosby, "Ride," 248.

13. William Campbell, "Stuart's Ride and Death of Latané," *Southern Historical Society Papers*, XXXIX (1911), 88. W. T. Robins, "Stuart's Ride Around McClellan," in Robert Underwood Johnson and Clarence Clough Buel, eds., *Battles and Leaders of the Civil War*, 4 vols. (New York, 1956), II, 271. There is a very good (loose) map of Stuart's route in H. B. McClellan, *The Life and Campaigns of Major-General J. E. B. Stuart* (Boston and New York, 1885). Stuart mentions his Jackson ruse in his report, *O.R.*, XI, pt. 1, 1036.

14. John Esten Cooke, *Wearing of the Gray*, ed. Philip Van Doren Stern (Bloomington, Indiana, 1959), 167; Douglas S. Freeman, *Lee's Lieutenants: A Study in Command*, 3 vols. (New York, 1942–44), I, 282.

15. Mosby, "Ride," 249; Stuart's Report, *O.R.*, XI, pt. 1, 1036; Richard E. Frayser, "A Narrative of Stuart's Raid in the Rear of the Army of the Potomac," *Southern Historical Society Papers*, XI (1883), 506.

16. Mosby, "Ride," 249; Stuart's Report, *O.R.*, XI, pt. 1, 1036.

17. Stuart's Report, *O.R.*, XI, pt. 1, 1037; Robins, "Stuart's Ride," 271–72.

18. Stuart's Report, *O.R.*, XI, pt. 1, 1037; Robins, "Stuart's Ride," 271–72; Campbell, "Stuart's Ride," 86–89; Frayser, "Stuart's Ride," 506–7.

19. Royall's successor in command, First Lieutenant Edward H. Leib, stated, "I felt most seriously the superiority of the enemy, who were armed with rifles and shot-guns, and had my command been furnished with carbines I would have been able to do him more injury and hold him back longer," *O.R.*, XI, pt. 1, 1022.

20. Campbell, "Stuart's Ride," 89; Emily J. Salmon, "The Burial of Latané: Symbol of the Lost Cause," *Virginia Cavalcade*, 28 (Winter 1979), 118–19; T. C. DeLeon, *Belles, Beaux and Brains of the 60's* (New York, 1907), 286–87.

21. Stuart's Report, *O.R.*, XI, pt. 1, 1037; McClellan, *Stuart*, 56–57.

22. Stuart's Report, *O.R.*, XI, pt. 1, 1037–38; Mosby ("Ride," 250) later insisted, "It would have been easy for Stuart to have retraced his steps; the way was open. . . ." But Stuart at the time did not know the way was open.

23. Stuart's Report, *O.R.*, XI, pt. 1, 1037–38; Mosby, "Ride," 250.

24. Stuart's Report, *O.R.*, XI, pt. 1, 1037–38.
25. Cooke, *Wearing of the Gray*, 169–70.
26. Mosby, "Ride," 251.
27. Cooke, *Wearing of the Gray*, 172–73.
28. Mosby, "Ride," 251.
29. Ibid.; Robins, "Stuart's Ride," 272–73; Von Borcke, *Memoirs*, I, 41–43; Stuart's Report, *O.R.*, XI, pt. 1, 1038–39.
30. Stuart's Report, *O.R.*, XI, pt. 1, 1038–39.
31. Cooke, *Wearing of the Gray*, 170, 174–75, 165.
32. Ibid., 175; Von Borcke, *Memoirs*, I, 43.
33. Frayser, "Stuart's Ride," 510–11; Robins, "Stuart's Ride," 273–74; Stuart's Report, *O.R.*, XI, pt. 1, 1039.
34. Mosby, "Ride," 253.
35. Robins, "Stuart's Ride," 274–75.
36. Frayser, "Stuart's Ride," 511–12. As Mosby remarked ("Ride," 252), "Stuart had done something without precedent in war, which was not provided for by the cavalry tactics they [the Federals] had been taught."
37. McClellan, *Stuart*, 66; Charleston *Mercury*, June 20, 1862.
38. Frayser, "Stuart's Ride," 512–13.
39. McClellan, *Stuart*, 67.
40. Cooke's reports and correspondence are in *O.R.*, XI, pt. 1, 1009–13.
41. Richmond *Enquirer*, June 16, 1862; Robins, "Stuart's Ride," 275; Richmond *Examiner*, June 16, 1862.
42. Richmond *Enquirer*, June 18, 1862.
43. General Orders No. 11, *O.R.*, XI, pt. 1, 1041–42; General Orders No. 74, *O.R.*, XI, pt. 1, 1042.
44. Stuart's Report, *O.R.*, XI, pt. 1, 1036–40.
45. Salmon, "The Burial of Latané," 122; DeLeon, *Belles, Beaux and Brains*, 288.
46. Gerald M. Garmon, *John Reuben Thompson* (Boston, 1979), 106–7 and n; the poem is printed in John S. Patton, ed., *Poems of John R. Thompson* (New York, 1920), 4–5.
47. Salmon, "The Burial of Latané," 118–29; DeLeon, *Belles, Beaux and Brains*, 285–302.
48. Richmond *Enquirer*, June 16, 1862.
49. Cooke, *Wearing of the Gray*, 166; Von Borcke, *Memoirs*, I, 22.
50. As Mosby wrote his wife at the time, "Stuart's name is in every one's mouth now." Mosby to Pauline, June 16, 1862, printed in Charles Wells Russell, *The Memoirs of Colonel John S. Mosby* (Boston, 1917), 120.

## VIII. *Major General Jeb*

1. Heros Von Borcke, *Memoirs of the Confederate War for Independence*, 2 vols. (New York, 1938), I, 47–48.
2. General Orders, No. 74, *War of the Rebellion: A Compilation of the Official Records of the Union and Confederate Armies*, 70 vols. in 127 (Wash-

ington, D.C., 1880–1901), Ser. I, XI, pt. 1, 1042 (hereafter cited as *O.R.*; all citations are Series I); General Orders No. 75, Clifford Dowdey and Louis H. Manarin, eds., *The Wartime Papers of R. E. Lee* (New York, 1961), 198–200.

3. Stuart's Report, *O.R.*, XI, pt. 2, 513–24.

4. Ibid.; Von Borcke, *Memoirs*, I, 52–53.

5. W. W. Blackford, *War Years with Jeb Stuart* (New York, 1945), 71.

6. Stuart's Report, *O.R.*, XI, pt. 2, 513–24.

7. Ibid.; Douglas S. Freeman, *Lee's Lieutenants: A Study in Command*, 3 vols. (New York, 1942–44), I, 503–16.

8. Freeman, *Lee's Lieutenants*, I, 655–59; Clifford Dowdey, *Seven Days: The Emergence of Lee* (Boston, 1964), 193–203; H. B. McClellan, *The Life and Campaigns of Major-General J. E. B. Stuart* (Boston and New York, 1885), 72–74.

9. Freeman, *Lee's Lieutenants*, I, 517–33.

10. Blackford, *War Years*, 72–74; Von Borcke, *Memoirs*, I, 53–58.

11. Stuart's Report, *O.R.*, XI, pt. 2, 513–24; McClellan, *Stuart*, 75–76.

12. Freeman, *Lee's Lieutenants*, I, 533–37; Dowdey, *Seven Days*, 236–42; Cooke's Report, *O.R.*, XI, pt. 2, 41–42; Jay B. Hubbell, ed., "The War Diary of John Esten Cooke," *Journal of Southern History*, VII (1941), 532.

13. Hubbell, ed., "War Diary," 532 and n; McClellan, *Stuart*, 76–77; Blackford, *War Years*, 74.

14. Stuart's Report, *O.R.*, XI, pt. 2, 513–24; Blackford, *War Years*, 74–75; McClellan, *Stuart*, 77.

15. McClellan, *Stuart*, 78.

16. Blackford, *War Years*, 75–77; Von Borcke, *Memoirs*, I, 66–69.

17. Stuart's Report, *O.R.*, XI, pt. 2, 513–24; McClellan, *Stuart*, 79–82; Freeman, *Lee's Lieutenants*, I, 588–604; Daniel H. Hill, "McClellan's Change of Base and Malvern Hill," in Robert Underwood Johnson and Clarence Clough Buel, eds., *Battles and Leaders of the Civil War*, 4 vols. (New York, 1956), II, 394.

18. Stuart's Report, *O.R.*, XI, pt. 2, 513–24; Pelham to Stuart, July 2, 1862, Stuart Papers, Manuscript Division, Duke University Library, Durham, North Carolina; McClellan, *Stuart*, 82–83; Blackford, *War Years*, 83–85. Lee to Davis, July 4, 1862, in Dowdey and Manarin, eds., *Wartime Papers*, 208.

19. Stuart to Flora, July 5, 1862, Stuart Papers on deposit Virginia Historical Society, Richmond, Virginia. This letter is also quoted in John W. Thomason, Jr., *Jeb Stuart* (New York, 1930), 206.

20. McClellan, *Stuart*, 83–85; Walter H. Taylor, *Four Years with General Lee* (New York, 1879), 41; Freeman, *Lee's Lieutenants*, I, 642–43.

21. General Orders, No. 75, July 6, 1862, in Dowdey and Manarin, eds., *Wartime Papers*, 210–11; Lee's Report, in Dowdey and Manarin, eds., *Wartime Papers*, 221.

22. Lee's Report, in Dowdey and Manarin, eds., *Wartime Papers*, 221; Freeman, *Lee's Lieutenants*, I, 605–13, 641–42, 658–59; Lee to Mrs. W. H. F. Lee, June 22, 1862, in Dowdey and Manarin, eds., *Wartime Papers*, 196–97.

23. Blackford, *War Years*, 87–88; Von Borcke, *Memoirs*, I, 82–91.
24. McClellan, *Stuart*, 86.
25. Ibid. The standard biography of Hampton is Manly Wade Hampton, *Giant in Gray: A Biography of Wade Hampton of South Carolina* (New York, 1949).
26. Freeman, *Lee's Lieutenants*, I, 433–34, II, 4–5; McClellan, *Stuart*, 91; Lee to Randolph, June 7, 1862, *O.R.*, XI, pt. 3, 580.
27. Thomas Cobb to Marion Cobb, June 20, 1862, and July 11, 1862, Thomas R. R. Cobb Collection, University of Georgia Libraries, Athens, Georgia, cited in William B. McCash, *Thomas R. R. Cobb: The Making of a Southern Nationalist* (Macon, Georgia, 1983), 303, 307.
28. Blackford, *War Years*, 90–92; Ball to Stuart, July 15, 1862, Stuart Papers, Huntington Library, San Marino, California.
29. On August 4–8, Stuart led Fitz Lee's brigade north and brushed with Federals at Massaponax Church. Then on August 9 Stuart again left Hanover Court House, this time to inspect Robertson's brigade, which was with Jackson. He arrived in the wake of the Battle of Cedar Mountain and conducted a reconnaissance for Jackson. Then he returned to his headquarters at Hanover Court House. McClellan, *Stuart*, 88–89; Blackford, *War Years*, 94–97; Stuart to Lee, August 5, 1862, *O.R.*, XII, pt. 3, 924–25; Freeman, *Lee's Lieutenants*, II, 42.
30. W. H. Taylor to Stuart, August 13, 1862, *O.R.*, XI, pt. 3, 674; Stuart to Lee, February 5, 1863, *O.R.*, XII, pt. 2, 725–28; Blackford, *War Years*, 97; Von Borcke, *Memoirs*, I, 100–104.
31. Von Borcke, *Memoirs*, I, 104–5; Charles Wells Russell, ed., *The Memoirs of Colonel John S. Mosby* (Boston, 1917), 135–36; Stuart to Lee, February 5, 1863, *O.R.*, XII, pt. 2, 724–28.
32. Stuart to Lee, February 5, 1863, *O.R.*, XII, pt. 2, 725–28; Von Borcke, *Memoirs*, I, 105–8; Russell, ed., *Mosby Memoirs*, 136–37; John Esten Cooke, *Wearing of the Gray*, ed. Philip Van Doren Stern (Bloomington, Indiana, 1959), 194–201.
33. Stuart to Lee, February 5, 1863, *O.R.*, XII, pt. 2, 725–28; Russell, ed., *Mosby Memoirs*, 137–42; McClellan, *Stuart*, 91; Freeman, *Lee's Lieutenants*, II, 60–62; Lee to Stuart, August 19, 1862, *O.R.*, XII, pt. 2, 728.
34. Von Borcke, *Memoirs*, I, 109; Stuart to Flora, August 19, 1862, Stuart Papers on deposit Virginia Historical Society, Richmond, Virginia. The hat Stuart lost he had very recently won from a Union general whom he had known at West Point. During a truce to bury the dead after Jackson's battle at Cedar Mountain, Stuart had met his old friend and bet a hat that Northern newspapers would claim the fight had been a Union victory. He won the bet and the hat (Blackford, *War Years*, 98n).
35. Stuart to Lee, February 23, 1863, *O.R.*, XII, pt. 2, 729–33; Von Borcke, *Memoirs*, I, 110–15; Blackford, *War Years*, 98.
36. Stuart to Lee, February 23, 1863, *O.R.*, XII, pt. 2, 729–33; Blackford, *War Years*, 98–99.

37. Stuart to Lee, February 23, 1863, *O.R.*, XII, pt. 2, 729–33.
38. Blackford, *War Years*, 99–100.
39. Stuart to Lee, February 23, 1863, *O.R.*, XII, pt. 2, 729–33; Blackford, *War Years*, 100–108; Von Borcke, *Memoirs*, I, 120–28; McClellan, *Stuart*, 94–95; "Raid on Catlett's," *Southern Historical Society Papers*, XXVII, 303–7.
40. Lee to Davis, August 23, 1862, *O.R.*, XII, pt. 3, 940–41; Lee to Davis, August 24, 1862, *O.R.*, XII, pt. 3, 942.
41. Stuart to Flora, August 25, 1862, Stuart Papers on deposit Virginia Historical Society, Richmond, Virginia; Freeman, *Lee's Lieutenants*, II, 71–72; W. Roy Mason, "Marching on Manassas," Johnson and Buel, eds., *Battles and Leaders*, II, 528; Henry Kyd Douglas, *I Rode with Stonewall* (Chapel Hill, North Carolina, 1940), 133–34.

## IX. *Knight of the Golden Spurs*

1. Douglas S. Freeman, *Lee's Lieutenants: A Study in Command*, 3 vols. (New York, 1942–44), II, 63–80.
2. Ibid., II, 81–91; Stuart's Report, February 28, 1863, *War of the Rebellion: A Compilation of the Official Records of the Union and Confederate Armies*, 70 vols. in 127 (Washington, D.C., 1880–1901), Ser. I, XII, pt. 2, 733–38 (hereafter cited as *O.R.*; all citations are Series I); W. W. Blackford, *War Years with Jeb Stuart* (New York, 1945), 109–112.
3. Blackford, *War Years*, 112–15.
4. Stuart's Report, February 28, 1863, *O.R.*, XII, pt. 2, 733–38; Trimble's report and letters are in *O.R.*, XII, pt. 2, 718–25; Stuart's response is in *O.R.*, XII, pt. 2, 741–43.
5. Heros Von Borcke, *Memoirs of the Confederate War for Independence*, 2 vols. (New York, 1938), I, 136–38.
6. Ibid.; Blackford, *War Years*, 115.
7. Stuart's Report, February 28, 1863, *O.R.*, XII, pt. 2, 733–38.
8. Ibid.; Blackford, *War Years*, 125–27.
9. Stuart's Report, February 28, 1863, *O.R.*, XII, pt. 2, 733–38; Blackford, *War Years*, 125–27.
10. James Longstreet, "Our March Against Pope," in Robert Underwood Johnson and Clarence Clough Buel, eds., *Battles and Leaders of the Civil War*, 4 vols. (New York, 1956), II, 525.
11. See the commentary of Vincent J. Esposito, ed., *West Point Atlas of American Wars*, 2 vols. (New York, 1959), I, maps 61–62.
12. Stuart's Report, February 28, 1863, *O.R.*, XII, pt. 2, 733–38.
13. Lee's Report, June 5, 1863, in Clifford Dowdey and Louis H. Manarin, eds., *The Wartime Papers of R. E. Lee* (New York, 1961), 285.
14. John Esten Cooke tells this story (to illustrate a different point) in *Wearing of the Gray*, ed. Philip Van Doren Stern (Bloomington, Indiana, 1959), 210–17.
15. Enclosure in Stuart's Report, February 28, 1863, *O.R.*, XII, pt. 2, 739;

Stuart to Flora, September 2, 1862, Stuart Papers, on deposit Virginia Historical Society, Richmond, Virginia.

16. Stuart to Flora, September 4, 1862, Stuart Papers, on deposit in Virginia Historical Society, Richmond, Virginia; R. Channing Price to Mother, September 5, 1862, R. Channing Price Papers, Southern Historical Collection, University of North Carolina at Chapel Hill.

17. Freeman, *Lee's Lieutenants*, II, 56, 68–69, 169–70.

18. See Blackford, *War Years*, 160–61; George Cary Eggleston, *A Rebel's Recollections* (Bloomington, Indiana, 1959), 12.

19. Frank M. Myers, *The Comanches: A History of White's Battalion, Virginia Cavalry* (Baltimore, 1871; new ed. Marietta, Georgia, 1956), 8, 87–88.

20. Ibid., 107–9.

21. Stuart's Report, February 13, 1864, *O.R.*, XIX, pt. 1, 814–21; Von Borcke, *Memoirs*, I, 182–83.

22. Stuart's Report, February 13, 1864, *O.R.*, XIX, pt. 1, 814–21; Von Borcke, *Memoirs*, I, 185–91; Stuart to Flora, September 12, 1862, Stuart Papers, on deposit Virginia Historical Society, Richmond, Virginia.

23. Von Borcke, *Memoirs*, I, 191–93; Blackford, *War Years*, 140; R. Channing Price to Mother, September 10, 1862, R. Channing Price Papers, Southern Historical Collection, University of North Carolina at Chapel Hill.

24. Blackford, *War Years*, 140–43; Von Borcke, *Memoirs*, I, 193–201.

25. Lee to Stuart, September 12, 1862, Stuart Papers, Henry E. Huntington Library, San Marino, California.

26. Dwight Dudley to Flora Stuart, November 27, 1875, Stuart Papers, Virginia Historical Society, Richmond, Virginia.

27. Stuart's Report, February 13, 1864, *O.R.*, XIX, pt. 1, 814–21; Esposito, ed., *West Point Atlas*, I, maps 67–69.

28. Von Borcke, *Memoirs*, I, 266–70; Henry Kyd Douglas, *I Rode with Stonewall* (Chapel Hill, North Carolina, 1940), 192–93; Blackford, *War Years*, 154–56.

29. Stuart's Report on the Seven Days is in *O.R.*, XI, pt. 2, 513–24; on Antietam, *O.R.*, XIX, pt. 1, 814–21.

30. Blackford, *War Years*, 156–59; Von Borcke, *Memoirs*, I, 270–72, 286–95.

31. Douglas, *I Rode with Stonewall*, 190; *Southern Illustrated News*, September 27, 1862.

32. Von Borcke, *Memoirs*, I, 272–76.

33. The quote is from George Hughes Hepworth, *The Whip, Hoe, and Sword: Or the Gulf-Department in 63* (Boston, 1864), 287–88, cited in Michael C. C. Adams, *Our Masters the Rebels: A Speculation on Union Military Failure in the East, 1861–1965* (Cambridge, Massachusetts, 1978), 161.

34. Douglas S. Freeman, *R. E. Lee: A Biography*, 4 vols. (New York, 1934–35), I, 646; IV, 306–7.

35. Douglas, *I Rode with Stonewall*, 196.

36. Von Borcke, *Memoirs*, I, 295–97.

37. Lee to Stuart, October 8, 1862, *O.R.*, XIX, pt. 2, 55.

38. Stuart's Report, October 14, 1862, *O.R.*, XIX, pt. 2, 52–56.

39. Blackford, *War Years*, 204–5; R. Channing Price to Mother, October 15, 1862, R. Channing Price Papers, Southern Historical Collection, University of North Carolina at Chapel Hill.

40. R. Channing Price to Mother, October 15, 1862, R. Channing Price Papers, Southern Historical Collection, University of North Carolina at Chapel Hill; Stuart to Flora, October 9, 1862, Stuart Papers, on deposit Virginia Historical Society, Richmond, Virginia.

41. Stuart's Report, October 14, 1862, *O.R.*, XIX, pt. 2, 52–56; Price to Mother, October 15, 1862, Southern Historical Collection, University of North Carolina at Chapel Hill; Hampton to Fisher, October 24, 1862, Hampton Family Papers, South Caroliniana Library, University of South Carolina, Columbia, S.C.; Blackford, *War Years*, 165.

42. Stuart's Report, October 14, 1862, *O.R.*, XIX, pt. 2, 52–56; John W. Thomason, Jr., *Jeb Stuart* (New York, 1930), 305–7.

43. Blackford, *War Years*, 169–70.

44. H. B. McClellan, *The Life and Campaigns of Major-General J. E. B. Stuart* (Boston and New York, 1885), 140–41.

45. Stuart's Report, October 14, 1862, *O.R.*, XIX, pt. 2, 52–56.

46. Blackford, *War Years*, 172–75, 178–80.

47. Ibid., 175–78; Stuart's Report, October 14, 1862, *O.R.*, XIX, pt. 2, 52–56; R. Channing Price to Mother, R. Channing Price Papers, Southern Historical Collection, University of North Carolina at Chapel Hill.

48. Thomason, *Stuart*, 316–17; Stuart to Flora, October 16, 1862, Stuart Papers, on deposit Virginia Historical Society, Richmond, Virginia.

49. McClellan to Halleck, October 11, 1862, *O.R.*, XIX, pt. 2, 66; Pleasonton's Report, October 13, 1862, *O.R.*, XIX, pt. 2, 38–40; Stoneman's Reports, October 13, 25, 1862, *O.R.*, XIX, pt. 2, 42–44; McClellan's Report, October 12, 1862, *O.R.*, XIX, pt. 2, 30–31.

50. Matthew Forney Steele, *American Campaigns*, 2 vols. (Washington, D.C., 1909), I, 286; Esposito, ed., *West Point Atlas*, I, map 70; William W. Hassler, ed., *The General to His Lady: The Civil War Letters of William Dorsey Pender to Fanny Pender* (Chapel Hill, North Carolina, 1965), 184; Hampton to Fisher, October 24, 1862, Hampton Family Papers, South Caroliniana Library, University of South Carolina, Columbia, S.C.; Julian T. Edwards to Lemuel and Mary Edwards, October 15, 1862, Julian T. Edwards Papers, Virginia Historical Society, Richmond, Virginia.

51. Lee's Report, October 14, 1862, *O.R.*, XIX, pt. 2, 51; Richmond *Examiner*, October 15, 1862; Richmond *Dispatch*, October 15, 1862.

52. Von Borcke, *Memoirs*, I, 299–301; Blackford, *War Years*, 181.

53. Stuart to Lily Parran Lee, December 5, 1862, quoted in Burke Davis, *Jeb Stuart: The Last Cavalier* (New York, 1957), 236–37; Alexander L. Tinsley, "General Stuart's Spurs," *Confederate Veteran*, XXXVII (May 1929), 198.

## X. Fame

1. Bell Irvin Wiley, *The Life of Johnny Reb: The Common Soldier of the Confederacy* (Indianapolis and New York, 1943), 169.

2. Heros Von Borcke, *Memoirs of the Confederate War for Independence*, 2 vols. (New York, 1938), II, 15–16.

3. *New York Times*, October 16, 1862; the Lincoln quote is cited in H. B. McClellan, *The Life and Campaigns of Major-General J. E. B. Stuart* (Boston and New York, 1885), 162.

4. Paul H. Hayne, "Stuart!" *Southern Illustrated News*, December 6, 1862.

5. John Esten Cooke, "The Song of the Rebel," *Southern Illustrated News*, January 24, 1863.

6. "Riding a Raid" is printed in Paul Glass, ed., *Singing Soldiers* (New York, 1964), 90–92; Richard B. Harwell describes the sheet music in *Confederate Music* (Chapel Hill, North Carolina, 1950), 139.

7. Fannie Lewis Adams Reminiscence, Virginia Historical Society, Richmond, Virginia; *New York Times*, October 11, 1962.

8. The incidents and quotes in this paragraph appear in earlier chapters. The reference to "puppy" is in Stuart to Flora, October 25, 1863; he wrote about a scrapbook December 11, 1862, and again February 26, 1863. Copies of these letters are on deposit at the Virginia Historical Society, Richmond, Virginia.

9. Stuart to Flora, October 22 and October 26, 1862, copies on deposit Virginia Historical Society, Richmond, Virginia; Von Borcke, *Memoirs*, II, 36–37.

10. Stuart to R. H. Chilton, Chief of Staff, October 24, 1862, Letterbook, Stuart Papers, Virginia Historical Society, Richmond, Virginia.

11. Stuart to Flora, October 26, 1862, copy on deposit Virginia Historical Society, Richmond, Virginia.

12. Stuart's Report, *War of the Rebellion: A Compilation of the Official Records of the Union and Confederate Armies*, 70 vols. in 127 (Washington, D.C., 1880–1901), Ser. I, XIX, pt. 2, 140–45 (hereafter cited as *O.R.*; all citations are Series I); McClellan, *Stuart*, 167–86; Douglas S. Freeman, *Lee's Lieutenants: A Study in Command*, 3 vols. (New York, 1942–44), II, 310–11; Von Borcke, *Memoirs*, II, 1–53.

13. Von Borcke, *Memoirs*, II, 59–61.

14. Stuart to Flora, November 2, 1862, copy on deposit Virginia Historical Society, Richmond, Virginia; H. H. Smith, "J. E. B. Stuart: A Character Sketch," Virginia Historical Society, Richmond, Virginia.

15. Von Borcke, *Memoirs*, II, 48–49.

16. Stuart to Flora, November 6, 1862, copy on deposit Virginia Historical Society, Richmond, Virginia; telegram, Stuart to Flora, November 8, 1862, Stuart Papers, Huntington Library, San Marino, California; John Esten Cooke, *Wearing of the Gray*, ed. Philip Van Doren Stern (Bloomington, Indiana, 1959), 16; Von Borcke, *Memoirs*, II, 49, 62–63.

17. Stuart to Flora, November 6, 1862, copy on deposit Virginia Historical Society, Richmond, Virginia.

18. Stuart to Lily Lee, November 16, 1862, Stuart Papers, Manuscript Department, Duke University Library, Durham, North Carolina.

19. *O.R.*, XXI, 544–45 and 1025.

20. McClellan, *Stuart*, 186–87n.

21. Lee to Cooper, November 22, 1862, and Lee to Jackson, November 23, 1862, *O.R.*, XXI, 1026–28.

22. Stuart to Flora, November 25, 1862, copy on deposit Virginia Historical Society, Richmond, Virginia; Von Borcke, *Memoirs*, II, 72–74, 80–85; W. W. Blackford, *War Years with Jeb Stuart* (New York, 1945), 186–87.

23. A. Tinsley to Stuart, November 25, 1862, Stuart Papers, Virginia Historical Society, Richmond, Virginia; Burke Davis, *Jeb Stuart: The Last Cavalier* (New York, 1957), 249–50; Stuart to Letcher, December 3, 1862, Stuart Papers, Virginia Historical Society, Richmond Virginia; Stuart to Lily Lee, December 5, 1862, Stuart Papers, Manuscript Department, Duke University Library, Durham, North Carolina.

24. Stuart to Flora, December 3, 1862, copy on deposit Virginia Historical Society, Richmond, Virginia; Blackford, *War Years*, 187–89; Von Borcke, *Memoirs*, II, 94–102.

25. Charles Minor Blackford III, ed., *Letters from Lee's Army* (New York, 1947), 143–45; McClellan, *Stuart*, 190; Von Borcke, *Memoirs*, II, 102–11; Blackford, *War Years*, 192–93.

26. Stuart to Flora, telegram, December 14, 1862, Stuart Papers, Virginia Historical Society, Richmond, Virginia; R. Channing Price to Mother, December 17, 1862, R. Channing Price Papers, Southern Historical Collection, University of North Carolina at Chapel Hill (this letter is quoted extensively in McClellan, *Stuart*, 191–95); Von Borcke, *Memoirs*, II, 112–34.

27. Von Borcke, *Memoirs*, II, 152–54.

28. Blackford, *War Years*, 199–200; Henry Kyd Douglas, *I Rode with Stonewall* (Chapel Hill, North Carolina, 1940), 207–9; Freeman, *Lee's Lieutenants*, II, 497–98.

29. Price to Mother, December 23, 1862, R. Channing Price Papers, Southern Historical Collection, University of North Carolina at Chapel Hill.

30. Freeman, *Lee's Lieutenants*, II, 397–99; Hampton's reports are in *O.R.*, XXI, 15–16, 690–91, 695–96.

31. Stuart's Report, *O.R.*, XXI, 731–35; McClellan, *Stuart*, 196–97.

32. Von Borcke, *Memoirs*, II, 158; R. Channing Price to Sister, January 2, 1863, R. Channing Price Papers, Southern Historical Collection, University of North Carolina at Chapel Hill; Freeman, *Lee's Lieutenants*, II, 399–400 and notes.

33. Freeman, *Lee's Lieutenants*, II, 399–400; R. Channing Price to Sister, January 2, 1863, R. Channing Price Papers, Southern Historical Collection, University of North Carolina at Chapel Hill; Stuart's Report, *O.R.*, XXI, 731–35.

34. Hampton's Report, *O.R.*, XXI, 735–36.

35. Stuart's Report, *O.R.*, XXI, 731–35; R. Channing Price to Sister, January 2, 1863, R. Channing Price Papers, Southern Historical Collection, University of North Carolina at Chapel Hill; McClellan, *Stuart*, 199–202; Freeman, *Lee's Lieutenants*, II, 401–7.

36. R. Channing Price to Sister, January 2, 1863, R. Channing Price Papers, Southern Historical Collection, University of North Carolina at Chapel Hill; Richmond *Examiner*, January 2, 1863; Richmond *Dispatch*, January 1, 7, 1863; *New York Times*, January 1, 1863.

37. Von Borcke, *Memoirs*, II, 167–68; Stuart completed his report of Second Manassas (Bull Run) on February 28, 1863 (*O.R.*, XII, pt. 2, 733–38) and reported operations after August 30, 1862, on February 13, 1864 (*O.R.*, XII, pt. 2, 743–45); Virginia Pelham Stuart was born October 9, 1863.

38. Hill to Stuart, November 14 [1862], Stuart Papers, Virginia Historical Society, Richmond, Virginia.

39. Stuart to G. W. C. Lee, December 18, 1862, Stuart Papers, Manuscript Department, Duke University Library, Durham, North Carolina; Von Borcke, *Memoirs*, II, 154; G. W. C. Lee to Stuart, February 5, 1863, and February 2, 1864, copies on deposit Virginia Historical Society, Richmond, Virginia.

40. Stuart to Flora, February 26, 1863, copy on deposit Virginia Historical Society, Richmond, Virginia.

41. Hampton to Mary Fisher Hampton, January 27, 1863, in Charles E. Cauthen, ed., *Family Letters of the Three Wade Hamptons, 1782–1901* (Columbia, South Carolina, 1953), 91–92; Hampton to Wigfall, February 16, 1863, Hampton Family Papers, South Caroliniana Library, University of South Carolina, Columbia, South Carolina.

42. Stuart to Cooper, January 13, 1863, and February 4, 1863, Stuart Papers, Virginia Historical Society, Richmond, Virginia; G. W. C. Lee to Stuart, February 5, 1863, copy on deposit Virginia Historical Society, Richmond, Virginia.

43. "Proceedings of the General Court Martial of Lt. Col. H. Clay Pate" in microfilm, Confederate Imprints collection.

44. For Rosser's battles with John Barleycorn, see his personal papers, 1171-a, Manuscripts Department, Alderman Library, University of Virginia, Charlottesville, Virginia; Stuart to Cooper, January 6, 1863, and Stuart to Walter H. Taylor, June 1, 1863, Stuart Papers, Virginia Historical Society, Richmond, Virginia.

45. Stuart to John R. Cooke, February 28, 1863, Cooke Family Papers, Virginia Historical Society, Richmond, Virginia.

46. Stuart endorsement, January 27, 1863, *O.R.*, XXI, 692.

47. Quoted in Freeman, *Lee's Lieutenants*, II, 409.

48. Stuart to John R. Cooke, February 28, 1863, Cooke Family Papers, Virginia Historical Society, Richmond, Virginia.

49. Blackford III, ed., *Letters from Lee's Army*, 157–58.

50. Blackford, *War Years*, 200–201; Cooke, *Wearing of the Gray*, 116–29.

51. Blackford, *War Years*, 200–201; Cooke, *Wearing of the Gray*, 116–

129; Harry Gilmor, *Four Years in the Saddle* (London, 1866), 58–60; McClellan, *Stuart*, 205–10.

52. Averell's Report, *O.R.*, XXV, pt. 1, 47–53; Stuart's Report and General Orders, No. 8, *O.R.*, XXV, pt. 1, 58–60; Fitz Lee's Report, *O.R.*, XXV, pt. 1, 60–63; Gilmor, *Four Years in the Saddle*, 61–65; Stuart to Lee, 7:00 P.M., March 17, 1863, quoted in Richmond *Examiner*, March 19, 1863.

53. Gilmor, *Four Years in the Saddle*, 61–62.

54. Ibid., 65–69; H. H. Matthewe, "Major John Pelham, Confederate Hero," *Southern Historical Society Papers*, XXXVIII, 379–84.

55. Stuart's General Orders, No. 9, *O.R.*, XXV, pt. 1, 60; Von Borcke, *Memoirs*, II, 188–90; Matthewe, "Pelham," 383; Blackford, *War Years*, 90; Stuart to Flora, March 19, 1863, and April 8, 1863, copies on deposit Virginia Historical Society, Richmond, Virginia.

56. Averell's Report, *O.R.*, XXV, pt. 1, 47–53; Fitz Lee's Report, *O.R.*, XXV, pt. 1, 60–63.

57. McClellan, *Stuart*, 218–20.

58. Ibid., 220–24; Lee to Stuart, April 19, 1863, *O.R.*, XXV, pt. 2, 736–37.

59. McClellan, *Stuart*, 225–31; Von Borcke, *Memoirs*, II, 202–17; Stuart's Report, *O.R.*, XXV, pt. 1, 1045–48.

60. Von Borcke, *Memoirs*, II, 218–22.

61. Freeman, *Lee's Lieutenants*, II, 538–62.

62. Stuart's Report, *O.R.*, XXV, pt. 1, 886–89; McClellan, *Stuart*, 235; Von Borcke, *Memoirs*, II, 227–28.

63. Rodes's Report, *O.R.*, XXV, pt. 1, 942–43.

64. Stuart's Report, *O.R.*, XXV, pt. 1, 886–89.

65. Lee to Stuart, 3:00 A.M., May 3, 1863, and 3:30 A.M., May 3, 1863, *O.R.*, XXV, pt. 2, 769.

66. Stuart's Report, *O.R.*, XXV, pt. 1, 886–89; McClellan, *Stuart*, 248–51; Freeman, *Lee's Lieutenants*, II, 584–99; H. P. Griffith, *Variosa* (n.p., 1911), 81–87.

67. Stuart's draft order is part of the Stuart Papers, Virginia Historical Society, Richmond, Virginia.

## XI. *"One of Those Fops"*

1. Douglas S. Freeman, *Lee's Lieutenants: A Study in Command*, 3 vols. (New York, 1942–44), II, 570 and n; Special Orders No. 123½, *War of the Rebellion: A Compilation of the Official Records of the Union and Confederate Armies*, 70 vols. in 127 (Washington, D.C., 1880–1901), Ser. I, XXV, pt. 2, 782 (hereafter cited as *O.R.*; all citations are Series I).

2. Stuart to Flora, May 20, 1863, copy on deposit Virginia Historical Society, Richmond, Virginia; Pender to Fanny, May 9, May 22, 1863, in William W. Hassler, ed., *The General to His Lady: The Civil War Letters of William Dorsey Pender to Fanny Pender* (Chapel Hill, North Carolina, 1965), 236, and Pender to Fanny, May 22, 1863, cited in Freeman, *Lee's Lieutenants*, II, 692n.

3. Lee to Stuart, May 11, 1863, *O.R.*, XXV, pt. 2, 792; Lee to Stuart, May 23, 1863, *O.R.*, XXV, pt. 2, 820–21; Pender to Fanny, May 23, 1863, in Hassler, ed., *General to His Lady*, 239.

4. Rosser to Betty Winston, May 12, 1863, Thomas Lafayette Rosser Papers, 1171-a, Manuscripts Department, Alderman Library, University of Virginia, Charlottesville, Virginia.

5. Lee to Davis, May 7, 1863, *O.R.*, XXV, pt. 2, 782–83; H. B. McClellan, *The Life and Campaigns of Major-General J. E. B. Stuart* (Boston and New York, 1885), 261, 293; Lee to Stuart, May 9, 1863, *O.R.*, XXV, pt. 2, 788–89.

6. Fitzhugh Lee to Stuart, April 6, 1863, Stuart Papers, Virginia Historical Society, Richmond, Virginia; Freeman, *Lee's Lieutenants*, II, 692–93 and n.

7. Hampton to Mary Fisher Hampton, May 19, 1863, in Charles E. Cauthen, ed., *Family Letters of the Three Wade Hamptons, 1782–1901* (Columbia, South Carolina, 1953), 93; *Christian Index*, May 18, 1863.

8. Heros Von Borcke, *Memoirs of the Confederate War for Independence*, 2 vols. (New York, 1938), II, 262–63; W. W. Blackford, *War Years with Jeb Stuart* (New York, 1945), 206; Burke Davis, *Jeb Stuart: The Last Cavalier* (New York, 1957), 299; Mary Jackson to Stuart, August 1, 1863, Stuart Papers, Virginia Historical Society, Richmond, Virginia.

9. McClellan, *Stuart*, 261, 293.

10. Von Borcke, *Memoirs*, II, 262–65; Blackford, *War Years*, 211–12.

11. Von Borcke, *Memoirs*, II, 265–67; Blackford, *War Years*, 211–12; Freeman, *Lee's Lieutenants*, III, 1–3; James Harrison Williams to Cora DeMovelle (Pritchartt) Williams, June 6, 1863, and George Henry Williams to Mary Julia (Williams) Wagner, June 6, 1863, Williams Family Papers, Virginia Historical Society, Richmond, Virginia.

12. Von Borcke, *Memoirs*, II, 266–67; the passage from *Childe Harold's Pilgrimage* is in Frederick Page, ed., *Byron: Poetical Works*, new ed. corrected by John Jump (London, 1970), 212.

13. McClellan, *Stuart*, 261–62.

14. George Henry Williams to Mary Julia (Williams) Wagner, June 6, 1863, and James Harrison Williams to Cora DeMovelle (Pritchartt) Williams, June 6, 1863, in Williams Family Papers, Virginia Historical Society, Richmond, Virginia; William N. McDonald, *A History of the Laurel Brigade* (Arlington, Virginia, 1907), 132; Frank M. Myers, *The Comanches: A History of White's Battalion, Virginia Cavalry* (Baltimore, 1871, new ed. Marietta, Georgia, 1956), 181; Francis Gilmer Diary, 8461, Manuscripts Department, Alderman Library, University of Virginia, Charlottesville, Virginia; Robert Krick, *9th Virginia Cavalry* (Lynchburg, Virginia, 1982), 18.

15. Von Borcke, *Memoirs*, II, 267; Freeman, *Lee's Lieutenants*, III, 3–5; John Esten Cooke, *Wearing of the Gray* (Bloomington, Indiana, 1959), 305–6; H. C. Burn to Father and Mother, June 11, 1863, Burn Family Papers, South Caroliniana Library, University of South Carolina, Columbia, South Carolina; Mobile *Daily Advertiser and Register*, June 19, 1863.

16. McClellan, *Stuart*, 262–63; Lee to Wife, June 9, 1863, in Clifford Dowdey and Louis H. Manarin, eds., *The Wartime Papers of R. E. Lee* (New York, 1961), 506–7.

17. Stephen Z. Starr, *The Union Cavalry in the Civil War*, 2 vols. (Baton Rouge, 1979–81), I, 366–73, 376–77.

18. Ibid., 378–80; McDonald, *Laurel Brigade*, 134–38; McClellan, *Stuart*, 264–69; Stuart's Report, *O.R.*, XXVII, pt. 2, 679–85; Blackford, *War Years*, 213–14.

19. Blackford, *War Years*, 214–15; Myers, *Comanches*, 183; Freeman, *Lee's Lieutenants*, III, 9–10, 13–14; Starr, *Union Cavalry*, I, 380–83.

20. McClellan, *Stuart*, 269–73.

21. Blackford, *War Years*, 215–16.

22. Ibid.; McClellan, *Stuart*, 273–79; Stuart's Report, *O.R.*, XXVII, pt. 2, 679–85; Starr, *Union Cavalry*, I, 383–87.

23. Freeman, *Lee's Lieutenants*, III, 12n.

24. Stuart's Report, *O.R.*, XXVII, pt. 2, 679–85; McClellan, *Stuart*, 281–92.

25. Blackford, *War Years*, 216; Freeman, *Lee's Lieutenants*, III, 11–12; Starr, *Union Cavalry*, I, 388–89.

26. General Orders, No. 24, June 15, 1863, *O.R.*, XXVII, pt. 2, 719–20; Casualties from McClellan, *Stuart*, 292–93, and quote 294; *Addresses of Gen'l T. L. Rosser* (New York, 1889), 39; John Newton Opie, *A Rebel Cavalryman with Lee, Stuart and Jackson* (Chicago, 1909), 147; Stuart's Report, *O.R.*, XXVII, pt. 2, 679–85.

27. Blackford, *War Years*, 217; Von Borcke, *Memoirs*, II, 280–81; Page, ed., *Byron*, 213.

28. H. C. Burn to Father & Mother, June 11, 1863, Burn Family Papers, South Caroliniana Library, University of South Carolina, Columbia, South Carolina; Charles Minor Blackford III, ed., *Letters from Lee's Army* (New York, 1947), 175; Pender to Fanny, June 12, 1863, in Hassler, ed., *General to His Lady*, 246; Hampton quote cited in Edwin B. Coddington, *The Gettysburg Campaign: A Study in Command* (New York, 1968), 60; Lee to Stuart, June 16, 1863, *O.R.*, XXVI, pt. 2, 687.

29. This incident is told in Freeman, *Lee's Lieutenants*, III, 51–52 and n.

30. Mobile *Daily Advertiser and Register*, June 19, 1863; Memphis *Appeal*, June 15, 17, 1863; Charleston *Mercury*, June 15, 17, 1863; Richmond *Enquirer*, June 13, 1863.

31. Richmond *Examiner*, June 12, 1863.

32. Richmond *Enquirer*, June 12, 1863; Stuart's Report, *O.R.*, XXVII, pt. 2, 679–85.

33. Newspaper file, Stuart Papers, Virginia Historical Society, Richmond, Virginia; Richmond *Enquirer*, June 19, 1863; John W. Thomason, Jr., *Jeb Stuart* (New York, 1930), 410: "If you are interested, you can find, in the files of the *Examiner* a few days later, a long, indignant letter, signed *Veritas*, or some such name. It purports to be from the pen of a staff officer of the cavalry division, and gives the Stuart side of it, and breathes a splendid indignation against slander, envy, and so forth. Tradition ascribes it to Stuart's good staff surgeon, Talcott Eliason. But the Style is much like Stuart's own."

34. Coddington, *Gettysburg*, 58–65; Starr, *Union Cavalry*, I, 391–93.

35. See Starr, *Union Cavalry*, I, 393–95.

## XII. Gettysburg

1. Stuart explained Brandy Station to Flora in Stuart to Flora, June 12, 1863, Stuart Papers, copy on deposit Virginia Historical Society, Richmond, Virginia.

2. Stuart to Flora, April 8, 1863, Stuart Papers, copy on deposit Virginia Historical Society, Richmond, Virginia.

3. W. W. Blackford, *War Years with Jeb Stuart* (New York, 1945), 205–6; *New York Times*, May 21, 1863.

4. Stuart's Report, *War of the Rebellion: A Compilation of the Official Records of the Union and Confederate Armies*, 70 vols. in 127 (Washington, D.C., 1880–1901), Ser. I, XXVII, pt. 2, 687–710 (hereafter cited as *O.R.*; all citations are Series I).

5. Ibid.; H. B. McClellan, *The Life and Campaigns of Major-General J. E. B. Stuart* (Boston and New York, 1885), 296–303; Stephen Z. Starr, *The Union Cavalry in the Civil War*, 2 vols. (Baton Rouge, 1979–81), I, 396–402.

6. McClellan, *Stuart*, 303–4; Heros Von Borcke, *Memoirs of the Confederate War for Independence*, 2 vols. (New York, 1938), II, 285–86.

7. Stuart's Report, *O.R.*, XXVII, pt. 2, 687–710; Starr, *Union Cavalry*, I, 403–4.

8. Blackford, *War Years*, 218; McClellan, *Stuart*, 306; Stuart's Report, *O.R.*, XXVII, pt. 2, 687–710.

9. Blackford, *War Years*, 218–20; Von Borcke, *Memoirs*, II, 292–95.

10. McClellan, *Stuart*, 306–7.

11. Von Borcke, *Memoirs*, II, 295–96; Blackford, *War Years*, 220.

12. McClellan, *Stuart*, 307; Starr, *Union Cavalry*, I, 407; S. Williams to Commanding Officer Fifth Corps, June 20, 1863, *O.R.*, XXVII, pt. 3, 229; Pleasonton to Gregg, June 20, 1863, *O.R.*, XXVII, pt. 3, 229–30.

13. Stuart's Report, *O.R.*, XXVII, pt. 2, 687–710; McClellan, *Stuart*, 308–12; Starr, *Union Cavalry*, I, 407–11.

14. Von Borcke, *Memoirs*, II, 297–302; Stuart's Report, *O.R.*, XXVII, pt. 2, 687–710.

15. Starr, *Union Cavalry*, I, 411–12; Roy P. Stonesifer, Jr., "The Union Cavalry Comes of Age," in John T. Hubbell, ed., *Battles Lost and Won: Essays from Civil War History* (Westport, Connecticut, 1975), 125–34; McClellan, *Stuart*, 312–14; Douglas S. Freeman, *Lee's Lieutenants: A Study in Command*, 3 vols. (New York, 1942–44), III, 52–53; Blackford, *War Years*, 221.

16. Stuart's Report, *O.R.*, XXVII, pt. 2, 687–710; Von Borcke, *Memoirs*, II, 296; John Newton Opie, *A Rebel Cavalryman with Lee, Stuart and Jackson* (Chicago, 1909), 281; Stuart to Flora, June 25, 1863, Stuart Papers, copy on deposit Virginia Historical Society, Richmond, Virginia; McClellan, *Stuart*, 314.

17. Freeman, *Lee's Lieutenants*, III, 54–55; McClellan, *Stuart*, 315–16; Longstreet to Stuart, June 22, 1865, *O.R.*, XXVII, pt. 3, 915; Lee to Stuart, June 22, 1863, *O.R.*, XXVII, pt. 3, 913.

18. McClellan, *Stuart*, 315; Stuart's Report, *O.R.*, XXVII, pt. 2, 687–710.

19. McClellan, *Stuart*, 316–17; Lee to Stuart, June 23, 1863, *O.R.*, XXVII, pt. 3, 923.

20. Stuart's Report, *O.R.*, XXVII, pt. 2, 687–710; Stuart to Robertson, June 24, 1863, *O.R.*, XXVII, pt. 3, 927–28; Charles Wells Russell, ed., *The Memoirs of Colonel John S. Mosby* (Boston, 1917), 216–17.

21. Stuart's Report, *O.R.*, XXVII, pt. 2, 687–710; McClellan, *Stuart*, 321–25.

22. Stuart's Report, *O.R.*, XXVII, pt. 2, 687–710; McClellan, *Stuart*, 321–25; Blackford, *War Years*, 224–25; Freeman, *Lee's Lieutenants*, III, 65–67; G. W. Beale, *A Lieutenant of Cavalry in Lee's Army* (Boston, 1918), 112.

23. Stuart's Report, *O.R.*, XXVII, pt. 2, 687–710; McClellan, *Stuart*, 326–27; Vincent J. Esposito, ed., *West Point Atlas of American Wars*, 2 vols. (New York, 1959), I, Map 95.

24. Stuart's Report, *O.R.*, XXVII, pt. 2, 687–710; McClellan, *Stuart*, 327–28; Blackford, *War Years*, 225–27; Starr, *Union Cavalry*, I, 528–29; G. W. Beale to Mother, July 13, 1863, printed in *Southern Historical Society Papers*, XI (1883), 320–27.

25. McClellan, *Stuart*, 329–30; Blackford, *War Years*, 228.

26. McClellan, *Stuart*, 329–30; Blackford, *War Years*, 228; G. W. Beale to Mother, July 13, 1863, printed in *Southern Historical Society Papers*, XI (1883), 320–27.

27. Stuart's Report, *O.R.*, XXVII, pt. 2, 687–710; N. K. Hitner to Mr. Hoofnagle, July 6, 1863, The Carlisle Barracks Collection, U. S. Army Military History Institute, Carlisle Barracks, Pennsylvania; McClellan, *Stuart*, 330–31; G. W. Beale to Mother, July 13, 1863, printed in *Southern Historical Society Papers*, XI (1883), 320–27; Sidney Herbert (Herbert Lancey), "Singular Criticism of 'Jeb' Stuart," *Confederate Veteran*, XVI (1908), 152; G. N. Saussy, "Color of His Uniform Misunderstood," *Confederate Veteran*, XVI (1908), 262.

28. McClellan, *Stuart*, 330–32; Starr, *Union Cavalry*, I, 430–31.

29. Freeman, *Lee's Lieutenants*, III, 139.

30. Stuart's Report, *O.R.*, XXVII, pt. 2, 687–710; McClellan, *Stuart*, 337.

31. Starr, *Union Cavalry*, I, 437–38.

32. Stuart's Report, *O.R.*, XXVII, pt. 2, 687–710; McClellan, *Stuart*, 337–40.

33. William E. Miller, "The Cavalry Battle Near Gettysburg," in Robert Underwood Johnson and Clarence Clough Buel, eds., *Battles and Leaders of the Civil War*, 4 vols. (New York, 1887–88), III, 404.

34. Ibid.; Starr, *Union Cavalry*, I, 436n.

35. Starr, *Union Cavalry*, I, 436; Miller, "Cavalry Battle," 404–5 and n.

36. Edwin B. Coddington, *The Gettysburg Campaign: A Study in Command* (New York, 1968), 522–23; McClellan, *Stuart*, 341–49; Blackford, *War Years*, 233; Stuart's Report, *O.R.*, XXVII, pt. 2, 687–710.

37. Stuart's Report, *O.R.*, XXVII, pt. 2, 687–710; Stuart to Flora, July 13, 1863, Stuart Papers, copy on deposit Virginia Historical Society, Richmond, Virginia.

38. McClellan, *Stuart*, 364–66.

39. Stuart's Report, *O.R.*, XXVII, pt. 2, 687–710; Stuart to Flora, July 30, 1863, Stuart Papers, copy on deposit Virginia Historical Society, Richmond, Virginia; Blackford, *War Years*, 235.

40. Charles Minor Blackford, III, ed., *Letters from Lee's Army* (New York, 1947), 195; Edward Younger, ed., *Inside the Confederate Government: The Diary of Robert Garlick Hill Kean* (New York, 1957), 90; Mobile *Daily Advertiser and Register*, August 11, 1863.

41. Lee's Report, *O.R.*, XXVII, pt. 2, 321; G. Moxley Sorrel, *Recollections of a Confederate Staff Officer* (New York, 1917), 162; Sir Frederick Maurice, ed., *An Aide-de-Camp of Lee, Being the Papers of Colonel Charles Marshall* ... (Boston, 1927), 209–11, 214–17, 224n; James Longstreet, *From Manassas to Appomattox* (Philadelphia, 1896), 341–43; "Causes of the Defeat of Gen. Lee's Army at the Battle of Gettysburg—Opinions of Leading Confederate Soldiers," *Southern Historical Society Papers* IV (1877), 80–87, 97–126, 151–60.

42. Charleston *Mercury*, September 12, 1863.

43. McClellan, *Stuart*, 325, 332–37; McClellan to Flora Stuart, February 19, 1887, Stuart Papers, Virginia Historical Society, Richmond, Virginia; McClellan to Flora Stuart, February 18, 1899, Stuart Papers, copy on deposit Virginia Historical Society, Richmond, Virginia.

44. Mosby to General Marcus J. Wright, February 22, 1896, John S. Mosby Papers, U.S. Army Military History Institute, Carlisle Barracks, Pennsylvania; John S. Mosby, *Stuart's Cavalry in the Gettysburg Campaign* (New York, 1908); Russell, ed., *Mosby Memoirs*, 201–57; John S. Mosby, "Longstreet and Stuart," *Southern Historical Society Papers*, XXVIII (1895), 238–47; John S. Mosby, "Heth Intended to Cover His Error ... ," *Southern Historical Society Papers*, XXXVII (1909), 369–72; John S. Mosby, "The Confederate Cavalry in the Gettysburg Campaign," Johnson and Buel, eds., *Battles and Leaders*, III, 251–52; Mosby to McClellan, February 15, 1887, Stuart Papers, Virginia Historical Society, Richmond, Virginia.

45. "A Review of the First Two Day's Operations at Gettysburg and a Reply to General Longstreet by General Fitz Lee," *Southern Historical Society Papers*, V (1878), 162–68; *Addresses of Gen'l T. L. Rosser* (New York, 1889), 42; Hampton to Thomas T. Munford, December 18, 1887, cited in Coddington, *Gettysburg*, 202n.

46. Stuart to Flora, July 10, 1863, July 13, 1863, and July 18, 1863, Stuart Papers, copies on deposit Virginia Historical Society, Richmond, Virginia.

47. Stuart's Report, *O.R.*, XXVII, pt. 2, 687–710.

48. "Address of Major H. B. McClellan ... ," *Southern Historical Society Papers*, VIII (1880), 453.

49. Coddington, *Gettysburg*, 207.

50. Blackford III, ed., *Letters from Lee's Army*, 195–96.

## XIII. *Stuart as Usual*

1. H. B. McClellan, "Address on the Life, Campaigns, and Character of Gen'l J. E. B. Stuart," *Southern Historical Society Papers*, VIII (1880), 452–53.

2. See Roy P. Stonesifer, Jr., "The Union Cavalry Comes of Age," in John T. Hubbell, ed., *Battles Lost and Won: Essays from Civil War History* (Westport, Connecticut, 1975), 125–39.

3. Stuart to Lee, May 27, 1863, Stuart Papers, Virginia Historical Society, Richmond, Virginia.

4. Douglas S. Freeman, *Lee's Lieutenants: A Study in Command*, 3 vols. (New York, 1942–44), III, 208–11.

5. Ibid., 206–13; Stuart to Flora, August 11, 1863, copy on deposit Virginia Historical Society, Richmond, Virginia; Stuart to Flora, August 28, 1863, and September 4, 1863, Stuart Papers, Virginia Historical Society, Richmond, Virginia.

6. Army of Northern Virginia, Special Orders, No. 226, September 9, 1863, in *War of the Rebellion: A Compilation of the Official Records of the Union and Confederate Armies*, 70 vols. in 127 (Washington, D.C., 1880–1901), Ser. I, XXIX, pt. 2, 707–8 (hereafter cited as *O.R.*; all citations are Series I).

7. Stuart to Flora, September 11, 1863, copy on deposit Virginia Historical Society, Richmond, Virginia; Peter Wilson Hairston to Fanny, October 30, 1863, Peter Wilson Hairston Papers, Southern Historical Collection, University of North Carolina at Chapel Hill; Freeman, *Lee's Lieutenants*, III, 211–12.

8. Freeman, *Lee's Lieutenants*, III, 208–15; Hampton to Mary Fisher Hampton, November 20, 1863, and December 8, 1863, in Charles E. Cauthen, ed., *Family Letters of the Three Wade Hamptons, 1782–1901* (Columbia, South Carolina, 1953), 96–98; Stuart Diary (1857), Stuart Papers, Virginia Historical Society, Richmond, Virginia; Stuart to Lee, September 11, 1863, Stuart Letterbook, Stuart Papers, Virginia Historical Society, Richmond, Virginia.

9. Stuart to Rosser, September 30, 1863, Rosser Papers, Manuscript Department, University of Virginia Library, Charlottesville, Virginia.

10. Rosser to Betty, September 15, September 16, September 24, 1863, Rosser Papers, Manuscripts Department, University of Virginia Library, Charlottesville, Virginia; Stuart to Alexander H. H. Stuart, December 18, 1863, Alexander H. H. Stuart Papers, Manuscripts Department, University of Virginia Library, Charlottesville, Virginia; Army of Northern Virginia, Special Orders, No. 256, October 15, 1863, *O.R.*, XXIX, pt. 2, 788.

11. Lee to Davis, October 5, 1863, *O.R.*, XXIX, pt. 2, 771–72; Lee to Cooper, October 9, 1863, *O.R.*, XXIX, pt. 2, 779; William N. McDonald, *A History of the Laurel Brigade* (Arlington, Virginia, 1969), 168–69.

12. Stuart to Flora, September 11, 1863, and August 26, 1863, copies on

deposit Virginia Historical Society, Richmond, Virginia; Stuart to Flora, September 17, 1863, Stuart Papers, Virginia Historical Society, Richmond, Virginia; John W. Thomason, Jr., *Jeb Stuart* (New York, 1930), 450–57.

13. H. B. McClellan, *The Life and Campaigns of Major-General J. E. B. Stuart* (Boston and New York, 1885), 372–73.

14. Ibid., 373–74; Rosser to Betty, September 15, 1863, Rosser Papers, Manuscripts Department, University of Virginia Library, Charlottesville, Virginia.

15. Buford to Pleasonton, September 22, 1863, and September 23, 1863, *O.R.*, XXIX, pt. 1, 140–41.

16. McClellan, *Stuart*, 374–75.

17. Stuart to Flora (telegram), September 23, 1863, Stuart Papers, Virginia Historical Society, Richmond, Virginia; Stuart to Flora, September 26, 1863, copy on deposit Virginia Historical Society, Richmond, Virginia; Lee to Stuart, September 23, 1863, *O.R.*, XXIX, pt. 2, 743; Buford to Pleasonton, September 23, 1863, *O.R.*, XXIX, pt. 1, 141; Rosser to Betty, September 24, 1863, Rosser Papers, Manuscripts Department, University of Virginia Library, Charlottesville, Virginia.

18. For a summary of the campaign, see Vincent J. Esposito, ed., *West Point Atlas of American War*, 2 vols. (New York, 1959), I, Map 118; Stuart's Report, *O.R.*, XXIX, pt. 1, 439–53.

19. Stuart's Report, *O.R.*, XXIX, pt. 1, 439–53; McClellan, *Stuart*, 376–83; Freeman, *Lee's Lieutenants*, III, 249–51.

20. Stuart's Report and enclosure A (G. M. Ryals to Stuart, February 4, 1864), *O.R.*, XXIX, pt. 1, 439–54.

21. Ibid.; McClellan, *Stuart*, 386–93; Freeman, *Lee's Lieutenants*, III, 251–60; W. W. Blackford, *War Years with Jeb Stuart* (New York, 1945), 238–42.

22. Esposito, ed., *West Point Atlas*, Map 118.

23. McClellan, *Stuart*, 393–94.

24. Blackford, *War Years*, 241.

25. Ibid., 241–42; McClellan, *Stuart*, 394–95.

26. McClellan, *Stuart*, 394–95; Stuart's Report, *O.R.*, XXIX, pt. 1, 438–54; Kilpatrick's Report, *O.R.*, XXIX, pt. 1, 380–83; Custer's Report, *O.R.*, XXIX, pt. 1, 389–92; Blackford, *War Years*, 242; the Richmond *Sentinel* mentions the captured letters (November 10, 1863), as does the Richmond *Dispatch* (October 27, 1863).

27. Stuart's Report, *O.R.*, XXIX, pt. 1, 438–54; Freeman, *Lee's Lieutenants*, III, 259–63; Frank M. Myers, *The Comanches: A History of White's Battalion, Virginia Cavalry* (Marietta, Georgia, 1956), 234; Lee to wife, November 5, 1863, in Clifford Dowdey and Louis H. Manarin, eds., *The Wartime Papers of R. E. Lee* (New York, 1961), 618–19.

28. Stuart to Flora, November 2, 1863, copy on deposit Virginia Historical Society, Richmond, Virginia.

29. Longstreet to Stuart, October 13, 1863 (copy), and Lawley to Stuart, November 21, 1863, Stuart Papers, Virginia Historical Society, Richmond, Virginia.

30. Richmond *Examiner*, August 13, 1863; see also Freeman, *Lee's Lieutenants*, III, 263, and Charles W. Ramsdell, "General Robert E. Lee's Horse Supply, 1862-65," *American Historical Review*, XXXV (1930), 758-77.

31. McClellan, *Stuart*, 257-61.

32. *O.R.*, XXIX, pt. 2, 709; pt. 1, 404; pt. 2, 898.

33. Stephen Z. Starr, *The Union Cavalry in the Civil War*, 2 vols. (Baton Rouge, 1979-81), II, 83; Lee to Davis, August 24, 1863, *O.R.*, XXIX, pt. 2, 664-65; Stuart to Seddon (endorsement of Hampton letter), February 15, 1864, *O.R.*, XXXIII, 1164.

34. Stuart to Flora, September 26, 1863, and McClellan to Flora, July 15, 1864, copies on deposit Virginia Historical Society, Richmond, Virginia; Stuart to Alexander H. H. Stuart, December 18, 1863, Alexander H. H. Stuart Papers, Manuscripts Department, University of Virginia Library, Charlottesville, Virginia.

35. Lee to Stuart, August 15, 1863, *O.R.*, XXIX, pt. 2, 648.

36. Lee to wife, November 5, 1863, in Dowdey and Manarin, eds., *Wartime Papers*, 618-19; Lee to Stuart, November 2, 1863, and November 4, 1863, *O.R.*, XXIX, pt. 2, 816, 820-21.

37. Stephen Z. Starr, *Colonel Grenfell's Wars: The Life of a Soldier of Fortune* (Baton Rouge, 1971), 107-12; Lee to Stuart, October 30, 1863, Stuart Papers, Huntington Library, San Marino, California; McClellan, *Stuart*, 375-76n.

38. Blackford, *War Years*, 25; Charles Wells Russell, *The Memoirs of Colonel John S. Mosby* (Boston, 1917), 48-49; Robert L. Krick, *Lee's Colonels: A Biographical Register of the Field Officers of the Army of Northern Virginia* (Dayton, Ohio, 1979), 338; Stuart to Flora, November 2, 1863, and October 25, 1863, copies on deposit Virginia Historical Society, Richmond, Virginia.

39. Richmond *Whig*, November 14, 1863.

40. Richmond *Enquirer*, November 19, 1863.

41. Richmond *Whig*, November 25, 1863.

42. *Southern Illustrated News*, November 28, 1863.

43. Blackford, *War Years*, 242; W. L. Fagan, coll., *Southern War Songs* (New York, 1889), 261.

44. Emory M. Thomas, *The American War and Peace, 1860-1877* (Englewood Cliffs, New Jersey, 1973), 151.

45. Stuart and Hampton Reports, *O.R.*, XXIX, pt. 1, 898-902.

46. See Freeman, *Lee's Lieutenants*, III, 278-79.

47. Stuart to Flora, November 1, 1863, copy on deposit Virginia Historical Society, Richmond, Virginia.

48. Stuart to Flora, October 25, 1863, copy on deposit Virginia Historical Society, Richmond, Virginia; Fitzgerald Ross, *Cities and Camps of the Confederate States*, Richard Barksdale Harwell, ed. (Urbana, Illinois, 1958), 168-69; Stuart to Flora, November 21, 1863, Stuart Papers, Virginia Historical Society, Richmond, Virginia.

49. Ross, *Cities and Camps*, 166-71.

50. Ibid., 174; Thomason, *Stuart*, 481–82.

51. Ross, *Cities and Camps*, 179–84; C. Vann Woodward, ed., *Mary Chesnut's Civil War* (New Haven, 1981), 539; ladder story is in Constance C. Harrison, *Recollections Grave and Gay* (New York, 1911), cited in Burke Davis, *Jeb Stuart: The Last Cavalier* (New York, 1957), 371.

52. Stuart to Flora, January 27, 1864, Stuart Papers, Virginia Historical Society, Richmond, Virginia; Martha B. Eskridge to Fanny (Frances Peyton [Stuart] Atkinson), May 24, 1864, Stuart Family Papers, Virginia Historical Society, Richmond, Virginia.

53. Thomason, *Stuart*, 480; Stuart Album, Virginia Historical Society, Richmond, Virginia.

54. Stuart to Flora, April 28, 1864; Agreement with Lewis M. Harbaugh, April 30, 1864, copies on deposit Virginia Historical Society, Richmond, Virginia.

55. Stuart to Flora, October 5, 1863, quoted in Davis, *Stuart*, 376; Stuart to Flora, February 8, 1864, Stuart Papers, Virginia Historical Society, Richmond, Virginia.

56. Blackford, *War Years*, 249–50; Stuart to Flora, January 30, 1864, Stuart Papers, Virginia Historical Society, Richmond, Virginia; Davis, *Stuart*, 376; Diary of Alexander R. Boteler (typescript), William E. Brooks Collection, Library of Congress, Washington, D.C.

57. Lee to Stuart (and Stuart note), February 3, 1864, original in possession of A. Stuart Campbell, Wytheville, Virginia.

58. Stuart to Cooper, March 28, 1864, Stuart Letterbook, Virginia Historical Society, Richmond, Virginia; Woodward, ed., *Mary Chesnut*, 588; Stuart to G. W. C. Lee, April 9, 1864, copy on deposit Virginia Historical Society, Richmond, Virginia.

59. T. C. DeLeon, *Belles, Beaux and Brains of the 60's* (New York, 1907), 221–22; Woodward, ed., *Mary Chesnut*, 531.

## XIV. *"I Had Rather Die Than Be Whipped"*

1. Stuart to Flora, August 26, 186? and April 26, 1864, copies on deposit Virginia Historical Society, Richmond, Virginia.

2. Stuart to Flora, April 28, 1864, copy on deposit Virginia Historical Society, Richmond, Virginia.

3. McClellan to Flora, July 15, 1864, copy on deposit Virginia Historical Society, Richmond, Virginia; Field Return for Army of Northern Virginia, *War of the Rebellion: A Compilation of the Official Records of the Union and Confederate Armies*, 70 vols. in 127 (Washington, D.C., 1880–1901), Ser. I, XXX, 1298 (hereafter cited as *O.R.*; all citations are Series I); Henry Kyd Douglas, *I Rode with Stonewall* (Chapel Hill, North Carolina, 1940), 275–76; Stephen Z. Starr, *The Union Cavalry in the Civil War*, 2 vols. (Baton Rouge, 1979–81), II, 82–86.

4. Starr, *Union Cavalry*, II, 68–80.

5. Ibid., 57–67; and Emory M. Thomas, "The Kilpatrick-Dahlgren Raid on Richmond," *Civil War Times Illustrated*, February, April, 1978.

6. Starr, *Union Cavalry,* II, 80–82.

7. Alexander R. Boteler Diary (typescript), William E. Brooks Collection, Library of Congress, Washington, D.C.

8. Ibid.; H. B. McClellan, *The Life and Campaigns of Major General J. E. B. Stuart* (Boston and New York, 1885), 406; Douglas, *I Rode with Stonewall,* 275–76.

9. Boteler Diary; Starr, *Union Cavalry,* 91–93.

10. Boteler Diary.

11. Ibid.; Douglas, *I Rode with Stonewall,* 275–76.

12. Boteler Diary; McClellan, *Stuart,* 406.

13. Edward Porter Alexander Memoir, ms. pp. 46–47, Edward Porter Alexander Papers, Southern Historical Collection, University of North Carolina at Chapel Hill.

14. Alexander R. Boteler Diary (typescript), William E. Brooks Collection, Library of Congress, Washington, D.C.; Stuart to Flora, May 6, 1864, Stuart Papers, Virginia Historical Society, Richmond, Virginia.

15. Douglas S. Freeman, *Lee's Lieutenants: A Study in Command,* 3 vols. (New York, 1942–44), III, 373–87; Stuart to Flora, telegram, May 7, 1864, Stuart Papers, Virginia Historical Society, Richmond, Virginia; Stuart to Lee, May 7 and May 7, 11 P.M., 1864, enclosure Fitz Lee to Stuart, May 7, 1864, *O.R.,* LXI, pt. 1, 248–50.

16. McClellan, *Stuart,* 407–9; Starr, *Union Cavalry,* II, 94–96; "Two Cavalry Chieftains," *Southern Historical Society Papers,* XVI (1888), 451–52.

17. Freeman, *Lee's Lieutenants,* III, 411–13; Starr, *Union Cavalry,* II, 97–102.

18. Starr, *Union Cavalry,* II, 99–101; Freeman, *Lee's Lieutenants,* III, 413–16; McClellan, *Stuart,* 410.

19. McClellan, *Stuart,* 410; Freeman, *Lee's Lieutenants,* III, 416.

20. McClellan, *Stuart,* 410–11; Freeman, *Lee's Lieutenants,* III, 416–17.

21. McClellan, *Stuart,* 411.

22. Ibid., 412.

23. Starr, *Union Cavalry,* II, 102–4; Freeman, *Lee's Lieutenants,* III, 420.

24. Starr, *Union Cavalry,* II, 104–5; Freeman, *Lee's Lieutenants,* III, 420–22; McClellan, *Stuart,* 412–13; "Stuart's Last Dispatch," *Southern Historical Society Papers,* IX (1881), 138–39.

25. McClellan, *Stuart,* 412–13; Starr, *Union Cavalry,* II, 105–6.

26. A. R. Venable to Fitz Lee, June 7, 1888, quoted in Freeman, *Lee's Lieutenants,* III, 423; C. T. Litchfield, dictated statement, September 15, 1908, copy on deposit Virginia Historical Society, Richmond, Virginia; J. R. Oliver, "J. E. B. Stuart's Fate at Yellow Tavern," *Confederate Veteran,* XIX (1901), 531; Frank Dorsey, "Gen. J. E. B. Stuart's Last Battle," *Confederate Veteran* XVII (1889), 76–77; "Fatal Wounding of General J. E. B. Stuart," *Southern Historical Society Papers,* XXX (1902), 236–38; I. Ridgeway Trimble, "Cause of Death of Maj. Gen. J. E. B. Stuart," appendix in Freeman, *Lee's Lieutenants,* III, 761–63; "The Death of General J. E. B. Stuart," Robert

Underwood Johnson and Clarence Clough Buel, eds., *Battles and Leaders of the Civil War*, 4 vols. (New York, 1956), IV, 194.

27. Venable to Fitz Lee, Freeman, *Lee's Lieutenants*, III, 425–27; Mc-Clellan, *Stuart*, 414–15; Theodore S. Garnett, "The Dashing Gen. J. E. B. Stuart," *Confederate Veteran* XIX (1911), 575; Trimble, "Cause of Death."

28. "The Wounding and Death of General J. E. B. Stuart," *Southern Historical Society Papers*, VII (1879), 140–41.

29. McClellan, *Stuart*, 416–17; Heros Von Borcke, *Memoirs of the Confederate War for Independence*, 2 vols. (New York, 1938), II, 312–14.

30. "Wounding and Death," 141.

31. Trimble, "Cause of Death."

32. McClellan, *Stuart*, 417; Venable to Fitz Lee, Freeman, *Lee's Lieutenants*, III, 430; Richmond *Examiner*, May 14, 1864.

33. "Wounding and Death," 141.

34. Richmond *Examiner*, May 14, 1864; Garnett, "Dashing," 575–76; [Judith W. McGuire], *Diary of a Southern Refugee* (New York, 1868), 267; Statement of Claude R. Scott, Spring Hill Cemetery Association, Lynchburg, Virginia, Stuart Papers, Virginia Historical Society, Richmond, Virginia.

35. A copy of Stuart's will is on deposit in Virginia Historical Society, Richmond, Virginia.

36. Statement of W. Gordon McCabe in Robert E. Lee, Jr., *Recollections and Letters of General Robert E. Lee* (Garden City, New York, 1904), 125; John Esten Cooke, *Wearing of the Gray*, ed. Philip Van Doren Stern (Bloomington, Indiana, 1959), 26.

37. Hampton to Mary Fisher Hampton, July 4, 1864 in Charles E. Cauthen, ed., *Family Letters of the Three Wade Hamptons, 1782–1901* (Columbia, South Carolina, 1953), 104–5; Frank M. Myers, *The Comanches* (Marietta, Georgia, 1956), 291.

38. William W. Blackford, *War Years with Jeb Stuart* (New York, 1945), 220–21.

39. There is a good collection of McClellan's papers at the Virginia Historical Society, Richmond, Virginia.

40. "Mrs. J. E. B. Stuart," *Confederate Veteran*, XXXI (1923), 244; Ben Butler to Flora, May 28, 1864, Stuart Papers, Virginia Historical Society, Richmond, Virginia; conversations with Mrs. Andrew J. Davis, who is Stuart's granddaughter (the daughter of Virginia Pelham Stuart Waller) and lived with her grandmother for many years.

*Metaphor as Man: Some Speculations by Way of Conclusion*

1. John S. Patton, ed., *Poems of John R. Thompson* (New York, 1920), 8–10, 238.

# Selected Bibliography

## Manuscript Material

At this moment, an undetermined number of Stuart papers are in private hands or under restricted access at manuscript repositories. During the course of research for this biography, Colonel James Ewell Brown Stuart IV did not permit me to see materials in his possession and imposed restrictions upon one collection he had deposited in the Virginia Historical Society. Mr. Stuart B. Campbell, Jr., on the other hand, was most generous with his time and the collection of Stuart letters in his possession. Mrs. Andrew J. Davis, Stuart's granddaughter, was also most gracious; she told me stories and answered questions. She permitted me to see papers she was in the process of donating to the Virginia Historical Society, some of the papers still in her possession, and copies of papers she had placed on deposit in the Virginia Historical Society.

The list that follows indicates manuscript collections consulted for this study. For more detail about the contents of these collections, consult *The National Union Catalog of Manuscript Collections* or the appropriate repository.

Fannie Lewis Adams: Virginia Historical Society
Edward Porter Alexander: University of North Carolina
Alexander Robinson Boteler: Duke University
Diary of Alexander R. Boteler (typescript), William E. Brooks Collection: Library of Congress
Burn Family: University of South Carolina
Cooke Family: Virginia Historical Society
Julian T. Edwards: Virginia Historical Society
Elliot G. Fishburne: University of Virginia
Francis Walker Gilmer: University of Virginia
Gordon and Rosser Family: University of Virginia

Grinnan Family: Virginia Historical Society
Peter Wilson Hairston: Southern Historical Collection, University of North Carolina
Wade Hampton: University of South Carolina
Atcheson L. Hench: University of Virginia
Fitzhugh Lee: University of Virginia
Henry B. McClellan: U.S. Army Military History Institute, Carlisle Barracks, Pennsylvania
Henry Brainard McClellan: Virginia Historical Society
John S. Mosby: U.S. Army Military History Institute, Carlisle Barracks, Pennsylvania
Elizabeth Byrd Nicholas: Virginia Historical Society
R. Channing Price: Southern Historical Collection, University of North Carolina
Thomas Lafayette Rosser: University of Virginia
H. H. Smith: Virginia Historical Society
Murray J. Smith: U.S. Army Military History Institute, Carlisle Barracks, Pennsylvania
Alexander Hugh Holmes Stuart: University of Virginia
James Ewell Brown Stuart: Duke University
James Ewell Brown Stuart: Henry E. Huntington Library
James Ewell Brown Stuart: Virginia Historical Society
James E. B. Stuart: University of Virginia
J. E. B. Stuart: Museum of the Confederacy, Richmond, Virginia
Stuart Family: Virginia Historical Society
Williams Family: Virginia Historical Society


*Newspapers and Periodicals*

Charleston *Daily Courier*
Charleston *Mercury*
*Christian Index*
Memphis *Appeal*
Mobile *Daily Advertiser and Register*
*New York Times*
Richmond *Dispatch*
Richmond *Enquirer*
Richmond *Examiner*
Richmond *Sentinel*
Richmond *Whig*
*Southern Illustrated News*


*Other Printed Sources*

W. L. Fagan, coll., *Southern War Songs* (New York, 1889).
Paul Glass, ed., *Singing Soldiers* (New York, 1964).

Richard B. Harwell, *Confederate Music* (Chapel Hill, North Carolina, 1950).

Robert L. Krick, *Lee's Colonels: A Biographical Register of the Field Officers of the Army of Northern Virginia* (Dayton, Ohio, 1979).

*Official Register of the Officers and Cadets of the United States Military Academy* (West Point, New York).

John S. Patton, ed., *Poems of John R. Thompson* (New York, 1920).

"Proceedings of the General Court Martial of Lt. Col. H. Clay Pate," Confederate Imprints (microfilm).

*War of the Rebellion: A Compilation of the Official Records of the Union and Confederate Armies,* 70 vols. in 127 (Washington, D.C., 1880–1901).

## Primary Material: Books

E. P. Alexander, *Military Memoirs of a Confederate* (New York, 1907).

G. W. Beale, *A Lieutenant of Cavalry in Lee's Army* (Boston, 1918).

R. L. T. Beale, *History of the Ninth Virginia Cavalry in the War Between the States* (Richmond, Virginia, 1899).

Charles Minor Blackford III, ed., *Letters from Lee's Army* (New York, 1947).

W. W. Blackford, *War Years with Jeb Stuart* (New York, 1945).

Heros Von Borcke, *Memoirs of the Confederate War for Independence,* 2 vols. (New York, 1938).

Charles E. Cauthen, ed., *Family Letters of the Three Wade Hamptons, 1782–1901* (Columbia, South Carolina, 1952).

"A Confederate," *The Grayjackets* (Philadelphia, 1867).

John Esten Cooke, *Wearing of the Gray,* ed. Philip Van Doren Stern (Bloomington, Indiana, 1959).

T. C. DeLeon, *Belles, Beaux and Brains of the 60's* (New York, 1907).

Henry Kyd Douglas, *I Rode with Stonewall* (Chapel Hill, North Carolina, 1940).

Clifford Dowdey and Louis H. Manarin, eds., *The Wartime Papers of R. E. Lee* (New York, 1961).

Jubal Anderson Early, *War Memoirs: Autobiographical Sketch and Narrative of the War Between the States,* Frank E. Vandiver, ed. (Bloomington, Indiana, 1960).

George Cary Eggleston, *A Rebel's Recollections* (Bloomington, Indiana, 1959).

Theodore S. Garnett, *J. E. B. Stuart* (New York, 1907).

Harry Gilmor, *Four Years in the Saddle* (London, 1866).

Ulysses S. Grant, *Personal Memoirs of U. S. Grant,* 2 vols. (New York, 1885–86).

H. P. Griffith, *Variosa* (n.p., 1911).

Constance C. Harrison, *Recollections Grave and Gay* (New York, 1911).

William W. Hassler, ed., *The General to His Lady: The Civil War Letters of William Dorsey Pender to Fanny Pender* (Chapel Hill, North Carolina, 1965).

Luther W. Hopkins, *From Bull Run to Appomattox: A Boy's View* (Baltimore, 1908).

Oliver Otis Howard, *Autobiography*, 2 vols. (New York, 1907).

Robert E. Lee, Jr., *Recollections and Letters of General Robert E. Lee* (Garden City, New York, 1904).

Elizabeth Lindsay Lomax, *Leaves from an Old Washington Diary, 1854–1863*, ed. Lindsay Lomax Wood (New York, 1943).

James Longstreet, *From Manassas to Appomattox* (Philadelphia, 1896).

Percival G. Lowe, *Five Years a Dragoon*, Don Russell, ed. (Norman, Oklahoma, 1965).

H. B. McClellan, *The Life and Campaigns of Major-General J. E. B. Stuart* (Boston and New York, 1885).

William N. McDonald, *A History of the Laurel Brigade* (Arlington, Virginia, 1907).

[Judith W. McGuire], *Diary of a Southern Refugee* (New York, 1868).

David Macrae, *The Americans at Home* (New York, 1952).

Sir Frederick Maurice, ed., *An Aide-de-Camp of Lee, Being the Papers of Colonel Charles Marshall* . . . (Boston, 1927).

Millard J. Miller, *My Grandpap Rode with JEB Stuart: Experiences of James Knox Polk Ritchie* . . . (Westerville, Ohio, n.d.).

Edward A. Moore, *The Story of a Cannoneer Under Stonewall Jackson* (Freeport, New York, 1971).

John S. Mosby, *Stuart's Cavalry in the Gettysburg Campaign* (New York, 1908).

Frank M. Myers, *The Comanches: A History of White's Battalion, Virginia Cavalry* (Marietta, Georgia, 1956).

George M. Neese, *Three Years in the Confederate Horse Artillery* (Washington, D.C., 1911).

John Newton Opie, *A Rebel Cavalryman with Lee, Stuart and Jackson* (Chicago, 1909).

Fitzgerald Ross, *Cities and Camps of the Confederate States*, Richard Barksdale Harwell, ed. (Urbana, Illinois, 1958).

[Thomas L. Rosser], *Addresses of Gen'l T. L. Rosser* (New York, 1889).

Louis Ruchames, ed., *A John Brown Reader* (London and New York, 1959).

Charles Wells Russell, ed., *The Memoirs of Colonel John S. Mosby* (Boston, 1917).

G. Moxley Sorrel, *Recollections of a Confederate Staff Officer* (New York, 1917).

Walter H. Taylor, *Four Years with General Lee* (New York, 1879).

George A. Townsend, *Rustics in Rebellion* (Chapel Hill, North Carolina, 1950).

Charles W. Turner, ed., *Old Zeus* (Verona, Virginia, 1983).

John C. West, *A Texan in Search of a Fight* (Waco, Texas, 1901).

C. Vann Woodward, ed., *Mary Chesnut's Civil War* (New Haven, 1981).

Edward Younger, ed., *Inside the Confederate Government: The Diary of Robert Garlick Hill Kean* (New York, 1957).

## Primary Material: Articles

G. W. Beale to Mother, July 13, 1863, *Southern Historical Society Papers*, XI (1883), 320–27.

William Campbell, "Stuart's Ride and Death of Latané," *Southern Historical Society Papers* XXXIX (1911), 86–90.

Frank Dorsey, "Gen. J. E. B. Stuart's Last Battle," *Confederate Veteran* XVII (1899), 76–77.

Bingham Duncan, ed., "Letters of General J. E. B. Stuart to His Wife, 1861," *Emory University Publications*, I (1943 [1]).

Richard E. Frayser, "A Narrative of Stuart's Raid in the Rear of the Army of the Potomac," *Southern Historical Society Papers*, XI (1883), 505–17.

Theodore S. Garnett, "The Dashing Gen. J. E. B. Stuart," *Confederate Veteran*, XIX (1911), 575.

Israel Green, "The Capture of John Brown," *North American Review*, December 1885, 564–69.

Peter W. Hairston, ed., "J. E. B. Stuart's Letters to His Hairston Kin, 1850–1855," *North Carolina Historical Review*, LI (July 1974), 261–333.

Sidney Herbert [Herbert Lancey], "Singular Criticism of 'Jeb' Stuart," *Confederate Veteran* XVI (1908), 152.

Daniel H. Hill, "McClellan's Change of Base and Malvern Hill," Robert Underwood Johnson and Clarence Clough Buel, eds., *Battles and Leaders of the Civil War*, 4 vols. (New York, 1956), II, 394.

Jay B. Hubbell, ed., "The War Diary of John Esten Cooke," *Journal of Southern History*, VII (1941), 526–40.

John D. Imboden, "Jackson at Harper's Ferry in 1861," Robert Underwood Johnson and Clarence Clough Buel, eds., *Battles and Leaders of the Civil War*, 4 vols. (New York, 1956), I, 111–25.

[Fitzhugh Lee], "A Review of the First Two Days' Operations at Gettysburg and a Reply to General Longstreet by General Fitz Lee," *Southern Historical Society Papers*, V (1878), 162–68.

Fitzhugh Lee, "Speech at A.N.V. Banquet, October 28, 1875," *Southern Historical Society Papers*, I (1876), 99–103.

James Longstreet, "Our March Against Pope," Robert Underwood Johnson and Clarence Clough Buel, eds. *Battles and Leaders of the Civil War*, 4 vols. (New York, 1956), II, 512–26.

W. Gordon McCabe, "Major Andrew Reid Venable, Jr.," *Southern Historical Society Papers*, XXXVII (1909), 61–73.

H. B. McClellan, "Address on the Life, Campaigns and Character of Gen'l J. E. B. Stuart," *Southern Historical Society Papers*, VIII (1880), 433–56.

H. W. Manson, "A. P. Hill's Signal Corps," *Confederate Veteran*, II (1894), 11–12.

W. Roy Mason, "Marching on Manassas," Robert Underwood Johnson and Clarence Clough Buel, eds., *Battles and Leaders of the Civil War*, 4 vols. (New York, 1956), II, 528–29.

H. H. Matthewe, "Major John Pelham, Confederate Hero," *Southern Historical Society Papers*, XXXVIII (1910), 379–84.

William E. Miller, "The Cavalry Battle Near Gettysburg," Robert Underwood Johnson and Clarence Clough Buel, eds., *Battles and Leaders of the Civil War*, 4 vols. (New York, 1956), III, 397–406.

Benjamin Blake Minor, "Jeb Stuart: How He Played Sheriff in a Lawyer's Bedroom," *Southern Historical Society Papers*, XXXVI (1908), 267–70.

John S. Mosby, "The Confederate Cavalry in the Gettysburg Campaign," Robert Underwood Johnson and Clarence Clough Buel, eds., *Battles and Leaders of the Civil War*, 4 vols. (New York, 1956), III, 251–52.

John S. Mosby, "Heth Intended to Cover His Error . . . " *Southern Historical Society Papers*, XXXVII (1909), 369–72.

John S. Mosby, "Longstreet and Stuart," *Southern Historical Society Papers*, XXVIII (1895), 238–47.

John S. Mosby, "The Ride Around General McClellan," *Southern Historical Society Papers*, XXVI (1898), 246–54.

J. R. Oliver, "J. E. B. Stuart's Fate at Yellow Tavern," *Confederate Veteran*, XIX (1901), 531.

W. T. Robins, "Stuart's Ride Around McClellan," Robert Underwood Johnson and Clarence Clough Buel, eds., *Battles and Leaders of the Civil War*, 4 vols. (New York, 1956), II, 271–74.

W. Stitt Robinson, ed., "The Kiowa and Comanche Campaign of 1860 as Recorded in the Personal Diary of Lt. J. E. B. Stuart," *Kansas Historical Quarterly*, 23 (1957), 382–400.

G. N. Saussy, "Color of His Uniform Misunderstood," *Confederate Veteran*, XVI (1908), 262.

Alexander L. Tinsley, "General Stuart's Spurs," *Confederate Veteran*, XXXVII (May 1929), 198.

"Causes of the Defeat of Gen. Lee's Army at the Battle of Gettysburg— Opinions of Leading Confederate Soldiers," *Southern Historical Society Papers*, IV (1877), 80–87, 97–126, 151–60.

"The Death of General J. E. B. Stuart," Robert Underwood Johnson and Clarence Clough Buel, eds., *Battles and Leaders of the Civil War*, 4 vols. (New York, 1956), IV, 194.

"Fatal Wounding of General J. E. B. Stuart," *Southern Historical Society Papers*, XXX (1902), 236–38.

"Mrs. J. E. B. Stuart," *Confederate Veteran*, XXXI (1923), 244.

"Raid on Catlett's," *Southern Historical Society Papers*, XXVII (1899), 303–7.

"Stuart's Last Dispatch," *Southern Historical Society Papers*, IX (1881), 138–39.

"Two Cavalry Chieftains," *Southern Historical Society*, XVI (1888), 451–52.

"The Wounding and Death of General J. E. B. Stuart," *Southern Historical Society Papers,* VII (1879), 140–44.

## Secondary Material: Books

Michael C. C. Adams, *Our Masters the Rebels: A Speculation on Union Military Failure in the East, 1861–1865* (Cambridge, Massachusetts, 1978).

Stephen E. Ambrose, *Duty, Honor, Country: A History of West Point* (Baltimore, 1966).

J. O. Beaty, *John Esten Cooke, Virginian* (New York, 1922).

F. N. Boney, *John Letcher of Virginia* (University, Alabama, 1966).

Edwin B. Coddington, *The Gettysburg Campaign: A Study in Command* (New York, 1968).

Burke Davis, *Jeb Stuart: The Last Cavalier* (New York, 1957).

William C. Davis, *Battle at Bull Run* (Garden City, New York, 1977).

Clifford Dowdey, *Seven Days: The Emergence of Lee* (Boston, 1964).

Vincent J. Esposito, ed., *West Point Atlas of American Wars,* 2 vols. (New York, 1959).

Sidney Forman, *West Point: A History of the United States Military Academy* (New York, 1950).

Douglas Southall Freeman, *Lee's Lieutenants: A Study in Command,* 3 vols. (New York, 1942–44).

Douglas Southall Freeman, *R. E. Lee: A Biography,* 4 vols. (New York, 1934–35).

Gerald M. Garmon, *John Reuben Thompson* (Boston, 1979).

Manly Wade Hampton, *Giant in Gray: A Biography of Wade Hampton of South Carolina* (New York, 1949).

Robert Krick, *9th Virginia Cavalry* (Lynchburg, Virginia, 1982).

William B. McCash, *Thomas R. R. Cobb: The Making of a Southern Nationalist* (Macon, Georgia, 1983).

William S. McFeely, *Grant: A Biography* (New York, 1981).

William S. McFeely, *Yankee Stepfather: General O. O. Howard and the Freedmen,* Norton Edition (New York, 1970).

James M. McPherson, *Ordeal by Fire: The Civil War and Reconstruction* (New York, 1982).

Stephen B. Oates, *To Purge This Land with Blood: A Biography of John Brown* (New York, 1970).

Virginia G. and Lewis G. Pedigo, *History of Patrick and Henry Counties Virginia* (Baltimore, 1977).

Stephen Z. Starr, *Colonel Grenfell's Wars: The Life of a Soldier of Fortune* (Baton Rouge, 1971).

Stephen Z. Starr, *The Union Cavalry in the Civil War,* 2 vols. (Baton Rouge, 1979–81).

Matthew Forney Steele, *American Campaigns,* 2 vols. (Washington, D.C., 1909).

Emory M. Thomas, *The American War and Peace, 1860–1877* (Englewood Cliffs, New Jersey, 1973).
Emory M. Thomas, *The Confederate Nation, 1861–1865* (New York, 1979).
John W. Thomason, Jr., *Jeb Stuart* (New York, 1930).
Bell Irvin Wiley, *The Life of Johnny Reb: The Common Soldier of the Confederacy* (Indianapolis and New York, 1943).

## Secondary Material: Articles

William R. Brooksher and David K. Snider, "Around McClellan Again," *Civil War Times Illustrated*, 13 (August 1974), 4–6, 8, 39–48.
William R. Brooksher and David K. Snider, "Stuart's Ride: The Great Circuit Around McClellan," *Civil War Times Illustrated*, 12 (April 1973), 4–6, 8–10, 40–47.
Churchill J. Gibson, "J. E. B. Stuart," *Southern Churchman*, February 11, 1934, 9.
William W. Hassler, "John Pelham of the Horse Artillery," *Civil War Times Illustrated*, 3 (August 1964), 10–14.
William W. Hassler, "Yellow Tavern," *Civil War Times Illustrated*, 5 (November 1966), 4–11, 46–48.
Frederick Shriver Klein, "Affair at Westminster," *Civil War Times Illustrated*, 7 (August 1968), 32–38.
Edward Longacre, "The Battle of Brandy Station . . ." *Virginia Cavalcade*, 25 (Winter 1976), 136–43.
Edward G. Longacre, "Cavalry Clash at Todd's Tavern," *Civil War Times Illustrated*, 16 (October 1977), 12–21.
Edward G. Longacre, "Stuart's Dumfries Raid," *Civil War Times Illustrated*, 15 (July 1976), 18–26.
James Lunt, "JEB Stuart," *History Today*, 1961, 11(8), 536–46.
Samuel H. Miller, "Yellow Tavern," *Civil War History*, 2(1956), 57–81.
Wilbur S. Nye, "How Stuart Got Back Across the Potomac," *Civil War Times Illustrated*, 4 (July 1966), 45–58.
Channing Price, "Stuart's Chambersburg Raid: An Eyewitness Account," *Civil War Times Illustrated*, 4 (January 1966), 8–15, 42–44.
Charles W. Ramsdell, "General Robert E. Lee's Horse Supply, 1862–1865," *American Historical Review*, XXXV (1930), 758–77.
Don Russell, "J. E. B. Stuart on the Frontier," *Civil War Times Illustrated*, 13 (April 1974), 12–17.
Don Russell, "Jeb Stuart's Other Indian Fight," *Civil War Times Illustrated*, 12 (January 1974), 10–17.
Emily J. Salmon, "The Burial of Latané: Symbol of the Lost Cause," *Virginia Cavalcade*, 28 (Winter 1979), 118–19.
Roy P. Stonesifer, Jr., "The Union Cavalry Comes of Age," John T. Hubbell, ed., *Battles Lost and Won: Essays from Civil War History* (Westport, Connecticut, 1975), 125–34.
Emory M. Thomas, "The Kilpatrick-Dahlgren Raid on Richmond," *Civil*

*War Times Illustrated*, 16 (February 1978), 4–9, 46–48; 17 (April 1978), 26–33.

Emory M. Thomas, "The Peninsula Campaign," *Civil War Times Illustrated*, 17 (February 1979), 4–9, 40–45; and 18 (April 1979), 28–35; 18 (May 1979), 12–18; 18 (June 1979), 10–17; 18 (July 1979), 14–24.

Glenn Tucker, "The Cavalry Invasion of the North," *Civil War Times Illustated*, 2 (July 1963), 18–22.

# Index

## About the Author

Emory M. Thomas, a native of Richmond, Virginia, is a professor of history at the University of Georgia. He earned his B.A. at the University of Virginia and his Ph.D. at Rice University. He is the author of *The Confederate Nation, 1861–1865* (a volume in the New American Nation series), *The American War and Peace, 1860–1877*, *The Confederate State of Richmond: A Biography of the Capital*, *The Confederacy as a Revolutionary Experience*, and numerous articles in both general and scholarly publications.